Soft Force

Princeton Studies in Muslim Politics

Dale F. Eickelman and Augustus Richard Norton, Series Editors

A list of titles in this series can be found at the back of the book.

Soft Force

WOMEN IN EGYPT'S ISLAMIC AWAKENING

Ellen Anne McLarney

PRINCETON UNIVERSITY PRESS
Princeton and Oxford

Published by Princeton University Press, 41 William Street,
Princeton, New Jersey 08540
In the United Kingdom: Princeton University Press, 6 Oxford Street,
Woodstock, Oxfordshire OX20 1TW

press.princeton.edu

Jacket art: Alaa Awad, *Women of Egypt*, 2012.
Photographed by Ossama Boshra.

Portions of chapter 6 were previously published as "Private Is Political: Women and Family in Intellectual Islam," *Feminist Theory* 11, no. 2 (August 2010): 129–48.
Portions of chapter 1 were previously published as "The Islamic Public Sphere and the Discipline of *Adab*," *International Journal of Middle Eastern Studies* 43, no. 3 (August 2011).

Library of Congress Cataloging-in-Publication Data

McLarney, Ellen Anne.
Soft force : women in Egypt's Islamic awakening / Ellen Anne McLarney.
pages cm.—(Princeton studies in Muslim politics)
Includes bibliographical references and index.
ISBN 978-0-691-15848-8 (hardcover : alk. paper)—ISBN 0-691-15848-7 (hardcover : alk. paper)—ISBN 978-0-691-15849-5 (pbk. : alk. paper)—ISBN 0-691-15849-5 (pbk. : alk. paper) 1. Women in Islam—Egypt. 2. Muslim women—Political activity—Egypt. 3. Feminism—Egypt. I. Title.
HQ1793.M4 2015
305.420962—dc23
2014026014

British Library Cataloging-in-Publication Data is available

This book has been composed in Charis SIL

Printed on acid-free paper. ∞

Printed in the United States of America

1 3 5 7 9 10 8 6 4 2

To my family,

especially my mother Martina Josephine McLarney

and my father Charles Patrick McLarney,

for their labor and their love

Contents

Acknowledgments

I have been unable to do these works, or their writers, justice, despite my desire to do so. I wanted to adequately convey the power and eloquence of their reinterpretations of the Islamic tradition, but it is something that perhaps can only be experienced by reading them in the original. Many of these works, however, are not widely available or accessible to many outside the Arabic-speaking world. Despite pioneering visions of transforming society with an Islamic gender justice, their voices have remained nearly inaudible in the West. Women embracing Islamic reform have been heard much less than those critical of Islam, likely because of persistent and seemingly intractable perceptions about Muslim women's oppression, measured in diametric opposition to presumed Western freedoms. These writers challenge these very stereotypes, perhaps the reason that they have been largely ignored in the West. This occlusion contrasts markedly with their vocality and visibility in global Muslim publics, a presence that is not just literary and scholarly but digital and visual as well.

By seeing submission as the path to liberation from gender oppression, these writers shake loose from normative liberal assumptions about the freedoms of the autonomous subject. Like Hannah Arendt, they see renouncing personal sovereignty as the key to a democratic politics. They believe in the political efficacy of an ethics of care. They launch articulate critiques of Western feminism, and especially of the emancipating power of economic self-determination, instead arguing for the connectivity of the "human capital" of family, community, and *umma*.

As a white girl from the Midwest, I know the problems my subject position poses for interpreting—and representing—these writings. Moreover, I come from a family of devout Catholics, albeit one of activist nuns with their own visions of gender justice (my Aunt Rose). I am named after one of those nuns (Sister Mary Hugh). Even in the face of crushing patriarchal oppression, they have been able to work for social justice not just from within but through their faith. In studying Muslim women's activism, I have been struck more by the commonalities of their mutual struggles—to live by the grace of God, fighting poverty and injustice, embracing an ethic of hospitality, and devoting oneself to others—rather than by any presumed clash in their worldviews. They lived and expressed their feminism through faith, but not always in the way a normative feminism recognizes or accepts. Nor is it a feminism that a normative faith often recognizes or accepts.

It is especially to my mother that I dedicate this book, for her feminism, mothering, homemaking, community building, affect, labor, and love. When I was growing up in the 1970s, it was the era of women's lib. My mother did not fit the mold of women's liberation at the time because she was a stay-at-home mom. But she was, nonetheless, a feminist. She invited my ERA-activist, lesbian fourth-grade teachers to our house for dinner; she hired women painters; she signed me up for soccer in the wake of Title IX; she organized sex education classes for my Campfire Girls' troop; she knew how to use a tool box better than my dad ever did; and there was no doubt who wore the pants in my house. Moreover, she told me that I was going to grow up and work and be a businesswoman. Like so many of my generation of middle-class white girls, I came to see paid labor as the path to true emancipation, and to see homemaking, motherhood, and femininity as backward and retrograde throwbacks to another era.

My mom made the business of being a mom look so effortless (and still does) that it seemed like it was not actually work. Only when I grew up did I realize how hard it is to take care of oneself, let alone others. It is partly an illusion of a formal economy that assigns this labor far less worth, even though it depends on this work for its very survival. And still we make the error in our language of saying that these women do not "work." In this project I sought to recuperate the power of motherwork and homespace elaborated in the writings of black feminists and Islamic activists alike. Both radically reimagine a new kind of democratic politics born of family and community, a politics that fights injustice—whether colonial, racial, economic, or patriarchal—through an ethic of care. They also recuperate work in the home and family as work, not just for an Islamic politics but also for a new kind of feminism.

My debts for this project run long, deep, and wide. I have relied on the patience of many people and institutions that have had faith in me, for reasons I sometimes cannot fathom. I thank Duke University for supporting, without reservation, my desire to have a family and a career, for granting me leave for the birth of each of my children, for keeping my family together, and for unwaveringly supporting my intellectual trajectory. Several people have been key to this: Dean of the Humanities Srinivas Aravamudan, my department chair Leo Ching, and Provost Peter Lange. I am grateful to have the opportunity to work at an institution like Duke, one that invests so fully in the humanities and that is serious about fostering interdisciplinary approaches to scholarship. This commitment enabled me to engage in new kinds of scholarship that allowed me to employ a literary and cultural studies approach to interpret popular Islamic religious texts. This intellectual freedom has made my job a true joy.

I thank my department, Asian and Middle Eastern Studies, and first and foremost my colleague and mentor miriam cooke, who has shown me unwavering support over the years. Her own scholarship has been a source of inspiration: it was from her essay on Muslim women's writing that I first discovered Bint al-Shatiʾ's lecture "The Islamic Understanding of Women's Liberation," the seed of this project. I am particularly indebted to Mbaye Lo, who has shown grace, patience, kindness, and understanding throughout the writing of this book. Thanks also to my other colleagues in the Arabic program, ʿAbd al-Sattar Jawad al-Mamouri, Maha Houssami, Muhammad Habib, and Amal Boumaaza. I could not have asked for a more supportive community. My good friends Aimee Nayoung Kwon and Eileen Cheng-yin Chow shepherded me through the writing of this book. I owe special thanks to Hae Young Kim, who has been an intellectual and professional mentor, as well as a neighbor.

This book would never have come to life if it were not for an Andrew W. Mellon Humanities Post-doctoral Fellowship in the Department of Religious Studies at Stanford University. For this fellowship, I have Seth Lerer and Beth Levin to thank. This project took shape and flourished under the tutelage and support of Joel Beinin, Bob Gregg, Arnold Eisen, and Hester Gelber, Salem Aweiss, Ramzi Salti, and Khalil Barhoum. It was further developed through participation in two faculty seminars at Duke, Michael Hardt and Robyn Wiegman's "Alternative Political Imaginaries" in the Franklin Humanities Institute and Frances Hasso's "Freedom and Feminism" seminar in the Program in Women's Studies. For their intellectual guidance, I am grateful. Most critical to the writing of this book was a fellowship at the National Humanities Center. Geoffrey Harpham provided advice and mentorship at key moments and showed me the light at the end of the tunnel.

I am indebted to the Department of Middle Eastern, South Asian, and African Studies at Columbia University, where I did my doctoral degree. It was that department and its stellar faculty that truly taught me the meaning of the politics of scholarship. I am particularly thankful for the mentorship and guidance of my advisers Magda al-Nawaihi and Muhsin al-Musawi, as well as Hamid Dabashi, George Saliba, Richard Bulliet, Maryse Condé, and Edward Said. They released me on my own recognizance, perhaps against their better judgement, to live, travel, study, and conduct research in Egypt, Tunisia, Syria, and Jerusalem. It was only because they did not give up on me that I was able to finally find my path. For that, I mainly have Magda to thank. Her indomitable spirit, intellect, political commitment, scholarship, and light continue to live on in this world. Then, at a critical point in my intellectual and professional development, Muhsin al-Musawi stepped in to guide me. I owe him so much.

Publishing this book with Princeton University Press was beyond my greatest dreams. Thanks to Fred Appel for giving me this present, one that arrived seemingly out of nowhere a few days shy of Christmas.

The transliteration system used in this book is based on that used by the *International Journal of Middle East Studies*. Thanks to Cole Bunzel for his diligent and meticulous review of the transliterations.

A number of feminist scholars I admire have been utterly formative to this project: Lila Abu-Lughod, Margot Badran, Beth Baron, Marilyn Booth, miriam cooke, Fedwa El Guini, Samira Haj, Sondra Hale, Frances Hasso, Mervat Hatem, Valerie Hoffmann, Saba Mahmood, Minoo Moallem, Valentine Moghadem, Afsaneh Najmabadi, Omnia El Shakry, Barbara Stowasser, and Sherifa Zuhur, among many others. Some have read parts of this project; some I only know through their scholarship. I deeply appreciated the blessing given this project by Niʿmat Sidqi's daughters Abeya and Naziha Rida and her granddaughters Amira and Heba Mashhour. They gave input, corrections, clarifications, and advice that helped me to be true to their memory of her. I thank my research assistant Andrew Simon for first leading me to them via the shaykhs at Jamaʿat Ansar al-Sunna al-Muhammadiyya. I am grateful to friends, colleagues, and collaborators Imam Abdullah Antepli, Laura Bier, Anne Enenbach, Carl Ernst, Luciana Fellin, Christof Galli, August Gering, Banu Gökarıksel, Erdağ Göknar, Dave Hardin, Andrew Janiak, Kelly Jarrett, Jeanette Jouili, Rebecca Joubin, Carmel Kooros (my Cairo coconspirator), Abeslam Maghraoui, Ebrahim Moosa, Negar Mottahedeh, Omid Safi, Rebecca Stein, and Nadia Yaqub. If there is one person who stands over this project, it is my guardian angel Engseng Ho. I am eternally grateful for his kind words of advice that acted as midwife to this project, only hours before the birth of my third child.

I owe special thanks to the Beth El moms for their support and friendship. They helped me survive this project with my humanity intact, showing me what it meant to fully inhabit the joys of motherhood. Mélida Guerrero has been my intuitive twin throughout; she loved and nurtured my children during my painful absences from them to write this book. I am thankful for her professionalism, her advice, her dependability, her good nature, and the model that she provided to me and my children.

It is to my family that I owe everything. My greatest debt is to my parents, who have shown unwavering faith and support me, even (and especially) when I do not deserve it. My parents' discipline, honesty, work ethic, kindness, generosity, hospitality, wisdom, and constant advice have been guiding stars in my work and in my life. My sister Megan is a daily solace, along with my brother Michael. I am especially grateful to my husband, Bruno Estigarribia, whose infallible faith in me has made me a better person and scholar. Sos mi balanza, mi equilibrio, mi delirio, mi esperanza, y mi camino. My children have given life, meaning, and urgency to this book. Through them I lived, breathed, and believed in its words. Nico, Mateo, and Catalina, you are the seed out of which this project grew; you are the heart of this book.

Soft Force

The Islamic Public Sphere and the Subject of Gender: The Politics of the Personal

One of the most visible public faces of the 2011 revolution in Egypt was Asmaʾ Mahfouz, a young woman who posted a video blog on Facebook calling for the January 25 protest in Tahrir Square "so that maybe we the country can become free, can become a country with justice, a country with dignity, a country in which a human can be truly human, not living like an animal."[1] She describes a stark imbalance of power: a lone girl standing against the security apparatus of the state. When she initially went out to demonstrate, only three other people came to join her. They were met with vans full of security forces, "tens of thugs" (*balṭagiyyīn*) that menaced the small band of protesters. Talking about her fear (*ruʿb*), she epitomizes the voice of righteous indignation against the Goliath of an abusive military regime. "I am a girl," she says, "and I went down." The skinny, small, pale girl bundled up in her winter scarf and sweater speaks clearly and forcefully, despite a slight speech impediment, rallying a political community to action against tyrannical rule. Mahfouz's vlog is not necessarily famous for actually sparking the revolution, as some have claimed in the revolution's aftermath. Rather, she visually embodies and vocally advocates what the Islamic activist Heba Raouf Ezzat calls "soft force," *al-quwwa al-nāʿima*. Raouf Ezzat uses the term to refer to nonviolent protest, or what she calls "women's jihad," wielded against "tyrannical government."[2] Connoting a kind of feminized smoothness, goodness, and grace, *niʿma*

[1] *Meet Asmaa Mahfouz and the Vlog That Helped Spark the Revolution*, 2011, http://www.youtube.com/watch?v=SgjIgMdsEuk&feature=youtube_gdata_player.

[2] Heba Raouf Ezzat, *al-Marʾa wa-l-ʿAmal al-Siyasi: Ruʾya Islamiyya* (Herndon, VA: Institute of Islamic Thought, 1995), 156–57; Heba Raouf Ezzat, "al-Quwwa al-Naʿima" (Al-Jazeera Center for Studies, October 13, 2011), http://studies.aljazeera.net/files/2011/08/20118872345213170.htm. Raouf Ezzat reinterprets Joseph Nye's concept of "soft power " but in a feminized sense and for an Islamic context. See Joseph Nye, *Soft Power: The Means to Success in World Politics* (New York: PublicAffairs, 2005).

is wielded as a weapon against what political scientist Paul Amar calls the "thug state."[3] Resonating with connotations of righteousness, it is a keyword used for imagining and creating a just society rooted in the grace of the right path.

"Soft force" is the gradual institutional change—and the war of ideas—that has been one of Islamic organizations' most powerful tools in Egypt. The concept of soft force found its way into the controversial 2012 constitution, authored by the Islamist government of Muhammad Morsi. The constitution's eleventh and final principle stated:

> Egypt's pioneering intellectual and cultural leadership embodies her soft force (*quwāhā al-nāʿima*), exemplified in the gift of freedom of her intellectuals and creators, her universities, her linguistic and scientific organizations, her research centers, her press, her arts, her letters, and her media, her national church, and her noble Azhar that was throughout its history a foundation of the identity of the nation, protecting the eternal Arabic language and the Islamic shariʿa, as a beacon (*manāra*) of enlightened, moderate thought.[4]

This book is about the soft force of Islamic cultural production in the decades leading up to the 2011 revolution in Egypt. It is about the passive revolution of Islamic popular culture, mass media, and public scholarship, a war of position developed within the structures of a semiauthoritarian, neoliberal state.[5] It is about the role women play in articulating that revolution, in their writings, activism, and discursive transformation of Egypt's social, cultural, and political institutions. It is intended as an antidote to dominant representations of women as oppressed by Islamic politics, movements, and groups. *Soft Force* details women's contribution to the emergence of an Islamic public sphere—one that has trenchantly critiqued successive dictatorships in Egypt, partly through a liberal ideology of rights, democracy, freedom, equality, and family values. Women's Islamic cultural production—their lectures, pamphlets, theses, books, magazines, newspapers, television

[3] Paul Amar, "Turning the Gendered Politics of the Security State Inside Out?" *International Feminist Journal of Politics* 13, no. 3 (2011): 299–328; Paul Amar, *The Security Archipelago: Human-Security States, Sexuality Politics, and the End of Neoliberalism* (Durham, NC: Duke University Press, 2013), 210–13.

[4] Jumhuriyyat Misr, "al-Dustur," December 26, 2012.

[5] Antonio Gramsci, *Selections from the Prison Notebooks*, trans. Quintin Hoare and Geoffrey Nowell Smith (London: Lawrence & Wishart, 1971), 289–300, 481–95; Asef Bayat, *Making Islam Democratic: Social Movements and the Post-Islamist Turn* (Stanford, CA: Stanford University Press, 2007), 132–38, 194–95.

shows, films, and Internet postings—has been a critical instrument of this soft revolution.

The Islamic family, a bastion of Islamic law and a site for the cultivation of Islamic subjectivities, has been a central axis of public discussions of an Islamic politics. The private sphere of intimate relations has been the site of a particularly intense process of creative self-fashioning, a place for cultivating the techniques of self so critical to Muslim piety in the age of the Islamic awakening.[6] In Islamist intellectual and cultural production, women are interpreted as having a privileged role in overseeing the transmission and reproduction of these techniques of self. They do this partly through the biological reproduction of the Islamic *umma* (the Islamic community) but also through its ideological reproduction. They not only participate in the inculcation of new Islamic citizen subjects through the labor of childrearing but also discursively construct new gendered subjects through their cultural production. The revivalist preacher and writer Niʿmat Sidqi describes this as the different dimensions of jihad, talking about jihad of the tongue, of the pen, of education, and even of childrearing.[7] She interprets the classical Islamic concept of jihad in novel ways, reorienting the struggle for an Islamic society in femininized spheres of influence, concepts that would be taken up by later Islamic thinkers like Heba Raouf Ezzat.

A women's jihad of childrearing assumes an essentialized femininity of biological motherhood, an essence that revivalist writers see as the *jawhar* (core, interior, gem, jewel) of a resplendent, luminous material world harmonized to the divine order. This jawhar, or essence, is also the core of a resplendent, luminous self—one that is enlightened, awakened, and revived by the divine word.[8] It is priceless and must be protected and safeguarded but also polished and hewn to shine. Jawhar is a kind of spiritual interior cultivated through proper Islamic practice but also refers, in an almost erotic way, to the female body's material beauty. The spiritual jawhar described in some of these writings suggests Qurʾanic images of paradise (55:22, 56–58), the rubies and coral that the Qurʾan likens to the chaste women that inhabit the garden, untouched by any man (55:56–58). Revivalist writers understand this feminine essence as a source of an instinct for the divine, constructing images that connect women's softness to God's grace (*niʿma*). They talk about *fiṭrat Allah*, the instinct that God implanted in the human breast, guiding human beings to peace, affection, and mercy (30:21, 30). In

[6] Nikolas S. Rose, *Powers of Freedom: Reframing Political Thought* (Cambridge: Cambridge University Press, 1999), 43, 74.

[7] Niʿmat Sidqi, *al-Jihad fi Sabil Allah* (Cairo: Dar al-Iʿtisam, 1975).

[8] Samah Hasan Maraʿi, *Yaqazat al-ʿIffa: Rihlati min al-Sufur ila al-Hijab* (Beirut: Dar al-ʿUlum li-l-Tahqiq wa-l-Tibaʿa wa-l-Nashr wa-l-Tawziʿ, 2004), 9, 15.

contrast to the stain of Christianity's original sin, *fiṭrat Allah* suggests an essential goodness in the material world of the female body, a feminine grace that smooths the path for the social, biological, and ideological reproduction of the Islamic community, the umma.

Women's Words: An Islamic Body of Texts

Through the life and work of a series of prolific public intellectuals, *Soft Force* chronicles women's role in the awakening of Islamic sentiments, sensibilities, and senses in Egypt. The authors are professors (Bint al-Shatiʾ) and preachers (Niʿmat Sidqi), journalists (Iman Mustafa) and theater critics (Safinaz Kazim), polemicists (Muhammad ʿImara, Muhammad Jalal Kishk) and activists (Heba Raouf Ezzat, Zaynab al-Ghazali), Azharis (ʿAbd al-Wahid Wafi) and muftis (ʿAtiyya Saqr), actresses (Shams al-Barudi) and television personalities (Kariman Hamza), wives and mothers. Their diverse nature—hailing from different disciplines, social milieus, and institutions; writing in different genres and styles; publishing in different outlets—speaks to the multifarious nature of the revival. Rather than a single movement, the *ṣaḥwa* (awakening) is a broad set of processes that has contributed to the revival of religious commitments and the circulation of religious materials articulating those commitments. I draw on a variety of forms: fatwas, sermons, lectures, theses, biographies, political essays, newspaper articles, scholarly essays, and exegeses of the Qurʾan, as well as websites, Facebook postings, Tweets, and YouTube videos. The echoing of a set of similar themes—about family, gendered identities, and women's rights and responsibilities in an Islamic society—suggests the consolidation of a hegemonic position around these issues in Islamic thought. Echoes of similar understandings of women's rights, roles, duties, and relationship to the family can be found across the umma.[9] It is through this shared world of Islamic letters that the revival has been able to imagine itself as an integral whole, cultivating gendered subjectivities understood to underpin both an Islamic cosmology and an Islamic praxis. Moreover, it is a vision of Islamic womanhood that has proliferated throughout the Islamic umma, as ideas about women's roles and women's work, women's knowledge, and women's bodies

[9] See Hibba Abugideiri, "On Gender and the Family," in *Islamic Thought in the Twentieth Century*, ed. Suha Taji-Farouki and Basheer M. Nafi (London: I. B. Tauris, 2004); Jeanette S. Jouili and Schirin Amir-Moazami, "Knowledge, Empowerment and Religious Authority among Pious Muslim Women in France and Germany," *The Muslim World* 96, no. 4 (2006): 617–42; Zakia Salime, *Between Feminism and Islam: Human Rights and Sharia Law in Morocco* (Minneapolis: University of Minnesota Press, 2011).

have been disseminated and reproduced, first through print media and Islamic presses and later through the digital circulation of images and words.

Soft Force chronicles the exponential rise in Islamic writings on women and gender that accompanied—and catalyzed—the revival in Egypt over the final decades of the twentieth century and the first decades of the twenty-first century. The reproduction and translation of these ideas in writings, blogs, and social media pages in Indonesia, France, Tunisia, Saudi Arabia, and postrevolutionary Iran attest to their far-reaching impact. Some of their main concepts have proliferated throughout the umma, influencing the very terms in which women's roles in contemporary society are conceptualized. Along with the revival of classical concepts like jihad, writers connected to a global Islamic awakening reinterpret and recycle older terms toward a new hermeneutics of the Qurʾan for modern Islamic society. These include key words like *tabarruj* (a kind of sensual adornment interpreted as sexual display from Qurʾan 33:59), *sakan* (peace, abode) and *mawadda* (affection, love, both from 30:21), and *fiṭra* (instinct, human nature from 30:30). Revivalist writers describe themselves as waging jihad in the family, in the home, in childbearing and childrearing, in their selves and souls, on their bodies, and in the body politic. They identify the conjugal family, gendered rights and duties, and women's bodies and sexuality as key pillars of Islam, equivalent to its five ritual practices, as the heart and soul of Islamic law, and as sacred domains for the cultivation of Islamic piety. This jihad is executed within the "social units of the Islamic umma," in Islamic organizations and groups, in communities, in the family, and in the home.[10] Reorienting Islamic politics in women's spheres of influence, these writers put gender justice in the family on par with ritual worship in Islam, make this justice the heart and soul of Islamic law, and understand the family as a sacred domain for cultivating Islamic piety. They describe biopower[11] from the ground up: grassroots forces harnessed against the oppressive weight of dominant political forces like secularism, militarism, authoritarianism, neoliberalism, and colonialism. Women are the crux of this biopower, as its very levers, mechanisms, and controls. Wielding this power, they contest the governmentality of the state through an Islamic politics of

[10] Raouf Ezzat, *al-Marʾa wa-l-ʿAmal al-Siyasi*, 161.

[11] This Islamic biopolitics became a "set of mechanisms through which the basic biological features of the human species became the object of a political strategy, a general strategy of power," one that contested the biopolitics of the secular state. See Michel Foucault, *The History of Sexuality, Vol. 1: An Introduction* (New York: Vintage, 1990), 140; Michel Foucault, *Security, Territory, Population: Lectures at the Collège de France 1977–1978*, ed. Michel Senellart, trans. Graham Burchell (New York: Picador, 2009), 1.

self-cultivation at the level of the body, soul, family, and community. Islamic *adab* (discipline) becomes a mechanism for challenging state control over the bodies of the population.

Can these writers be considered as constituting a movement? They are surprisingly disconnected from one another. Despite reiterating a consistent set of themes and motifs, they rarely cite, acknowledge, or refer to one another, though they are clearly influenced by concepts, terms, and interpretations that circulate among them. Instead they copiously draw on other, male authorities, who write introductions to their works and whom they invoke for the purposes of legitimization, cite in footnotes, and pay tribute to in the course of their writings.[12] These women writers reject female solidarity, making clear that their discursive framework is Islamic, not feminist. Though there are clearly historical, stylistic, and generic parallels among their writings, they consistently assert that they are connected through Islam, not gender. They are connected by the rise in Islamic ethos and sensibility characterizing the Islamic revival in Egypt.[13] Moreover, they are connected through an Islamic public sphere emerging through the boom in the production, circulation, and consumption of religious writings and materials. These writers might be considered Islamic feminists, though they do not use this assignation themselves and often explicitly reject it.[14] They develop less a feminist theology for Islam than a gendered one, recentering Islamic knowledge around spheres of experience coded as feminine.

The writers are also connected by class. For the most part, they constitute an intellectual elite: Islamic professionals who romanticize the family; upper-middle-class citizens demanding their rights to self-government. They live comfortable lives of social status and are, for the most part, invested in concepts of private property and the family as an economic unit. (Kariman Hamza is described wearing fur; Niʿmat Sidqi had houses in Garden City, Alexandria, and Zamalek and is from a family of pashas, Bint al-Shatiʾ and Heba Raouf Ezzat have PhD degrees

[12] Fedwa Malti-Douglas, *Medicines of the Soul: Female Bodies and Sacred Geographies in a Transnational Islam* (Berkeley: University of California Press, 2001), 16–22, 86, 112, 173.

[13] Saba Mahmood, *Politics of Piety: The Islamic Revival and the Feminist Subject* (Princeton, NJ: Princeton University Press, 2005), 3.

[14] See Safinaz Kazim, "al-Fiminizm: Harakat al-Ghetto al-Nisaʾi." *al-Muqattam* (24 June, 1994), 45; Shahrzad Mojab, "Theorizing the Politics of 'Islamic Feminism,'" *Feminist Review* no. 69 (2001): 124–46; Valentine M. Moghadam, "Islamic Feminism and Its Discontents," *Signs: Journal of Women in Culture and Society* 27, no. 4 (2002): 1135–71; Margot Badran, "Islamic Feminism: What's in a Name?" *al-Ahram Weekly Online*, January 17, 2002; Ziba Mir-Hosseini, "Beyond 'Islam' vs 'Feminism,'" *IDS Bulletin* 42, no. 1 (2011): 67–77.

and university positions; Iman Mustafa and Safinaz Kazim are journalists and cultural critics; Shams al-Barudi emphasizes that she is from a "good family" and did not work out of need.) Their preoccupation with the good economic, disciplinary, and pedagogical management of the family reflects their bourgeois concerns with the home as a "purified, cleansed, moralized, domestic space" for the "moral training" of children. In this way their visions of the Islamic family have played "a key role in strategies for government through freedom," with women as experts in cultivating Islamic techniques of self.[15]

Even though "political Islam" critiques the political marginalization of religion to social life and to the sphere of private relations, these writers demonstrate an extraordinary investment in religiosity expressed through the family, reproduction, childrearing, and private sexuality.[16] The family and its gendered division of labor have become a crux of public definitions of Islamic practice—the site of the practice and embodiment of religiosity. The politics of the personal, these writers assert, is where the heart, soul, and body of the Islamic citizen have their most primary formation and articulation. Women play leading roles in the inculcation of modern Islamic subjects and selves; they are lynchpins in the cultivation of an Islamic society, especially in their roles as mothers. These writings convey a sense of the family and its intimate relations as the sphere of feminine affect, emotion that becomes closely connected to faith as an interior experience, mediated through the body and the senses. Revivalist authors ground their descriptions of faith in the affective plane of the self and the sensory realm of the body. They describe healing the split between outer appearance and inner self, conduct and conviction, public politics and private spirituality. They are preoccupied with the moral construction of the self at the level of emotions, senses, and instincts, how these shape the structure of the family, and their centrality to the social and political practice of Islam.

The family becomes the nodal point through which the adab—the ethics and the literature—of the Islamic community is inhabited and expressed. This is what ethnographers of revivalist movements have referred to as "political motherhood," where family life and the domestic sphere constitute a private space with public or political importance.[17] Women use knowledge to transform definitions of religious

[15] Rose, *Powers of Freedom*, 43, 74.

[16] Samira Haj, *Reconfiguring Islamic Tradition: Reform, Rationality, and Modernity* (Stanford, CA: Stanford University Press, 2008), 112–13, 163–65.

[17] Pnina Werbner, "Political Motherhood and the Feminisation of Citizenship," in *Women, Citizenship and Difference*, ed. Pnina Werbner and Nira Yuval Davis (London: Zed Books, 1999).

authority, emphasizing the political and social importance of women's authority over home and family. In public discourse, the private sphere is envisaged as "a space that should be the basis for the creation of a collective subject, based on Islamic virtues."[18] The home has been the site for the cultivation of imagined communities, a central axis along which human identity is newly defined and affirmed in public space. "This critical exchange" around new human identities "itself came to constitute a public sphere."[19]

Overlapping literary, legal, economic, political, and religious discourses on the nature of intimate relations structured the emergence of an Islamic public sphere in Egypt. Only recently have Western theorists shifted their attention to the central role of religion in constructing public spheres, a subject that has been a central concern in recent anthropological and sociological scholarship of the Middle East.[20] Not only has religion been crucial to the emergence of modern secular public spheres, but Islam has been a central point of reference for the politics of both the colonial and postcolonial nation-state. These modern public spheres tend to engage Islam as a religion (and as a form of politics) through its private practices—focusing on women, their bodies, sexuality, and family life. This has been as true for early colonial and missionary (and orientalist) discourses as it has been for contemporary France and for the United States, and for imperialist wars in Afghanistan and Iraq. Despite compelling research theorizing the emergence of an "Islamic public sphere,"[21] little scholarship has looked at its gendered nature in depth, even though debates over women's rights, roles, and responsibilities have been a cornerstone of revivalist writings on religion.[22] Though women writers actively contribute to public discourse and participate in the public sphere, they conceive of women's

[18] Jouili and Amir-Moazami, "Knowlege, Empowerment, and Religious Authority," 623.

[19] Charles Taylor, *Modern Social Imaginaries* (Durham, NC: Duke University Press, 2003), 105–6.

[20] Michael Warner, "'An Evangelical Public Sphere' (lecture)" (presented at the Critical Speaker Series, University of North Carolina, Chapel Hill, September 23, 2011); Eduardo Mendieta and Jonathan VanAntwerpen, eds., *The Power of Religion in the Public Sphere* (New York: Columbia University Press, 2011).

[21] Dale Eickelman and Jon Anderson, eds., *New Media in the Muslim World: The Emerging Public Sphere* (Bloomington: Indiana University Press, 2003); Armando Salvatore and Dale F. Eickelman, "Muslim Publics," in *Public Islam and the Common Good* (Leiden: Brill, 2004); Armando Salvatore and Mark LeVine, eds., *Religion, Social Practice, and Contested Hegemonies: Reconstructing the Public Sphere in Muslim Majority Societies* (New York: Palgrave Macmillan, 2005); Charles Hirschkind and Brian Larkin, "Media and the Political Forms of Religion," *Social Text* 26, no. 3 (2008): 1–15.

[22] Notable exceptions include Fariba Adelkhah, "Framing the Public Sphere: Iranian Women in the Islamic Republic," in *Public Islam and the Common Good*, ed. Dale

place as principally within the domain of intimate relations—in the family, the conjugal couple, a gendered division of labor, and private sexualities.[23] Many of these writers conceptualize these roles through the trope of a liberation situated within the family, achieved through the processes of childbearing, motherhood, and childrearing.[24] Their writings identify affect, family, and gendered roles as the site for the cultivation of religion.[25] Motherwork and homespace become ways of nurturing Islamic community outside the reach of the secular state, military intervention, and foreign ideologies, even though these practices are clearly conditioned by the politics of domination within which they are proscribed and against which they mobilize.[26] This seeming paradox in contemporary Islamic thought—of liberation in the family and home—is at the heart of this project. It is a politics of the private sphere, a private piety cultivated in the public eye, women's inner life

---

Eickelman and Armando Salvatore (Leiden: Brill, 2006), 227–41; Haifaa Jawad, "Islamic Feminism: Leadership Roles and Public Representation," *Hawwa* 7, no. 1 (2009): 1–24.

[23] Margot Badran, "Competing Agendas: Feminists, Islam, and the State in Nineteenth- and Twentieth-Century Egypt," in *Women, Islam and the State*, ed. Deniz Kandiyoti (Philadelphia: Temple University Press, 1991), 219; Yvonne Yazbeck Haddad, "The Case of the Feminist Movement," in *Contemporary Islam and the Challenge of History* (Albany: State University of New York Press, 1982); Barbara Freyer Stowasser, "Religious Ideology, Women, and the Family: The Islamic Paradigm," in *The Islamic Impulse* (Washington, DC: Georgetown University Press, 1987).

[24] Haddad, "Case of the Feminist Movement," 56; Mervat Hatem, "Secularist and Islamist Discourses on Modernity in Egypt and the Evolution of the Postcolonial Nation-State," in *Islam, Gender, and Social Change*, ed. Yvonne Yazbeck Haddad and John L. Esposito (Oxford: Oxford University Press, 1997), 92–94. Hatem describes how Islamic activists (both women and men) "presented a romantic ideal of domesticity" embedded in the "familiar language of individual liberties and rights." This represents "a convergence between Islamic and modern discussions of the sexual division of labor that assigned women to the private (family) sphere and men to the public sphere."

[25] Lila Abu-Lughod, "The Marriage of Feminism and Islamism in Egypt: Selective Repudiation as a Dynamic of Postcolonial Cultural Politics," in *Remaking Women: Feminism and Modernity in the Middle East*, ed. Lila Abu-Lughod (Princeton, NJ: Princeton University Press, 1998), 243; Margot Badran, *Feminism in Islam: Secular and Religious Convergences* (Oxford: Oneworld, 2009); Sherine Hafez, *An Islam of Her Own: Reconsidering Religion and Secularism in Women's Islamic Movements* (New York: NYU Press, 2011); Mervat Hatem, "Egyptian Discourses on Gender and Political Liberalization: Do Secularist and Islamist Views Really Differ?" *Middle East Journal* 48, no. 4 (1994): 661–76; Hatem, "Secularist and Islamist Discourses on Modernity."

[26] Two black feminists use the terms motherwork and homespace to refer to the family as a place of refuge from white racial oppression and a place for inculcating politically conscious subjectivities and collectivities. Patricia Hill Collins, "Shifting the Center: Race, Class, and Feminism Theorizing about Motherhood," in *Motherhood: Ideology, Experience, and Agency*, ed. Evelyn Nakano Glenn, Grace Chang, and Linda Rennie Forcey (New York: Routledge, 1994); bell hooks, "Homeplace: A Site of Resistance," in *Yearning: Race, Gender, and Cultural Politics* (Boston: South End Press, 1990).

at the crux of public debate, a family where an Islamic biopower is both performed and transformed.

Controlling the visibility or the visuality of the intimate sphere has been critical to public debates about its Islamic nature. Despite prevalent representations of Muslim women as invisible, relegated to the domestic sphere, and condemned to a life of biological reproduction, proliferating discourses about women's rights and roles only highlight their centrality to national politics. These discourses revolve explicitly around women's actual visibility, what they reveal and conceal, what they veil and unveil, their presences and absences in public life. The outward sign of the veil has been critical to cultivating inner, pious selves, where the female body takes on a certain sacred inviolability. Moreover, veiling has been critical to public performances of an Islamic self—whether in print media, on television, or in the film industry. In fact, veiling narratives and veiled women have been key players in the emergence of an Islamic public sphere. This is perhaps as true in Egypt as it has been in France and Turkey, where veiling has been legally banned, and in Iran, where the veil is officially prescribed. The hijab has been a screen on which women have projected pious selves, writing new life stories through a classical signifier of Islamic faith. Proliferating veiling narratives dramatize new roles for women, cultivate an inner spirituality bounded by the hijab, but also facilitate movement between private and public spheres.

Revivalist writings on gender have not been translated; they are poorly understood; and their ideas have been flagrantly misrepresented or not represented at all, especially in European and American public discourse. Substantive scholarship has chronicled women's roles in mobilizing public piety and the performance of gendered identities within the movement. Much of this research has concentrated on the bodily cultivation associated with veiling, women's visible activism, and their intellectual production.[27] Writings on the proper practice of women's Islamic roles have been central to the movement. Yet there has been little deep or systematic analysis of this corpus of texts in general, or of how these writings help produce gendered subjectivities associated with the rise in Islamic sensibilities, even though scholars

[27] Fadwa El Guindi, "Veiling Infitah with Muslim Ethic: Egypt's Contemporary Islamic Movement," *Social Problems* 28, no. 4 (April 1, 1981): 465–85; Valerie J. Hoffman-Ladd, "Polemics on the Modesty and Segregation of Women in Contemporary Egypt," *International Journal of Middle East Studies* 19, no. 1 (1987): 23–50; Hatem, "Secularist and Islamist Discourses on Modernity"; Abu-Lughod, "Marriage of Feminism and Islamism"; Mervat Hatem, "Gender and Islamism in the 1990s," *Middle East Report* no. 222 (2002): 44–47; Mahmood, *Politics of Piety*; Badran, *Feminism in Islam*; Hafez, *Islam of Her Own.*

have stressed their importance.[28] I use literary analyses to do justice to these writers' intellectual contributions, the sources of their wide popular appeal, and their texts' fertile content and aesthetic impact. I detail not only *what* these writers say but *how* they say it (through style, genre, medium), and the texts and contexts with which they are in dialogue. I showcase the writers and their writings, situate them in the sociopolitical contexts that helped produce them (and that they helped produce), and use theoretical literature on the revival to interpret their influence on contemporary Egyptian politics. I closely chronicle their oeuvres, interlocutors, arguments, publishing houses, and fields, and the political context in which their writings were formulated. Through a holistic look at each author's body of writings, I detail the progression of their ideas, the evolution of their private and public personas, the political and social issues that they address, and how they position themselves as Islamic thinkers in the intellectual reformism associated with the revival. Through a thick description of the lives and writings of some of the most important Islamic intellectuals associated with the ṣaḥwa (awakening), I trace the tangled roots of their intellectual lineages and chart the political, economic, and legal contestations that their writings address and aim to influence. The Iranian scholar Ziba Mir-Hosseini calls for precisely such an approach, for a close examination of "the personal and sociopolitical trajectories of so-called Islamic feminists, in their own specific contexts."[29]

Drawing on processes initiated earlier in the twentieth century, these writers deploy new genres, disciplines, and stylistic approaches toward the production of Islamic knowledge. *Soft Force* focuses on how the language, texts, and concepts of the Islamic discursive tradition are reinterpreted and reconfigured through new, modernist hermeneutics. The writers use Arabo-Islamic disciplines, lexicons, literatures, and ethical systems to reinterpret not only ideas of rights and freedom but also the key position of women in a modern Islamic political community—a community that has for so long been strangulated by different forms of authoritarian secularism (or secular authoritarianism). Though formulated within the modernist project of secular liberalism (and in dialogue with it), these Islamic discourses challenge its key biases—about its grounding in Western political and cultural forms, its relationship

[28] Hoffman-Ladd's article "Polemics on the Modesty and Segregation of Women" pioneered this field. Malti-Douglas's impressive *Medicines of the Soul* focuses on Islamist women's autobiographical production. Her incisive literary analyses inspired this book, even though I focus more specifically on the texts' relationship to Egyptian politics and their broader impact on popular Islamic discourse across the umma.

[29] Mir-Hosseini, "Beyond 'Islam' vs 'Feminism.'"

to religion and to the church in particular, and the political power of the private sphere.

The Islamic writings examined here envision the Islamic family—with mothers at the helm—as wielding biopower that shapes governmentality on a larger scale, as the root source of political community, and as an informal economy that stands over the most precious resources of the umma, its reproductive capacity. Rather than a sentence to subservience, women's submission to God becomes the chain that makes them free, a renunciation of sovereignty that is—however paradoxically—"the condition of democratic politics."[30] The writers see the family as the site for the construction of a common (Islamic) world, the realization of an Islamic ethics (its adab), and the practice of social justice on a microcosmic level. As Walaʾ ʿAbd al-Halim of Bayt al-ʿAʾila (Family House) said, "This is part of the reformist methodology of the Muslim Brotherhood. Shaping a righteous individual leads to shaping a righteous family, and by shaping a righteous family, you get a righteous society that can choose a righteous leader."[31] Family becomes the very basis (cell or unit) of political community—and its ethics of duty, self-sacrifice, care, and compassion, the basis for an ethical politics. Local networks of home and family foster an Islamic community outside the reach of the secular state, even though these realms are clearly conditioned by the politics of domination within which they are proscribed and against which they mobilize. A space for the cultivation of religious freedom became key for the practice of a modern Islamic politics at a grassroots level, through the inculcation of Islamic sensibilities and an Islamic ethics. These thinkers interpret "*family* or *personal life* as *natural to woman* and in some formulations *divinely ordained*; it is a domain governed by needs and affective ties, hence a domain of *collectivity*; and the hierarchy within it also constitutes the domain of 'real political life' for feminists."[32]

I focus on towering public figures, prominent contributors to debates over the nature of intimate relations, the people whose ideas and works have been widely circulated, disseminated, and reiterated in public discourse. I examine the ripple effect of their ideas, how their contributions influence new generations of writers and writings, as certain concepts "go viral" through the mechanical reproduction of the

[30] Linda Zerilli, *Feminism and the Abyss of Freedom* (Chicago: University of Chicago Press, 2005), 16, 19.

[31] Mona El-Naggar, "Family Life According to the Brotherhood," *New York Times*, September 4, 2012, http://www.nytimes.com/2012/09/05/world/middleeast/05iht-letter05.html.

[32] Wendy Brown, "Liberalism's Family Values," in *States of Injury: Power and Freedom in Late Modernity* (Princeton, NJ: Princeton University Press, 1995), 147.

digital age. Each chapter is organized around a seminal figure or set of related figures, proceeding roughly chronologically through a thematic history of the ṣaḥwa in Egypt. I trace each writer's individual trajectory but also explore how their personal experiences transect with the larger discursive narratives of their age. They engage the overarching historical debates of their time, weaving them into their narratives, arguments, and worldviews. Moreover, their personal relationships are often closely interconnected with their intellectual sparring partners and with their spiritual guides. Sometimes the tangled narratives of personal lives overlap with the public dialogues in which these figures engage. Their ideas merge, converge, and conflict in both private and public, sometimes dictating their geographical and intellectual trajectories. The connective tissue of interconnected lives provides the very fabric of this revivalist Islam, through relationships with spouses, potential lovers, fathers, sisters, friends, colleagues, teachers, and mentors.

The book proceeds through a set of interlocking thematic debates about the continuing relevance of the early community and the Qurʾan for the modern world of letters and modern society (chapter 1); the nature of Islamic law and personal status laws (chapter 2); motherhood and childbearing (chapter 3); veiling and cultivating the self (chapter 4); women's labor in the face of developmentalist narratives, neoliberal expansion, free market reform, and structural adjustment (chapter 5); and the family as the political unit of the umma (chapter 6). The three parts show how an Islamic politics, a theology of emancipation from the grip of secular authoritarianism (part 1), helped foster new kinds of Islamic selves and identities (part 2), as well as new "cells" of modern society like a nuclear family (part 3). I analyze the cultural production of the revival with a cultural studies approach. Drawing on interdisciplinary scholarship of the revival, I use sociology, political science, women's studies, religion, and history to interpret how popular writings on gender function as powerful tools of social and political mobilization.

Soft Force focuses mainly on the awakening of the final decades of the twentieth century and the first decades of the twenty-first century. But I also examine how these revivalist debates originated in the earlier, nineteenth-century awakening known as the *nahḍa*. Nahḍa ideas, books, and texts have been resuscitated for the late twentieth-century revival known as the ṣaḥwa. Through a process of publication and republication, new redactions, collections, and editions, newer works recycle the Islamic intellectual tradition for new political contexts and for ever wider popular audiences. The word *nahḍa* is often translated as the Arab "renaissance," but the word's true meaning is "awakening" or "arising," with both political and spiritual connotations.[33] The more formal word *yaqaẓa*, which also connotes "awakening," has been used in literary texts but eventually gave way to the more colloquial ṣaḥwa.[34] The word *baʿth* (uprising or rebirth) was connected with the more secular era of Arab nationalism and its political parties in Syria and Iraq (especially with its pan-Arab connotations of Christian resurrection). Ṣaḥwa eventually won out for the late twentieth- and early twenty-first-century revival, even though this ṣaḥwa has continued to connect itself to the earlier nahḍa as both a movement and a concept. In the aftermath of the 2011 uprisings in the Arab world, the use of nahḍa intensified, coming to refer to political parties, platforms, organizations, and movements for the postrevolutionary era. Nahḍa is often coupled with the concept of a dawn (*fajr*), suggesting a new era but also carrying connotations of "enlightenment." Enlightenment (*tanwīr*) has been a related concept widely circulated in revivalist texts, a light (*nūr*) of Islam that is part of a new Islamic vision (*ruʾya*) and a new Islamic weltanschauung (*taṣwīr*), conveyed through new modes of representation and new kinds of imagery. This taṣwīr connotes a new way of seeing and looking at the world, an Islamic worldview enlightened, awakened, and revived by the word of God, the Qurʾan, *al-bayān*.

Islamic Adab: The Context of the Texts

Soft Force engages in a qualitative analysis of new forms of cultural production so critical to producing an Islamic communal identity and to conceptualizing new kinds of Islamic selves, subjectivities, and sensibilities. Vivid dramatizations of the politics of the personal have been critical to imagining "new definitions of human identity."[35] *Soft Force* explores the political implications of this "signifying action"[36] and also how religion is constituted through these processes of representation, how it is lived, embodied, and experienced. Precisely because of the marginalization of Islamic groups from state power, they have

[33] The translation of the word as "renaissance" misleads with its Christian overtones of rebirth, glossing the ritualistic, Islamic connotations of awakening.

[34] Muhammad ʿImara, *Tayyarat al-Yaqaza al-Islamiyya al-Haditha* (Cairo: Dar al-Hilal, 1982) and *al-Tariq ila al-Yaqaza al-Islamiyya*, (Cairo: Dar al-Shuruq, 1990).

[35] Taylor, *Modern Social Imaginaries*, 106.

[36] Carrie Rosefsky Wickham, *Mobilizing Islam: Religion, Activism, and Political Change in Egypt* (New York: Columbia University Press, 2002), 120. Wickham describes *daʿwa* as promoting "a new ethic of civic obligation that mandated participation in the public sphere . . . movement organizers act partly as 'signifying agents,' articulating and transmitting ideas that can serve as the basis for action."

been able to effect long-lasting grassroots mobilization at the level of civil society, local networks, associations, community groups, and Islamic nongovernmental organizations (NGOs).[37] Cultural production, or "print Islam," has been critical to articulating this "parallel Islamic sector"—popular pamphlets, tracts, books, journals, and newspapers that later extended to audiocassettes, cable channels, Internet sites, social media, and YouTube videos. "Islamic ideological outreach was typically a personal, even intimate process . . . relationships reinforced by the wide range of Islamic books, pamphlets, and cassette tapes produced in the parallel Islamic sector," writes Carrie Wickham in *Mobilizing Islam*. She argues that

> the dissemination of Islamist *daʿwa* through print and audio technologies at the microlevel was intricately related to institutional developments at the macrolevel. Beginning in the mid-1970s and accelerating in the 1980s, independent Islamic publishing houses and bookstores launched new forms of cultural production and created channels through which their output could be distributed to a mass market. . . . If such technologies have assisted in the formation of broad national or communal identities, they have served equally well to disseminate more specific ideological frames, including, in this case, a new, activist conception of Muslim faith and observance.[38]

Soft Force examines how an Islamic public sphere developed within the specific national context of Egypt and charts its far-reaching significance for transnational politics. Scholarly, polemical, digital, and visual production in Egypt helped disseminate Islamic ideas across national boundaries, first through print media and more recently through new technologies, where they proliferate in new contexts. Certain keywords and concepts have taken root in new soils, in places as diverse as postcolonial France, postrevolution Iran, Indonesia, Tunisia, and Saudi Arabia, a process chronicled in this book. The Islamic public sphere developed in response to the local politics of Egypt but became closely tied to Islam's central importance to different public spheres across the globe. A close look at the mechanisms of Islamic cultural production in the specific case of Egypt helps demonstrate how it affected both national and transnational politics.

In Egypt the shift to a neoliberal economy in the mid-1970s helped contribute to the emergence of the revival during this same period.

[37] Ibid.; Bayat, *Making Islam Democratic.*

[38] Wickham, *Mobilizing Islam*, 135.

Economic liberalization was accompanied by political liberalization mandated by international governing bodies like the International Monetary Fund and USAID. When Anwar Sadat took power in 1970, he reversed his predecessor Gamal ʿAbd al-Nasser's oppressive policies toward Islamic groups, freeing Islamic political prisoners, allowing Islamic presses to resume publication, loosening restrictions on Islamic cultural production, and permitting Islamic organizations and groups to thrive. Sadat's campaign of partial political liberalization famously aimed at using the Islamists to counter the weight of the leftists, helping to contribute to a surge of Islamic textual production that accompanied and precipitated the Islamic Awakening.[39] Though Islamic groups were still marginalized from direct participation in state politics, the space that they were allowed to inhabit—in an increasingly Islamic public sphere, an Islamic civil society, informal networks, and the family and community—gave the Islamic movement powerful means to mobilize the populace, as it came to inhabit institutions that the state was unable to fully manipulate toward its own ends.[40]

Islamic politics has had a contentious relationship with the political core or center of the Egyptian state. The state's approach has ranged from cooptation (of religious institutions) and outright persecution under Nasser to accommodation under Sadat's and Mubarak's policies of partial (economic and political) liberalization.[41] The state's contra-

[39] Yves Gonzalez-Quijano, *Les gens du livre: édition et champ intellectuel dans l'Égypte républicaine* (Paris: CNRS Éditions, 1998); Wickham, *Mobilizing Islam*, 134–47; Dale Eickelman and Jon Anderson, "Redefining Muslim Publics," in *New Media in the Muslim World: The Emerging Public Sphere* (Bloomington: Indiana University Press, 2003), 1; Armando Salvatore and Mark LeVine, eds., *Religion, Social Practice, and Contested Hegemonies: Reconstructing the Public Sphere in Muslim Majority Societies* (New York: Palgrave Macmillan, 2005), 15; Mahmood, *Politics of Piety*, 3; Bayat, *Making Islam Democratic*, 33. Mahmood defines the Islamic Revival as a "term that refers not only to the activities of state-oriented political groups but more broadly to a religious ethos or sensibility that has developed within contemporary Muslim societies. This sensibility has a palpable public presence in Egypt, manifest in the vast proliferation of neighborhood mosques and other institutions of Islamic learning and social welfare[,] . . . a brisk consumption and production of religious media and literature, and a growing circle of intellectuals who write and comment upon contemporary affairs in the popular press from a self-described Islamic point of view."

[40] Diane Singerman, *Avenues of Participation: Family, Politics, and Networks in Urban Quarters of Cairo* (Princeton, NJ: Princeton University Press, 1996). Singerman describes the power of popular forms of mobilization among "informal networks" in Egypt, a power the Islamic movement has cultivated toward its own ends.

[41] Laura Bier, *Revolutionary Womanhood: Feminisms, Modernity, and the State in Nasser's Egypt* (Stanford, CA: Stanford University Press, 2011), 107. Nasser dismantled the shariʿa courts while integrating personal status law into the new national courts. At the same time, he nationalized the Islamic university al-Azhar, putting it under the control of the state, the "centripetal consolidation" referred to by Hirschkind in *Ethical Soundscape* (55).

dictory—or, one might say, paradoxical—approach to Islamic law has mediated its relationship with Islamic groups and institutions. Successive constitutions have slipped between defining shariʿa as *a* source of legislation (in 1971) to shariʿa as *the* source of legislation (in a 1981 amendment). The relegation of shariʿa to the laws of personal status has created a seeming paradox of "'the family' as both a private space and one that was central to the political order." The confinement of shariʿa "to domestic matters politicized the family both as a sphere of intimate, affective relations and as a repository of group identity of which religious affiliation was a defining legal and moral characteristic."[42] The relationship between secular and religious law, foreign and indigenous systems of government, and social and sexual contracts, along with the question of religious liberties and religious politics, have been constantly negotiated through public contestations over the personal status laws in Egypt and elsewhere in the Muslim world.[43] The official domain of shariʿa in Egyptian state law, these laws mainly concern the intimate sphere of gendered relations, family, and marriage (even though the *waqf*, or "religious endowments," and the economic and political autonomy of religious property are also governed by these laws). Through these laws, a tight historical bond has been forged among the family, gendered relationships, Islamic law, and religious politics, authority, and governance. Moreover, it has been closely connected to an economy of Islamic property that lies in the informal networks of private life.

The identification of family matters (and religious property) with religious law appears as a secular understanding of religious law's proper jurisdiction in the private sphere. These laws have the effect of creating the family as the sphere of religion, in which religion is both concentrated and confined. In *Formations of the Secular*, Talal Asad calls the personal status laws the expression of a "secular formula for 'privatizing' religion." Family is defined as an autonomous sphere of freedom seemingly outside the domain of the state, even while circumscribed and codified by state (religious) law. "The family becomes the unit of 'society' in which the individual is physically and morally reproduced and has his or her primary formation as a 'private' [or one might say 'religious'] being."[44] Asad views the reproduction of the private individual in terms of "citizen's rights," where the individual is understood

[42] Bier, *Revolutionary Womanhood*, 104.

[43] Talal Asad, *Formations of the Secular: Christianity, Islam, Modernity* (Stanford, CA: Stanford University Press, 2003), 205–56; Wael B. Hallaq, *An Introduction to Islamic Law* (Cambridge: Cambridge University Press, 2009), 145–46; Bier, *Revolutionary Womanhood*, 101–20.

[44] Asad, *Formations of the Secular*, 227.

as self-governing, self-regulating, and autonomous "as befits the citizen of a secular, liberal society."[45] It becomes a means of creating (an illusion of) the private domain of the family as an "extrapolitical" space of freedom outside of government rule—a space key not just to the free practice of religion but also to the critique of arbitrary government.[46] Because the seeming apolitical nature of the private has been so central to secularism's mythology of itself, Islamic thinkers have been able to capitalize on this assumption to build a safe space for the articulation of Islamic politics outside the reach of the secular state. The freedom of this sphere has been critical to the articulation of an Islamic public sphere predicated on both the free practice of religion and freedom of (religious) expression. Through this "freedom of public exchange," Asad says, "debates about Islamic reasoning and national progress, as well as about individual autonomy, could now take place publicly."[47] These "intellectual technologies" so key to governing have mediated the relationship between the law and the family, government and religion, public and private.[48] Asad understands this freedom as the condition of a secular modernity, but it is also the condition of a modern Islamic liberalism ("a national nonsecular modernity") that has challenged the very legitimacy of the secular state, even while operating within and against this secularism.[49] Islamic thinkers developed a critique not only of the state's illiberal authoritarianism but of secularism's inherent illiberality. Secular liberalism is not just hypocritical and tyrannical, they assert, but unenlightened and backward.

The identification of the family, and Islamic law, as sacrosanct domains outside of state control was a key maneuver performed within Islamic intellectual production. This is what the Islamic thinker Heba Raouf Ezzat terms a "politics of informality" mobilized through the "power of public spheres in Egypt."[50] Intellectuals like Raouf Ezzat play on—and subvert—secularism's core assumptions about the separation of church and state and of private and public, using these assumptions to define family relations as Islamic territory. Revivalist writings em-

[45] Ibid., 226.

[46] Rose, *Powers of Freedom*, 72–74; Taylor, *Modern Social Imaginaries*.

[47] Asad, *Formations of the Secular*, 236.

[48] Rose, *Powers of Freedom*, 27.

[49] Omnia El Shakry, "Schooled Mothers and Structured Play: Child Rearing in Turn-of-the-Century Egypt," in *Remaking Women: Feminism and Modernity in the Middle East*, ed. Lila Abu-Lughod (Princeton, NJ: Princeton University Press, 1998), 128; Dipesh Chakrabarty, *Provincializing Europe: Postcolonial Thought and Historical Difference* (Princeton, NJ: Princeton University Press, 2007), 11–14.

[50] Heba Raouf Ezzat, "Politics of Informality: On the Power of the Public Spheres of Egypt," Alwaleed Bin Talal Center for Muslim-Christian Understanding, Georgetown University, Washington, DC, February 15, 2012.

phasize the crucial importance of the family's intimate relations to the cultivation of Islamic sensibilities, Islamic selves, Islamic subjectivities, and gendered Islamic bodies. They root this process in the classical tradition of adab, where the cultivation of bodily sensibilities, habits, and disciplines is critical to constructing an ethical Islamic self. Adab is a kind of pedagogy that cultivates virtue. Ebrahim Moosa defines it as "both the education itself and the internalization of norms in order to ingrain into the psyche a certain virtue (*faḍīla*). . . . *Adab* is that learning acquired for the sake of right living, a knowledge that goes beyond knowing. It is the disposition that enables one to experience the effects of knowledge and be transformed by its animation in the self."[51] Adab also means "literature," the actual body of texts, the *belles lettres* that discursively outline the parameters of the ethical self. New kinds of Islamic adab have helped cultivate an Islamic sensibility for the modern age, a sensibility that entails certain liberal understandings of gendered rights and duties. This literature has been critical as well to outlining the role of love, desire, intimacy, and sexuality in the cultivation of a sacred self. Since this literature largely focuses on the family as the site of production of gendered Islamic identities and subjectivities, this self is always bound into a community of believers, over which the mother (the *umm*) stands as the sign of the Islamic community (the umma).

Even as Islamic thought challenges the secularist opposition between private and public, personal faith and politics, religion and state, the private realm provided religious discourse with a refuge from the predations of the secular state, a safe haven for opposition discourse.[52] This is what the Freedom and Justice Party calls the "oasis of the family" in the "Social Issues" section of *IkhwanOnline*.[53] This privacy has provided religious discourse with a place *within* the secular state and the logic of secularism that confines religion to the private sphere. The family, gendered identities, women's bodies, the sexual division of labor, and the domestic sphere have become sacrosanct, partly because they are conceptually outside the secular state's sphere of influence. As debates over "private" issues played out in the Islamic public sphere,

[51] Ebrahim Moosa, *Ghazali and the Poetics of Imagination* (Chapel Hill: University of North Carolina Press, 2005), 210.

[52] Christopher Lasch, *Haven in a Heartless World: The Family Besieged* (New York: Norton, 1995); Brown, "Liberalism's Family Values," 159–61; Raouf Ezzat, *al-Marʾa wa-l-ʿAmal al-Siyasi*, 173–81. See chapter 6 for a fuller discussion of the family as a haven and an oasis in Raouf Ezzat's writings.

[53] See, for example, an article on Manal Abu al-Hassan, the Freedom and Justice Party's "minister of women." Ahmad Jamal, "Manal Abu al-Hassan: The Security of Woman in the Freedom and Justice Party Focuses on All Groups of Women," *IkhwanOnline*, accessed October 12, 2012, http://www.ikhwanonline.com/new/Article.aspx?ArtID=123235&SecID=323.

they helped to define the intimate domain in religious terms. But they also infused public discourse with discussions of religion. The private sphere (of family relations, gendered identities, and women's roles) has been a critical "extrapolitical" space in which religion has a sacred place—a space in which Islamic politics has become inordinately invested. In Egypt the world of Islamic letters "was appropriated by the public of private people making use of their reason and was established as a sphere of criticism of public authority," a process described by Jürgen Habermas in *The Structural Transformation of the Public Sphere*. Islamic intellectuals drew on a world of letters already well equipped with forums for discussion, public institutions, "intellectual technologies," and epistemologies.[54] The religious authority of the ʿulamaʾ (religious scholars) continued to be critical to these epistemologies, but religious writings by intellectuals outside the formal institutions of the Islamic public sphere brought new, experimental hermeneutics to the interpretation of traditional texts. The appropriation of religious discourse by "lay" writers was part of the process of decentralization of religious knowledge so important to the rise of modern "Muslim publics" in Egypt. These writers adapted genres, disciplines, and narrative styles associated with secular modernity to the Islamic intellectual tradition.[55] These representatives—and purveyors—of public opinion battled with political power over regulation of the social. Their political task was the regulation of civil society. "With the background experience of a private sphere"—interpreted as "humanity's genuine site"—they "challenged the established authority of the monarch," aided by the "illusion of freedom evoked by human intimacy." This is how "the experiential complex of audience-oriented privacy made its way into the political realm's public sphere."[56]

Scholarly characterizations of the ṣaḥwa in Egypt emphasize the dissemination of religious knowledge among the general populace, leading to what some have understood as a "democratization of religious

[54] Jürgen Habermas, *The Structural Transformation of the Public Sphere: An Inquiry into a Category of Bourgeois Society*, trans. Thomas Burger (Cambridge, MA: MIT Press, 1991), 51–52.

[55] Charles D. Smith, "The Crisis of Orientation: The Shift of Egyptian Intellectual to Islamic Subjects in the 1930s," *International Journal of Middle Eastern Studies* 4 (1973): 382–410; Charles D. Smith, "'Cultural Construct' and Other Fantasies: Imagined Narratives in Imagined Communities," *International Journal of Middle Eastern Studies* 31 (1999): 95–102; Israel Gershoni and James P. Jankowski, "Print Culture, Social Change, and the Process of Redefining Imagined Communities in Egypt," *International Journal of Middle Eastern Studies* 31 (1999): 81–94; Sabry Hafez, *The Genesis of Arabic Narrative Discourse* (London: Saqi Books, 2001); Israel Gershoni and James P. Jankowski, *Redefining the Egyptian Nation, 1930–1945* (Cambridge: Cambridge University Press, 2002).

[56] Habermas, *Structural Transformation of the Public Sphere*, 52.

authority."[57] Recent scholarship on Muslim publics discusses the "fragmentation of religious and political authority" facilitated by the development of mass education, spread of literacy, and expansion of print capitalism and other media.[58]

> These transformations increase the range of participants in discussions about Islamic values and practice. Women and minorities find their way into arenas of political and religious discourse. . . . Educated people who are not religious scholars increasingly contribute to the discussion of legal issues and create alternative sites for religious discourse and representation. Many of them claim legitimacy on the basis of simplified, systematized, and downmarket interpretations of basic texts. . . . The new media engage wider and more public communities with claims to interpret and to provide additional techniques of interpretation.[59]

A new kind of intellectual Islam, presented in a vernacular readily accessible to wider publics, enjoyed immense popularity, circulating widely in multiple editions, reprints, and translations. Revivalist writings have developed a popular intellectual Islam for the masses by opening up Islamic scholarship to a wide swath of the population. Groups previously marginalized from religious scholarship—by training, access, and gender—have burst to the fore of public debate, among them, women. Women writers emphasize the importance of religious knowledge, training, and education to the formation of the pious self. But they also shift emphasis to other kinds of intuitive knowledge, training, and education (like that of childrearing) that they suggest are more "natural" to women—an intuition of affect rooted in the biological experience of motherhood. (And these writings are careful to identify motherhood as a kind of training and "preparation.") More secular feminists criticize this as trapping women in a biological essentialism and condemning them to family life. Nonetheless, the identification with family and motherhood is one revivalist writers clearly revel in developing, cultivating, and expanding. It is a way of not only legitimizing their cultural production that deals with these issues but also infusing other aspects

[57] Charles Hirschkind, *The Ethical Soundscape: Cassette Sermons and Islamic Counter publics* (New York: Columbia University Press, 2009), 105.

[58] Eickelman and Anderson, "Redefining Muslim Publics," 1; Armando Salvatore and Mark LeVine, "Reconstructing the Public Sphere in Muslim Majority Societies," in *Religion, Social Practice, and Contested Hegemonies: Reconstructing the Public Sphere in Muslim Majority Societies* (New York: Palgrave Macmillan, 2005), 15.

[59] Eickelman and Anderson, "Redefining Muslim Publics," 11.

of their life work with value and cultural capital, along with religious significance.

Scholars of the revival interpret the ṣaḥwa through tropes of political center and periphery. In political theory, women are often seen as marginalized from political power, along with home, family, and informal networks.[60] In a brilliant metaphor, Charles Hirschkind interprets the revival as a "vast centrifugal countermovement" decentralizing—and democratizing—religious authority and knowledge.

> The centripetal consolidation of religious authority and knowledge by the Egyptian state from the 1950s onward occurred simultaneously with a vast centrifugal countermovement, what both observers and participants often refer to as the Islamic Revival movement, *al-Ṣaḥwa al-Islāmiyya*. The revival has had the net effect of dispersing the loci of religious authority across a variety of new locations, media, and associational forms. Because the protagonists of this movement have adopted modes of organization, communication, and technology ushered in by political modernization, they hastened those processes of transformation promoted by the state that aimed at developing a modern public sphere.[61]

Revivalist cultural and intellectual production has aimed more at transforming the social life of the populace than the state. And women, family, home, and informal networks are powerful forces driving this centripetal movement. The revival succeeded in entrenching its aims of social transformation at a grassroots level—in bodily subjectivities and affect—something that political revolution would not be able to achieve. A "civil Islam" rooted in the institutions of civil society (such as private mosques, Islamic voluntary associations, welfare societies, cultural organizations, schools, and commercial enterprises like Islamic banks and publishing houses) has been key to this mobiliza-

[60] In the introduction to *Avenues of Participation*, Diane Singerman launches a searing and eloquent critique of political theory that locates political power only in state institutions. Wickham, *Mobilizing Islam*, 94, defines the periphery as "encompassing all other potential arenas for collective action, including religious institutions, local community and youth centers, schools, and even private households."

[61] Hirschkind, *Ethical Soundscape*, 55. Other scholars contest this view of a division between al-Azhar as religious center and Islamic activists as a periphery, arguing more for a continuum and fluidity. See Ebrahim Moosa, "The Ethical Soundscape: Cassette Sermons and Islamic Counterpublics. By Charles Hirschkind," *Journal of the American Academy of Religion* 80, no. 1 (2012): 252–54; and Muhammad ʿAbd al-ʿAziz Dawud, *al-Jamʿiyyat al-Islamiyya fi Misr wa-Dawruha fi Nashr al-Daʿwa al-Islamiyya* (Cairo: al-Zahraʾ li-l-Iʿlam al-ʿArabi, 1992).

tion.[62] One of the most important parts of this civil Islam was an Islamic public sphere that emerged in tandem with a flourishing of Islamic bookstores, presses, and literature, helping form a new kind of imagined community not necessarily rooted in secular rationality. Yet the revival still employed critical tools of the semiliberal secular state to rally for political participation through grassroots democratic mobilization on the margins of the state. On this periphery are households, families, and community networks that become reoriented in revivalist discourse as a "center" of religious inculcation and education. For women largely marginalized from the formalized political structures of the state, the civic domains of social life become sites for the cultivation of new modes of religious authority.[63]

Soft Force examines specifically how a gendered vision of a free and equal family imbued with reciprocal rights and duties became a cornerstone, or a pillar, of Islamic politics in the modern age. Through their central importance to the Islamic family, women have been at the crux of the tense relationship between secular and religious law, secular and religious government(alities), secular and religious forms of political citizenship. This relationship has been consistently framed through recourse to a language of religious rights, freedoms, and liberties that will free an Islamic politics from secular tyrannies. Islam's place in modern governance has been constantly negotiated in modern Egyptian history through the laws of personal status and through contestations over the nature of gendered relations, family, and marriage.[64] Operating within and against a regime of secular authoritarianism, Islamic intellectual production and political mobilization took "the family" as one of the most important sites in which the issue of liberty was "problematized and technologized." The family was celebrated as the essential basis of an Islamic politics but was also a key counterweight to the tyranny of

[62] Wickham, *Mobilizing Islam*, 97; Bayat, *Making Islam Democratic*, 33; Gonzalez-Quijano, *Les gens du livre*, 171–98.

[63] The political power of these private (and peripheral) places has been at the center of feminist critiques of the public sphere. Nancy Fraser, "What's Critical about Critical Theory? The Case of Habermas and Gender," in *Unruly Practices: Power, Discourse and Gender in Contemporary Social Theory* (Cambridge: Polity Press, 1989); Nancy Fraser, "Rethinking the Public Sphere: A Contribution to the Critique of Actually Existing Democracy," in *Habermas and the Public Sphere*, ed. Craig Calhoun (Cambridge, MA: MIT Press, 1992), 109–42; Joan B. Landes, "The Public and the Private Sphere: A Feminist Reconsideration," in *Feminists Read Habermas: Gendering the Subject of Discourse* (New York: Routledge, 1995); Michael Warner, *Publics and Counterpublics* (New York: Zone Books, 2002).

[64] Asad, *Formations of the Secular*, 205–56; Frances Susan Hasso, *Consuming Desires: Family Crisis and the State in the Middle East* (Stanford, CA: Stanford University Press, 2010), 24–60; Bier, *Revolutionary Womanhood*, 101–20.

the secular state.[65] Women, so closely connected to the family, became critical to the expression of this religious freedom, to embodying its ethics, and to inculcating its disciplines.

Awakening, Revival, Revolution

In her vlog, Mahfouz articulately deploys a language of rights and freedoms to critique government corruption and tyranny. "To live like humans, to live like *banī Ādam* (children of Adam)," she says, "we've got to go down and protest on January 25th, go down to protest to demand our right as children of Adam. . . . Go down and demand your right, my right, your people's right, and the right of us all." Her images of the dehumanizing effects of authoritarian rule—of the self-immolation of Muhammad Bouʿazizi in Tunisia and the four Egyptians who set themselves on fire in front of Parliament—suggest the bare life of living without rights, the extinction of self in subjection to oppression.[66] But her words also evoke rights as the threshold of the human, and the exercise of those rights in a community as a condition of both political and personal sovereignty.[67] Mahfouz is known as one of the founding members of the April 6th movement that helped start the revolution, but she is also a member of the Muslim Brotherhood's Freedom and Justice Party. Easily slipping between religious and secular registers of political rationality, she says, "Don't fear the government, fear God," drawing on a classic argument from Islamic political thought equating submission to an earthly (secular) political authority as a form of tyranny, as the subjugation of man by man, and of subjection to God as a form of freedom. She then quotes verse 13:11 of the Qurʾan: "And among God's commands are that he will not change the condition of a people until they change what is in themselves," a verse that ends with "And there is no other leader for them except Him."

[65] Rose describes the importance of moral agency in constructing subjects capable of governing themselves; they are free only by subjecting themselves to certain disciplines. The family, he asserts, was one of the most important sites "in which the issue of liberty was problematized and technologized . . . celebrated as the essential basis and counterweight to government." Rose, *Powers of Freedom*, 72–74.

[66] Giorgio Agamben, *Homo Sacer: Sovereign Power and Bare Life*, trans. Daniel Heller-Roazen (Stanford, CA: Stanford University Press, 1998); Judith Butler, *Precarious Life: The Powers of Mourning and Violence* (New York: Verso, 2006), 128–52.

[67] Analyzing Hannah Arendt's writings, Linda Zerilli stresses that humans do not have rights because they are human, but only through their membership in political community. Hannah Arendt, *The Origins of Totalitarianism* (New York: Harcourt, Brace, Jovanovich, 1973), 298, 300; Zerilli, *Feminism and the Abyss of Freedom*, 173.

A discourse of a free and equal Islam emerged out of—and in response to—a history of secular authoritarianisms in the region, under first colonialism, then the Ottoman monarchy, and finally successive military dictatorships. At the heart of this discourse has been a rights language calling for women's freedom and equality, drawing on the terminology and ideology of women's liberation, and calling for women's participation in public life, even while asserting their critical importance to the family. This paradox at the heart of liberalism—its freedoms and coercions, rights and duties, public and private spheres—structures revivalist writings on gender and religion. Women simultaneously signify the limits of secular political citizenship, the productivity of cultural reproduction, and the sacred realm of family relations. *Soft Force* chronicles a series of key Islamic writers, thinkers, and activists who employ what Talal Asad calls "new discursive grammars" to reinterpret the Islamic intellectual tradition for a modern Islamic politics. These writers aim to produce "a theological vocabulary . . . about how a contemporary state of affairs should be configured."[68] They do so by drawing deeply on the Islamic discursive tradition, on its language, texts, thinkers, laws, and hermeneutics, reviving and reinterpreting these sources for new contexts, social problems, and forms of government and governmentalities.

New lexicons are created for new political imaginaries, even as they draw on older vocabularies, Asad observes. The concept of nahḍa is a case in point, a word that refers to the older "awakening" but has been revived for the more recent awakening, as well as the aftermath of the 2011 revolutions in the Arab world. After the uprisings in Egypt, the Islamist presidential candidate Muhammad Morsi elaborated an Islamic platform for instating "true democracy . . . with Islam as a reference" known as the Nahda Project. The document protests "despotism, oppression, and injustice" and calls for the restoration of a framework of rights and liberties and for peace and security (*amn*) in the face of a "brutal state, corrupt regime, or foreign power." One of the most important ways of safeguarding democracy, the document says, is by protecting the autonomy of (civil) society and the private sphere, the Egyptian family and "freedom of speech guided by genuine Egyptian values," to check state power.[69] The Islamic liberalism suggested in the platform of the Nahda Project (and by the language of the Freedom and Justice Party) draws on a history of Islamic criticism of secularism's undemocratic nature, both at home and abroad. Bending liberal

[68] Asad, *Formations of the Secular*, 220.

[69] Hizb al-ʿAdala wa-l-Hurriyya, "General Features of the Nahda (Renaissance) Project," *IkhwanWeb*, April 28, 2012, http://www.ikhwanweb.com/article.php?id=29932.

ideology toward its own ends, Islamic thought in Egypt has claimed, among other rights, self-determination (and self-rule), political autonomy, freedom of religion, and freedom of expression as the foundations of an Islamic polity.

Part of this rhetoric has involved calls for women's equality and participation in public life, in conjunction with repeated acknowledgments of women's central and critical importance to the family. The Nahda Project calls for the "empowerment (*tamkīn*) of the Egyptian woman to facilitate her fruitful participation in every aspect of life, what helps the woman realize a balance between her contribution to her home and to her society."[70] The promotion of work/life balance for women has been a part of Egyptian state discourse since the 1952 revolution, with successive constitutions calling for the coordination of "women's duties toward the family" with "her work in society and her equality with men in the fields of social, political, cultural, and economic life, without infringing on the dictates of the Islamic shariʿa."[71] The Nahda Project diverges from earlier state language that suggested that women's "work in society and equality with men" were somehow at odds with the shariʿa. In contrast, the Nahda Project asserts women as "totally equal to men in position and status, in work and importance"—an assertion of gender equality that became one of the core principles of the 2012 constitution.

The Nahda Project's understanding of women's equality was critical to its vision of not only political democratization but also economic development. The document signals the Muslim Brotherhood's commitment to a free market economy and to economic, social, and political liberalization through language that advocates and supports privatization and private property. One section, entitled "A Comprehensive Human Development Program," echoes earlier state (and developmentalist) initiatives that conceived of women as the "entryway to total development" in the region.[72] This section of the Nahda Project calls for "protecting woman from discrimination in her work, whether pri-

[70] Hizb al-ʿAdala wa-l-Hurriyya, "Ihtimam Khass bi-l-Marʾa fi Mashruʿ al-Nahda," *IkhwanOnline*, April 28, 2012, http://www.ikhwanonline.com/new/president/Article.aspx?ArtID=107305&SecID=470.

[71] Ellen McLarney, "Women's Rights in the Egyptian Constitution: (Neo)Liberalism's Family Values," May 22, 2013, http://www.jadaliyya.com/pages/index/11852/womens-rights-in-the-egyptian-constitution_(neo)li.

[72] League of Arab States, UNICEF, and Markaz al-Dawli li-l-Taʿlim al-Wazifi li-l-Kitab fi al-ʿAlam al-ʿArabi, *al-Marʾa al-ʿArabiyya wa-l-Tanmiya al-Qawmiyya: Halqa Dirasiyya* (Cairo: UNICEF, 1972); Lajnat al-Khidmat, *Tanmiyat al-Marʾa ka-Madkhal li-l-Tanmiya al-Shamila*, Silsilat Taqarir Majlis al-Shura (Cairo: Matbuʿat al-Shaʿb, 1984); *Nadwat al-Marʾa wa-l-Tanmiya al-Qawmiyya: Cairo, 10–11 Nufimbir 1984*. (Cairo: UNESCO: al-Markaz al-Iqlimi al-ʿArabi li-l-Buhuth wa-l-Tawthiq fi al-ʿUlum al-Ijtimaʿiyya, 1984).

vate or public," but also for supporting "women's participation in economic work beginning from micro-enterprise of women in the family and extending to free private enterprise for pioneering women."[73] The document ends with an assertion of the importance of private property, a clear signal to Western governments about where an Islamic democracy would stand in a transnational neoliberal economy. From the outset, Morsi signaled his receptivity to loans from the International Monetary Fund through clear declarations of commitment to economic liberalization, structural adjustment, privatization, and free market exchange. This neoliberal economy depends on both liberal understandings of economic and political rights and freedoms and on the value—economic and otherwise—of women's work in the family.[74] The family is a critical engine of the national economy, and its organization becomes central to the management of that economy. Women are thus envisioned in leadership roles, roles for which they must be cultivated and groomed, fostering the development of an Islamic moral economy rooted in the "political unit" of the family.

Scholars of the gendered politics of the revival observe the close relationship between liberal secularism and the revival. Saba Mahmood describes this relationship as one of "proximity and coimbrication." *Soft Force* closely analyzes the gendered dimensions of what Mahmood calls "the historically shifting, ambiguous, and unpredictable encounters that this proximity has generated."[75] Through a textual ethnography of some of the revival's most important thinkers, I trace a rhizome-like lineage of this shifting, ambiguous, and unpredictable relationship. Intellectuals associated with the revival advocate freedom as an Islamic political ideal, calling for resistance against the encroachment of Western political and cultural domination. Yet Mahmood understands the revival as a "nonliberal" movement, even as she acknowledges the

[73] Hizb al-ʿAdala wa-l-Hurriyya, "Ihtimam Khass bi-l-Marʾa"; Hizb al-ʿAdala wa-l-Hurriyya, "Nahda Project."

[74] Wendy Brown, "American Nightmare: Neoliberalism, Neoconservatism, and De-Democratization," *Political Theory* 34, no. 6 (2006): 690–714. Brown's distinction between political liberalism and economic neoliberalism is curious, especially in light of her broader work more generally, which links the rise of political and personal rights to the importance of property and to the development of a capitalist economy. The connection of "rights" discourses to neoliberal expansion has been a central feature of both rights theory and feminist critiques of developmentalism. See, for example, Maria Mies, *Patriarchy and Accumulation on a World Scale: Women in the International Division of Labour* (London: Palgrave Macmillan, 1999); and Samuel Moyn, *The Last Utopia: Human Rights in History* (Cambridge, MA: Belknap Press of Harvard University Press, 2012). See chapter 5 on women's work for a fuller discussion of neoliberal capitalism's family values.

[75] Mahmood, *Politics of Piety*, 5.

interplay between classical Islamic concepts and pervasive liberal—and neoliberal—political ideologies.[76] Critiques of Mahmood's *Politics of Piety* observe how the Islamic revival emerged out of economic and political liberalization in Egypt.[77] Other scholars have analyzed how Islamic thinkers deploy liberal political ideals in their call for Islamic self-determination, self-rule, and liberation from secular forms of authoritarianism, ideals that also shape their conceptions of gender relationships, the family, and the couple.[78] Revivalist literature draws on liberal concepts of freedom as a political ideal, freedom as a discipline that entails gendered duties as much as gendered political rights. Yet understandings of how Islamic thinkers have adapted, adopted, and transformed liberal concepts have been tainted by neoimperial prescriptions for politics in the Muslim world and the Middle East.[79] Imperial and neoimperial projects have used the language of democracy, freedom, and women's rights in inflammatory, hypocritical, and dishonest ways—what theorists understand as a racialized authoritarian governmentality at the heart of liberalism.[80] Moreover, classic scholarship on Islamic liberalism has assumed that it is secular and antithetical to a religious ("scripturalist") politics, an assumption that this project dismantles.[81]

The tensions and dichotomies between a private Islam cultivating submission and piety and a public Islam of political mobilization (for freedoms and rights) are what political theorists understand as the

[76] Ibid.

[77] Samah Selim, "Politics of Piety: The Islamic Revival and the Feminist Subject," *Jadaliyya* (October 13, 2010), http://www.jadaliyya.com/pages/index/235/politics-of-piety_the-islamic-revival-and-the-femi.

[78] Haddad, "Case of the Feminist Movement"; Hatem, "Egyptian Discourses on Gender"; Lila Abu-Lughod, "Feminist Longings and Postcolonial Conditions," in *Remaking Women: Feminism and Modernity in the Middle East* (Princeton, NJ: Princeton University Press, 1998); Badran, *Feminism in Islam*; Hafez, *Islam of Her Own*.

[79] Saba Mahmood, "Secularism, Hermeneutics, Empire: The Politics of Islamic Reformation," *Public Culture* 18, no. 2 (2006): 323–47.

[80] Mitchell Dean, *Governmentality: Power and Rule in Modern Society* (New York: Sage Publications, 1999), 131–48; Uday Singh Mehta, *Liberalism and Empire: A Study in Nineteenth-Century British Liberal Thought* (Chicago: University of Chicago Press, 1999), 46–76; Jennifer Pitts, *A Turn to Empire: The Rise of Imperial Liberalism in Britain and France* (Princeton, NJ: Princeton University Press, 2006); Karuna Mantena, *Alibis of Empire: Henry Maine and the Ends of Liberal Imperialism* (Princeton, NJ: Princeton University Press, 2010); Domenico Losurdo, *Liberalism: A Counter-History*, trans. Gregory Elliott (London: Verso, 2014).

[81] Leonard Binder, *Islamic Liberalism: A Critique of Development Ideologies* (Chicago: University of Chicago Press, 1988). Binder sees liberalism as indicative of an "open society" predicated on the separation of religion and state, and fundamentalism and scripturalism as markers of a "closed society." These are dichotomies coded into liberalism's own division of spheres.

paradoxes, or "constitutive dualisms," of liberalism. This creates a "division of labor" between the private as a feminized realm of difference and relationality and the public domain as the sphere of political autonomy, rights, and freedoms. The intimate domain is structured by a sexual contract in which an ethics of care and self-sacrifice serve as an essential counterweight to a public discourse of individual rights and freedoms.[82] This paradox has been explored not only in feminist theory[83] but also in Middle Eastern scholarship on the gendered discourses of the revival.[84] I draw specifically on this particular body of literature that probes liberalism's gendered contradictions, ones epitomized by the dichotomization between the private and the public domains, the personal and the political, feminine and masculine spheres. *Soft Force* explores the sexual contract at the heart of a new, Islamic social contract, one that has been elucidated through a discourse of intimacy articulated in the Islamic public sphere. This social contract has called for citizenship rights, freedom of expression and conviction, freedom of press, freedom of congregation, freedom of political participation, and freedom of democratic self-rule under successive military dictatorships that have sought to manage and control religion and religious expression. The public sphere of Islamic letters has tried to wrest itself free of excessive control over these religious discourses. The sexual contract, sanctioned by Islamic law, becomes an expression of a "free" domain outside state control, considered a repository of Islamic politics, and the "natural" domain of religion. Women become signifiers of this sexual contract but also of the power of this sacrosanct domain as a bastion against—and within—the secular state, an inviolable domain of Islamic politics and an Islamic religious citizenship. In the writings

[82] Carole Pateman, *The Sexual Contract* (Stanford, CA: Stanford University Press, 1988); Seyla Benhabib, *Situating the Self: Gender, Community, and Postmodernism in Contemporary Ethics* (New York: Routledge, 1992); Seyla Benhabib, "Autonomy, Modernity, and Community: Communitarianism and Critical Social Theory in Dialogue," in *Cultural-Political Interventions in the Unfinished Project of Enlightenment*, ed. Axel Honneth (Cambridge, MA: MIT Press, 1992); Lasch, *Haven in a Heartless World.*

[83] For some of the feminist theory on the subject, see Carole Pateman, "Feminist Critiques of the Public/Private Dichotomy," in *Public and Private in Social Life*, ed. S. I. Benn and G. F. Gaus (London: St. Martin's Press, 1983); Brown, "Liberalism's Family Values"; Joan Wallach Scott, *Only Paradoxes to Offer: French Feminists and the Rights of Man* (Cambridge, MA: Harvard University Press, 1997); Joan Wallach Scott, *Parite!: Sexual Equality and the Crisis of French Universalism* (Chicago: University of Chicago Press, 2005).

[84] A wide body of scholarship on gender in Islamic discourses notes the "convergence" between the language of liberal secularism and contemporary Islamic ideology. See, for example, Haddad, "Case of the Feminist Movement"; Stowasser, "Religious Ideology"; Hatem, "Egyptian Discourses on Gender"; Abu-Lughod, "Marriage of Feminism and Islamism"; Jouili and Amir-Moazami, "Knowlege, Empowerment, and Religious Authority"; Badran, *Feminism in Islam*; Hafez, *Islam of Her Own.*

analyzed here, the sexual contract, the sphere of intimate relations, family, home, motherhood, and marital sexuality are invested with an extraordinary power to transform both community and politics. Revivalist women focus inward on self, home, family, and the intimate domain, calling for the cultivation of this natural unit of the Islamic umma. This inward focus might be interpreted as one of the effects of the Islamic movement's coimbrication with liberalism in Egypt, as the production of a privatized religion that has become the outpost of religious sensibilities within the secular state. These religious sensibilities are cultivated within an idealized family form that has been the site for the expression of women's piety.

Soft Force explores the roots of "assertive women's subjectivities" through a deep history of the writings of "alternative Islamic feminist voices" that have worked to "re-politicize a politics of piety" during the last half of the twentieth century and into the early twenty-first century.[85] "Egypt," political scientist Paul Amar writes, "is not and never has been simply an end-point for vectors of the 'dissemination' of internationalist feminism; to the contrary, Egypt has been an originator, center, and disseminator of modern internationalist feminism, of both the 'maternal' and radical varieties."[86] Is there a paradox between the Nahda Project's assertion of women's fundamental political equality with men and revivalist emphasis on the primacy of women's roles as mothers and preoccupation with the family? This "paradox" at the heart of liberalism is the subject of this book—paradoxes of sovereignty and submission, equality and difference, rights and duties, freedom and coercion that have structured Islamic politics in Egypt. This is not merely a "derivative discourse"[87] but a conscious use of the master's tools to dismantle the master's house[88] through an Islamici-

[85] Amar, "Turning the Gendered Politics of the Security State Inside Out?" 320, 321.

[86] Ibid.

[87] Partha Chatterjee, *Nationalist Thought and the Colonial World: A Derivative Discourse* (Minneapolis: University of Minnesota Press, 1993); Partha Chatterjee, *Texts of Power: Emerging Disciplines in Colonial Bengal* (Minneapolis: University of Minnesota Press, 1995), 8. "Fortunately for history, modern power and the scientific practices of the disciplines spilled over their colonial embankments to proliferate in the native quarters. Energized by the desires and strategies of entirely different political agencies, the intellectual project of modernity found new sustenance in those densely populated parts; and in the process, it took on entirely new forms. . . . we will find that it was not as though the 'pure fluid' of European enlightenment was merely mingled with a few drops of the 'muddy but holy Ganges water'; the 'claims of conscience,' as indeed the strategies of power, opened to question some of the very procedures of the practice of modernity."

[88] Using the tools of racist patriarchy means that "only the most narrow perimeters of change are possible and allowable." Audre Lorde, *Sister Outsider: Essays and Speeches* (New York: Ten Speed Press, 1984), 111.

zation of the ideological tools of modern governmentalities. Yet the question remains: if these thinkers are caught in the contradictions of liberalism, can this ever truly lead to a genuine emancipatory politics? The writers discussed in this book all probe the contradictions at the heart of liberalism. They understand its "tyranny" and "coercions" (its racial, gendered, and imperial hypocrisies).[89] For them, this contradiction is epitomized by the emancipating power of submission to God. Islam is the chain, they argue, that makes an Islamic polity truly free.

Islam is not an "unchanging essence" with an ossified lexicon but a tradition that carries within it the mechanisms for its own renewal, reform, and reinterpretation according to changing political and historical circumstances.[90] Islamic thinkers of the past decades have employed new terminologies—and technologies—to engineer the revival of Islamic thought and practice, as well as to ensure the social and political survival of Islam within successive secular authoritarianisms. Partly because of their disenfranchisement from state politics, revivalist thinkers adopted and adapted the language of democratic mobilization, language that goes back to the nahḍa, the Arab awakening of the late eighteenth and early nineteenth centuries. An Islamic language of rights and freedoms has served as a powerful tool for critiquing various forms of secular authoritarianism in the region—colonial, monarchical, dictatorial, and military—regimes that have systematically, and sometimes brutally, repressed Islamic groups, movements, and writings.[91]

[89] Brown writes about "contradictions," while Scott talks about "paradoxes" in the gendered politics of liberalism. See Brown, "Liberalism's Family Values"; Scott, *Only Paradoxes to Offer*. Similarly, Rose writes about the "despotism . . . at the heart of liberalism"; Dean, about liberalism's authoritarianism. See Rose, *Powers of Freedom*, 43; Dean, *Governmentality*, 131–48. Mehta and Losurdo write about the liberalism's hypocrisy with regard to colonialism and slavery. See Mehta, *Liberalism and Empire*; Losurdo, *Liberalism*.

[90] John O. Voll, "Renewal and Reform in Islamic History: Tajdid and Islah," in *Voices of Resurgent Islam*, ed. John L. Esposito (Oxford: Oxford University Press, 1983); Shakry, "Schooled Mothers and Structured Play"; Asad, *Formations of the Secular*, 222; Haj, *Reconfiguring Islamic Tradition*.

[91] To name just a few of the most important critiques: ʿAbd al-Rahman Kawakibi, *Tabaʾiʿ al-Istibdad wa-Masariʿ al-Istiʿbad*, ed. Muhammad ʿImara (Cairo: Matabiʿ Ruz al-Yusuf, 2011); ʿAbd al-ʿAziz Jawish, *al-Islam Din al-Fitra wa-l-Hurriyya* (Cairo: Dar al-Maʿarif, 1968); ʿAbd al-ʿAziz Jawish, *Athar al-Qurʾan fi Tahrir al-Fikr al-Bashari*, ed. Muhammad ʿImara (Cairo: Majallat al-Azhar, 2012); Muhammad al-Khidr Husayn, *al-Hurriyya fi al-Islam* (Cairo: Dar al-Iʿtisam, 1982); Sayyid Qutb, *al-ʿAdala al-Ijtimaʿiyya fi al-Islam* (Cairo: Maktabat Misr, 1949); ʿAli ʿAbd al-Wahid Wafi, *Huquq al-Insan fi al-Islam* (Cairo: Maktabat Nahdat Misr, 1957); Jamal al-Banna, *Qadiyyat al-Hurriyya fi al-Islam* (Cairo: al-Ittihad al-Islami al-Dawli li-l-ʿAmal, 1985); Jamal al-Banna, *al-Hurriyya fi al-Islam* (Beirut: Muʾassasat al-Intishar al-ʿArabi, 2011); Hasan Hanafi, *al-Din wa-l-Thawra fi Misr* (Cairo: Maktabat Madbuli, 1988). For the ripple effect of this Islamic discourse throughout the Islamic world, see, e.g., Asgharali Engineer, *Islam and Liberation Theology: Essays on Liberative Elements in Islam* (New Delhi: New Delhi Sterling Publishers,

Infringements on the free practice of religion, free expression, the freedom to congregate, freedom of the press, freedom of conviction, freedom to form a family, and so forth have become an intrinsic part of how Islamic thinkers have come to express their moral and ethical indignation at excessive restraints on rights.

Islamist writers of the past decades have revived key thinkers from the nahḍa to legitimize an Islamist liberalism that has been critical to political mobilization. This resuscitation has been performed through multiple republications of older material, new redactions and interpretations, and reinjections of nahḍa thought into the landscape of popular Islamic scholarship. This scholarly production constructs an intellectual genealogy that connects the nahḍa to the ṣaḥwa. It also imparts an a priori legitimacy to more recent conceptualizations of Islamic liberalism—a liberalism that includes notions of individual liberty, democratic and representative institutions, guarantees of individual rights, freedom of expression, and freedom of conviction. It is a liberalism that has been formulated in indigenous terms, not only against foreign colonial tyrannies but also in response to local ones, used to articulate protest against unjust rule.

Islamic language of democratic mobilization challenges the very foundations of liberalism's home in secularism and in the West. These writings wrest liberalism from its own imperial xenophobia, expose liberalism's hypocrisy about its own grounding in religion, and question liberalism's disavowal of the political power of the private sphere. But they also reinscribe certain assumptions about the masculine nature of political power, about the role of private property in securing rights, and about women and mothers as presiding over social reproduction in the private sphere.[92] *Soft Force* explores the intimate link between the language of citizenship rights and freedoms, gendered roles (and re-

---

1990); and Hamid Dabashi, *Islamic Liberation Theology: Resisting the Empire* (New York: Routledge, 2008). These are but a small sliver of a vast literature. These discourses have been tools of political change precisely at revolutionary moments—at the turn of the century (as protest against colonialism), after the 1921 revolution, prior to and just after the 1952 revolution, during the revival in the 1980s and 1990s, and during and after the revolution in 2011. Muhammad ʿImara, so essential to the discursive production of the revival in the 1970s and 1980s, reemerged right after the 2011 revolution with a set of republications on the liberating nature of Islam. This body of literature on Islamic "freedom" is the subject of a second book project intimately connected to the present one. It traces a genealogy of Islamic liberalism from the nahḍa to the ṣaḥwa.

[92] Haddad, "Case of the Feminist Movement"; Stowasser, "Religious Ideology"; Hatem, "Egyptian Discourses on Gender"; Hatem, "Secularist and Islamist Discourses on Modernity"; Brown, "Liberalism's Family Values"; Abu-Lughod, "Marriage of Feminism and Islamism"; Abugideiri, "On Gender and the Family"; Badran, *Feminism in Islam*; Hafez, *Islam of Her Own*.

sponsibilities) in the family, and a neoliberal vision of women's special role in cultivating the family as a critical unit of the global economy.[93] This is what Mona El-Naggar of the *New York Times* calls "family values according to the Muslim Brotherhood." These values emphasize a woman's "authentic role as wife, mother, and purveyor of generations," a political platform that has—however paradoxically—"gained followers by extolling subservience."[94] Asmaʾ Mahfouz tweeted El-Naggar's article "Family Life According to the Muslim Brotherhood" to her nearly 350,000 followers, receiving responses like this one written in colloquial Egyptian: "The Brothers are hearing us—the sweetest peace for the woman is the house of her husband and her family."[95]

Conclusion: Liberalism's Contradictions

Islamic thinkers constantly interrogate the terms and premises of liberalism—that it is the exclusive monopoly of the West; that it is inherently secular rather than rooted in religion; that it is relentlessly individualistic rather than promoting a kind of political (and economic) community. These thinkers subject "liberal notions of justice, autonomy, tolerance, and individual rights" to critical scrutiny "from the standpoint of Islamic traditions."[96] They reinscribe certain liberal assumptions about the masculine nature of the state, the role of the private sphere in safeguarding personal freedom, and women and mothers as providing a haven in a heartless world. They do this while drawing deeply on Islamic sources—Qurʾan and hadith, *fiqh* (jurisprudence) and shariʿa, interpretations old and new—to interpret the role of women in a new Islamic politics. As many theorists have noted, liberalism is an ideological system that carries within it its own antitheses, making it difficult to rupture with its own internal logic[97]—antitheses like the West versus Islam, freedom versus subjection, state versus religion, individual versus community, political versus personal, public versus private, male versus female.

[93] Mies, *Patriarchy and Accumulation*, 100–144. Mies calls this the "housewifization of the global economy."

[94] El-Naggar, "Family Life According to the Brotherhood."

[95] khaled a elnaser to Asmaʾ Mahfouz, https://twitter.com/khalidaelnaser/status/245175159349182465.

[96] Saba Mahmood calls for this in her article "Questioning Liberalism, Too: A Response to 'Islam and the Challenge of Democracy,'" *Boston Review* (May 2003).

[97] Slavoj Zizek, *Did Somebody Say Totalitarianism? Five Interventions in the (Mis)Use of a Notion* (New York: Verso, 2001), 3, 5; Jodi Dean, *Zizek's Politics* (New York: Routledge, 2006), 104.

Revivalist interpretations of gender and the family worked within the terms set by a dominant state secularism but deployed a liberal discourse of the modern family as a site from which to critique the increasing secularization of society. This discourse of domesticity and the family has functioned as a platform for women's participation in the project of Islamic nationalism, as they have inhabited a space within discourses of modernity to perform a modern ideal of Islamic womanhood. Islamist women highlight the centrality of home and family, reorienting Islam within a sphere newly designated as the realm of women's authority. In these Islamic writings, women's sphere of influence becomes integral to the shaping of Islamic subjects and, accordingly, an Islamic society. Their vision of the family has been used as a strategic tool to challenge both local and neoimperial forms of political tyranny and injustice and to generate an indigenous politics at a grassroots level, in the sphere of the most intimate relations of community. "Like we have said a thousand times," the Islamic thinker Muhammad Jalal Kishk writes, "liberalism does not grow under the wing of colonialism but begins in the clash with it, the struggle against it, and demanding freedom from it."[98]

[98] Muhammad Jalal Kishk, *Jahalat ʿAsr al-Tanwir: Qiraʾa fi Fikr Qasim Amin wa-ʿAli ʿAbd al-Raziq* (Cairo: Maktabat al-Turath al-Islami, 1990), 78. See chapter 2 for a fuller discussion of Kishk's ideas.

CHAPTER 1

The Liberation of Islamic Letters

Bint al-Shati᾽'s Literary License

Bint al-Shati᾽'s writings crystallize some of the most salient themes of the modern Islamic public sphere and illustrate the power of adab in formulating modern Islamic ethics and politics. A public intellectual, political activist, chaired professor, journalist, and *adība* (woman of letters), Bint al-Shati᾽ (the penname of ʿA᾽isha ʿAbd al-Rahman) synthesized discursive trends for a broad spectrum of readers that included both intellectual elites and popular audiences. Enjoying an illustrious career as an Islamic intellectual, she drew on the authority of revivalist discourses and traditional religious disciplines like *tarājim* (religious biography), *tafsīr* (Qur᾽anic exegesis), and the sciences of the Arabic language. Yet she was neither of al-Azhar (although she was the first woman invited to lecture there) nor of the Muslim Brotherhood but of Cairo University and ʿAin Shams. From these more secularly oriented institutions, she mainstreamed ideas of the Islamic intellectual sphere—in the press, lectures, and popular publications. She helped reconfigure adab, literature, for the adab—the ethics, morals, and values—of the emergent Islamic awakening. Perhaps most important, she articulated the gendered dimensions of this Islamic public sphere, writing about women in the Prophet's family, women's emancipation in Islam, women's rights, women in Islamic law, and women writers. Her writings contributed to making the world of letters, religion, and women the very axis for articulating an Islamic body politic.

Bint al-Shati᾽ (1913–1998) circulated in the most eminent intellectual circles of her time, among figures whose lives and careers were defined by the intersection of religion and literature. Like her, they used literary techniques to reinterpret classical religious sources; like her, they brought new kinds of training to traditional scholarship. She expanded the intellectual legacy of intellectual foremothers like Labiba Ahmad and Fatima Rashid, even as she clearly emulated her male colleagues—her husband Amin al-Khuli, her dissertation adviser Taha

فى السودان تلقى محاضرة عام 1967

Bint al-Shati' lecturing at the Islamic University of Omdurman in 1967. Image courtesy of Hasan Jabr.

Husayn, her colleague ʿAli ʿAbd al-Wahid Wafi, her sparring partner ʿAbbas Mahmud al-ʿAqqad, and his protégé Sayyid Qutb. Although clearly influenced by and refracting intellectual currents of these circles, she was no mere "copy" of these thinkers, as the novelist and playwright Tawfiq al-Hakim accused her of being.[1] On the contrary, she was able to synthesize intellectual arguments for popular audiences, meld literary creativity and religious scholarship, build on theories of the liberating nature of Islam, and put the intimate domain in the front center of Islamic cultural production. The Islamic world of letters articulated middle-class values as Islamic ones through gendered interpretations of intimate relations in the private sphere.

Epitomizing a new kind of Islamic intellectual not formally educated in religious institutions or disciplines, Bint al-Shatiʾ became a popular authority on the Qurʾan and religious literature. The spread of public education and literacy created literate audiences for these writings, opening up religious knowledge and religious texts to portions of the populace for whom they had previously been inaccessible. By deploying new approaches and techniques, she reconfigured religious knowledge for the modern middle class. One of the most important parts of the spread of education was the increased literacy of women, and Bint al-Shatiʾ was one of the first fruits of this generation. Even as she firmly situated herself as an Islamic scholar, she was not trained in Islamic institutions but at Cairo University. She did not (officially) specialize in Islamic studies but earned her degree in Arabic literature. She used alternate channels (Arabic literature and poetry, the press, literary writings, popular literature) to access domains of Islamic learning largely closed to women of her age. In doing so, she helped throw its doors open to women's religious scholarship and to the women's Qurʾanic exegesis that followed. One of the ways she did this was by rewriting classical Islamic stories into new, popular literary forms. Her biographies of women in the Prophet's family read like romance novels, even though they are carefully grounded in rigorous religious scholarship. Through new modes of popular writings, she helped disseminate formal religious learning among a newly emergent reading public.

A lion(ess) of the literary establishment, Bint al-Shatiʾ enjoyed an intellectual trajectory that spanned eras and genres. Through her own publishing career, she connected the surge in Islamic literature of the 1930s and 1940s to the awakening of the later 1970s and 1980s. Literary writing played a key role in catalyzing the rise of an Islamic public

[1] C. Kooij, "Bint al-Shatiʾ: A Suitable Case for Biography?" in *The Challenge of the Middle East*, ed. Ibrahim El-Sheikh, C. Aart van de Koppel, and Rudolph Peters (Amsterdam: University of Amsterdam, 1982), 70.

sphere, connecting the awakening (nahḍa) of the late nineteenth century to the later awakening known as the ṣaḥwa. Precisely because of her position at the center of public institutions, she was able to visibly sustain a newly decentralized Islamic discursive tradition throughout the secularly oriented Nasser era. Her writings provided a public outlet for religious discourse at a time when the Muslim Brotherhood was driven underground, the religious courts were abolished, and al-Azhar was put under the control of the state. Her literary production during the Nasser years laid the foundation for the intellectual Islam of the later revival, especially the gendered politics that became so critical to the literature of the ṣaḥwa.

Bint al-Shatiʾ drew on classical models of adab, the Qurʾan, *sunna*, tafsīr, literature, and poetry, yet she also formulated a contemporary vision of the "Islamic personality," one rooted in political lexicons of freedom and responsibilities, rights and duties.[2] She used new kinds of Islamic humanities to envision new kinds of Islamic selves. Her primary frame of reference is *al-bayān*, the Qurʾan. Throughout her career, the concept of al-bayān is a constant and multivalent point of reference. The word, language, speech, eloquence, the very articulation that God gave to humanity (al-bayān) becomes the path to human enlightenment, the means of emancipation from ignorance, the way of awakening the self through knowledge. In a pivotal lecture that she presented at the Islamic University of Omdurman, "al-Mafhum al-Islami li-Tahrir al-Marʾa" (The Islamic Understanding of Women's Liberation, 1967), she quotes a verse from the Qurʾan referring to al-bayān no fewer than three times: to open the lecture, to drive her point home in the lecture's climax, and to close the lecture. "The merciful. Taught the Qurʾan. Created humanity. Taught it eloquence (al-bayān)" (55:1–4).[3] These verses could be said to encapsulate Bint al-Shatiʾ's Islamic humanism, realized through the practice of eloquent speech, through God's word, and through His signs. Bint al-Shatiʾ uses this Islamic humanism to articulate a political project of women's rights in Islam—to knowledge, to education, to participation in the world of letters, to public scholarship, to free speech, to debate and deliberation about Islam's "established principles." The human, she says, becomes complete only through the power of intelligence and articulation (al-bayān: also, "the Qurʾan"), distinguishing the human from the "mute beast." This human right to knowledge is "our intrinsic and authentic right to life, this is not extrinsic to us, nor is it a foreign import. It is the book of Islam in us" (6).

[2] Bint al-Shatiʾ, *al-Shakhsiyya al-Islamiyya* (Beirut: Jamiʿat Bayrut al-ʿArabiyya, 1972).

[3] Bint al-Shatiʾ, *al-Mafhum al-Islami li-Tahrir al-Marʾa: Muhadara ʿAmma* (Cairo: Matbaʿat Mukhaymir, 1967), 3, 8, 16.

The Adab of Islamic Humanities

Bint al-Shati' came of age during a time of literary flourishing, when secular intellectuals were tackling religious themes. They used modern narrative techniques—journalism, short stories, novels, theater, contemporary biography, family romance—to reinterpret classical sources for popular audiences. In Egyptian public life, especially between the late 1920s and late 1940s, literary writing helped develop a modernist hermeneutics for Islamic thought.[4] Literary treatments of religious texts dominated the world of letters during this time, as the most illustrious innovators of Arab literature in the twentieth century treated scriptural subjects through modern genres.[5] This approach developed largely from intellectuals who had come from secular backgrounds, written on secular topics, and emulated Western models of knowledge earlier in their careers.

Discourses of revival (*iḥyā'*, nahḍa, *ba'th*) were integral to Islamic publishing during this time, with the aim of "awakening" classical literature, generating new kinds of literary production, and building the new on the basis of the old. Historians proffer a number of explanations for the shift toward religious themes in the 1930s and 1940s, among them the "revival of the Islamic-Arab cultural legacy as the basis of modern society and culture" and "the desire to appeal to new literate publics . . . through the use of popular forms and themes of literary production."[6] Integral to this process was the formulation of a "non-Western national ideology based on indigenous values which could be accepted as a modern framework of identity by broad sectors of society."[7] These writers drew on a spiritualist paradigm that sought to counter the dehumanizing effects of colonial modernity with

[4] The most important literary interpretations of the Qur'an during this time were Amin al-Khuli, *al-Tafsir: Ma'alim Hayatihi, Manhajuhu al-Yawm* (Cairo: Jama'at al-Kitab, 1944); Sayyid Qutb, *al-Taswir al-Fanni fi al-Qur'an* (Cairo: Dar al-Ma'arif, 1945); Muhammad Ahmad Khalaf Allah, *al-Fann al-Qisasi fi al-Qur'an al-Karim* (Cairo: Maktabat al-Nahda al-Misriyya, 1950). Earlier, Taha Husayn's *Fi al-Shi'r al-Jahili* (Cairo: Matba'at Dar al-Kutub al-Misriyya, 1926) used literary criticism to comment on certain inconsistencies in the Qur'an, causing an uproar. On the debates over literary interpretations of the Qur'an at the time, see Nasr Abu-Zayd, "The Dilemma of the Literary Approach to the Qur'an," *Alif: Journal of Comparative Poetics* 23, no. Literature and the Sacred (2003): 22–34; and Rachid Benzine, *Les nouveaux penseurs de l'Islam* (Paris: Albin Michel, 2004), 149–72.

[5] Hafez, *The Genesis of Arabic Narrative Discourse*, is a brilliant analysis of how new genres evolved out of the classical Arabic (and Islamic) literary tradition.

[6] Gershoni and Jankowski, *Redefining the Egyptian Nation*, 65, esp. 54–78; Charles D. Smith, *Islam and the Search for Social Order in Modern Egypt: A Biography of Muhammad Husayn Haykal* (Albany: State University of New York Press, 1983), 97.

[7] Gershoni and Jankowski, *Redefining the Egyptian Nation*, 70.

a newly enchanted humanistic approach (what these thinkers call a "revival of the spirit"). This new literary movement infused religious "aura" into supposedly secular forms of technological reproducibility, belying Lukács's formulation that modern narrative forms like the novel depict "a world . . . abandoned by God."[8] This new kind of literature reinterpreted traditional religious sources for the modern age, imagining a religious community in terms accessible to a broad, contemporary reading public. New genres and narrative styles did not so much break with the Islamic intellectual tradition as reconfigure it in new forms of communicability. Theorists like Benedict Anderson and Walter Benjamin interpret modern mass media as secular and as destroying sacred and traditional modes of art. But more recent scholarship by thinkers like Charles Hirschkind and Brian Larkin analyzes the power of new technologies to communicate religious sensibilities and create "anew the grounds for communal belonging."[9] The affective site of the family has been a particularly powerful vehicle for communicating—and reproducing—religious sensibilities, a realm of intimate relations continually defined and redefined in public discourses.

A new genre of religious writing known as *islāmiyyāt* emerged during this period, deploying artistic license to paint idealized portraits of the early Islamic community (the *aslāf*). Using a modernist humanism to reinterpret religious texts, this literature emphasized the Prophet's humanity and the "divine inspiration" that produced the miracle of the Qurʾan. There were several principal genres of islāmiyyāt, the main ones being travelogues of the pilgrimage, biographies of the Prophet, biographies of the aslāf, and eventually, literary interpretations of the Qurʾan. One of the first exemplars of this kind of literature was Muhammad Husayn Haykal's biography of the Prophet, *Hayat Muhammad* (Life of Muhammad, 1935), which drew on classical sources but was narrated as a modern biography—a response to and reformulation of orientalist portraits of the Prophet. An earlier proponent of (the secularly inflected) Pharaonism and an author of Egypt's "first" novel, Haykal emphasized that the miracle of the Qurʾan was a "human" and "rational" one, even as he drew on romantic notions of the Prophet as divinely inspired. Through this approach, writers like Haykal employed a modernist humanism toward reinterpreting the divine miracle of the Qurʾan. Haykal characterized his biography as "striving for freedom of

[8] Georg Lukács, *The Theory of the Novel: A Historico-Philosophical Essay on the Forms of Great Epic Literature*, trans. Anna Bostock (Cambridge, MA: MIT Press, 1974), 88.

[9] Hirschkind and Larkin argue that religion circulates through media, creating new kinds of imagined communities for the contemporary world, contradicting Walter Benjamin's understanding of mass technology as destroying religious aura. Hirschkind and Larkin, "Media and the Political Forms of Religion," 3.

thought. However strange it may sound, this is the message of Muhammad and the foundation of his preaching."[10] The humanistic freedom of Islam would become both the central theme of Bint al-Shatiʾ's later religious writings and a foundational concept of writings connected to the ṣaḥwa.

Bint al-Shatiʾ would almost methodically master the different genres of islāmiyyāt, using it as a path to guide her own popular cultural production. She first wrote about her experience of the *ʿumra* (the lesser pilgrimage), then composed extensive *tarājim* (biographies) of women from the Prophet's family, and finally ventured her own literary exegeses of the Qurʾan. Through vivid portraits of the early Islamic community, Bint al- Shatiʾ and other leading intellectuals of her time employed a kind of literary Salafism to imagine an idealized umma, principally through biographies of the aslāf. Curiously, Bint al-Shatiʾ would start writing other works on Islam only after the death of her husband, the Islamic scholar Amin al-Khuli. In her autobiographical work *ʿAla al-Jisr* (On the Bridge, 1967), published just after al-Khuli's death, Bint al-Shatiʾ describes how she wanted to pursue Islamic studies at the university. Al-Khuli encouraged her to instead study Arabic language and literature—perhaps because of her gender—arguing that she had to first master this primary tool for understanding religion.[11] Master this tool she did, completing her dissertation on the eleventh-century poet Abu al-ʿAlaʾ al-Maʿarri. Her dissertation was supervised by the great literary scholar Taha Husayn, another intellectual who experimented with literary approaches to religious texts. He, too, had written his dissertation on al-Maʿarri at the newly opened Cairo University (then called Fuʾad University), after leaving his religious studies at al-Azhar.[12] From the beginning of her scholarly career, Bint al-Shatiʾ had fought for the right to go to school, first against her own father's opposition. She garnered support from her mother and maternal grandfather,

[10] Muhammad Husayn Haykal, *Hayat Muhammad* (Cairo: Matbaʿat Misr, 1935), 71–73, 202–9; Gershoni and Jankowski, *Redefining the Egyptian Nation*, 57.

[11] Bint al-Shatiʾ, *ʿAla al-Jisr: "Usturat al-Zaman"* (Cairo: Dar al-Hilal, 1967), 34.

[12] Al-Maʿarri, the "blind skeptic," was known for his atheism and vegetarianism as much as for his literary reputation. His *Risalat al-Ghufran* (Message of Forgiveness) was thought to have influenced Dante's *Inferno*. Husayn published eight works on al-Maʿarri; Bint al-Shatiʾ, four. In the late 1930s and early 1940s, at the height of the boom in *islāmiyyāt* literature, al-Maʿarri experienced a renaissance, with Taha Husayn's *Tajdid Dhikrat Abi al-ʿAlaʾ* (Cairo: Matbaʿat al-Maʿarif, 1937); ʿAbbas Mahmud al-ʿAqqad's *Rajʿat Abi al-ʿAlaʾ* (Cairo: Dar al-Kutub al-Haditha, 1939); Bint al-Shatiʾ's *al-Hayat al-Insaniyya ʿind Abi al-ʿAlaʾ al-Maʿarri* (Cairo: Matbaʿat al-Maʿarif, 1939); and Amin al-Khuli's, *Raʾyi fi Abi al-ʿAlaʾ* (Cairo: Jamaʿat al-Kuttab, 1945). Why the revival of al-Maʿarri? Did his use of poetry and prose to probe religious and existential questions serve as model for these literary scholars turning to theological matters?

an Azhari shaykh, whom she often credits when invoking her own intellectual lineage. Her intellect was fiercely precocious. Even before beginning the university in 1934, she acted as editor-in-chief for Labiba Ahmad's Islamically inflected journal for women, *al-Nahda al-Nisaʾiyya* (Women's Awakening).[13] No sooner had Bint al-Shatiʾ entered Cairo University than she became al-Khuli's spiritual and intellectual companion—and his second wife. While still in college, she published two well-received books on the Egyptian countryside (one of which won a state prize) even while giving birth to her first two children, Amina and Adiba. In her final year of college, she published a book on al-Maʿarri's humanism before going on to write both her master's thesis and her dissertation (both on al-Maʿarri). Meanwhile, she also published a novella and a collection of short stories. Giving birth to her third son Akmal as she began her doctorate, she also worked for the Ministry of Education and wrote for the newspaper *al-Ahram*. Her literary, popular, and scholarly production was vast, as she published more than thirty works on classical Arabic poetry, the Prophet, Qurʾanic exegesis, contemporary Arabic literature, women from the Prophet's family, and linguistics.

Almost immediately after completing her doctoral thesis, Bint al-Shatiʾ turned to religious themes with the publication of *Ard al-Muʿjizat: Rihla fi Jazirat al-ʿArab* (Land of Miracles: Journey in the Arabian Peninsula, 1951), a memoir of performing the ʿumra (lesser pilgrimage) on a school trip with students and teachers. This work marks a definite transition in her scholarship, as she moved away from poetics and toward religious themes. Over the next decade, she would move from poetics to publishing almost exclusively on religious subjects, with few exceptions. With *Land of Miracles*, Bint al-Shatiʾ jumps into the "new Islamic mood" of the Egyptian intelligentsia, situating herself directly in what had by then become a genre of religious travel writing mainly by male literati.[14] But she also drew on the writings of her mentor Labiba Ahmad, the founding editor of *Women's Awakening*,

[13] In her chapter on Labiba Ahmad, "The Path of an Islamic Activist," Beth Baron describes how Ahmad kept the spirit of the women's press alive, even though it had begun to wane in the 1940s. Beth Baron, *Egypt as a Woman: Nationalism, Gender, and Politics* (Berkeley: University of California Press, 2005), 189–214.

[14] "Where in the 1920s the intellectual fashion had been to visit the Pharaonic ruins of Upper Egypt in order to realize one's Egyptian identity, in the 1930s a new trend took its place: that of proceeding to the Hijaz to experience personally the full effects of participation in the hajj. The content of such accounts usually combined description of the formal ceremonies of the Pilgrimage with analysis of the social and emotional meaning of taking part in this central event of the Muslim umma." Gershoni and Jankowski, *Redefining the Egyptian Nation*, 60.

who performed the pilgrimage almost yearly and wrote detailed accounts of her experiences. In *Land of Miracles*, Bint al- Shatiʾ describes a transformative, personal experience of Islamic history in Mecca, interspersing her travelogue with erudite references to pre-Islamic and Islamic poets, hadith, and the Qurʾan. The miracle in the title is clearly the Qurʾan, but she also used other literary forms, like poetry, to interpret her experiences. The travelogue style is punctuated by a ritualistic narrative reenactment of her ʿumra. She composes the narrative vertically and horizontally, synchronically and diachronically, historically and in a newly (hyper) modernized Saudi Arabia. Alongside her narration of the rites of the ʿumra performed in Mecca, she tells the story of the airplane taking them to the "land the awakening" (*ard al-mabʿath*) and later, the story of oil in Dhahran. The synchronic and diachronic play out stylistically, as she writes in a direct, journalistic, reportage style, with footnotes on hadith and pre-Islamic poetry. Her personal experience of the pilgrimage, woven in with scripture and poetry, attests to both textual and emotional authenticity, as she intersperses mundane details of travel with witnessing the transformative power of ritual and sacred space. Her modern scholarly style (of meticulous footnotes, for example) combines literary references simplified for a general audience and explanations in a clear vernacular of citations that would be familiar to more educated readers of Arabic. The book enjoyed immense popularity, with over six printings between 1951 and 1985.

Bint al-Shatiʾ would perhaps become most famous for the biographies of the women in the Prophet's family, published between 1956 and 1961, during critical years of the government of Gamal ʿAbd al-Nasser. In the wake of a struggle for power between Nasser and the Muslim Brotherhood, one that ended in an assassination attempt on Nasser's life in 1954, Nasser cracked down on Islamic groups through a campaign of mass incarcerations, censorship of religious publications, and outlawing of the Muslim Brotherhood. Between 1956 and 1961, he put religious institutions like al-Azhar University under state control, abolished the religious courts, and brought the personal status laws (grounded in religious law) under the jurisdiction of the civil courts. At the same time, Nasser initiated a campaign to reform the personal status laws, which was so contentious that it would be over a decade before the issue was finally dropped in the aftermath of the Six-Day War with Israel in 1967. A bastion of Islamic law within the secular state, the personal status laws created "'the family' as a private space that was central to political order." But they also "politicized the family both as a sphere of intimate, affective relations and as a repository of group identity of which religious affiliation was a defining legal and moral characteristic."[15] During the Nasser years, especially between 1956 and 1967, the family became a locus of political contestation between secular and religious modes of governmentality. Bint al-Shatiʾ's narratives of women in the Prophet's family distilled elements of the tumultuous political context, treating—in seemingly indirect ways—contentious questions about the relationship between religion and political power, religion and state law, religion and the family.

Her tarājim's appearance during this time is anachronistic: they do not belong to the earlier boom in this literature (in the 1930s and 1940s), nor do they belong to the surge in religious biographies during the later ṣaḥwa.[16] Bint al-Shatiʾ's writings bridged these epochs of religious writing, serving to sustain and reinvent the islāmiyyāt for a new generation, occupying an "exceptional place" in the "chronological map" of biographical writing about women.[17] Anticipating the themes of Salafi domesticity that would come to dominate writings associated with the revival, Bint al-Shatiʾ's biographical writings would continue to enjoy great popularity during the ṣaḥwa, through multiple republications well into the 1990s. In the midst of the Iranian Revolution, her biography of Zaynab bint al-Zahraʾ would be republished in Farsi.[18] Family ties and identities are central to these narratives, where "modern forms of subjectivity" are constructed with women in roles of mother, daughter, and wife.[19] Yet they are hardly "traditional" interpretations of scripture. These narratives imagine a modernized nuclear family and domestic sphere, one that became a site for the production of Islamic knowledge as a new middle-class elite staked out this territory as its own.[20]

[15] Bier, *Revolutionary Womanhood*, 104.

[16] Al-ʿAqqad's popular biographies of the Prophet and his companions, known as his *ʿabqariyyāt* (genius) series, are good examples: ʿAbbas Mahmud al-ʿAqqad, *ʿAbqariyyat Muhammad* (Cairo: Matbaʿat al-Istiqama, 1942); ʿAbbas Mahmud al-ʿAqqad, *ʿAbqariyyat ʿUmar* (Cairo: Matbaʿat al-Istiqama, 1942); ʿAbbas Mahmud al-ʿAqqad, *ʿAbqariyyat al-Siddiq* (Cairo: Matbaʿat al-Maʿarif wa-Maktabatuha, 1943); ʿAbbas Mahmud al-ʿAqqad, *ʿAbqariyyat al-Imam* (Cairo: Dar al-Maʿarif, 1943). Al-ʿAqqad's biographies of ʿAʾisha and Fatima, written during the same period, do not carry "genius" in their titles.

[17] Booth, *May Her Likes Be Multiplied*, 416n15.

[18] Bint al-Shatiʾ, *Zaynab Banu-yi Qahraman-i Karbala*, trans. Naini (Hisan) Ayat Allah'zadah and Habib Chaychiyan (Tehran: Amir Kabir, 1979); Bint al-Shatiʾ, *Batalat Karbala: Zaynab Bint al-Zahraʾ* (Beirut: Maktabat al-Andalus, 1956).

[19] Booth, *May Her Likes Be Multiplied*, 285.

[20] Stowasser, *Women in the Qurʾan, Traditions, and Interpretation* (New York: Oxford University Press, 1996), 120. For a brilliant discussion of modern discourses of Islamic domesticity, see Shakry, "Schooled Mothers and Structured Play."

Under the Nasser government's exercise of authoritarian control over religious groups and institutions, Bint al-Shatiʾ's writings helped keep the spirit of Islamic letters alive in popular consciousness, despite a climate in which Islamic thinkers and groups were under siege. By focusing her attentions on Islamic private life—the household of the Prophet, the family, and gender relations—she formulated a space both within the secular state for the practice of religion and beyond its reach. This tactic would become a powerful tool of the Islamic movement as religious thinkers claimed institutions like the family as Islamic territory, governed by both Islamic law and literature, both legally and discursively. Secularism itself defines the sphere of intimate relations and private beliefs as outside the purview of the state, even though recent theorists demonstrate secularism's contingency on religion, specifically via the formulation of religion as private belief and practice.[21] By focusing on the family, Islamic thinkers like Bint al-Shatiʾ helped create a space for the free practice of an authentic religion—a nostalgic, idealized, originary space for religion under siege by an authoritarian secularism. The freedom of this space was critical to the discourse of the revivalist writers, as were other principles like freedom of conviction, freedom of speech, freedom of opinion, and women's freedom. Islamic conceptions of human rights—of political self-determination, freedom, and equality—were critical elements of this new Islamic humanities. Even as these thinkers challenged liberalism's very foundations in secularism, they deployed liberal concepts toward creating a free and open deliberative space for the practice of an Islamic society, shaped by Islamic law, defined by Islamic letters, and forming the critical basis of an Islamic polity. The concept of umma, of the Islamic homeland, with its feminine etymology connected to the word for mother, *umm*, gave expression to this vision of a modern Islamic politics of the intimate sphere. Formulated in the shadow of the secular authoritarianism of successive military regimes—Gamal ʿAbd al-Nasser, Anwar Sadat, and Hosni Mubarak—the "soft force" of informal institutions like the family, waged as a war of persuasion, became the most powerful weapon of the Islamic movement's passive revolution.

Women of the Prophet: Politics of the Islamic Family

Bint al-Shatiʾ's understanding of the family as a space for the free (and equal) practice of religion would become a critical rhetorical instrument of revivalist politics. Drawing on the literary humanism of the

[21] Asad, *Formations of the Secular*, 230–31.

islāmiyyāt, she portrayed Muhammad as a human prophet-husband and his relationship to his wives as bound by affective love. The "rational" and "free" hermeneutic described by Haykal informed Bint al-Shatiʾ's interpretation of the free and consensual household of the Prophet. Bint al-Shatiʾ's biographies of women of the Prophet's family—his daughters, granddaughters, mother, and wives—package impeccable *sīra* scholarship (biographical literature) in an engaging narrative. Her *Banat al-Nabi* (Daughters of the Prophet, 1956), *Zaynab Bint al-Zahraʾ* (1956), *Umm al-Nabi* (Mother of the Prophet, 1958), *Sukayna Bint al-Husayn* (1958), and *Nisaʾ al-Nabi* (Wives of the Prophet, 1961) are novelistic dramatizations of the Prophet's domestic life. The biographies evoke the inner life, both emotional and domestic, of women in the Prophet's family, as Bint al-Shatiʾ constructs modern images of these historical figures. She infuses domestic space with romantic love, wifely devotion, and narrative suspense, painting intimate portraits of her subjects, with inferences to their emotional life and psychological states (feminine jealousy, motherly tenderness, wifely worry, daughterly devotion). In the introduction she describes using creative license and the flow of the literary process ("I let my pen imagine") to flesh out details of the classical material. Her clear, lucid style makes the writing and its material broadly accessible for a general audience. Her romantic characterization of the dramas of the Prophet's love life and relationships turn these books into modern narratives, intelligible to her contemporary audiences, and partly accounting for their vast and persistent popularity. This new kind of religious biography, combining domestic fiction with sīra literature, would become a dominant mode of literary production in the revival of later decades.[22] In *Women in the Qurʾan*, Barbara Stowasser implies that Bint al-Shatiʾ's modern storytelling style is antithetical to her "traditional" focus on domesticity. "Even though Muhammad's wives are presented with a modern focus, their exemplary qualities are found in their supportive strengths in the domestic arena . . . Bint al-Shatiʾ's work is based squarely on the medieval sources, even though its often romantic style is that of the storyteller."[23] Marilyn Booth, however, recognizes that this domesticity is less "traditional" than it is a modern discourse of femininity, where women and the intimate sphere become identified as repositories of communal identification. More important, the intimate life of

[22] Gonzalez-Quijano, *Les gens du livre*; Booth, *May Her Likes Be Multiplied*, esp. 281–310. In *Mobilizing Islam*, Wickham quotes one bookseller as saying that "anything on the Prophet's wives" was popular (135).

[23] Stowasser, *Women in the Qurʾan*, 120.

the Prophet becomes seen as the very locus of his humanity, the place where the divine meets the world.

In *Wives of the Prophet*, Bint al-Shati' describes the Prophet's household as a place where "earth was connected with Heaven . . . a house in which human passion mingle with a flow of sublime light and femininity. . . . Some of these currents pulled this femininity to earth, others exalted it to Heaven and as a result we have a balance between the Divine and the human."[24] This juncture of heaven and earth, divine and human, finds its embodiment in the home and in Muhammad as the "Prophet Husband." The emphasis, as in Haykal's and al-ʿAqqad's biographies of the Prophet as well as in the orientalist biographies, is on Muhammad as human being.[25] Orientalist biographies interpreted this as evidence against his prophethood. For Haykal and al-ʿAqqad, this humanity becomes the source of his genius as a kind of romantic poet-hero who channels the divine into human language. Bint al-Shati'’s humanistic vision of the prophet is as "Muhammad the husband, the man of human limbs, within whose protection these honorable ladies lived and whose private world embraced them all." This humanity, which the Islamic message insists on, has no parallel among other religions, she says. She quotes from the Qur'an 41:6: "Say: I am human like yourselves." The epitome of this humanity is Muhammad's involvement in family life, his relationship with his wives, desire, love, and attraction.[26] The Prophet's sensuality, seen by the orientalists as evidence of his degeneracy, becomes here the *sunna* (model) of the ideal husband. When Bint al-Shati' quotes al-Tabari's description of Muhammad's physical characteristics, his physicality leaps off the page: "A handsome young man with distinctive features, a radiant color, neither too tall nor too short, with a fine head and noble brow, a flowing beard and graceful neck, deep chested, with strong hands and feet. Thick, dark hair crowned his head, and his deep-set, brilliant dark eyes glowed with a magical charm under long dark eyelashes. His white, well-spaced teeth sparkled whenever he spoke or smiled." Another quote talks about the "sweat [that] beaded on his forehead just above his eyebrows" when he became angry (9). Prophetic history, in Bint al-Shati'’s hands, becomes a history of "married life" that "dazzles with its vitality that knows no sterile passion." Khadija, witness and midwife to the inception of the message (*al-ʿalaq*, the embryo, to which the first verses of

[24] Bint al-Shati', *Wives of the Prophet*, trans. Matti Moosa and D. Nicholas Ranson (Lahore: Sh. Muhammad Ashraf, 1971), xix.

[25] Stowasser, *Women in the Qur'an*, 120.

[26] Bint al-Shati', *Wives of the Prophet*, 4.

the Qurʾan to come down refer), is described as mothering the Prophet through his fear.

The sphere of intimate relations would play a central role in defining the humanity of the Prophet and the humanism of Islam, just as it had played a central role for orientalists in discounting the divine nature of the message. Rather than a secular humanism, though, this humanism is divinely sanctioned, a central message in Islamic history, and an integral part of the Qurʾan. New kinds of prophetic history countered orientalist fixations on the Prophet's sensuality and his relationship with women. Instead they turned this humanism into key elements for spreading the message, through a human sensuality that appealed to followers of the message. The Prophet's sensual qua human self reemerged as one of the central focuses of these narratives. It was a critical component of a new kind of intellectual Islam but also of a new hermeneutics of scripture that drew on humanism, the humanities, and gendered relations as interpretive tools. In Bint al-Shatiʾ's biographies, the hero-prophet, a romantic conceptualization of an immanent prophet, becomes the prophet-husband.[27] In her chapter on Zaynab bint Jahsh, she quotes Zaynab as saying that she was unique among Muhammad's wives because she was married to him by God and by the Qurʾan. Bint al-Shatiʾ interprets the events leading up to the marriage as a "love story," drawing on both traditional sources and orientalist squabbles over Muhammad's sensuality.[28] Haykal, she notes, rejected the notion of a love story as an "orientalist invention." But Bint al-Shatiʾ roots the Prophet's very humanity in this love. "The sign of greatness in our Prophet's personality is that he is a human being who eats and walks in the market-place like anyone else. We know of no other great man . . . who has insisted that he was so human as did Muhammad; neither has humanity known such a divine book which so clearly affirms, as does the inimitable book of Islam, the human quality of the man entrusted with the Message." And again, she repeats the verse from the Qurʾan 41:6 that she cites in her chapter on "Muhammad: The Prophet Husband": "Say: I am human like yourselves" (148). The attraction between Zaynab and Muhammad was not an orientalist invention; it was recorded in the most important classical sources: in al-Tabari, al-Isaba, tafsīr, and in *al-Simt al-Thamin*. The key to this human nature (*fiṭra*) was desire: "The Prophet came looking for Zayd and there was over the chamber door a curtain made of hair. The wind

[27] Ibid., 1.

[28] Gershoni and Jankowski, *Redefining the Egyptian Nation*, 65. In a section on the "motives and intentions" of the islāmiyyāt, Gershoni and Jankowski observe that one of the very first "motives and intentions" of the islāmiyyāt literature was responding to orientalist critiques of Islam.

blew aside the curtain and revealed Zaynab as she was naked in her chamber. Immediately he felt love for her in his heart" (143). "How could the Prophet, as a man, resist?" Bint al-Shati' asks.

The family as the site of freedom and equality becomes the expression of an idealized community whose bonds are not only sacred but governed by rights and responsibilities that are part of a divine order. The notion of companionate marriage was a "shared point of reference" for both reformers and their opponents, as historian Laura Bier notes about this period. In particular, the notion of *muʿāshara*, meaning "intimacy," "was often used to depict the normative affective bonds of marital and familial life and evoked the constellation of subjectivities and practices associated with companionate marriage." Both reformers and their opponents "not only linked companionate marriage to the preservation of the social and political order but also saw it as integrally linked to issues of rights, freedom, and citizenship." Public debate employed a "new language of rights, which argued that unions violating the tenets of marital intimacy were antithetical to women's status as enfranchised citizens in a modern nation-state."[29] In Bint al-Shati'’s *Wives of the Prophet,* she characterizes the loving, erotic relationship between Zaynab and Muhammad as explicitly based on free will. Moreover, such a relationship, she says, is a marriage arranged in heaven, "revealing the will of God."[30] The rest of the chapter is devoted to describing the "love story" between Zaynab and the Prophet—testament not just to the Prophet's humanity but to Islam's humanistic message of consensual marital relations.

In Bint al-Shati'’s chapter on Khadija, she describes a love marriage—"the happiest marriage that Mecca had seen for a long while—and time would tell how they sipped the nectar of a deep and pure love" (30). This time, though, she quotes orientalist biographies like Bodley's *The Messenger*, Emile Dermenghem's *The Life of Muhammad*, Regis Blachère's *Le problème de Mahomet*, and William Muir's *The Life of Muhammad.* She quotes Bodley as saying that Khadija "married for love," which was a reflection of her "trust in the belief" of Islam (40). Dermenghem likewise emphasized Khadija's love for Muhammad, describing her comforting him after he returned from Hira, frightened and trembling after having received the first verses of the Qur'an. "She restored him to peace and calm and lavished on him the devotion of a lover, the loyalty of a wife, and the compassion of a mother. She drew him to her breast where he found the peace and tranquility of childhood" (41). These orientalist accounts also emphasize Khadija as not

[29] Bier, *Revolutionary Womanhood,* 113.
[30] Bint al-Shati', *Wives of the Prophet,* 140.

only the mother of Muhammad's children but a mother figure for him as well because of her age and his orphanhood. Bint al-Shatiʾ emphasizes this love and motherly affection in Khadija's story—Khadija as "mother and housewife," the chapter's title. This depiction of Khadija as domestic creature rather than powerful merchant would become the dominant characteristic of revivalist biographical literature. The sentiment of home life, "the emotional construct of monogamous heterosexual love as underlying the ideal Muslim couple, and by extension, the ideal community. . . . Marriage as portrayed here and in most other contemporary biographies of women of Muhammad's time, is companionate, harmonious, emotionally fulfilling for both partners, a partnership that unites religious duty in the larger community with the duty of maintaining the family as the basic unit of society."[31] But besides being harmonious, this family and these gender relations provide the framework for women's rights, "saving women from tyranny and oppression . . . centuries before the world ever heard of women's awakening and women's rights" (23). In *Women in the Qurʾan*, Stowasser discusses how this literature on the Prophet's domestic affairs emphasized women's rights in Islam. "Dignity, honor, and rights both spiritual and material provided for the woman in Islam are contrasted with woman's chattel status in the Arabian Jahiliyya and other past and present societies, especially of the West. . . . Women's rights in Islam verify the collective dignity of all Muslims, indeed of the whole Islamic system that the West (missionaries and Orientalists) had set out to defame."[32] The Prophet founded a society based on a set of laws that finally granted women not only honor and respect but also their rights.

The Home of Public Debate

Bint al-Shatiʾ wrote her *tarājim* during key years of the Nasser government, between the promulgation of the constitution in 1956 and the National Charter in 1961. This period was one of heated public contestation over the nature of women's public and private roles in the new republic, as citizens, wives, and mothers. These writings, first published during postrevolution debates over women's citizenship rights versus their familial responsibilities, went on to enjoy great popularity in subsequent decades. The constitution had declared equal rights one of the principles of the republic: all citizens are "the same before the law. They are equal in their rights and public obligations and there

[31] Booth, *May Her Likes Be Multiplied*, 303.
[32] Stowasser, *Women in the Qurʾan*, 120–21.

should be no discrimination among them based on sex, origin, language, religion, or faith.” It connected this equal opportunity to “social liberty which is specified as the basic rights of all citizens.”[33] In contrast, the laws of personal status delineated a relationship between husband and wife—and man and woman—as one of male authority and female obedience, fundamentally contradicting the ideals of freedom and equality espoused in the constitution. Debates tended to focus on a more abstracted relationship between men and women, even when they were talking about the specific relationship between husbands and wives.[34] In 1957 Amina Shukri, one of the first women to be elected to Parliament, proposed amending the principle of *bayt al-ṭāʿa* or “house of obedience” in the personal status laws, the compulsory return of a “rebellious” (*nāshiz*) wife to her husband’s household, even against her will.[35] She also proposed subjecting decisions of divorce, polygamy, and child custody to a judge’s mediation, giving the wife a say in these domestic matters.[36] Bint al-Shatiʾ, with Suhayr Qalamawi and Mufida ʿAbd al-Rahman, would present a nearly identical proposal in 1960. A professor of literature, Qalamawi was the first woman to receive her doctorate from Cairo University (also under the supervision of Taha Husayn). Mufida ʿAbd al-Rahman was the first woman to practice law in Cairo, served in the United Arab Republic’s National Assembly, and defended the feminist activist Doria Shafiq in the trial against her after she stormed Parliament calling for reform of the personal status laws and for equal rights for women.[37] In this coalition, we see the world of letters and the letter of the law negotiating the nature of government in the private and public domains. At stake were women’s public and private rights, seemingly differentially defined. Public discourse depicted these roles as complementary and overlapping, even as they were characterized by contradictory ideals: freedom, equality, and rights on one side, dependencies, hierarchies, and responsibilities on the other.

Public attention was riveted by debates over the personal status laws. At issue were not only the relationship between family and state but the nature of gendered rights and responsibilities in the new republic. In December 1959 Bint al-Shatiʾ published an editorial in *al-Ahram* about the laws of personal status, arguing for a revolutionary liberation of the family from the despotism of *bayt al-ṭāʿa*, which she compared to

[33] Jumhuriyyat Misr, “al-Dustur,” 1956, 11.

[34] See, for example, chapters on “Aspects of Discrimination between Women and Men” in Wafi, *Huquq al-Insan fi al-Islam*, 121–216.

[35] Bier, *Revolutionary Womanhood*, esp. 101–20.

[36] Ibid., 112.

[37] Cynthia Nelson, *Doria Shafik, Egyptian Feminist: A Woman Apart* (Cairo: University of Cairo Press, 1996), 171–74.

prerevolutionary feudalism and colonialism.[38] The principle of forced obedience contrasted with Bint al-Shatiʾ's vivid model of the loving, consensual couple in *Wives of the Prophet* and contradicted the liberal concepts of consent and freedom that would become so important to revivalist discourses around the Islamic family. In the editorial, Bint al-Shatiʾ argued for Islam as a religion of freedom and equality. Drawing on the Qurʾanic verse stating that there is no compulsion in religion (2:256), she wrote that "just as the Qurʾan stated that there was no compulsion in religion, there was also no compulsion in a marriage concluded according to correct Islamic principles."[39] She also framed the question of freedom in the family in larger political terms, as a kind of foreign despotism crushing the true spirit of Islam, violating its sacredness with erroneous interpretations of its dictates. "When Arab society was sinking under feudalism, despotic rule exploited a reactionary army in the battle for the umma. . . . Under the auspices of this feudalism, statutes on the family were put in place, violating all that is sacred in it and maliciously ripping it apart. These statutes still exist and paralyze every attempt to conserve family and society." Bint al-Shatiʾ adapts a socialist framework in this passage, applying a revolutionary discourse of liberation to the conservation of the sacred family. The liberation is from various forces: colonial, feudal, reactionary, and patriarchal.

In the middle of these debates over women, the family, and the personal status laws, Bint al-Shatiʾ's immensely popular writings on religious domesticity depicted the family as the natural domain of women's work, the Prophet's family as a model of idealized domesticity, and the private sphere as the repository of religion. In his work on the laws of personal status, Talal Asad describes secularism as producing the family as a sphere of religiosity (and, analogously, circumscribing religious law in the family).

> It is because the legal formation of the family gives the concept of individual morality its own "private" locus that the sharīʿa can now be spoken of as "the law of personal status"—*qānūn al-aḥwāl al-shakhṣiyya*. In this way it becomes the expression of a secular formula, defining a place in which "religion" is allowed to make its public appearance through state laws. And the family as concept, word, and organizational unit acquires a new salience.[40]

[38] Bint al-Shatiʾ, "Fi al-Ahwal al-Shakhsiyya," *al-Ahram*, December 3, 1959.
[39] Ibid.; Bier, *Revolutionary Womanhood*, 117.
[40] Asad, *Formations of the Secular*, 230–31.

As scholars have noted, the personal status laws had the contradictory effect of relegating religion to the domain of intimate relations while also maintaining its very visible place in public politics.[41] During this period, such "private" definitions of religion, whether in literary letters or in the letter of the law, served less to relegate religion to the margins than to secure its visibility in the public eye.

One of Bint al-Shatiʾ's main interlocutors in debates over the personal status laws was ʿAli ʿAbd al-Wahid Wafi, then dean of the faculty of education at al-Azhar. Educated at the Sorbonne by one of Durkheim's acolytes (Paul Fauconnet), Wafi's most famous work was the widely circulated *Huquq al-Insan fi al-Islam* (Human Rights in Islam, 1957). This work incorporates elements from his dissertation *Contribution a une théorie sociologique de l'esclavage* (Contribution to a Sociological Theory of Slavery, 1931) comparing slavery among the ancient Greeks and Romans, the Hebrews, in medieval Islam, and in the French Antilles. Although he employed the classic philological "comparison of cultures" approach, his conclusion inverts notions of Islam's "oriental despotism" that characterized such philological treatises. In contrast to premodern and modern Europe, Wafi writes, liberty in Islam is "imprescriptible": free people cannot have their liberty stripped of them; no person can voluntarily surrender his or her freedom; slaves enjoy certain basic freedoms; and Islam encourages the emancipation of slaves as an act of piety.[42] From this Wafi deduces an understanding of common law of free birth in Islam, a "*liberté de naissance*" and a "*naissance libres de droit.*"[43] Wafi characterizes the institution of slavery in Islam not as one of bondage but as an institution securing the specific rights of slaves, encouraging emancipation as a religious duty, and asserting freedom as an ultimate ontological value in Islam. Wafi's own writings "Islamicized" the discipline of sociology by drawing on religious sources and the Islamic intellectual tradition, combining them with the disciplinary conventions of sociology as a field.

Although educated in more secular institutions—the Sorbonne and Dar al-ʿUlum—Wafi would be appointed dean of al-Azhar's faculty of education and later, dean of the faculty of arts and sciences at the

[41] Ibid., esp 226–35; Bier, *Revolutionary Womanhood*, 149.

[42] ʿAli ʿAbd al-Wahid Wafi, *Contribution à une théorie sociologique de l'esclavage: étude des situations génératrices de l'esclavage* (Paris: A. Mechelinck, 1931). Wafi bases this interpretation on several premises: that Islam never practiced the capture of free men (114); slavery was not used as a juridical punishment (115); neither apostasy nor sacrilege was punished with slavery (117); a free child is not appropriable for the purposes of slavery (118); and paternal power cannot reduce any person to slavery (122). Finally, slavery was not by birth to a slave woman but only by birth to a slave father.

[43] Ibid., 34–35.

Islamic University of Omdurman. He would host Bint al-Shatiʾ in 1967 and 1968, perhaps courting her—intellectually and otherwise—in the aftermath of al-Khuli's death. In the opening words of "The Islamic Understanding of Women's Liberation," she acknowledges that they "had already met in other homelands, spiritually, intellectually, and affectively," but she headed to "your good lands desiring to meet you" (3). Wafi's ideas would leave their own mark on Bint al-Shatiʾ. The following year they would present in tandem—Wafi on "al-Hurriyya al-Madaniyya fi al-Islam" (Civil Liberty in Islam, 1968), an excerpt from the "Freedom in Islam" section of *Human Rights in Islam*, and Bint al-Shatiʾ on "al-Qurʾan wa-Huquq al-Insan" (The Qurʾan and Human Rights, 1968), which drew on Wafi's ideas about liberty in Islam as "imprescriptible."

Family, gender, and the laws of personal status are pivotal to Wafi's conception of *Human Rights in Islam*. The book is framed as a general discussion of Islamic freedom and equality, but at the heart of the section on equality is a long exploration of the "aspects of discrimination between men and woman" that addresses point by point the core issues in the debates over the personal status laws: divorce, *bayt al-ṭāʿa*, and polygamy. Published just when Nasser abolished the religious courts and put al-Azhar under the control of the state, the book defends the personal status laws as a domain of freedom, rights, and equality. The book makes a claim to a democratic politics of Islam but, however paradoxically, simultaneously inscribes gender discrimination into a "free and equal" Islam. Wafi interprets gender discrimination in the shariʿa, codified under colonial rule in Egypt, as a vestige of an authentic and original Islam.

Human Rights in Islam would be republished several times between 1956 and 1967 as the personal status laws were ardently debated. Wafi's section on "Equality in Islam" addressing these laws would be reissued as a separate book many times over the subsequent decade.[44] Wafi argues that practical—or incidental—discrimination between a man and woman (husband and wife) does not compromise a woman's intrinsic freedom and human equality.[45] On the contrary, these ele-

[44] ʿAli ʿAbd al-Wahid Wafi, *Bayt al-Taʿa wa-Taʿaddud al-Zawjat wa-l-Talaq fi al-Islam*, Maʿa al-Islam (Cairo: Muʾassasat al-Matbuʿat al-Haditha, 1960); ʿAli ʿAbd al-Wahid Wafi, *al-Musawaa fi al-Islam*, Iqraʾ (Cairo: Dar al-Maʿarif, 1962); ʿAli ʿAbd al-Wahid Wafi, *al-Marʾa fi al-Islam* (Cairo: Maktabat Gharib, 1971).

[45] This argument can be found in Sayyid Qutb, *Social Justice in Islam* (Oneonta, NY: Islamic Publications International, 2000), 73: "As for the relation between the sexes, Islam has guaranteed women complete equality with men with regard to their sex; it has permitted no discrimination except in some incidental matters connected with physical

ments of discrimination ensure certain rights to financial support (*nafaqa*). Wafi draws on classical arguments about women and men's complementary rights and duties in the family but infuses them with new political concepts of freedom, equality, and human rights.[46] These contradictions are characteristic of liberal discourse, the political scientist Wendy Brown argues—what she calls its "constitutive dualisms," with freedom, equality, and rights on one side and obligation, hierarchies, and duties on the other. These dualisms are emblematic of a gendered division of labor in society, between a free and equal citizenship, balanced by the obligations and duties required for communal cohesion. "The social contract to make civil society and the state *cannot come into being* without a sexual contract that subordinates women in marriage," writes Brown.[47] The historian Joan Scott refers to contradictions as the "paradox" at the heart of liberalism, of free and equal citizenship in public compounded by gendered difference.[48] Wafi would reiterate his argument in *Human Rights in Islam* countless times over his career: in his republications, in his lecture in Omdurman, and in his public debates with Bint al-Shatiʾ over the personal status laws.

Wafi published an editorial in *al-Ahram* responding to Bint al-Shatiʾ, taking a passage verbatim from *Human Rights in Islam*. Wives, he argues, have a *duty* to obey their husbands, one that corresponds to their *right* to financial maintenance. Similarly, husbands have a *right* to women's obedience, just as they have a *duty* to provide economic support for them.

> Both husband and wife are bound by a number of rights and mutual duties. For each right for each of them, there is a duty that has to be carried out. Due to this exchange in rights and duties a good deal of balance is achieved between the married couple in

capacity, customary procedure, or responsibility, in all of which the human status of the two sexes is not in question." Qutb quotes Wafi's *Human Rights in Islam* at length in his exegesis of Surat al-Nisaʾ, and Wafi's *Human Rights* clearly owes a big debt to *Social Justice in Islam*. Sayyid Qutb, *In the Shade of the Qurʾan*, trans. Adil Salahi and Ashur Shamis (Leicester: Islamic Foundation, 2001), 125.

[46] Barbara Freyer Stowasser, "Women and Citizenship in the Qurʾan," in *Women, the Family, and Divorce Laws in Islamic History*, ed. Amira El Azhary Sonbol (Syracuse, NY: Syracuse University Press, 1996), 23–38; Kecia Ali, "Progressive Muslims and Islamic Jurisprudence: The Necessity for Critical Engagement with Marriage and Divorce Laws," in *Progressive Muslims: On Gender, Justice, and Pluralism* (Oxford: One World, 2003), 163–89.

[47] Brown, "Liberalism's Family Values." Her argument draws on Pateman, *The Sexual Contract*. For a discussion of the sexual contract in the context of Egypt, see Hatem, "Egyptian Discourses on Gender and Political Liberalization."

[48] Scott, *Only Paradoxes to Offer*.

> social and civil aspects and in the smooth running of family life. One of the main tasks that fall on the husband is to look after the family and its financial expenditure. . . . This is exchanged by certain duties from the side of the wife.[49]

Wafi’s description is more than just an articulation of different duties and obligations within the family structure: it encodes wifely obedience and male authority through differential tasks. His argument adopts the paradoxes and contradictions of liberal discourse, where freedom, rights, and equality are asserted as universal ideals but are differentially defined for women and men, and for private and public spheres.

These debates testify to how the model of the free and equal family became a vehicle for nascent Islamic discourses around religious law, women’s rights, and political participation in a secular polity. The family—based in the *sunna* of the early community—becomes a political model for righteous governance. Yet it enjoys an “extrapolitical” status within the secular state, giving it both a legitimacy and a conceptual inviolability from state control.[50] This form of political expression was particularly important during this period of mass incarceration of Muslim Brothers, executions, and censorship of religious materials. Sayyid Qutb, who continued to use his own rights language against what he described as the tyranny of the secular state, faced nearly a decade in prison and eventually execution. The subtle language of the “gentle sex,” and the seemingly innocuous subject of the Muslim family, served as a vehicle for a nascent Islamic rights discourse. The family also became a repository for something more—a place for the inculcation of modern religious subjectivities, cultivated through affect and contracted through choice. Women and family were critical to constructing modern Muslim subjectivities and a sense of Islamic citizenship. Wafi’s extensive sociological writings on the pedagogical role of the family and Bint al-Shati'’s literary treatments of the Islamic family performed different but analogous functions for imagining and creating a world of Islamic sensibilities as much as Islamic politics.

[49] Wafi, *Human Rights in Islam*, 132.

[50] “With the modern public sphere comes the idea that political power must be supervised and checked by something outside.” Charles Taylor, *Modern Social Imaginaries* (Durham, NC: Duke University Press, 2003), 90.

The Private Life of the Public Intellectual

Bint al-Shatiʾ's writings functioned as a kind of literary *daʿwa* for the reading public: they were widely disseminated and circulated among popular audiences but also performed the pedagogical role of inculcating Islamic knowledge and fostering Islamic practice. Her adab, her literary production, helped cultivate the proper comportment associated with Islamic adab. Her writings are preoccupied with defining the nature of the private sphere in public, what Habermas calls "privateness oriented toward an audience" and Charles Taylor describes as the shaping of the sphere of intimate relations through public debate.[51]

> The intimate domain had to be defined through public interchange, both of literary works and of criticism. This is only superficially a paradox. A new definition of human identity, however private, can become generally accepted only through being defined and affirmed in public space. And this critical exchange itself came to constitute a public sphere. We might say that it came to constitute an axis of the public sphere, along with, even slightly ahead of, the principal axis of exchange around matters of public (in the first sense) policy.[52]

The world of letters plays a critical role in constituting the bourgeois nature of the public sphere in Habermas's formulation, with the literary domain intersecting with the letter of the law to make middle-class mores and values normative. Habermas observes how the patriarchal conjugal family acts as the "home" of public debate; that is, as a public of private individuals whose "audience-oriented privacy made its way into the political realm's public sphere."[53] The world of letters is the mode through which this experience of privateness is publicly articulated.

Political upheavals in the region, as well as upheavals in Bint al-Shatiʾ's personal life, shaped a new kind of weltanschauung in her work, what Sayyid Qutb called a new kind of Islamic taṣwīr, a mode of seeing and a mode of representation. In the late 1960s Bint al-Shatiʾ shifts, almost abruptly, from her focus on poetry and women in the Prophet's family to tackling Qurʾan exegeses, writing a biography of the Prophet, and formulating theories of the "Islamic self" and Islamic

[51] Habermas, *Structural Transformation of the Public Sphere*, 43.
[52] Taylor, *Modern Social Imaginaries*, 105–6.
[53] Habermas, *Structural Transformation of the Public Sphere*, 51.

freedom. She suddenly begins experimenting with new literary interpretations of the Qurʾan, revolutionizing her intellectual production. This religious turn anticipated the kinds of writings that would come to dominate the awakening in the 1980s and 1990s. As a literary scholar—and perhaps also as a woman—Bint al-Shatiʾ worked outside the political radar of the state, which most likely enabled her to sustain this Islamic discourse with impunity. Sayyid Qutb, who abandoned literary scholarship for Islamic activism in the Brotherhood, is a counter-example, suffering a decade in prison, torture, and eventual execution (in 1966). She also first presented these ideas far from the political fray in Cairo, at the Islamic University of Omdurman in the Sudan. Between her first set of lectures in February 1967 and the second in February 1968, Egypt went through a seismic change after its loss to Israel in the Six-Day War, marking the physical and political decline of Nasser and his political ideology of Arab nationalism and the rise of Islamic political and intellectual mobilization. Nasser's political demise affected not only Bint al-Shatiʾ's own cultural production but also the broader cultural production of Egyptian intellectuals, as they turned from Arab nationalism to a more Islamic orientation. From then on, Carrie Wickham observes, "calls for political freedom, social justice, and confrontation with Zionism and imperialism could still be heard, but they were henceforward cast in an Islamic idiom."[54]

The Omdurman lectures also marked a transition in Bint al-Shatiʾ's personal life: it was her first public appearance after the death of her husband, Amin al-Khuli. In her first lecture, "The Islamic Understanding of Women's Liberation," Bint al-Shatiʾ expresses gratitude for the warmth of her reception in people's homes, at the university, and by the crowded audience. This welcome protects her from the "ferocity [*waḥsha*: wilderness] of alienation." "We have already met in other homelands, spiritually, intellectually, and emotionally," she says. She talks about the letters written to her in the newspapers, words that touched her, shook her, and flooded her with feelings of protection (*riʿāya*) and welcome. But she also talks about her hidden grief, emotions that she tried to "fold" into her interior so that the audience would not see her pain ("so that you would not perceive [what lies] behind what I show you of myself"). Using evocative literary language, she says, "I have lost the taste for life since the person that granted all my existence life, value, and meaning has gone" (3). Enveloped by the humanity of the world of letters, Bint al-Shatiʾ exposes her inner emotional world to the crowd in poetic language that aesthetically evokes her mourning. Yet these public lectures—given almost a year after al-

[54] Wickham, *Mobilizing Islam*, 34.

Khuli's death—vocally call for liberation from mourning back into the light of day and into "living emotion." Bint al-Shatiʾ finds liberation in the world of Islamic letters through a poetics of affect for God, Prophet, Qurʾan, and for her departed lover.

Al-Khuli's death seemed to free Bint al-Shatiʾ intellectually, as she began writing almost single-mindedly on the Qurʾan, publishing seven works of Qurʾan interpretation in just three years.[55] During al-Khuli's lifetime, Bint al-Shatiʾ published just one slim volume of exegesis, a meticulously executed reading of the mystical suras at the end of the Qurʾan, in which she closely followed al-Khuli's method of Qurʾan interpretation. The book, *al-Tafsir al-Bayani li-l-Qurʾan al-Karim* (Clear Interpretation of the Noble Qurʾan, 1962), is a cautious work with the methodical rigor of an ambitious student—and the tentativeness born of the gendered (and perhaps personal) boundaries she was breaking down.[56] Just before al-Khuli died, Bint al-Shatiʾ would republish *Clear Interpretation* with a second volume's worth of material added to the original, a volume she republished as a separate book in 1968.[57] The first Qurʾan interpretation written by an Egyptian woman, this work opened the way for women's exegeses of the Qurʾan written by Islamic intellectuals like Niʿmat Sidqi, Zaynab al-Ghazali, and Kariman Hamza during the ṣaḥwa.[58] Even though Bint al-Shatiʾ had written scores of biographies of women in the Prophet's family, she never ventured her own biography of the Prophet until after al-Khuli's death. The Omdurman lectures are her first foray into some of these experimental ideas, as she leaps out of the tight frame of the hermeneutical approach of her earlier writings. The first lecture she presented, "The Islamic Understanding of Women's Liberation," calls for liberating women's literary expression from

[55] Bint al-Shatiʾ, *al-Tafsir al-Bayani li-l-Qurʾan al-Karim*, vol. 2 (Cairo: Dar al-Maʿarif, 1968); Bint al-Shatiʾ, *Maqal fi al-Insan* (Cairo: Dar al-Maʿarif, 1969); Bint al-Shatiʾ, *al-Qurʾan wa-l-Tafsir al-ʿAsri "Hadha Balagh li-l-Nas,"* Iqraʾ (Cairo: Dar al-Maʿarif, 1970); Bint al-Shatiʾ, *Muqaddima fi al-Manhaj* (Cairo: Maʿhad al-Buhuth wa-l-Dirasat al-ʿArabiyya, 1971); Bint al-Shatiʾ, *al-Iʿjaz al-Bayani li-l-Qurʾan wa-Masaʾil Ibn al-Azraq* (Cairo: Dar al-Maʿarif, 1971); Bint al-Shatiʾ, *al-Qurʾan wa-Qadaya al-Insan* (Beirut: Dar al-ʿIlm li-l-Malayin, 1972); Bint al-Shatiʾ, *al-Shakhsiyya al-Islamiyya.*

[56] Bint al-Shatiʾ, *al-Tafsir al-Bayani li-l-Qurʾan al-Karim*, Maktabat al-Dirasat al-Adabiyya (Cairo: Dar al-Maʿarif, 1962).

[57] Bint al-Shatiʾ, *al-Tafsir al-Bayani li-l-Qurʾan al-Karim*, 2 vols., 2nd ed. (Cairo: Dar al-Maʿarif, 1966).

[58] Niʿmat Sidqi, *Muʿjizat al-Qurʾan* (Cairo: ʿAlam al-Kutub, 1971); Zaynab al-Ghazali and ʿAbd al-Hayy Faramawi, *Nazarat fi Kitab Allah* (Cairo: Dar al-Shuruq, 1994); Kariman Hamza, *al-Luʾluʾ wa-l-Marjan fi Tafsir al-Qurʾan* (Cairo: Maktabat al-Shuruq al-Dawliyya, 2010).

mourning poetry (*rithāʾ*), often considered the traditional domain of women's poetry.

The first Qurʾan exegesis that Bint al-Shatiʾ wrote after al-Khuli's death develops a theory of Islamic freedom revolving around questions of free will, freedom of belief, freedom of thought and opinion.[59] She reaches these conclusions partly by employing al-Khuli's method of literary interpretation of the Qurʾan, treating the text as a whole and looking at every instance of a word or idea (rather the classical approach of line-by-line analyses).[60] Her exegetical method (*manhaj*) focuses "on the text itself—guidance provided by the book of Islam . . . the original source that guides us to the core of Islamic thought on freedom."[61] This approach frees her from tradition, from the "opinions" of philosophers and religious scholars (ʿulamaʾ), from hadith and *turāth* (heritage). Engaging in a kind of literary Salafism, she calls for a textual analysis that asserts the primacy of the Qurʾan as revelation, returns to the guidance of the original text, and uses a form of literary *ijtihād* to reinterpret scripture. She argues for letting "the Qurʾan speak for itself and be understood in the most direct of ways," and for eliminating extratextual elements (such as biblical material, historical accounts, and prior exegeses). Her close readings treat the text as an "organic whole," drawing on romantic understandings of the literary work's organicity but also on al-Khuli's understanding of the Qurʾan as literature.[62] In *Maqal fi al-Insan: Dirasa Qurʾaniyya* (Treatise on the Human: A Qurʾanic Study, 1969), she engages in literary analysis of key Qurʾanic terms, namely, those related to willing, wanting, determining, and desiring. She observes that their subjects are always predicated by humans, not by God. Through a careful lexical analysis, she argues for an Islamic conception of free will

[59] Bint al-Shatiʾ, *Maqal fi al-Insan,* 61–118. For more information on the method and its conclusions about free will, see Issa J. Boullata, "Modern Qurʾan Exegesis: A Study of Bint al-Shatiʾ's Method," *Muslim World* 64 (1974): 112–13; Yudian Wahyudi, "Ali Shariati and Bint al-Shatiʾ on Free Will: A Comparison," *Journal of Islamic Studies* 9, no. 1 (1998): 35. Boullata's excellent scholarship focuses extensively on literary approaches to the Qurʾan. Some of his students have focused on the development of the method but not its cultural, social, and political implications nor its gendered politics. Muhammad Amin, "A Study of Bint al-Shatiʾ's Exegesis" (MA thesis, McGill University, 1992); Syamsuddin Sahiron, "An Examination of Bint al-Shatiʾ's Method of Interpreting the Qurʾan" (MA thesis, McGill University, 1998).

[60] Amin al-Khuli, *Manahij Tajdid fi al-Nahw wa-l-Balagha wa-l-Tafsir wa-l-Adab* (Cairo: Dar al-Maʿarif, 1961), 305–12.

[61] Bint al-Shatiʾ, *Maqal fi al-Insan,* 63.

[62] Qutb's mentor ʿAbbas Mahmud al-ʿAqqad made romantic ideas about the text as an organic whole and the poet as divinely inspired into an influential school of literary thought in the late nahḍa. See ʿAbbas Mahmud al-ʿAqqad and Ibrahim al-Mazini, *al-Diwan: Kitab fi al-Naqd wa-l-Adab* (Cairo: Maktabat al-Saʿada, 1921). Al-ʿAqqad and Bint al-Shatiʾ would square off in public over the question of women in the Qurʾan.

through chapters on freedom of belief, freedom of thought, and freedom of opinion in the Qurʾan.

Bint al-Shatiʾ opens *Treatise on the Human* with an intensely personal description of her mourning. She describes retreating to her childhood home seeking solace in the Qurʾan: "Seeking isolation, I withdrew into the remains of my self, trying to gather its scattered fragments, from which I began to walk on the path of existence." She talks about regaining her humanity by facing death and reading the Qurʾan. The specter of death forces humanity to endure "the furthest of what she can bear, in order to realize her ideal existence, making us face our final destiny that encloses all that exists, as if an illusory dream or vision."[63] Slipping between the collective "us" of humanity and the singular pronoun of the feminine humanity, "she," Bint al-Shatiʾ encloses herself in a collective human experience even as she recounts her own intensely personal experience of death, mourning, life (*wujūd*), and emotion (*wijdān*, from the same root). Publishing this account of her grief in the introduction to her Qurʾan interpretation, she describes it as a dream or a vision that helped her understand the "secret of being." The Qurʾan, she says, tells this story of the human being from beginning to end, a story of struggle and effort (84:6), using the word *mujāhada*, an alternate rendering of jihad.[64] Her analytic labor, alone with the text, is an existential, ontological, spiritual, and literary struggle to interpret the Qurʾan, one that led to an illumination she describes as liberation. The fruit of her jihad is *Treatise on the Human*, where she probes the "story of the human," exploring how language grants humanity its special status among God's creatures, and the way knowledge ultimately frees humanity from enslavement to ignorance and false gods. Melding Enlightenment concepts with revivalist ones, she writes about the primacy of knowledge and the darkness of human ignorance, ignorance (*jāhiliyya*) equated with unbelief (*jaḥd*).

The Islamic Understanding of Women's Liberation

In Bint al-Shatiʾ's first lecture at Omdurman, "The Islamic Understanding of Women's Liberation," she describes Islam as liberating humanity from the shackles of ignorance, drawing on classical imagery of the time before Islam as one of ignorance (jāhiliyya). For her, the path to

[63] Bint al-Shatiʾ, *Maqal fi al-Insan,* 7. "Her" refers to the feminine "humanity" (*insāniyya*), an intentional literary double entendre.

[64] "O humanity, you strive toward your Lord and you will meet him" (Qurʾan 84:6) (my translation).

human liberation lies in education and knowledge, as a human right granted by the Qurʾan: "It is not the modern West that lends us this right, but it is a fundamental legal right of women on the authority of her humanity. The first verse of the revelation that came down indicates that knowledge is the special province of humanity" (8).[65] Connecting the authority of women's humanity to the authority of divine revelation, she develops a notion of Islamic humanism as enlightening humanity through the word of God. Bint al-Shatiʾ says that women have a fundamental ("original and intrinsic") human right to participate in the world of Islamic letters (5). She describes literacy, knowledge, eloquence, and the clear signs of God's word (al-bayān) as liberating women from the "veil of ignorance (*ḥijāb al-jahl*) imposed on their minds" and from "the wilderness of blind illiteracy." This is the only way, she says, that women will "awaken to horizons of light and consciousness" and "escape the confines of the harem so that we can share in the public life of our people" (4, 8, 14). To refer to the Qurʾan, she consistently uses the word al-bayān, meaning speech, eloquence, and illumination. Through this Islamic intellectual terminology, she justifies her own presence speaking before the audience at the Islamic University of Omdurman as a liberated, educated, knowledgeable, enlightened, vocal, articulate woman of Islamic letters. The Islamic language literally makes her *shine*, through the eloquence of her own literary style, by drawing on the power of the Qurʾan's signs, demonstrating her mastery of the scriptural tradition, and debating "the deep-rooted principles established by the righteous *salaf*, the men of religion" (16). Deploying orientalist imagery of harems and veils, she subverts underlying assumptions about the backwardness and superstition of Islam. The light of Islamic knowledge liberates women from the shackles of ignorance; this is the "Islamic understanding of women's liberation."

Even after asserting that a woman's right (to self-determination: "my right to life") is equal to that of a man, not contingent on the will of man, Bint al-Shatiʾ avows men's right to "guardianship" over women. In the second part of the lecture on women's emancipation, she moves seemingly diametrically from freedom and equality in the world of letters to dependency and difference in the intimate sphere of the family. Nonetheless Bint al-Shatiʾ is less diverging from her liberal paradigm than reasserting it, continuing to draw on language of freedom, equality, and rights, even as she asserts hierarchies, dif-

[65] Here Bint al-Shatiʾ quotes the first verses of the Qurʾan to come down (96:1–5): "Recite and your Lord is most bountiful, who taught with the pen, taught humanity what it did not know."

ference, and duties. "Our understanding of the equality between men and women has been liberated," she says, "with the return to the origin of Islam [the Qurʾan]. The equal, instinctual (*fiṭrī*) woman admits that man has a legal and natural right to guardianship over her" (12). She shifts from the language of human rights to instinct and natural law, substantiated with verses from the Qurʾan. She does not abandon the liberal framework structuring her argument. On the contrary, the argument about the family and gender relations is counterpoised—like the private sphere is to the public—to her discussion of the liberating potential of the public sphere, women's right to equal participation, and the illuminating nature of the world of letters. Even as women's "instinct (fiṭra) submits" to male authority in the family, she says, women do not revoke their "legal right to equality" (13). Liberation, Bint al-Shatiʾ asserts, "does not call for obliterating all differences between men and women." She relates this to different biological and reproductive functions of women and men, as well as to differences in the marriage contract. Can women, she asks,

> in accordance with the right to equality, have multiple husbands? Why does the woman alone carry the burden of pregnancy and breastfeeding? Is it not incumbent upon the man to share the burden in accordance with the right to equality? Does he become pregnant, give birth, and breastfeed one time and then the next time she becomes pregnant, gives birth, and breastfeeds? In truth, the new woman has liberated her understanding of this equality. The situation is not ambiguous, only distortions eliminate the natural differences between male and female and the social differences between man and woman. Equality does not go beyond equivalent rights and duties" (10).

While continuing to evoke rights and equality, Bint al-Shatiʾ does so through gendered binaries that strike a balance between equivalent rights and duties. Organically structuring this balance is the partnership between man and woman, husband and wife. The conjugal couple becomes the unit of this social structure, with gendered differences balancing the private sphere. "We, modern emancipated women, believe that the man and the woman are complementary, that each of them needs the other to realize a complete existence. The two partners are . . . companions in the journey of the lifespan" (11).

Bint al-Shatiʾ draws on the Qurʾanic concept of fiṭra to provide her own interpretation of the true nature of equality in the family. "Equality," she says, "remains sentenced to the severe judgment of the logic of instinct (fiṭra) and the law of nature that does not know complete equality between one man and another nor between one woman and another, let alone between one sex and the other" (11). Fiṭra connotes the creation of God and human nature but also can mean instinct of intuition when referring to the human being's innate character or natural disposition.[66] "Raise your face truly toward religion the creation of God (*fiṭrat Allah*) according to which he created (*faṭara*) people" (Qurʾan 30:30). This idea of divine fiṭra connected to human instinct would become associated with the conjugal couple and the family in revivalist thought.

Bint al-Shatiʾ understands the couple as "a single social cell . . . shared life beating with a single pulse, united in congruity and harmony in an integral whole" (11). In an essay on family law in Egypt, Talal Asad describes a process whereby the family becomes

> the unit of "society" in which the individual is physically and morally reproduced and has his or her primary formation as a "private" being. It is often assumed that colonial governments were reluctant to interfere with family law because it was the heart of religious doctrine and practice. I argue, on the contrary, that the sharīʿa thus defined is precisely a secular formula for privatizing "religion" and preparing the ground for the self-governing subject.

A citizen's rights, Asad argues, are "integral to the process of governance, to the normalization of social conduct in a modern, secular state. In this scheme of things the individual acquires his or her rights mediated by various domains of social life—including the public domain of politics and the private domain of the family—as articulated by the law."[67] My aim is not to depict liberal Islam's view of gender relations as merely a derivative discourse but to contextualize its relationship to liberalism and secularism. Wendy Brown talks about liberalism resting on "mechanical foundations," as a sense of duty that "prowls about in our lives like the ghost of dead religious belief." Liberalism, she argues, continues to mechanically reproduce itself, whether in "Chinese post-Confucian post-Maoism" or in "Iranian Islamic fundamentalism. In this way, its Protestant 'origins' live somewhere in a cultural—as opposed to substantively economic—modality that capitalism is and generates."[68] In the same way, a global economic and political liberal-

[66] Edward William Lane, *Arabic-English Lexicon* (Beirut: Librairie du Liban, 1968), 2416.

[67] Asad, *Formations of the Secular*, 227–28.

[68] Brown, "Liberalism's Family Values," 136–37.

ism operates through and within particular local configurations, even as these local "dialects" speak back to the global discourse.[69] These cultural origins, transmitted through the vehicle of colonial dominance and capitalist expansion, would plant a seed in the fertile ground of Islamic intellectual thought. These seeds grew, becoming the tangled roots of an Islamic modernity, the fruit of these mixed origins.

In Bint al-Shatiʾ's second lecture, "The Arab Literary Woman: Yesterday and Today," education, writing, voice, and expression are still keys to awakening and emancipation. She calls for women's participation in public but not for exposing too much or for proclaiming too loudly. Emancipation—whether emotional or intellectual—takes place within very specific literary and moral bounds. The moral bounds are of chastity and modesty; the literary bounds are the limits on what should be expressed. In short, some things should not be made public. Her use of fiṭra is key; it is another word, like *wijdān*, that evolved in modernist religious and literary writings.[70] Bint al-Shatiʾ uses fiṭra in a double, almost conflicting, way to express emotion and modesty. Women's instinctual connection with emotion makes them fit for the field of literature, but part of this "instinctual [*fiṭrī*] inheritance" is also the "chastity, abstention, and modesty" that women must preserve with their own hands. Those who do not will go from being the "personal property of their husbands to being common property [*shuyūʿ*] in the streets."[71] The word she uses for "common property," *shuyūʿ*, has connotations not just of a kind of prostitution but also of the circulation of goods and news (as well as the "common property" of communism). She defines the "licit" in self-expression as love, emotion, spiritual desires, and intellectual liberation. Liberated literary women

> recognized with soundness of their instinct (fiṭra) the limits of what is licit (*mubāḥ*) in what Eve disclosed (*bawḥ*) of her affection. . . . Even today it is impossible for us to rebel against what is in our femininity of chastity and modesty, either instinctually or genetically. It is impossible to rebel against the feelings of limits

[69] Lila Abu-Lughod, "Against Universality: Dialects of (Women's) Human Rights and Capabilities," in *Rethinking the Human*, ed. J. Michelle Molina and Donald K. Swearer (Cambridge, MA: Harvard University Press, 2010).

[70] Over subsequent editions of *Social Justice in Islam*, Qutb changes his use of fiṭra from meaning a natural, animal-like instinct of needs (the vernacular, lay sense of fiṭra) to the sense of God-given nature. William E. Shepard documents these changes in *Sayyid Qutb and Islamic Activism: A Translation and Critical Analysis of* Social Justice in Islam (Leiden: E. J. Brill, 1996), 33n82, 35n95, 42n17, 71n202.

[71] Bint al-Shatiʾ, *al-Adiba al-ʿArabiyya Ams wa-l-Yawm: Muhadara ʿAmma* (Cairo: Matbaʿat Mukhaymir, 1967), 24.

> that we know we will not surpass, either in disclosure or in exposure. There is a difference between our freedom in expressing our selves and our feelings, and those who go beyond these limits. (20)

Bint al-Shatiʾ calls for a measure of "repression and reserve (*kitmān*: also meaning silence) during this phase of our emancipation" and for "chastity in behavior and in words. . . . The tearing of the veil is a rebellion against our femininity that still controls us with modesty and abstention, thanks to a long inheritance. We should proudly reject this current loudly voiced exposure that sullies our femininity . . . with nakedness and degradation" (20). Yet Bint al-Shatiʾ acknowledges that this "instinctual [*fiṭrī*] inheritance" has shackled women mentally and emotionally, shackles that they have not been able to discard.

Bint al-Shatiʾ writes about this chastity, abstention, and modesty in the context of "our emancipated reality and our equal instinct" (20). This is similar to the set of contradictions in "The Islamic Understanding of Women's Liberation," where she talks about "liberating our understanding of equality" while still arguing that the "equal instinctual woman admits that a man has a legal and natural right to guardianship over her." Men have a degree over women "to which instinct (fiṭra) submits and measurements are balanced, without revoking our legal right to equality" (13). This formulation assumes a liberation of women's literary voice and a correlated liberation of their emotions, but boundaries and restraints in their relationships to men, to sexuality, and in the family. Similarly, Bint al-Shatiʾ asserts equality even while describing gendered hierarchies. Wendy Brown's "constitutive dualities of liberalism" become, in the literary world, feminized emotion, instinct, love, intimacy, and affection that public discourse declares are women's natural domain and, moreover, "liberate" women into their true nature. In "The Islamic Understanding of Women's Liberation," Bint al-Shatiʾ juxtaposes and connects the biological "instinct" of reproduction, childbearing, and breastfeeding[72] with the God-given gifts infused in human nature: of knowledge, intelligence, speech, eloquence, and so on. This gift of speech becomes the medium for ex-

[72] Writers associated with the revival similarly combine this sense of fiṭra as God-given nature and fiṭra as human instinct governing family relations. Heba Raouf Ezzat draws on Qurʾanic language nearly verbatim (which she renders in italics): "The foundation of the family is connected *to the creation of God according to which he created people*, from the desire of each of the sexes for the other. And this drive is what makes the family one of the social models [*sunan*]. The importance of legislation is in its preservation of *love, mercy, and tranquility*. This is a trait at the core of human nature [fiṭra] according to God's creation." Raouf Ezzat, *al-Marʾa wa-l-ʿAmal al-Siyasi*, 187.

pressing human nature, defined differentially for a woman, as mother, chaste, emotional, instinctual, and also literary. Writing of the Qurʾan, Bint al-Shatiʾ says, "The freedom of the Muslim woman returns to this established origin. In the Islamic understanding, this freedom is the completeness of woman's humanity in all the rights connected with this humanity, and all it carries of tasks and responsibilities . . . knowledge is her legal human right" (7). Ideals of freedom and equality become gendered rights and duties, not just cast in the romantic hue of instinct, nature, and biological essentialism but also given an ontological spiritual status. Here scriptural language of fiṭra, Islamic legal definitions of equivalent rights and duties, and gendered virtues become interpreted through liberal discourses of rights, freedom, and equality, which clearly encode a particular vision of gendered relationships.

"The Islamic Understanding of Women's Liberation" asserts freedom, equality, and rights as the legal entitlement of the (Muslim) citizen-subject. But this freedom entails a corresponding set of hierarchies and dependencies within the family. In this way, Islamic citizenship is publicly defined through reference to a set of "family values." Bint al-Shatiʾ's later work assumes a gender-neutral (male?) citizen-subject imbued with freedom and rights but also envisions an Islamic family that is simultaneously free and equal but structured by obligations and hierarchies. Women's work in the family assumes a key role in building community, shaping ethics, and claiming political autonomy from the state. This is the foundation of their liberation in an Islamic politics, as they define the "common world" of the Islamic populace, a plurality of persons connected by their commitment to the free practice of religion.

Conclusion

Bint al-Shatiʾ's Omdurman lectures reinterpreted the concept of "women's liberation" for an Islamic politics, nearly seventy years after Qasim Amin first ventured his interpretation of "women's liberation" in Islam in 1899. Like Amin, she has unmitigated faith in the power of education and knowledge—scientific, Islamic, and literary—to elevate the political community from its political chains. Like Amin, she defines women's rights and roles in this political community through the structure of the family unit. But she also surpasses Amin in imagining the force of women's literary voices in transforming the umma, just as she surpassed him in literary accomplishment, stature, and recognition. Just before her death in 1998, nearly twenty years after "The Islamic Understanding of Women's Liberation," Bint al-Shatiʾ presented a lecture on "Islam and the New Woman" at a conference in Italy. The two lectures play on the language of Qasim Amin's two seminal books—*Tahrir al-Marʾa* (The Liberation of Woman, 1899) and *al-Marʾa al-Jadida* (The New Woman, 1900)—during a time that Amin's contribution was being reevaluated by the revival.[73] She begins, as she does in "The Islamic Understanding of Women's Liberation," by delineating the accomplishments and progress of women in the professions, in the workplace, government and politics, and education. "So what is the problem?" she asks, in a preacher-like repetitive fashion. Though women have entered the public sphere, she argues, the true nature of liberation and equality has become deformed, creating a "distorted vision of women's rights."[74] The work of motherhood has been devalued; it was a mistake for the movement to focus on women's public roles. This misplaced focus has produced a false understanding of women's liberation since mothers are not valued for their productive labor.

> Our failure to recognize the true value of the mother's great role was a major stumbling block in the early stages of the movement for which our generation paid a terrible price. Thus I hope that we may spare our daughters from falling into the same trap, and enable them to realize their full potential in society as Islam—the religion of the deepest insight and intuition (fiṭra)—has taught us. (198)

Women's leadership and example comes from this maternal function, she argues. "I remind people of this," she says, "in order to correct mistaken ideas about the position of woman and the role of motherhood in Islam, the religion of insight and deepest intuition (fiṭra)" (201). Islam protects women from "mental and emotional burial" by making marriage free from compulsion and characterized by "affection and compassion, spiritual and mental compatibility, and a peaceful home" (202). Bint al-Shatiʾ's "new Islamic woman" is the mother, whose labor, role, and contribution have been grossly underestimated and misrecognized. These words suggest a corresponding Islamicization of liberal discourse, or perhaps a liberalization of Islamic discourse. The world of letters used Islamic terms, ideas, and texts to articulate a public sphere governed by rights, freedoms, and equality and a private sphere gov-

[73] Kishk, *Jahalat ʿAsr al-Tanwir*; ʿAbd al-Halim Muhammad Abu Shuqqa, *Tahrir al-Marʾa fi ʿAsr al-Risala: Dirasa ʿan al-Marʾa Jamiʿa li-Nusus al-Qurʾan al-Karim wa-Sahihay al-Bukhari wa-Muslim* (Kuwait: Dar al-Qalam, 1990); Yusuf al-Qaradawi et al., *Tahrir al-Marʾa fi al-Islam: Muʾtamar 22–23 Fabrayir 2003* (al-Safat, Kuwait: Dar al-Qalam, al-Lajna al-Islamiyya al-ʿAlamiyya li-l-Marʾa wa-l-Tifl, 2004).

[74] Bint al-Shatiʾ, "Islam and the New Woman," trans. Anthony Calderbank, *Alif: Journal of Comparative Poetics* 19 (1997): 197.

erned by affection, compassion, spirituality, self-sacrifice, and devotion—the social and sexual contracts of modern Islamic thought. Bint al-Shati''s writings helped develop specific notions of women's rights, roles, and emancipation that would become central to the Islamic revival. She did so partly by cultivating, like many of the literary intelligentsia, an Islamic imaginary that envisioned an idealized private sphere through public debate over the Islamic world of letters.

Though Bint al-Shati' and her circle of interlocutors argue extensively and eloquently for the free will, free speech, freedom of opinion, freedom of conviction, and political freedom of the Muslim subject, this freedom is bound to the political community of the umma, of which the family and religious law have become emblematic. In her seminal essay on the nature of freedom, Hannah Arendt writes about the paramount importance of the public sphere to a democratic politics. Yet the building of a free political community, she argues, requires a certain renunciation of individual freedom. "If men wish to be free, it is precisely sovereignty that they must renounce."[75] For Bint al-Shati', the *umm*, the mother, is a powerful emblem of this collective membership. The sign of the mother, and her power within the Islamic community, has come to define the umma in the shade of secularism. The free practice of religion in the family symbolizes a political sovereignty that is gained through the autonomy of a sacred community free to express, articulate, and practice its beliefs. Freedom is attained through submission to Islam, a contract bound by Islamic law and expressed through the world of Islamic letters.

[75] Hannah Arendt, "What Is Freedom?" in *Between Past and Future: Eight Exercises in Political Thought* (New York: Penguin Books, 1993), 165. For a discussion of this concept, see Zerilli, *Feminism and the Abyss of Freedom*, 16.

CHAPTER 2

The Redemption of Women's Liberation

Reviving Qasim Amin

At the turn of the millennium, two major conferences in Cairo commemorated women's liberation. The two conferences appeared as competing interpretations of women's liberation, one secular and the other religious.[1] The first, *Miʾat ʿAm ʿala Tahrir al-Marʾa* (One Hundred Years of Woman's Liberation, 1999), was sponsored by the state and brought together mainly secular intellectuals to celebrate the hundredth anniversary of Qasim Amin's *Tahrir al-Marʾa* (The Liberation of Woman, 1899). The second, *Tahrir al-Marʾa fi al-Islam* (The Liberation of Woman in Islam, 2003), gathered the most prominent luminaries of intellectual Islam to memorialize the exiled Muslim Brother ʿAbd al-Halim Abu Shuqqa, author of the six-volume work *Tahrir al-Marʾa fi ʿAsr al-Risala* (The Liberation of Woman in the Age of the Message, 1990).[2] The second conference brought together scholars from diverse ideological orientations within Islamic thought, among them Shaykh Muhammad Sayyid Tantawi from al-Azhar, the popular preacher Shaykh al-Shaʿrawi, the revivalist shaykh Muhammad al-Ghazali, and popular intellectuals Yusuf al-Qaradawi and Muhammad ʿImara. Though the two conferences appear as a call and response, they represent more of a consensus reached between religious and secular camps on the question of women's liberation. The two conferences represent the wholesale acceptance, if not the institutionalization, of the idea of women's emancipation in Islam across ideological and institutional boundaries. Yet the Islamic conference retained its sense of an oppositional discourse, one marginalized and repressed by a dominant secularism. What had been understood as a Western idea and a threat to Islam was

[1] al-Majlis al-Aʿla li-l-Thaqafa, *Miʾat ʿAm ʿala Tahrir al-Marʾa* (Cairo: al-Majlis al-Aʿla li-l-Thaqafa, 2001); al-Qaradawi et al., *Tahrir al-Marʾa fi al-Islam*.

[2] Abu Shuqqa, *Tahrir al-Marʾa fi ʿAsr al-Risala*.

Muhammad Jalal Kishk's *Ignorances of the Age of Enlightenment*, an extinguished candle on Qasim Amin's book *The Liberation of Woman*. Image courtesy of Maktabat al-Turath al-Islami.

now incorporated into the very textual bases of Islam and projected back into the first moments of the religion's founding.

The concept of women's liberation has become an integral part of a transnational Islamic discourse, deployed in contexts as diverse as debates over the freedom to wear the headscarf in France, in the writings of exiled Muslim Brothers in Kuwait and Saudi Arabia, and in the rhetoric of the Ennahda Party in postrevolutionary Tunis.[3] The idea of women's liberation, identified as growing out of colonial feminism and an imperialist secular liberalism, has now become part of a popular Islamic discourse reiterated by activists and scholars alike. This chapter charts the origins of a discourse of women's liberation in Islam during the nineteenth-century awakening known as the nahḍa and its revival for the late twentieth-century ṣaḥwa. The concept of women's liberation was vilified in the nahḍa, with Qasim Amin's *Liberation of Woman* being called a "sermon of the devil." The later ṣaḥwa, however, would appropriate the concept and language of women's liberation, making it a most potent ideological weapon.[4] I look at the first instantiations of this religious discourse in the 1960s and 1970s in the writings of Islamic thinkers Muhammad ʿImara and Muhammad Jalal Kishk, two writers who did much of the intellectual labor to revivify the concept for the Islamic awakening. I trace the flourishing of this idea in the boom in Islamic cultural production in the 1980s and 1990s. In the new millennium it became a way of grappling with a newly emergent imperialist militarism, one that once again took the Muslim woman as its object of liberation.[5]

[3] Muhammad Qutb, *Qadiyyat Tahrir al-Marʾa*, Nahw Fiqh Rashid (Fairfax, VA: Maʿhad al-ʿUlum al-Islamiyya wa-l-ʿArabiyya fi Amrika, 1990); Mayanthi L. Fernando, "Reconfiguring Freedom: Muslim Piety and the Limits of Secular Law and Public Discourse in France," *American Ethnologist* 37, no. 1 (2010): 19–35; Jeanette S. Jouili, "Beyond Emancipation: Subjectivities and Ethics among Women in Europe's Islamic Revival Communities," *Feminist Review* 98, no. 1 (July 2011): 47–64; Lauren E. Bohn, "Tunisia's Forgotten Revolutionaries," *Foreign Policy*, July 14, 2011; Hizb al-ʿAdala wa-l-Tanmiya, "Qiyada bi-l-Nahda al-Tunisiyya: Tahrir al-Marʾa wa-Taʿziz Huquqiha Juzʾ min Risalat al-Islah wa-Binaʾ li-Harakatina," *Harakat al-Nahda*, March 7, 2013.

[4] Mukhtar ibn Ahmad Muʿayyid ʿAzmi, *Fasl al-Khitab aw Taflis Iblis min Tahrir al-Marʾa wa-Rafʿ al-Hijab* (Beirut: al-Matbaʿa al-Adabiyya, 1901); Muhammad Farid Wajdi, *al-Marʾa al-Muslima* (Cairo: Matbaʿat al-Taraqqi, 1901).

[5] Lila Abu-Lughod, "Do Muslim Women Really Need Saving? Anthropological Reflection on Cultural Relativism and Its Others," *American Anthropologist* 104, no. 3 (September 2002): 783–90; Christine McCarthy McMorris, "Grappling with Islam: Bush and the Burqa," *Religion in the News* 5, no. 1 (Spring 2002); United Nations Development Programme, Regional Bureau for Arab States and Arab Fund for Economic and Social Development, *The Arab Human Development Report 2005: Towards the Rise of Women in the Arab World* (New York: United Nations, 2005).

In the mid-1960s there were initial, tentative forays into a discourse of women's liberation in Islam, with Bint al-Shati''s lecture in Omdurman "The Islamic Understanding of Women's Liberation," Kishk's *al-Hurriyya fi al-Usra al-Muslima* (Freedom in the Muslim Family, 1965), and Muhammad ʿImara's republications of Qasim Amin's *Liberation of Woman*. These works, all written between 1965 and 1968, were marginalized in public discourse, partly because of a secular state hostile to ideas of Islamic liberation (or what Kishk calls Islamic revolution). Sayyid Qutb, theorist of Islamic notions of emancipation (Islam as "a universal declaration of emancipation from the tyranny of man over man"), was executed in 1966 for his polemics against the state. Muhammad al-Khidr Husayn, one of the first Islamic thinkers to develop a theory of freedom in Islam, quietly stepped down as the grand shaykh of al-Azhar in 1953, becoming a recluse. ʿAbd al-Wahid Wafi, author of *Human Rights in Islam*, left his position as dean at al-Azhar, becoming dean of the Islamic University of Omdurman. Bint al-Shatiʾ ventured her theory of women's liberation in Islam only at the Islamic University of Omdurman in the Sudan, far from the center of Egypt's political fray. Kishk's *Freedom in the Muslim Family* would remain unpublished until 1979. ʿImara first offered his theories of an Islamic liberation of women by projecting them back in time to the nahḍa and stamping them with the religious authority of Muhammad ʿAbduh. Under the government of Gamal ʿAbd al-Nasser, the family became the site for larger struggles over the role of Islamic law within the secular state. By the 1980s and 1990s, this discourse would move from the margins of Islamic cultural production, becoming an integral part of popular discourse about the liberating nature of Islam.

Although Kishk was essentially blacklisted from publishing in the 1960s and ʿImara first had to publish his writings in Beirut, their works would eventually find mainstream publishers in Egypt when they became massively popular. Their texts were republished over and over again by various presses, putting their circulation into hundreds of editions. As the intellectual production connected to the revival skyrocketed, new Islamic publishing houses emerged (among them Dar al-Iʿtisam, Dar al-Shuruq, Dar al-Daʿwa, al-Turath al-Islami, al-Mukhtar al-Islami, and Dar al-Qalam) to cater to the wide readership of this popular scholarship. These presses created the institutional infrastructure of an Islamic public sphere, with a large body of writings devoted to discussions of women, family, and gender relations in Islam. As Carrie Rosefsky Wickham writes of "print Islam" in the Islamic public sphere in Egypt, anything related to women in the Prophet's family was massively popular.[6] Works on women's liberation in Islam demonstrate a striking consensus on

[6] Wickham, *Mobilizing Islam*, 134.

the topic: that it is situated within the family, within women's roles as mothers, and within the framework of religion. These ideas circulated through a process of publication, republication, and new editions; texts recycled under different titles and reiterated by different authors. The Islamic book industry and its extensive network of Islamic publishing houses came to support a critical mass of Islamic intellectuals writing popular treatises in the 1980s and 1990s.[7] The sheer volume of publications on "women's liberation in Islam" speaks to a wide readership, just as the number of republications and new editions (sometimes by multiple houses) testifies to the scope of its audience.

Wafi's *Human Rights in Islam*, Kishk's *Freedom in the Muslim Family*, and ʿImara's writings on Qasim Amin all use the trope of "women's liberation in Islam" as a way of talking about the liberal nature of Islamic law, the personal status laws, and the Islamic family. They are ostensibly discussing the politics of Islamic law in the secular state, but their focus on the family reinforces the circumscription of Islamic law in the private realm, reemphasizing the family as the "natural nursery" of good Islamic governance and interpreting the family as the "natural" sphere for religion. The family appears as the microcosm of an Islamic politics, and the umma as a macrocosm of the family, an image reinforced through constant reference to the family as the first "cell" of society in the writings of both the nahḍa and the ṣaḥwa. This relationship is shaped by what Foucault calls a kind of "double conditioning" between the intimate sphere and the politics of the state. Even as the private realm appears as insulated from the state, the family is invested with some of the most important mechanisms of power, becoming an instrument for society, politics, and economics at large.[8] Foucault focuses on how new forms of knowledge like psychiatry, the economy, and political science are deployed to control reproduction and population. In Egypt assertions of the repression of an Islamic family served as an incitation to discourse, provoking a proliferation of writings calling for its emancipation and, accordingly the emancipation of Muslim women, from the encroachment of a predatory secularism. New forms of religious knowledge were instrumental for the "greatest Malthusian maneuvers of the age," deployed toward shaping a productive Islamic family for the age of revival.

The discourse of women's liberation in Islam—and women's liberation in the Islamic family—reemerged just as the Nasser government turned its attention to reform of the family through (1) a national

[7] Ibid.; Wickham, *Mobilizing Islam*, 134–35.

[8] Michel Foucault, *Histoire de la sexualité I: la volonté de savoir* (Paris: Gallimard, 1976), 132.

family-planning initiative and (2) reform of the personal status laws. Both projects were launched in the early 1960s but would be interrupted by the tumult following Egypt's defeat in the 1967 war with Israel and Nasser's subsequent death. The family-planning initiatives would increase in breadth and scope under the government of Anwar Sadat in the 1970s. In conjunction with Sadat's program of economic liberalization, his rapprochement with Israel, and his agreements with the International Monetary Fund, the role and influence of foreign funding agencies and aid organizations greatly increased. Organizations like USAID not only embarked on campaigns for free market reforms but also targeted the family for reform, beginning with a set of efforts at population control. NGOs such as United Nations Children Fund (UNICEF) and the Ford Foundation forged connections with Islamic institutions like al-Azhar to create centers for population control that connected women to economic development (see chapter 5.) These efforts to promote reform of the family through women's development, equality, and liberation were paralleled by calls to reform the personal status laws, which Sadat did by "emergency decree" in 1980, causing an uproar. As the sphere of social and biological reproduction, the family became a particularly dense node of ideological investment, as international aid organizations, the state, Islamic institutions, and Islamic groups vied for control over the family and women's bodies.

In the midst of these contestations emerged an Islamist discourse that sought to maintain control over the management and reform of the family. In Islamist writings the reform of the family becomes understood as the revival of an ontological family form in Islam, a family emancipated from foreign (secular) domination. They call for an emancipation from this global—and local—secularism, through entrenchment in an Islamic family seen as a bastion of religious law. ʿImara and Kishk, for example, develop an understanding of the family as a sacrosanct domain for the free practice of religion, partly by interpreting Islamic law—and the personal status laws—as emancipating women. This discourse strove to strengthen the family as the seat of religion (religious politics and religious law) in a secular society, reifying its focus on the family as the core of Islamic society and polity. The family becomes the natural place for the free practice of religion, an authentic, sacrosanct domain "insulated" (in Foucault's words) from a foreign secularism. The family, however, is perhaps one of secular liberalism's most powerful tools of social reproduction, as feminist critiques of liberalism have observed.[9] As emblematic of family life, women have

[9] Pateman, *The Sexual Contract*; Brown, "Liberalism's Family Values."

been sites of particularly intense investment in the fate of religion, as keys to its reproduction in a secular society.

Women's Liberation in Islam: From Nahḍa to Ṣaḥwa

Both ʿImara and Kishk drew on nahḍa ideas to construct their understandings of women's liberation, recycling, reinterpreting, and reframing the concept for the final decades of the twentieth century—partly through a set of intertextual dialogues between themselves, with other revivalist writers, and with writers from the nahḍa. They were two of the main authors responsible for the revitalization of the "Islamic liberation of woman" motif for the ṣaḥwa. Both Kishk and ʿImara tailored their intellectual Islam to popular audiences, marketed their works to mass audiences, and circulated their works in both print and digital media. They published extensively, with Kishk writing nearly thirty books and ʿImara almost eighty. Both were prolific producers of Islamic cultural material in the public sphere, from newspapers to satellite television (CBC Egypt, al-Hafiz, al-Fajr, and AzhariTV). ʿImara, who appears frequently on Egyptian television and al-Jazeera, has more than four hundred videos posted on YouTube. His lectures and interviews repackage his writings for television audiences, with videos on "Men and Women's Equality in Islam," "Leadership and Guardianship of Women in Islam," "Women's Rights in Islam," "Liberalism and Secularism," "The Relationship of the State with Religion," "Politics and Morals," and "The Civil and Religious State." In the aftermath of the 2011 revolution, he reemerged as a public commentator, partly by republishing nahḍa works on the liberating nature of Islam. Kishk, a prolific contributor to the popular press, passed away in the public eye. He died in the midst of a heated debate on Arab American television with Nasr Hamid Abu Zayd, the Egyptian intellectual accused of apostasy (and forcibly divorced from his wife) for his literary interpretations of the Qurʾan.[10]

Both Kishk and ʿImara were bright stars of the Marxist Left who defected from the party to become bright stars of the Islamic revival. Neither was educated in religious institutions, but at Cairo University. ʿImara received his degree in Arabic language and Islamic sciences from Dar al-ʿUlum (1965) and later, his doctorate in Islamic philoso-

[10] Muhammad Jalal Kishk and Nasr Hamid Abu Zayd, "Akihr Ma Nutiqa bihi Jalal Kishk," *al-Shaʿb*, December 17, 1993; Charles Hirschkind, "Heresy or Hermeneutics: The Case of Nasr Hamid Abu Zayd," *Stanford Electronic Humanities Review* 5, no. 1, Contested Polities (February 26, 1996).

phy (1975). Kishk, born in a village in Upper Egypt, came to Cairo (at the time Fu'ad) University to study at the business school, even though—or perhaps because—he was already a member of the Marxist Party. There is a palpable shift in their writings from Arab nationalism to Islamism in the mid-1960s, as both became disillusioned with Arab nationalism as an ideology and turned to writing in an Islamic vein. Nonetheless, their lay training in secular institutions continued to inform their ideological framework, just as their move away from Marxism informed their adoption and adaptation of a liberal discourse (and their ideas about liberating religion from secularism). Much like Kishk's early writings, ʿImara's first publications in the 1960s were largely Arab nationalist works that blended a vocabulary of Arab and Islamic nationalism.

ʿImara's early works—*al-Umma al-ʿArabiyya wa-Qadiyyat al-Tawhid* (The Islamic Umma and the Issue of Unity, 1966), *Fajr al-Yaqaza al-Qawmiyya* (Dawn of the Nationalist Awakening, 1967), and *al-ʿUruba fi al-ʿAsr al-Hadith: Dirasat fi al-Qawmiyya wa-l-Umma* (Arabism in the Modern Age: Studies in Nationalism and the Umma, 1967)—couched the keywords of Arabism in an Islamic idiom, of *tawḥīd* (unity), *qawmiyya* (nationalism), and the umma (nation or the Islamic community). ʿImara would reshape this terminology of Arabism to Islamism, as he shifted from the secular ideology of socialism to the religious politics of the revival (and the era of economic liberalization), each involving different kinds of supranational forms of communal identification. Critical to this shift was a greater emphasis on the religious nature of certain key ideas and concepts, where the *qawm*, the "people" of qawmiyya refer to the Muslims rather than the Arabs. The tawḥīd is no longer Arab solidarity but the "unity" of a monotheistic God. The umma now specifically refers to the Muslim community, not to a more general "national community." Kishk and ʿImara begin to openly embrace an Islamic-based solidarity in the 1960s, moving from *al-qawmiyya al-ʿarabiyya* of Arab nationalism to *al-umma al-islāmiyya* of the Islamic community, from *al-ghazw al-fikrī* (intellectual conquest) to *jihad* as "eternal revolution," from *al-mujtamaʿ al-ʿarabī* (Arab society) to *al-Islām wa-l-ijtimāʿ* (Islam and society). ʿImara's early work employs the word *yaqaẓa* to refer to the "nationalist awakening" of Arabism, a word that was also used to refer to the intellectual awakening of the nahḍa.[11] The formal, literary Arabic term *yaqaẓa* anticipates the more colloquial *ṣaḥwa*, which became the common word for the awakening, although

[11] Muhammad ʿImara, *Tayyarat al-Yaqaza al-Islamiyya al-Haditha* (Cairo: Dar al-Hilal, 1982); and *al-Tariq ila al-Yaqaza al-Islamiyya* (Cairo: Dar al-Shuruq, 1990).

there has also been a revival of nahḍa, especially during the 2011 revolutions. Nahḍa is often translated as the Arab "renaissance," but the word's true meaning is "awakening" or "arising," with both political and spiritual connotations.[12] Striking is the malleability of these concepts as they were adapted to the different of Arab nationalism to the Islamism in the 1980s and 1990s.

The revival of women's liberation for the later awakening can be attributed to Muhammad ʿImara, who dedicated his career to a full-scale excavation of the works of the nahḍa. When ʿImara was a graduate student at Cairo University in the mid-1960s, he began reinjecting nahḍa ideas into popular consciousness through widely circulated compilations of the nahḍa's most important texts. ʿImara became famous for his complete works of the nahḍa's most illustrious thinkers: Jamal al-Din al-Afghani, ʿAbd al-Rahman al-Kawakibi, ʿAli ʿAbd al-Raziq, Muhammad ʿAbduh, Qasim Amin, and many others. Through a process of massive republication, ʿImara constructed an intellectual heritage for the ṣaḥwa whose point of departure (*munṭalaq*) was the nahḍa. One of the first of these was his complete works of the Islamic reformer Muhammad ʿAbduh published in the early 1970s. In his introduction to the six-volume work, he caused a stir by arguing that ʿAbduh authored parts of *The Liberation of Woman*. He reiterated this assertion many times in a series of publications on the subject.[13] Ultimately the question of whether ʿAbduh actually wrote the book is less relevant than the urgency of ʿImara's recuperative project and his tireless commitment to showing Islam's compatibility with Amin's vision of women's liberation. ʿAbduh's name served to legitimize the concept of women's liberation for Islam, which would come to dominate revivalist writings on women, writings that consistently situate this liberation within the Muslim family. This liberation is described as the freedom to choose a husband, to own property, to receive financial maintenance (and hence, to devote oneself to motherhood), and to dissolve a marriage (which is mainly a male right). The patriarchal conjugal bourgeois family described in Amin's text becomes a critical unit of not just an Islamic society but also Islamic law and politics. ʿAbduh and Amin epitomize the tension between secular and religious ideology, politics, law, family, and gender relations, an opposition that is collapsed (and reproduced) in the assertion of their joint authorship of *The Liberation of Woman*. A number of scholars of gender in the revival have insightfully analyzed the overlap between secular and religious discourses around

[12] The translation of the word as "renaissance" misleads with its Christian overtones of rebirth, glossing the ritualistic, Islamic connotations of awakening.

[13] al-Qaradawi et al., *Tahrir al-Marʾa fi al-Islam*.

gender, situated in a family described as free and equal but governed by male leadership.[14] Even though ʿAbduh and Amin appear as opposite poles in the ideological clash of civilizations, they more accurately epitomize the mutually constitutive binaries, dualism, and paradoxes of secular liberalism.

Liberalism's Two Faces: Amin and ʿAbduh

Qasim Amin's *Liberation of Woman* is characterized by what Muhammad Jalal Kishk calls a "double approach." His oeuvre as a whole epitomizes the sense of battling ideologies over the issue of women's rights (Hourani's "division of spirits")—a Western secular modernity versus an indigenous Islamic identity.[15] This, Kishk writes, is the "secret of the attention paid to Qasim Amin," the "celebration" of his ideas, and the "insistence on digging up his thought."[16] Kishk says that Amin suffered from "schizophrenia" (*infiṣām*), a concept that he borrows from the Islamic thinker Safinaz Kazim, a friend and colleague whom he spoke with every day on the phone. In her famous essay "ʿAn al-Sijn wa-l-Hurriyya" (On Prison and Freedom, 1986), published a few years earlier, Kazim describes a schizophrenia of the self, a split between her religious and secular identities that she struggles to close. She suffered this split on an individual level, she says, "yet our society as a whole suffers from this schizophrenia."[17] Kishk uses similar language: "Like Egypt, Qasim Amin is more than one personality."[18]

Qasim Amin is an emblem of women's emancipation in the Arab world, however much his contribution is disputed. Many contest his status as "the first feminist" in Egypt, arguing that attention to *The Liberation of Woman* eclipsed the voices of women writing at the same time. Others recognize that his version of women's emancipation was merely a modernist vision of the bourgeois family form—valorizing a

[14] Hatem, "Egyptian Discourses on Gender and Political Liberalization"; Abu-Lughod, "The Marriage of Feminism and Islamism in Egypt;" Stowasser, "Religious Ideology"; Margot Badran, "Gender Activism: Feminists and Islamists in Egypt," in *Identity Politics and Women: Cultural Reassertions and Feminisms in International Perspective*, ed. Valentine M. Moghadam (Boulder, CO: Westview Press, 1994).

[15] Albert Habib Hourani, *Arabic Thought in the Liberal Age, 1798–1939* (Cambridge: Cambridge University Press, 1962), 138.

[16] Kishk, *Jahalat ʿAsr al-Tanwir*, 54, 57; Leila Ahmed, *Women and Gender in Islam: Historical Roots of a Modern Debate* (Cairo: American University in Cairo Press, 1993), 159. Ahmed calls the text "turgid and contradictory."

[17] Safinaz Kazim, *ʿAn al-Sijn wa-l-Hurriyya* (Madinat Nasr, Cairo: al-Zahraʾ li-l-Iʿlam al-ʿArabi, 1986), 33.

[18] Kishk, *Jahalat ʿAsr al-Tanwir*, 45.

companionate wife, an educated mother, and a well-organized household.[19] Lila Abu-Lughod traces Islamist discourses of women's emancipation and their "bourgeois vision of women's domesticity" back to Amin's text. He was more interested, she argues, in promoting a "modern bourgeois family with its ideal of conjugal love and scientific childrearing" as emblems of a new kind of Egyptian elite.[20] This turn-of-the-century discourse envisioned the family as a key institution for producing a rational, disciplined, and self-governing citizen subject—self-government at the microcosmic level that was a precondition for independence at the level of politics. Colonists and missionaries imagined they were liberating the colonized from "oriental despotism," both in government and in the home. In response, nationalist reformers began focusing on the family as the site for cultivating new disciplines and rationalities that would foster self-rule on a larger scale. Freedom became the operative concept of this liberal ideology, idealized as a principle of political transformation of the self, human relations, and the polity. Women, as mothers of the future, presided over the transition to a new kind of governmentality within the family.[21] This liberation had several key elements that repeatedly reappear in reformist writings. Among them was the modernist call for freedom from tradition, for shaking off outdated customs, for renewal and reform—which meant the revival of true religion for modern society.[22] An important aspect of this freedom entails education that leads to enlightenment about the nature of true religion. This freedom is from ignorance and jāhiliyya. It is accordingly the precondition for participation in the world of letters and in the rights and duties of citizenship.

Another freedom is freedom from the harem, which entails restructuring the elite household along the lines of the nuclear family and the conjugal couple. Romantic love, in this formulation, becomes the expression of choice powered by individual affect. Finally, the rights and freedoms structuring the family unit are indicative of the rights and

[19] Juan Ricardo Cole, "Feminism, Class, and Islam in Turn-of-the-Century Egypt," *International Journal of Middle East Studies* 13, no. 4 (November 1, 1981): 387–407; Ahmed, *Women and Gender in Islam.*

[20] Abu-Lughod, "Marriage of Feminism and Islamism," 255–56; Shakry, "Schooled Mothers and Structured Play," 131, 137, 148–49; Cole, "Feminism, Class, and Islam."

[21] Shakry, "Schooled Mothers and Structured Play," 132–35, 143; Foucault, Michel, "Governmentality," in *The Foucault Effect: Studies in Governmentality*, ed. Graham Burchell, Colin Gordon, and Peter Miller (Chicago: University of Chicago Press, 1991), 87–104.

[22] Writers envisioned "true Islam" as the religion of modernity, "unadulterated by 'traditional' accretions." Shakry, "Schooled Mothers and Structured Play," 148; Voll, "Renewal and Reform in Islamic History," Voll talks about this process as internal to the Islamic tradition—renewal and reform as being part of Islamic tradition itself, an argument made by Samira Haj in *Reconfiguring Islamic Tradition.*

freedoms of the polity. Freedom from coercion is critical to this family unit, with duties assumed willingly, a subjectivation to the scheme of rights as the path to political participation. This model of political participation through rights and duties in the family begins in the nahḍa, flourishes in the rights discourses of the 1950s and 1960s (in the work of Sayyid Qutb, ʿAbd al-Wahid Wafi, and Bint al-Shatiʾ), and then finds its full expression in the work of Heba Raouf Ezzat, where the family is envisioned as a political unit.[23] The kind of society is not in dispute; it is a free and equal one mediated by rights. What is in dispute is the kind of rationality—secular or religious, Western or Islamic, indigenous or foreign—that will govern this process of transformation.

Qasim Amin's intellectual trajectory vividly illustrates the ideological contestation between these binaries. In his three main works, he moves from a defense of indigenous culture, to an Islamic intellectual framework mixed with secular liberal ideals of rights, to a wholesale adoption of a Western model. His first work, *Les Égyptiens*, was written in French, a response to the Duc d'Harcourt's *L'Égypte et les Égyptiens* (1893) and a defense of Egyptian cultural practices. His most famous work, *Tahrir al-Marʾa* (The Liberation of Woman, 1999), is composed in the vein of an Islamic modernism, as he locates the path to women's rights, equality, and emancipation in a properly understood original Islam. He criticizes how tradition has corrupted the true Islam and calls for reform. If Islam had remained unaffected by local tradition, he writes, "then Muslim women today should have been at the forefront of free women on earth. The Islamic legal system, the shariʿa, stipulated the equality of women and men before any other legal system. Islam declared women's freedom and emancipation, and granted women all human rights."[24] The book deploys an Islamic intellectual framework to argue for legal and social reforms—in seclusion, veiling (of the face), education, and polygamy. The text draws on Islamic sources as diverse as the Qurʾan, hadith, Islamic jurisprudence (*fiqh*), and exegesis (*tafsīr*). Amin also advocates a specific vision of the bourgeois family, based on companionate marriage and with women as household managers. He connects citizenship to the right to own property and roots women's rights in their right to be cared for financially by a male breadwinner.

Amin's *al-Marʾa al-Jadida* (The New Woman, 1900), published the following year, completely abandoned any reference to the Islamic discursive tradition and turned wholesale to a Western intellectual framework. Interpreting a woman's freedom and her "obligation to her family"

[23] See chapters 1 and 6 for discussions of these figures and their works.

[24] Qasim Amin, *The Liberation of Woman and the New Woman*, trans. Samiha Sidhom Peterson (Cairo: American University in Cairo Press, 2000), 7.

with reference to European and American history, culture, and scholars, he holds up the West, and Western rationality, as a model for the emancipated modern girl, implicitly positing an unbridgeable divide between modernity and Islamic tradition. It is this that most irks Islamic reformers, as they continually assert that Islam provides the surest path to a just society, to securing political rights, to democracy, and to women's emancipation. Yet *The Liberation of Woman* remains an intellectual blueprint for reinterpreting classical Islamic texts and arguments, even as the book continues to be a site of deep conflict and ambivalence. Future Islamic authors condemn Amin's eventual intellectual treason, even as they still draw on his rhetorical devices and arguments about women's emancipation in Islam. Amin's wholesale turn to a Western, secular intellectual framework in *The New Woman* becomes a model of what not to do.

This intellectual struggle plays out vividly in the writings of Islamic intellectuals like ʿImara and Kishk, who both wrote extensively on the subject of women's liberation in Islam. They simultaneously vilify Qasim Amin for "channeling" the call of the "Western missionaries of women's liberation," even as they draw directly on his understanding of women being liberated by true Islam. In Kishk's book *Jahalat ʿAsr al-Tanwir: Qiraʾa fi Fikr Qasim Amin wa-ʿAli ʿAbd al-Raziq* (Ignorances of the Age of Enlightenment: A Reading in the Thought of Qasim Amin and ʿAli ʿAbd al-Raziq, 1990), he argues that Amin's *Les Égyptiens* was written by "the Islamic Qasim Amin" who "found himself defending Islam's intellectual and historical reputation." He calls Qasim Amin of *Les Égyptiens* "Shaykh Qasim," "an extremist (*mutaṭarrif*) or even fanatic (*mutaʿaṣṣib*) Muslim." (In Kishk's book, this is a compliment.) Playing on ʿImara's argument that the nineteenth-century Islamic reformer Muhammad ʿAbduh actually wrote *The Liberation of Woman*, Kishk (satirically) writes that it is more likely that Muhammad ʿAbduh wrote *Les Égyptiens*. Or, he says, *Les Égyptiens* could just as well have been written by the Islamic reformers ʿAbd al-ʿAziz Jawish or Rashid Rida.[25] In Kishk's *Freedom in the Muslim Family*, he directly quotes the passage from Amin's *Liberation of Woman* asserting women's rights, freedom, and independence in Islam.

[25] Rida was Muhammad ʿAbduh's more conservative disciple; ʿAbd al-ʿAziz Jawish, an educational reformer who wrote on Islam as a "religion of instinct and freedom." *Islam: Din al-Fitra (wa-l-Hurriyya)* was initially published in 1910 but would be republished in 1952 and 1968 by the Islamic publishing house Dar al-Maʿarif, in 1983 by the more mainstream publisher Dar al-Hilal, and in 1987 by the Islamist press al-Zahraʾ li-l-Iʿlam al-ʿArabi.

> If religion had power over customs, then Muslim women today would be the most advanced women of the earth. The Islamic shariʿa preceded all other legal systems in establishing woman's equality with man, proclaiming her freedom and independence at a time when she was at the depth of inferiority among all nations, granting her human rights and considering her the equal of man in all civil statutes. . . . Some Western women have not obtained this type of rights. All this testifies that at the foundations of the liberal shariʿa is a respect for woman and equality between her and man.[26]

This is what Kishk calls "the miracle of personal freedom" (*muʿjizat al-ḥurriyya al-shakhṣiyya*) in Islam.

Freedom in the Muslim Family: Muhammad Jalal Kishk

Kishk became most famous for his publications on the West's "intellectual invasion" of the Muslim world, drawing on a Gramscian concept of a war of ideas to cultivate his own (passive) Islamic revolution. Kishk began his intellectual career as a Marxist, publishing his first book, *al-Jabha al-Shaʿbiyya* (The Popular Front, 1951), while still studying at the university, a book that led to his incarceration; he took his final exams while in prison. Released when Nasser came to power, Kishk eventually became disillusioned, as he came to understand Marxism as another implement of imperial rule.[27] While writing polemics against Russian influence in Egypt under the socialist government of Nasser, he was effectively banned from publishing in the mid-1960s. It was during this time that he wrote his most famous works, developing his signature idea of "intellectual invasion" (*al-ghazw al-fikrī*). No fewer than four different presses issued his book *al-Ghazw al-Fikri* (Intellectual Invasion, 1964), and he would write a number of other works that used the idea of intellectual invasion to analyze nationalism, Marxism, and Zionism. It also became a term widely used in the popular press by writers like Bint al-Shatiʾ and Safinaz Kazim.

Intellectual Invasion represents Kishk's turn to an Islamic nationalism as an indigenous mode of revolutionary protest. "It has long been

[26] Qasim Amin, *Tahrir al-Marʾa wa-l-Marʾa al-Jadida* (Cairo: al-Markaz al-ʿArabi li-l-Bahth wa-l-Nashr, 1984), 12; Muhammad Jalal Kishk, *al-Hurriyya fi al-Usra al-Muslima*, Nahw Waʿy Islami (Cairo: al-Mukhtar al-Islami, 1979), 24.

[27] Muhammad Ilhami, "Muhammad Jalal Kishk," *Majallat al-Mujtamaʿ al-Kuwaytiyya*, August 26, 2009; Muhammad Jalal Kishk, *Rusi wa-Amriki fi al-Yaman* (Cairo: Wakalat al-Sihafa al-Afriqiyya, 1957).

preached," he writes, "that Islam and religion are the enemies of revolution, but the greatest revolutions of the age had a fully Islamic spirit."[28] Kishk deftly implements the concepts and lexicons of these ideologies toward his own conception of an "Islamic revolution," linking what Talal Asad refers to as "new vocabularies" and new "discursive grammars" to older ones.[29] He uses certain Western "tools" to "build a modern, developed Arab Islamic civilization distinct from the civilization of the Europeans," as ʿImara says.[30] Kishk structures his argument according to what Leila Ahmed calls the antithesis to the colonial thesis.[31] In his own analyses of this antithetical discourse of the revival, Charles Hirschkind uses the concept of a "counterpublic," drawing on Nancy Fraser's understanding of alternative publics, or what she calls "parallel discursive arenas," resonating with Carrie Wickham's analysis of "print Islam" as critical to the "parallel Islamic sector" in Egypt.[32] These counterpublics are self-consciously oppositional, displaying an awareness of their subordination within the dominant order, carrying within themselves elements of the dominant discourse, what Foucauldians call a "reverse discourse."[33] Kishk's writings reflect a kind of inverted mirroring, where the Islamic family becomes the source of an indigenous, revolutionary, liberated Islam wielded against a foreign, secular colonialism that threatens to liberate women *from* Islam.

In Kishk's advocacy of an Islamic revolution against foreign domination, women and the family are critical fronts in defining the character of an Islamic nationalism. In *Intellectual Invasion* he devotes a chapter entitled "Jamila . . . or Simone?" to the Algerian revolutionary Jamila Bouhrid, posing her against Simone de Beauvoir, the French Marxist who denounced motherhood as oppressive. Kishk writes about the Algerian war of independence as an "Arab Islamic revolution" against the French and Western "crusades."[34] The book's epigraph—taken from this chapter on Jamila—calls colonialism a "rejection of Islam" and a form of undemocratic political oppression. He quotes a revolutionary in the Algerian war of independence (during which the book was written): "The rejection of Islamic ideology in colonized nations oppresses the religion of the overwhelming majority of its people. . . .

[28] Muhammad Jalal Kishk, *al-Ghazw al-Fikri*, Mafahim Islamiyya (Cairo: Maktabat Dar al-ʿUruba, 1964), 7.

[29] Asad, *Formations of the Secular*, 222.

[30] Muhammad ʿImara, *Qasim Amin wa-Tahrir al-Marʾa wa-l-Tamaddun al-Islami* (Beirut: Dar al-Wahda, 1985), 157.

[31] Ahmed, *Women and Gender in Islam*, 162.

[32] Fraser, "Rethinking the Public Sphere," 123; Hirschkind, *Ethical Soundscape*.

[33] Foucault, *History of Sexuality*, 101; Warner, *Publics and Counterpublics*, 121.

[34] Kishk, *al-Ghazw al-Fikri*, 102.

Those steeped in Westernized life and thought are party to the ideology of the enemy colonizer" (101). Kishk's work hinges on claiming freedom for an Islamic politics and unmasking Western claims to freedom as oppressive, backward, and reactionary. His polemics focus on the coercions of Western agendas to liberate Muslim lands, arguing that reclaiming Islam for Muslim society is true liberation—from the tyranny of Western regimes and back to a truly free originary Islam. Kishk inverts the emancipatory promise of enlightenment modernity, turning it into a form of oppression.

In the closing pages of *Intellectual Invasion*, Kishk criticizes the literary critic Louis ʿAwad for arguing that the word *ḥurriyya* (freedom), "in its complete political and social sense," is derived from the Western concept of "liberty." Kishk takes up this Western concept of liberty in *al-Hurriyya fi al-Usra al-Muslima* (Freedom in the Muslim Family, 1965), published the following year, writing of Libertas in the opening pages of the book. The word jumps out from the Arabic, capitalized in Roman letters. "A generation was raised believing that it was indebted to Europe for its freedom, but it lost its freedom when Europe occupied their lands and annihilated their freedom."[35] Kishk moves from this world-historical, geopolitical framing of the question of Islamic freedom to the question of more local contestations over the personal status laws. In so doing, he shifts the focus to contestations over those laws, a struggle between secular government and Islamic law that plays out at the most intimate level of family relations. Kishk continues to use some of the same language—of liberating Muslim lands from the tyranny of an imperial secularism—but now concentrated within the sphere of the family.

Freedom in the Muslim Family is a seventy-nine-page polemic against the proposed changes to the personal status laws under Nasser. Written in 1965, at the height of debate over these reforms, the work would not be published until 1979 with a fresh set of proposed reforms over the laws, but now under the government of Anwar Sadat. Kishk essentially recycled this older text for the new context. In 1979 the Sadat government amended the personal status laws by emergency decree. Popularly known as Jihan's law (because of the supposed influence of Sadat's wife Jihan), controversial reforms that had been debated for decades were pushed through in one fell swoop—a wife's automatic right to divorce if her husband married another woman; a divorced wife's right to custody of minor children, to alimony, and to the

[35] Ibid., 137.

marital home.[36] *Freedom in the Muslim Family* was published in conjunction with another, analogous pamphlet, *Tahrir al-Marʾa al-Muharrara* (Liberation of the Liberated Woman, 1979), both with the Islamist press al-Mukhtar al-Islami (the Islamic Choice).[37] These polemics against changes to the existing laws of personal status depict the laws as representing a true, original Islam that liberates women and the family from the true oppressor, the imperialistic West and its handmaiden, the secular state. Kishk is particularly critical of how foreign conceptions of freedom infringe on the free practice and expression of Islamic societies and Islamic laws. Quoting Qasim Amin, Kishk argues that true Islam liberated women fourteen centuries ago, giving women freedom, rights, and equality long before the West did.

Kishk relentlessly adheres to a liberal framework, opening *Freedom in the Muslim Family* by asserting the freedom and equality of the Muslim family. Like ʿAbd al-Wahid Wafi's *Human Rights in Islam* (see chapter 1), his argument proceeds with a point-by-point defense of the existing personal status laws. He begins with divorce, arguing that the principal marker of freedom in the family is freedom to choose a mate, as much as to dissolve the bonds of marriage without restriction. "The Islamic family is based on the free will of two equal parties. It remains on the basis of a shared desire that unites two equal parties. And it separates on the basis of free will. The family is based—in the first instance—on the free will of the man and the woman."[38] He depicts proposed limits on men's unilateral right to divorce as infringing on the natural freedoms of the family, as well as the freedom of a properly Islamic society. Divorce is a right and a freedom; curbs on divorce become unnecessary restrictions on God-given rights and freedoms. Yet he says nothing about women's lack of equivalent freedom to divorce. Instead he interprets any changes in the personal status laws as the imposition of a Western model of liberation, which reenacts the intellectual invasion of colonialism.

Part of Kishk's approach depends on the implication that state legislation of the personal status laws constitutes a form of foreign (secular) interference in Islamic law. Kishk claims a violation of human rights, describing Nasser's Committee to Amend the Personal Statute as attacking Muslims' rights and obstructing the free practice of religion, "freedom of conviction," and "the right to freely choose a religion" (4).

[36] Fayza Hassan, "Women's Destiny, Men's Voices," *Al-Ahram Weekly*, February 3, 2000, 467 ed.; Lynn Welchman, ed., *Women's Rights and Islamic Family Law: Perspectives on Reform* (New York: Zed Books, 2004), 30–37; Lama Abu-Odeh, "Modernizing Muslim Family Law: The Case of Egypt," *Oxford University Comparative Law Forum* (2004).

[37] al-Qaradawi et al., *Tahrir al-Marʾa fi al-Islam.*

[38] Kishk, *al-Hurriyya fi al-Usra al-Muslima*, 3.

He also interprets these violations as a kind of repression. Putting restrictions on divorce, he says, is a Western, Christian ideology, where even a king (Henry VIII of England) was prohibited from divorcing his wife. He bitterly attributes limits on divorce to the "stupidity of the missionaries," an attitude he connects to Christian repression of sexual freedom. Christians want to impose their vision of divorce on Muslims to strip Islam of its freedoms and hence its superiority. This, he says, is an example of the West's "intellectual invasion" (25) and of "ideas plagiarized" (33) from the West. "These rights have been in the Muslim family for four centuries," he writes. "Do we really need to make a fuss about the liberation of woman, who has been free for fourteen centuries, so that we can merely resemble Europe? How Europe has been shackled in centuries of darkness and oppression until they arrived at what has been self-evident in Islam!" (6). In contrast to the "subjection of woman in Western civilization," Kishk invokes women's right to property in Islam, much like Qasim Amin, orienting citizenship rights in private property (7). Women's right to property, he writes, has been the basis of her complete economic liberation, her freedom, and her complete equality in economic rights and is a pillar of her social equality.

A hermeneutic amalgam of liberal ideas structure these writings—about the importance of rights, equality, freedom, family, and private property to an Islamic citizenship situated, however paradoxically, in the family. Critical to exercising these freedoms, Kishk argues, is sexual and psychological emancipation. Another fundamental dimension of women's liberation in Islam is the freedom to sexual pleasure within the Muslim family. Kishk graphically describes this pleasure, of the body, the appetite, and the five senses, citing the "literature of sex" in Islamic civilization. In contrast, the West and Christianity have understood the body as corrupt and women as "guilty" for Adam and Eve's fall from grace. This understanding of the body and of sexuality, he argues, has had a nefarious effect on Western society. "This inhibition (*iḥtibās*)," he writes, "injures the body . . . sexual pleasure is an end in itself. . . . Europe had to discover Psychology and fill its mental hospitals with the sick of the two sexes," before it learned what Muslims had known since the seventh century (11, 15). Unlike in the West, this sexual freedom is strictly confined to the marital bond, on the pain of severe punishment. Even the punishment for adultery (stoning) is described as the expression of "a deep respect for women, and a deep regard for sex. . . . the organization of Islamic marriage reaches the summit of emancipation, simplicity, and sacredness at the same time" (6).

Central to this liberal hermeneutic of self is choice. Romantic love becomes the expression of choice (of partner) powered by individual affect, expressed in revivalist writings through reference to Qurʾanic terms like peace, affection, and mercy (from 30:21).[39] The freedom to divorce is important in Islam, Kishk reiterates, because the Muslim family is founded on free choice and dissolved on free choice. "The Muslim family," he writes, "is the only family that is founded on the basis of complete freedom because, as we have seen, it comes into existence through free choice, is based on complete equality of its parts. More importantly than all of this, the continuity of the marriage means consent to that continuity, because the right to annul it is guaranteed. This is the Islamic miracle known by the name of divorce" (25). Here Kishk understands divorce as a sacred right and freedom and the Muslim family as simultaneously sacrosanct and free. He uses the word *muʿjiza* to refer to the "miracle" of divorce, making divorce a miracle like that of the Qurʾan. Divorce is "at the same time, the miracle of personal freedom" (*muʿjizat al-ḥurriyya al-shakhṣiyya*) and an example of Islam's "humanistic understanding of human behavior." This is exactly Qasim Amin's argument, he says, in *The Liberation of Woman.* Personal freedom, in this iteration, is put on par with the miracle of the Qurʾan.

Though Kishk formulated *Freedom in the Muslim Family* in response to the 1965 debates over the personal status laws, the booklet would not be published until 1979, when it easily slipped into debates over Jihan's law. The most critical legislation related to divorce, including a woman's right to seek divorce if her husband took an additional wife without her consent, to retain custody of her children, to receive alimony, and to retain the marital home until she remarried or until the period of child custody ended.[40] Simultaneous to the publication of *Freedom in the Muslim Family*, the Islamist publishing house al-Mukhtar al-Islami issued *Liberation of the Liberated Woman*, a ten-point refutation of Jihan's law, describing it as infringing on Muslim women's freedoms. Using the same vocabulary of liberation and repression, Kishk begins by saying that Muslim men and women are both sinking "under the yoke of foreign power" and that the aim is "liberation of them all through unified struggle against foreign dominance and social backwardness."[41] Again, Kishk equates the amendments to the personal status laws with foreign dominance. This argument was not difficult to make, given that Sadat made the amendments under emergency decree

[39] Niʿmat Sidqi, *Niʿmat al-Qurʾan* (Cairo: Matbaʿat al-Sunna al-Muhammadiyya, 1968), 210; Iman Muhammad Mustafa, *Imbaraturiyyat al-Nisaʾ al-ʿAmilat* (Madinat Nasr, Cairo: al-Zahraʾ li-l-Iʿlam al-ʿArabi, 1991), 21; Raouf Ezzat, *al-Marʾa wa-l-ʿAmal al-Siyasi*, 75–76; Abu-Lughod, "Marriage of Feminism and Islamism."

[40] Hassan, "Women's Destiny, Men's Voices."

[41] Muhammad Jalal Kishk, *Tahrir al-Marʾa al-Muharrara*, Nahw Waʿy Islami (Cairo: al-Mukhtar al-Islami, 1979), 5.

in the wake of the Camp David Accords. Kishk argues that calling for "forbidding divorce" is a reactionary position, in contrast to the "right to divorce," which is a progressive one. Deploying trenchant satire, one of Kishk's most formidable (and oftentimes humorous) stylistic tools, he describes the scene of a "hippie den" he visits in Italy, with black lights, the air thick with smoke, and an androgynous (female) couple. One of these is a leader in the Italian "women's liberation movement." He asks her, "Liberation from what? What is left?" (9). Women in Italy, she responds, gained the right to divorce only two weeks ago (in 1974). He laughs, saying that the progressives in his country are against divorce. Confused, the woman says that the smoke must have gone to his head.

Kishk's topic is the personal status laws, but his objection is mainly to the state's interference in what he calls the private domain of religion. The government, he says, has no right to legislate in personal affairs, which are beyond its jurisdiction (11). Kishk describes in detail what he calls "a division of labor" between rules and interdictions relating to "civil, criminal, and political" matters and those relating to religion. Through this division of labor, he both reenacts the division of spheres assumed by secular ideology and claims the private sphere of the family for religion. "There are rules subject to the authority of belonging to a particular religion. This is what is termed 'the personal status.' On the foundation of freedom of conviction and the free right to belong to religion, these rules become a private matter to those who belong to that religion" (15–16). "Civil marriage" is a contradiction in terms because marriage, he assumes, is a private matter relating to religion. For Kishk, religion then becomes ontologically private, ontologically related to gendered relationships, heterosexual marriage, and conjugal affairs. There can be no marriage without religion.

Kishk's writings reproduce the assumptions of secular liberalism about the place of religion in the private sphere. But this private sphere also provides a home for this religious discourse, a site beyond the reach of the secular state's legislative power. The family and its gendered relations also seem to have become a place of refuge for the articulation of an Islamic society, as well as the jurisdiction of Islamic government. This is what Habermas describes as the public sphere's "privacy oriented toward an audience," because the public sphere is where private relations are negotiated and defined. This was not merely the "privatized domain of the market economy," though under Sadat and Mubarak's neoliberal economic reforms this was a key element in reifying the middle-class family for the Egyptian revival. The private sphere of the family was also a legal construct. The "intimate sphere of the conjugal family" is understood as "humanity's genuine site."

Habermas describes the battle of public opinion with political power for control of "the social." "With the background experience of a private sphere that had become interiorized human closeness, it challenged the established authority of the monarch; in this sense its character was from the beginning both private and polemical at once."[42] In contrast, earlier models of the public sphere depended on "domination without any illusion of freedom evoked by human intimacy," since the dispute was against an external enemy, not with a people's own government, as with the modern public sphere.[43] Kishk claims this private sphere of human intimacy as not only humanity's but also religion's "genuine site." He deploys this realm as a site of legitimacy from which to launch his critique of government encroaching on human freedom. The Islamist desire for a "national nonsecular modernity" was embodied in the personal statute, becoming an emblem of religious freedom, even as it enshrined religious law in the family.[44] Any tampering with this realm was seen as an infraction on the rights of Muslims and their freedom of practice. While Islamist discourse used liberal language against the politics of the semiauthoritarian secular state, it did so to bolster its extrapolitical authority within the very structure of this secularism.

An Islamic family becomes, for Kishk, a site for cultivating a grassroots democracy that stands against foreign domination and its instrument, authoritarian secularism. The Islamic Qasim Amin argument was not just for women's liberation but also for democracy. "Qasim Amin in his Muslim role believes, like us exactly, in democracy indigenous to Islam, springing from the belief that we are all from Adam and that Adam comes from dust. Qasim Amin, member of the Islamic movement (*al-jamāʿāt al-islāmiyya*), stands proudly over the European Duc d'Harcourt with the democracy of Islam that stands on belief in equality."[45] Kishk quotes Qasim Amin in *Les Égyptiens* arguing that all inhabitants of any Muslim country are equal under the law regardless of sex, religion, wealth, or birth. Islamic society cannot be founded on anything but a democratic order, "because it arises [*yanhaḍ*: awakens] from the foundation of equality and fraternity (*al-ikhāʾ*)" (46). Kishk recuperates not just Amin's discussion of the Egyptian woman for Islamic thought but also Amin's defense of Islam as a fair and just system

[42] Habermas, *Structural Transformation of the Public Sphere*, 51–52.

[43] Ibid., 52; Taylor, *Modern Social Imaginaries*, 87, 91. As Charles Taylor observes about the public sphere, its integrity depends on its autonomy from political power and its freedom from subjection.

[44] Shakry, "Schooled Mothers and Structured Play," 152–53; Chakrabarty, *Provincializing Europe*, 11–14.

[45] Kishk, *Jahalat ʿAsr al-Tanwir*, 46.

of government. Through the trope of "woman," these writings simultaneously revolve around the question of the free practice of Islamic law in an Islamic society and accordingly in an Islamic politics. In the second section of the book, on ʿAbd al-Raziq, Kishk drives this point home. His call for liberation here is from the incursions of Western governmentality through colonialism and its handmaiden, secular liberalism. "Like we have said a thousand times," Kishk writes, "liberalism does not grow under the wing of colonialism, but begins in the clash with it, the struggle against it, and demanding freedom from it" (78).

The Liberation of Islamic Law and Letters: Muhammad ʿImara

ʿImara first articulated his claim that ʿAbduh wrote *The Liberation of Woman* in *The Complete Works of the Imam Muhammad ʿAbduh* in 1972, but he would go on to reiterate this argument in numerous publications, republications, new editions, and new volumes over the next decades. ʿImara's aim is less proving ʿAbduh's authorship of *The Liberation of Woman* than demonstrating that a liberal family and women's liberation are compatible with Islam and especially with Islamic law. He uses Muhammad ʿAbduh as not just an emblem of reformist Islam, whose ideas were grounded in reinterpretation of the early texts of Islam, but also a legal authority. ʿAbduh had been head of the religious courts, the "native tribunals" that governed the personal status laws. While he held this position, he began venturing some of his reformist ideas, about polygamy not being condoned by the Qurʾan, for example, ideas that found their way into *The Liberation of Woman*. ʿImara's extended meditation on *The Liberation of Woman* becomes a way of showing that a liberal family is compatible with Islamic law. "The opinion of Islamic law in issues of the hijab, marriage, divorce, and polygamy, included in *The Liberation of Woman*," ʿImara states, "is the opinion of the Professor Imam Muhammad ʿAbduh."[46]

In his writings, ʿImara is very concerned with disavowing the secular nature of this liberation and with distinguishing the Islamic family (and women's liberation in Islam) from secular influence. He sets up an antithetical binary between Amin's secular Western weltanschauung and ʿAbduh's Islamic worldview of women and the family. But he also recognizes their imbrication and overlap, their mutual influence, analyzing what he calls a "division of labor" within the text. The division

[46] Muhammad ʿImara, *al-Aʿmal al-Kamila li-Qasim Amin: Dirasa wa-Tahqiq* (Beirut: al-Muʾassasa al-ʿArabiyya li-l-Dirasat wa-l-Nashr, 1976), 130.

of labor is between religion and secularism but is also a bid to delineate the jurisdiction of Islamic law over the private sphere. *The Liberation of Woman,* ʿImara asserts, not only has two authors but also has "two goals." One goal, he says, pertains purely to Islamic law and jurisprudence and how they relate to women and the family. The other goal is the secular ideas attributed to Amin. This division of labor is intended to create a distinction, embodied in the two different authors and thinkers, between the Islamic and the Western, the religious and the secular. But the juxtaposition of the two thinkers and the two systems of thought speaks more forcefully to how they mutually constitute each other and are connected through the concept of liberation. Who is doing the repressing, and the liberating, remains a shifting (or perhaps a vacillating) target, moving between the two poles of secularism and religion. But the assertion of repression appears to drive these writings. The proliferation of publications around the subject appears as a consciousness-raising effort to reeducate the public about their rights and duties in the republic, the family, and the home.

The division between a Western secularism (embodied in the state) and an Islamic family appears as what Foucault calls the "double conditioning" between family and state, public and private. But in these revivalist writings, it is also a double conditioning between religion and secularism, Islam and the West, ʿAbduh and Amin. Wendy Brown calls this dualism the "constitutive binaries of liberalism"; Slavoj Zizek refers to it as the binaries of liberal discourse. Brown writes more of the double relationship between the sexual and social contracts, between private and public, family and state, feminine and masculine. But Zizek is more concerned with secular liberalism's messianic nature and how its own religiosity is projected onto an Islamic other, as its diametric (inverted and mirroring) opposite, as the very specter of itself.[47] ʿImara's and Kishk's writings inhabit that space of liberal secularism's "reverse discourse," a counterpublic grounded in the private sphere, where religion in the family becomes the promise of refuge from a pervasive and invasive secularism.

ʿImara appears as primarily concerned with emphasizing the juridical aspects of the liberation of woman, and particularly legitimizing a liberal family and a liberated woman as compatible with Islamic law. He does this by emphasizing the legal dimensions of *The Liberation of Woman* and connecting them to ʿAbduh. The parts written by ʿAbduh, he writes, are dedicated to studies in jurisprudence (fiqh) and

[47] Zizek, *Did Somebody Say Totalitarianism?*, 3–5, 152. Also see Roxanne L. Euben, *Enemy in the Mirror: Islamic Fundamentalism and the Limits of Modern Rationalism* (Princeton, NJ: Princeton University Press, 1999).

are aimed mainly at jurists and Islamic scholars. ʿImara redeems *The Liberation of Woman* with the stamp of ʿAbduh's juridical authority and also by legitimizing the text as an important contribution to Islamic legal studies. Earlier thinkers did not take the text seriously in this way, instead denouncing it as "un-Islamic."[48] ʿImara, in contrast, calls the book an urgent "call—to well-regarded people in Islamic law and those knowledgeable of its dictates—to protect the needs of the Islamic umma and its requirements with respect to women. No one, except an imam *mujtahid* in Islam, could write these parts; and there was no one of that age that could do so except the Professor Imam" (139). ʿImara talks about the thorough religious argumentation within the text. The author, he says, possesses a comprehensive knowledge of all the schools of law, all the branches of the shariʿa, all the books of jurisprudence. "Especially in the chapters dealing with the perspective of the shariʿa and religion in the matter of women's liberation, there are a series of juridical opinions and discussions of which a writer like Qasim Amin is not capable . . . more important, we find comprehensive legal opinions that point to their author and their source had penetrated deeply into research in this matter in all the principal sources of Islamic thought, its different schools and intellectual movements" (144). This is ʿImara's main evidence that ʿAbduh wrote the text.[49] ʿImara is preoccupied with delineating the sphere of the family as a specifically Islamic domain, one governed by the laws of shariʿa. He calls for the "protection [*ṣiyāna*, a word also denoting chastity]" of the household with a law "that all individuals abide by, limits imposed on the special domain (*ikhtiṣāṣ*) between a husband and a wife" (140). Using the legal term *ikhtiṣāṣ*, ʿAbduh demarcates the specific jurisdiction or sphere of authority of the shariʿa in regulating the household, the marriage bond, and gendered relations, staking out the home and family as the territory governed by Islamic law.

ʿImara projects a liberal Islamic family, women's rights and duties, and a social and political "division of labor" into the past, imparting it with a timeless legitimacy, even as his ideas were formulated in

[48] ʿAzmi, *Fasl al-Khitab*; Wajdi, *Al-Marʾa al-Muslima*.

[49] Claims that Muhammad ʿAbduh wrote parts of *The Liberation of Woman* had long circulated, but ʿImara was the first to make a protracted argument for ʿAbduh's direct hand in its composition. Yet ʿImara relies on weak circumstantial evidence: that the two men moved in the same social circles, that they believed in the same ideas, and that shared authorship and the use of pseudonyms were common at the time. The only real piece of evidence is a quote from Doria Shafiq, printed in bold: "It was said that some paragraphs in *The Liberation of Woman* are evidence of the style of the Shaykh Muhammad ʿAbduh himself." Doria Shafiq and Ibrahim ʿAbduh, *Tatawwur al-Nahda al-Nisaʾiyya fi Misr min ʿAhd Muhammad ʿAli ila ʿAhd al-Faruq* (Cairo: Maktabat al-Adab, 1945); ʿImara, *al-Aʿmal al-Kamila li-Qasim Amin*, 139.

response to current politics. His *Complete Works of Muhammad ʿAbduh,* in which he first made his claim for ʿAbduh's authorship of *The Liberation of Woman,* was written at the end of the 1960s, in the waning years of the Nasser regime. The six-volume collection would not be published until 1972, however, coinciding with a massive conference held in Cairo on Arab Women in National Development, sponsored by the League of Arab States and UNICEF. ʿImara would follow a pattern of publishing on "woman and Islam," "women's liberation in Islam," women and the family, and Qasim Amin and Muhammad ʿAbduh in response to international initiatives focusing on reform of women and the family. He issued a flurry of writings on women and Islam in 1975 and 1976 in the aftermath of the International Women's Year conference in Mexico City, to which Jihan Sadat led a delegation of Egyptian representatives. During that time he published a compilation of ʿAbduh's writings on "Islam and woman," as well as *The Complete Works of Qasim Amin,* in which he reiterated verbatim the claim that Muhammad ʿAbduh wrote *The Liberation of Woman.* Both Islamic (like Dar al-Rashad and Dar al-Shuruq) and mainstream (like Dar al-Hilal) presses would reissue these two works many times over subsequent decades, in addition to related works on Amin and ʿAbduh under different titles but with similar material. Clearly the audience and reception of these works were vast, warranting multiple editions by many different presses.

In the wake of Jihan's law in 1979, ʿImara republished *Islam and Woman* twice. The book, a collection of ʿAbduh's articles and writings, focuses principally on the family and the marriage contract. ʿImara's interpolations in the text—its framing, the chapter titles, the epigraphs, the introduction, and the commentary—most illustrate the uses to which he bends ʿAbduh's writings. In this we see the interpretive role played by the redactor and interpreter as these texts are recycled for a new era. ʿImara follows the first chapter of the book on Islamic gender "equality" with a chapter on divorce and another on polygamy—the two main issues debated in discussions over the reform of the personal status laws. The contradictions between an imagined ontological equality and the inequalities of divorce and polygamy in Islamic law are stark, but they also represent a revivalist drive to reconcile the politics of the family with the contradictions (of equality and inequality, rights and duties, freedom and submission) inherent in liberal thought. ʿImara's arguments reiterate some of the fundamental contradictions seen in the liberal discourse around the family during the Nasser period—of a gendered hierarchy in the family framed by assertions of freedom and equality. ʿImara's argument in *Islam and Woman in the Opinion of Muhammad ʿAbduh* depends on an extended analogy between the Islamic family and the umma, becoming a commentary on the nature of Islamic governance both inside and outside the home. The epigraph to the book is a quotation from ʿAbduh about the family as the "building block" of the umma: "The umma is made up of families. The reform of one is the reform of the other. Whoever does not have a home does not have an umma."[50] ʿImara's collection of ʿAbduh's writings on gender is a means of envisioning Islamic political liberty and Islamic government through the trope of the family as the political unit of the umma. ʿImara dedicates the book to the "Egyptian, Muslim, and Eastern family," arguing that the only way to cure the social ills plaguing the region is to cure the ills plaguing the family (4). To answer these questions, he turns to ʿAbduh, "who was and still is—in our contemporary age—the most important *mujtahid* in Islamic reasoning from the greatest Islamic mind, who stood in front of the book of God and the Sunna of the prophet in order to see in them—with an enlightened mind—the cure for the ills of our contemporary society, ills in the life of the family in particular." The solution, ʿImara says, is the Islamic shariʿa. And he rues those who see the shariʿa as something "backward or calcified." The book is dedicated to those who "search for the true meaning of the suitability of Islamic law in the progression of time and space" (4).

After Jihan's law ʿImara also republished his commentary from *The Complete Works of Qasim Amin* under the title *Qasim Amin wa-Tahrir al-Marʾa* (Qasim Amin and Woman's Liberation, 1980), at the same time writing another commentary on ʿAbduh and his school of thought, including Amin, and their relationship to "Islamic renewal." Both works would be republished in 1985 when the Mubarak government issued its own set of personal status laws.[51] These works take the material from *The Complete Works of Qasim Amin* nearly verbatim but omit the sections claiming ʿAbduh authored *The Liberation of Woman.* Instead ʿImara Islamicizes the text in a new way: by rehabilitating Amin. Suddenly Amin becomes a *salafi*, calling for a return to the simplicity of Islam by stripping it of its cultural accretions, returning to the Qurʾan and the true hadith, dispensing with the corruptions of the "men of religion" and the "jurists," and focusing on the political work of the message (140, 141, 144). Amin is no longer emblematic of the un-Islamic (social, literary, Western) aspects of the text; instead he becomes a political and religious reformer. "His Islamic intellectual background did

[50] Muhammad ʿImara, *al-Islam wa-l-Marʾa fi Raʾy al-Imam Muhammad ʿAbduh* (Cairo: Dar al-Hilal, 1979), 6.

[51] Muhammad ʿImara, *Qasim Amin wa-Tahrir al-Marʾa* (Cairo: Dar al-Hilal, 1980); ʿImara, *Qasim Amin wa-Tahrir al-Marʾa.*

not qualify him to be an Islamic writer rather than an Islamic reformer. But his particular nature and individual formation called him to be a writer specializing and interested in religious matters and he was proud of Islam and the attacks on Islam . . . provoked him" (134)" A chapter on "Islamic Civilization" is structured as a six-part discussion of "Qasim Amin's Islamic viewpoints and opinions." ʿImara writes: "As for Islam, as a religion, Qasim Amin had a simple and good understanding of it at that time. He saw that religion was innocent of what had been added to it with the passing of the ages . . . those committed to this simple religion should return to its most trusted source: the Qurʾan and then to a few sound hadiths" (140–41). What kind of reform does ʿImara envision? His chapter "The Freedom of Woman" revolves around a central analogy in Amin's work: that the oppression of women in the home is like the oppression of men by the government. The chapter begins with a quote from *The Liberation of Woman*: "There is overlap between the political situation and the familial situation . . . for the type of government is reflected in household manners and household manners are reflected in social forms. In the East we find woman is the slave of man and man is the slave of the government. When women enjoy their personal freedom then men enjoy their political freedom. The two situations are completely linked" (105). In his discussion of freedom, ʿImara continually returns to Amin's analogy between tyranny in the home and tyranny in politics, reiterating, rephrasing, and requoting the original passage. ʿImara, drawing on Amin, frames women's emancipation as eradicating tyranny in the home. But it is also an argument against state interference in the domain of religious governance—in the family and elsewhere.

ʿImara ideologically aligns his argument with the thought of Sayyid Qutb, in particular, with respect to questions of religious and political freedom. Qutb associates servitude to anything but God—that is, to human, secular forms of government—with *shirk* and jāhiliyya. In one specific passage, ʿImara directly draws on Qutb's language of subjugation (*ʿubūdiyya*) and despotism (*istibidād*); emancipation (*taḥarrur*) and intrinsic freedom (*wijdān al-ḥurriyya*); justice (*ʿadāla*) and dominance (*siyāda*). Echoing Qutb, ʿImara writes: "We perceive Qasim Amin's depth when he connected women's backwardness and subjugation to the dominance of a tyrannical order. . . . It was not Islam . . . but tyranny made women one of its preys and shackled her with fetters and chains. Her emancipation is connected to the emancipation of man from tyranny and the emancipation of society as a whole" (111). The emancipation of women becomes one battlefield in the fight against secular tyranny and political oppression, and Islam, the means to that emancipation. ʿImara returns to the book's epigraph about man treating woman as a "slave," depriving her of "intrinsic freedom" (*wijdān al-ḥurriyya*)—a term referencing Qutb's first pillar of social justice "intrinsic freedom" (*al-taḥarrur al-wijdāni*). Even as he deploys the liberal language of freedom, ʿImara seeks to distinguish this freedom from secularism, as a form of human tyranny on earth.

With new legislation around the personal status laws in 2001 and 2004, ʿImara published no fewer than four new books on the "movement for women's emancipation in Islam," including republications of *Islam and Woman* and *The Complete Works of Qasim Amin*.[52] The legal authority of ʿAbduh, combined with Amin's conceptualization of the bourgeois family form as emancipating, created a gendered space central to revivalist discourses. This "social structure of the public sphere"—the family and private space—was discursively produced through the overlapping world of letters and the letter of the law. These two forms of public sphere "blended with each other in a peculiar fashion. In both, there formed a public consisting of private persons whose autonomy . . . wanted to see itself represented as such in the sphere of the bourgeois family and actualized inside as love, freedom, and cultivation—in a word, as humanity."[53] In Habermas's *Structural Transformation of the Public Sphere*, he interprets the autonomy of the bourgeois family as residing in its "private property." In revivalist writers' assertions of women's freedom and equality in Islam, the right to private property is one of the most important. But the right to religious freedom, one infringed on by the secular authoritarian state, is more primary in these writings. The religious autonomy of this family, as the site of freedom, choice, and rights, is a primary tenet of both secularism and liberalism. These writings use liberalism as an ideological weapon to protect its territory, on secularism's own terms.

ʿImara's claim about *The Liberation of Woman* has been widely accepted as truth in scholarship on Amin, reifying assumptions about the diametric opposition between Islamic and Western thought, the religious and the secular.[54] Leila Ahmed's widely used *Women and*

[52] Muhammad ʿImara, *Shubuhat wa-Ijabat hawl Makanat al-Marʾa fi al-Islam* (Cairo: al-Majlis al-Aʿla li-l-Shuʾun al-Islamiyya, 2001); Muhammad ʿImara, *al-Tahrir al-Islami li-l-Marʾa* (Cairo: Dar al-Shuruq, 2002); Muthni Amin Nadir and Muhammad ʿImara, *Harakat Tahrir al-Marʾa min al-Musawaa ila al-Jindir: Dirasa Islamiyya Naqdiyya* (Cairo: Dar al-Qalam, 2004); Ahmed, *Women and Gender in Islam*.

[53] Habermas, *Structural Transformation of the Public Sphere*, 55.

[54] Ahmed, *Women and Gender in Islam*, 159, 270n16; Margot Badran, *Feminists, Islam, and Nation: Gender and the Making of Modern Egypt* (Princeton, NJ: Princeton University Press, 1996), 18; Haj, *Reconfiguring Islamic Tradition*, 146, 246–47n92, 249n3; Cole, "Feminism, Class, and Islam in Turn-of-the-Century Egypt." In ʿImara's writings, Amin's chapter "Hijab al-Nisaʾ min al-Jiha al-Diniyya" in *Liberation of Woman* is attributed to Muhammad ʿAbduh.

Gender in Islam is structured in this way, through diametric oppositions between native and imported discourses on gender, one associated with religion and the other with Westernization. Like ʿImara, Ahmed builds her argument through sets of dichotomous personalities—Huda Shaʿrawi and Malak Hifni Nasif, Doria Shafiq and Zaynab al-Ghazali, Qasim Amin and Muhammad ʿAbduh—with one embodying indigenous values and the other, imported ones. Ahmed characterizes Huda al-Shaʿrawi, founder of the Egyptian Feminist Union, as supporting "the adoption of Western political institutions and a secularist understanding of the state . . . by her close connections with Western women and Western feminism, her perspective was informed by a Western affiliation and a westernizing outlook and apparently by a valorization of Western ways as more advanced and 'civilized' than native ways."[55] She contrasts Shaʿrawi with Zaynab al-Ghazali, the founder of the Muslim Women's Association, who had a long relationship with the Muslim Brotherhood. In her youth al-Ghazali was a member of Shaʿrawi's Egyptian Feminist Union, but she broke away, believing that "the women's liberation movement is a deviant innovation," because Islam already provides women with their freedom, freedom in "economic rights, political rights, social rights, public and private rights" (198). Citing ʿImara, Ahmed repeats the claim that ʿAbduh wrote parts of *The Liberation of Woman*. Ahmed, like Kishk, plays on this concept, saying that the Western, colonial parts were written by Lord Cromer, the consul general of Egypt. "Given the wholehearted reproduction of views common in the writings of the colonizers," writes Ahmed, "that idea was not perhaps altogether farfetched" (159). Like ʿImara, Ahmed imagines an unimpeachable version of feminism stamped by the religious authority of Muhammad ʿAbduh. Even though both argue for unveiling, Amin's analysis represents "the internalization and replication of the colonialist perception," whereas ʿAbduh's is rationally and fairly argued. Amin argues against equality, whereas ʿAbduh argues for it.[56]

The discourse of rights and freedoms of the Islamic private sphere was framed not just by legal contestations over the family but also by economic liberalization under Sadat and Mubarak. In a groundbreaking essay on Qasim Amin, Juan Cole argued for the compatibility of the bourgeois family form espoused in Amin's text with the economic interests of the secular intelligentsia at the turn of the century. Cole argues that *The Liberation of Woman* idealizes the private home, nu-

[55] Ahmed, *Women and Gender in Islam*, 178.

[56] "Every person has the natural right to develop their talents" and "What difference is there between men and women . . . when we see children of both sexes equal in their curiosity?" (161).

clear family, and conjugal couple associated with a class that arose in conjunction with the transition to a capitalist economy.[57] The revival of Qasim Amin served to legitimize just such a bourgeois family form for the Islamic Awakening, at a time when the Islamic student movement leaders came of age, becoming the doctors, lawyers, and engineers who dominated the revival.[58] What effect did Sadat's neoliberal reforms have on helping produce a bourgeois family form for the Islamic revival, one with "Islamic family values"? Kishk and ʿImara repeatedly assert the characteristics of the bourgeois family form, one based on free consent, companionate marriage, and the integrity of (women's) personal property, and made up of educated (and "enlightened") subjects.[59] This literature emphasizes the right to private property as one of the core elements of the "freedom" of the Muslim family and the rights of its members, namely, women. Muslim women's rights to manage their own assets, to personal property, to buying and trading, and to financial maintenance are stressed in revivalist writings as key to women's liberation in Islam.

Other Islamic thinkers and activists, such as Hasan al-Hanafi and Jamal al-Banna, crystalized a philosophy of Islamic rights and freedoms during this period. Similarly, older texts, like the nahḍa philosopher Muhammad al-Khidr Husayn's *Freedom in Islam* (originally published in 1909) and the Muslim Brother Sayyid Qutb's *Social Justice in Islam,* were republished and circulated in new editions.[60] Islamic groups worked to expand the freedoms wrested through the process of partial liberalization under Sadat and Mubarak, but the Islamic nature of these freedoms was contingent on distancing the Islamic movement from the secular state. In the absence of the Islamic movement's free participation in state politics, Islamic thinkers were able to inhabit a space conceptually outside the secular state, an extrapolitical status that gave them a mark of legitimacy. The Islamic family was both part of the secular state and understood to be beyond its reach. Maintaining the Islamic nature of the Islamic family depended on continual disavowal that it was a "secular formula," or an invention of colonial modernity, rather than a preservation of a precolonial vestige of Islamic law. The writings analyzed here exploit—and become caught in—the ineluctable binaries of secular liberalism: of state and religion,

[57] Cole, "Feminism, Class, and Islam in Turn-of-the-Century Egypt," November 1, 1981; Abu-Lughod, "Marriage of Feminism and Islamism."

[58] Wickham, *Mobilizing Islam.*

[59] Abu-Lughod, "Marriage of Feminism and Islamism," 252.

[60] Gonzalez-Quijano, *Les gens du livre*; al-Banna, *Qadiyyat al-Hurriyya fi al-Islam*; Hanafi, *al-Din wa-l-Thawra fi Misr*; Husayn, *al-Hurriyya fi al-Islam.* Originally published in 1949, *Social Justice in Islam* was republished fifteen times between 1952 and 2002.

public and private, political and personal. Because the Islamic family was already territory ceded by the secular state to Islamic law, the family became a sacred outpost in the public discourse of political Islam. The family, as one of the pivotal social structures of the public sphere, was discursively produced through these overlapping domains: the world of letters and the letter of the law. Kishk and ʿImara, as well as a flood of other public commentators that followed, formulated a public hermeneutics in which legal norms pertaining to the family became expressed, critiqued, and interpreted through the Islamic world of letters.[61]

Conclusion

The cultivation required for participation in the world of letters, the adab, the discipline, ethics, and literary knowledge, is a key tenet for what both ʿImara and Kishk understand as the emancipating power of religious enlightenment. Their repeated emphasis on religious enlightenment, a motif taken from earlier revivalist texts on gender, becomes a means of illustrating the power of religious knowledge for the modern age.[62] Through this argument, these writers underscore their own importance to the hermeneutical process of interpreting an Islamic modernity. This Islamic intelligentsia and their scholarship become keys to an Islamic enlightenment promising to eradicate jāhiliyya. The *salafī* identification of an educated, enlightened, textual Islam, untainted by custom and culture, is a critical element of the Islamic enlightenment. It brings religious scholars to the fore in defining a modern, universalist Islam, imparting to them the authority of Islam's foundational texts but granting them license to dispense with traditional interpretations and authorities. Inevitably these arguments become trapped in the inexorable logic of modernist progress, obliging ʿImara, Kishk, and their contemporaries to reverse secular modernity's assumptions about religion. This reversal, or inversion, turns the writings into a mirroring discourse of secular liberalism, where instead of being reactionary and retrograde, Islam becomes the pinnacle of enlightenment progress. The issue of women's status becomes a means of discussing, at length, Islam as enlightened, progressive, and compatible with modernity and modern society. The books focus on the liberation of woman as a barometer of civilization, the problem of secular modernity (versus

[61] Habermas, *Structural Transformation of the Public Sphere*, 55; Fraser, "Rethinking the Public Sphere."

[62] Bint al-Shatiʾ, *al-Mafhum al-Islami li-Tahrir al-Marʾa*; Sidqi, *Niʿmat al-Qurʾan*, 13–16.

Islamic mores) as a measure of progress, and the role of intellectual Islam in the renewal (*tajdīd*) and reform (*iṣlāḥ*) of Islamic society. Much of this narrative depends on inversions and mirrorings of not just liberal secular narratives of emancipation but also enlightenment narratives of reason, knowledge, and education. In Kishk's *Jahalat ʿAsr al-Tanwir*, for example, colonial secularism becomes a form of ignorance, and Islam, the path to enlightenment. The *jahālāt* of the title is "ignorance that has spread and is still spreading in our country in the name of enlightenment."[63] This has led to "an age of darkness" and "an age of oppression" (*ʿaṣr al-ẓalām*), a modern jāhiliyya that calls for a second coming of Islam and true enlightenment. ʿImara's intellectual production revolves around conceptualizing Islam as the path to enlightenment, but it is also the way these Islamic intellectuals legitimize their own pedagogical role in leading the umma out of ignorance and jāhiliyya.[64]

Even as ʿImara demonstrates an intellectual imbrication in the presumed joint authorship between ʿAbduh and Amin and a convergence of Western, secular and Islamic, religious worldviews on the subject of "women's liberation," he sets up dichotomies between East and West, religious and secular, legal and cultural, Islamic and un-Islamic. ʿImara identifies two nahḍas—one calling for the wholesale adoption of Western civilization and the other for "benefiting from the 'tools' of the European Renaissance and civilization, making its point of departure Arab-Islamic and its character Arab-Islamic" and "building a modern, developed Arab Islamic civilization distinct from the civilization of the Europeans."[65] Amin's age, ʿImara writes, was split between two kinds of renaissance. ʿImara describes Arab and Islamic contemporary civilization as "reliant on a model of progress and development," using the words nahḍa, tajdīd, and yaqaẓa, comparing them to the European Renaissance, Reformation, and Enlightenment (156). Instead of modeling the Islamic awakening on the European Enlightenment, however, he roots the Enlightenment in Islam. "The Protestant Reformation borrowed from the spirit of Islam and its teachings. Europe's path to enlightenment and rationalism propel its enlightened little by little to Islam" (143). Amin, he writes, had an "enlightened understanding" of the Islamic religion and "one of his important references was to the unbounded and open possibility of the spread of Islam to Europe. Only

[63] Kishk, *Jahalat ʿAsr al-Tanwir*, 9.

[64] Muhammad ʿImara, *al-Islam bayn al-Tanwir wa-l-Tazwir* (Cairo: Dar al-Shuruq, 1995); Muhammad ʿImara, *Fi al-Tanwir al-Islami* (Cairo: Dar Nahdat Misr, 1997); Muhammad ʿImara, *Rifaʿa al-Tahtawi: Raʾid al-Tanwir fi al-ʿAsr al-Hadith* (Cairo: Dar al-Mustaqbal al-ʿArabi, 1984).

[65] ʿImara, *Qasim Amin wa-Tahrir al-Marʾa*, 1980, 157.

a religion distinguished by such simplicity and rationalism harmonizes with their people, with the Renaissance, Enlightenment, and Rationalism that prevailed and prevail in European societies. This religion is Islam" (142). Using European history as a model, ʿImara argues that *tajdīd* will bring about *tanwīr*, enlightenment, just as the Reformation brought about the Enlightenment.

These writings on women's liberation in Islam use the master's tools to dismantle the master's house. This, Audre Lorde famously argued, prevents any real change in the terms. "The master's tools will never dismantle the master's house," she writes. "They may allow us temporarily to beat him at his own game, but they will never enable us to bring about genuine change."[66] She calls for a kind of genuine flourishing outside the structures of this dominant discourse. She asks for more than just a "reverse discourse" but a reconceptualization of the very terms of the debate. Women writers of the period would take the terms of this dominant discourse and transform it, mainly by reconceptualizing the political nature of the private sphere as a site for the mobilization of a women's movement and a women's consciousness but also as the site of the "genuine conditions of women's lives." Lorde quotes Simone de Beauvoir: "It is in the knowledge of the genuine conditions of our lives that we must draw our strength to live and our reasons for acting." The Islamic political theorist Heba Raouf Ezzat would write something nearly identical in her book *Woman and Political Work: An Islamic Vision*, arguing for the family as a vast site for the political mobilization of the umma. It is not only the place of the actual conditions of women's most important work but a place where they draw their strength, she argues. Even if this "focus on the family" is framed by the economic liberalization of society and by the encroachment of a secular world, these women writers develop the family as the site of a vivid Islamic imaginary and a place of human flourishing.

[66] Lorde, *Sister Outsider*, 112.

CHAPTER 3

Senses of Self

NIʿMAT SIDQI'S THEOLOGY OF MOTHERHOOD

In her wildly popular booklet *al-Tabarruj* (Adornment, 1967), the revivalist preacher Niʿmat Sidqi describes how she was afflicted with a terrible abscess in her mouth, an abscess (*dummal*: also, inveterate evil) that is a symptom of spiritual decay.[1] *Tabarruj* comes from verse 33:33 of the Qurʾan, addressed in the feminine plural to the Prophet's wives: "Stay in your homes and do not adorn (*tabarrajna*) yourselves with the adornment (*tabarruj*) of jāhiliyya." Connoting sensual enhancement, *al-tabarruj* becomes a kind of sickness associated with the "sickness" of unbelief, a corruption in the body and of the social body cured by faith. Sidqi describes God as treating her spiritual affliction with a painful illness, one that restores her heart and soul to health (12). This bodily sickness is a gift from God, a pain cleansing her of corruption. Lucky to have this purifying fire, she can escape this punishment in the afterlife. It comes as a warning. A friend of Sidqi's comments that she, of all people, did not deserve such a punishment from God. "God," Sidqi replies, "does not ever oppress anyone; people oppress themselves."

> I, the sinner, deserved this punishment and more. This mouth that God disciplined (*addaba*) with sickness and pain was painted red and did not enjoin the good and forbid evil. This abscessed face beautified itself with makeup. This abject body adorned itself with fine cloth. This head burning with hot pain did not cover with the veil as God commanded. So now it is wrapped in medical bandages just like the veil. I did not cover with the veil of modesty, so God covered me with the veil of pain. My mouth and face were beautified with paint and oil, so God slapped my face with the slap of shame and disgrace. (14)

[1] Niʿmat Sidqi, *al-Tabarruj* (Cairo: Matbaʿat al-ʿAsima, 1971), 10.

An undated photograph of Niʿmat Sidqi, provided by her daughters Abeya and Naziha Rida and granddaughters Hiba and Amira Mashhur, who attended the religious lessons at her home. Image courtesy of Abeya and Naziha Rida.

She describes her recovery (*al-shifāʾ*) as a miracle, as the hand of God reaching out and wiping away sickness and pain and draining the abscess.

Al-Tabarruj describes the physical ugliness of being out of sync with God's design, a sickness and a blight whose cure is Islam. A negative vision of how the eye can be led astray, the booklet describes vision clouded by corruption. *Al-Tabarruj* starkly contrasts with Sidqi's later work celebrating synchronicity—both physical and spiritual—with divine commands. In later writings she calls herself a doctor of the Qurʾan. "I have harvested the best of what the minds of the ʿulamaʾ had to offer and took its nectar to nourish the reader, cure her heart, revive her, and heal her."[2] Quoting Muhammad al-Ghazali, a revivalist known for his writings on gender, she compares different kinds of Qurʾan exegeses to different kinds of doctors who work to cure the human body. Sidqi begins *Niʿmat al-Qurʾan* (Grace of the Qurʾan, 1968) by calling the Qurʾan a "cure for the heart from the illness of ignorance (*jahl*), a light and guidance, lighting up insight with the radiance of its verses (*āyāt*: also, signs). It is mercy when it brings people out of the gloom of error and darkness and leads them with its light to truth and righteousness. It is a wholesome cure!" she exclaims, "A shining light and an absolute proof!"[3] For Sidqi, the Qurʾan is medicine, enlightenment, and knowledge.

The metaphor of knowledge as medicine and light speaks to its corporeal effects and particularly its disciplinary powers to cultivate righteous bodily practices and sensibilities. The sermon goes on to elaborate on the power of knowledge to unlock the treasures of adab—here meaning righteous comportment, but a word that also means literature, discipline, and ethics. This jihad of the mind for God, she says, is a form of education (*tarbiya*), discipline (*tahdhīb*), and enlightenment (*tanwīr*). "Whoever is not enlightened by the reflection of its verses," a reflection that is intellectual, disciplinary, and sensory, "remains lost in the darkness of ignorance, however wide his knowledge" (16). This light of the Qurʾan penetrates the core of the heart and disciplines with the discipline of God. Unless knowledge is of religion, it is useless in instructing morals and rectifying society. Sidqi describes the Qurʾan as written on the heart and speaking with the heart's voice, a heart that "submits to its discourse." "You must know from the Qurʾan: who created you, and what created you, and how to worship Him. You must understand the text's every command, every prohibition, every rule, and every expression, and you must listen to you your heart: what God

[2] Sidqi, *Muʿjizat al-Qurʾan*, 15.
[3] Sidqi, *Niʿmat al-Qurʾan*, 13–14.

says, submit to His discourse, fear His punishment, and hunger for His reward" (18). In the middle of this passage, Sidqi switches from talking about "people" in the abstract third person to a more direct second person form of address. She uses "you" copiously and repetitively for emphasis—"you must listen to you your heart"—doubling up the object of address as "you your heart." Listening to the heart becomes listening to God, what God says, and to God's discourse. You must see the miracle of the Qurʾan with your own eyes and your own will, she says; it is religious knowledge that speaks through the heart. With this knowledge, the eyes see God's signs, the ears hear His message, and the mouth speaks His word. Sidqi's contribution is a corporeal reading of the Qurʾan through the female body. What Elizabeth Grosz calls a "corporeal feminism" gives the body the "explanatory power of the mind" that functions as an "inscriptive surface."[4] Encoding the body with the microphysics of God's power, Sidqi also reshapes the discursive terrain of Islamic thought by interpreting the female body as embodying God's word. She depicts a soul produced within the body, articulated through knowledge of God, the Qurʾan, and His word.[5]

The eye is at the center of a satellite of senses attuned to God's will, command, and presence. Like desire itself, it is a portal to both good and evil.[6] In *al-Tabarruj*, Sidqi emphasizes how these senses can be led astray, through the sight of a woman's body, smell (of a woman's scent), sound (of a woman's voice), and taste (of a woman as flesh, *ladhdhat al-laḥm*). These are all ways that a woman touches the sensory realm, and that a woman's sensuality is touched. In this section on the senses, she again switches to the second-person form of address, exhorting her audience directly to heed God's verses and "what is in them of wisdom and adab." The verse commands women "to not please an eye other than her husband's with her beauty, no ear other than his ear with the sweetness of her voice, no nose other than his nose with the strength of her scent, and no imagination other than his imagination with what she hides of beauty (*zīna*) and attractiveness. She must be a fortified fortress, a strong and secure bastion of chastity, far from the exposure of corrupt looks" (24). Playing on the word *ʿayn*'s double meaning as "source" and "eye," she elaborates, in explicit terms, on the eye as the source of desire and as kindling for appetites. A vivid passage describes how the eye awakens the mouth's desire to taste flesh, like wolves'

[4] Elizabeth A. Grosz, *Volatile Bodies: Toward a Corporeal Feminism* (Bloomington: Indiana University Press, 1994), vii, 138–59.

[5] Michel Foucault, *Discipline and Punish: The Birth of the Prison*, trans. Alan Sheridan (London: Allen Lane, 1977), 26, 28.

[6] Sidqi, *Niʿmat al-Qurʾan*, 279.

hunger at the sight of meat or like consumers' craving of products that attract with pretty papers and colors in the market. The booklet revolves around how tabarruj leads the senses astray through the enhancement of sensuality and seductiveness. Latent within this vision is a conception of spiritual beauty in alignment with God's word. If a

> *mutabarrija* (a woman who engages in tabarruj) reflected with the eye of her inner vision (*baṣīra*), if she had a heart that was aware, she would find that she, with her fake fabricated beauty and her excessive adornment (*tazyīn*), gains nothing of beauty or attractiveness, but sullies her face and hides what God has given her of instinctual beauty (*al-jamāl al-fitrī*) with a mask (*qināʿ*: also, veil) of showy colors unnatural to nature and offensive to good taste. Heedlessly, she does not comprehend what she fabricated of distortion and ugliness. (35)

This falseness blinds the vision of both men and women together (46). Only through *al-adab al-Islāmī*, or Islamic comportment, can a woman truly see.

Scholarly discussions of *al-Tabarruj* argue that Sidqi understands the body as *ʿawra*, or shameful.[7] Despite the brilliance of these analyses, the emphasis on *ʿawra* as a negative taint distorts Sidqi's positive vision of the body in tune with Islamic practice and with God's design. Unfortunately, *al-Tabarruj* has been analyzed in isolation from Sidqi's wider oeuvre, which scholarship has virtually ignored. From this vantage point, revivalist discourse appears to treat the female body as corrupting and needing to be covered. Sidqi's other writings turn from the sick, ignorant, tainted body of *al-Tabarruj* to an enlightened, sound, serene, discerning body in tune with God's vision, commands, and word. These later books describe harmonious unity with the cosmic design through Islamic practice and through the embodiment of an Islamic weltanschauung. The ethical labor of bodily discipline synchronizes the body

[7] For definitions of *ʿawra*, see Fedwa Malti-Douglas, "Faces of Sin: Corporeal Geographies in Contemporary Islamist Discourse," in *Religious Reflections on the Human Body*, ed. Jane Marie Law (Bloomington: Indiana University Press, 1995), 70; Valentine M. Moghadam, *Modernizing Women: Gender and Social Change in the Middle East* (Boulder, CO: Lynne Rienner, 2003), 173. Valerie Hoffman-Ladd discusses the meaning of *ʿawra* with respect to contemporary debates over modesty in the Islamic movement. "*ʿAwra* is that which ought to be covered and protected, because of the shame of having it show. But the *ʿawra* of woman is not limited to her pudenda. Rather, Hadith insists that woman herself is *ʿawra*, and traditional exegetes such as al-Baydawi state that the entire body of the free woman is *ʿawra*—even her voice is *ʿawra*—and must be covered with the same care as the pudenda of men." Hoffman-Ladd, "Polemics on the Modesty and Segregation of Women," 28.

and senses with the soul (*nafs*), creating an Islamic self (*nafs*). Being out of sync results in an obscured perception of true beauty—artificial, superficial adornment that "distorts" (*yushawwih*) true beauty. Sidqi's images evoke certain ideas from classical literary criticism, about *al-maẓhar wa-l-jawhar* (appearance and essence), *al-lafẓ wa-l-maʿnā* (style and meaning), *al-maṣnūʿ wa-l-maṭbūʿ* (artificiality and naturalness). In *al-Tabarruj* these are at odds, in opposition, the body in contradistinction to the soul. Sidqi's later writings describe a synchronicity of body and soul in which the senses are properly attuned to the divine order. She imagines Islamic adab for the Muslim woman of her time—not just an ethics of good conduct but also a literature expressing that ethics.[8]

This chapter explores Sidqi's literary and social vision of Islam through her writings. I look at all her works but focus mainly on *Muʿjizat al-Qurʾan* (Miracle of the Qurʾan) published in 1971. Her vision of the Qurʾan grounds religiosity in the human body and the sensory realm as the site in which faith is embodied, lived, and practiced. Sidqi uses words for "vision" (*baṣar* and *baṣīra*) that most strongly evoke the physical dimensions of spiritual seeing, more than words like *shahāda* (witnessing) or *ruʾya* (vision).[9] In Sidqi, physical and spiritual seeing are deeply contingent. Spiritual seeing is intimately connected to the body's physical experience of the world and especially to a particular disciplining of the senses that shapes religious subjectivity. Just as *al-Tabarruj* evokes how seeing, hearing, taste, smell, and touch act as vehicles for vice, her later writings emphasize the senses' capacity for attunement to the divine word. To recognize God's bounty and goodness on earth is to develop an inner spiritual vision. These later writings turn on spiritual seeing and hearing, *al-baṣar wa-l-samʿ*, which appear many times in the Qurʾan as the means of hearing, seeing, and understanding the message (or for blocking it and misunderstanding it). These sensory channels become the means of apprehending the dual aspect of the Qurʾan as both recitation and scripture. As both preacher and writer, Sidqi lived and worked to exemplify the dual sensory approaches though which the message is conveyed, as both speech and text.

My broader focus is revivalist disciplining of the body, through the discursive experience of scripture, recitation, sermon, and exegesis. These texts explore how religion is lived and experienced through the senses, shaping a religious subjectivity and self through religious sensibilities. I end by examining Sidqi's social vision for this Islamic body, and particularly for the Muslim woman's body. Her gendered

[8] Mahmood, *Politics of Piety*, 100.
[9] Sidqi, *Niʿmat al-Qurʾan*, 16, 21, 27, 212, 228, etc.

theology of the Qurʾan envisions the divine as embodied in the female body but also constructs a Muslim female subjectivity rooted in bodily disciplines and sensibilities. Sidqi describes the attuning of bodily sensibilities as a form of religious discipline, religious discourse that also produces (and is produced by) a particular social vision of women's roles as mothers. Sidqi interprets motherhood as the epitome of religious practice, the female body at one with the divine order of things. She embeds her vision of motherhood within the matrix of the conjugal couple and the patriarchal family, a vision that she reproduces both in her individual works and over the course of her entire oeuvre. In her second work, *Grace of the Qurʾan*, for example, she intersperses sermons on the two parents, the two spouses, desire (*al-hawā*: also meaning love and affection), and children within sermons on the five ritual practices of Islam.[10] She frames the conjugal patriarchal family within her discussions of the most basic ritual practices and virtues of Islam. One of her later books, *al-Jihad fi Sabil Allah* (Struggle for the Sake of God, 1975), centers the doctrinal obligation of jihad within the self, body, and family (and "with the tongue and pen"). Chapters on "Raising Children Is Jihad," "Religious Education," childhood, and motherhood envision familial duties as a form of jihad, reorienting jihad in new domains of religious struggle. In these writings, the female body becomes a site of the reproduction of religion, less *ʿawra* than sacred. Moreover, Sidqi situates the Islamic sensibilities she describes within a sacralized family and domestic space, connecting it to the pedagogical role of the mother. Even as she concentrates this Islamic jihad within the family, it has far-reaching potential for transformation of not just society but the very world. But politics is not so much Sidqi's object, even if the currents of revivalist politics made her own publications possible and perhaps even popular. She ties the disciplined body to a larger division of social roles that are interpreted through the adab of the (modern conjugal patriarchal) family. But this discipline is also a product of the adab of the Islamic intellectual tradition, the adab of Islamic practice, and the adab of the revival. Sidqi envisions her own sermons and writings within this adab, as its own mode of discipline and education. The pedagogy of her sermons would prove to be far-reaching, extending far beyond the home where she conducted her religious lessons.[11] Her ideas and influence clearly made their mark on

[10] Sidqi begins with a chapter entitled "The Grace of the Qurʾan," moves to chapters on the five pillars (belief, prayer, alms, fasting, and pilgrimage), and then turns to chapters on "The Two Parents," "The Two Mates," "Property and Children," and "Desire."

[11] In a book about the awakening of her Islamic awareness, Kariman Hamza describes Sidqi as a focal point of attention at a conference on "The Position of Women in Islam." Kariman Hamza, *Rihlati min al-Sufur ila al-Hijab* (Cairo: Dar al-Iʿtisam, 1981), 188–94;

the landscape of Egyptian social life, as well as the body politic of the larger Islamic umma.

Texts and Contexts

Though the illness precipitating Sidqi's deepened commitment to Islam occurred in the early 1940s, *al-Tabarruj* was not published until nearly thirty years later, the first in a flood of eight books that appeared between 1967 and 1977. After her sickness in the 1940s, Sidqi went on the hajj with her husband Muhammad Rida. On the boat traveling to Mecca, she met Muhammad Hamid al-Fiqi, founder and leader of the powerful preaching and welfare organization Jamaʿat Ansar al-Sunna al-Muhammadiyya (Association for the Partisans of Muhammad's Model).[12] Formed about the same time (and in the same region) as the Muslim Brotherhood, the Jamaʿat was the Brotherhood's intellectual counterpart, publishing revivalist books, manuscripts, and journals on al-Fiqi's private press.[13] Beginning in the late 1920s, al-Fiqi published new editions with critical commentary of classics by thinkers like Ibn Taymiyya and his disciple Ibn al-Qayyim, earlier reformers who became key referents for later revivalist thought.[14] Al-Fiqi became Sidqi's spiritual guide and mentor, directing her readings of the books of jurisprudence, tafsīr, Qurʾan, and hadith. On Fridays al-Fiqi conducted religious lessons in Sidqi's home, gatherings in which the whole family participated.[15] Sidqi eventually asked al-Fiqi's permission to assemble women for the purpose of sharing the story of her own "conversion." These meetings of friends and acquaintances grew by word of mouth into congregations, becoming the early seeds of women's *ḥalaqāt*, or religious study groups that came to dominate the revival in subsequent

---

Malti-Douglas, *Medicines of the Soul*, 36–38. By 1975 Sidqi's book *al-Tabarruj* had gone through at least nineteen printings. As Malti-Douglas observes, her narrative would resurface in other contemporary revivalist materials, often without attribution. Sidqi's family mentions that *al-Tabarruj* was used as a textbook in Saudi Arabia.

[12] Abeya Rida to Shaykh Fathi Amin Uthman, "Sira Dhatiyya li-l-Sayyida Niʿmat Sidqi."

[13] Dawud, *al-Jamʿiyyat al-Islamiyya fi Misr wa-Dawruha fi Nashr al-Daʿwa al-Islamiyya*, 175–98; Brynjar Lia, *The Society of the Muslim Brothers in Egypt: The Rise of an Islamic Mass Movement 1928–1942* (Reading, UK: Ithaca Press, 2006), 142, 147n67.

[14] Al-Fiqi's press Matbaʿat al-Sunna al-Muhammadiyya revived many books by Ibn Taymiyya through multiple republications and new editions accompanied by critical commentaries. Some of these include *Kitab al-Nubuwat* (1927), *ʿAqidat Ahl al-Sunna wa-l-Firqa al-Najiya* (1939), *al-Risala al-Qubrusiyya* (1946), *al-ʿUbudiyya* (1947), and *Radd ʿala al-Mantiqiyyin*, which Matbaʿat al-Sunna al-Muhammadiyya published under the title *Naqd al-Mantiq* (1951, 1970, 1980).

[15] Rida, "Sira Dhatiyya li-l-Sayyida Niʿmat Sidqi."

decades.[16] These are what Niʿmat Sidqi's daughter Abeya calls "faith sessions" (*jalasāt īmāniyya*) held in Sidqi's homes in Alexandria and in the upscale Cairo neighborhoods of Zamalek and Garden City. Sidqi's narrative circulated in increasingly wider circles, spreading by word of mouth, until she became a preacher of renown and a figurehead of the early revival.[17] The gatherings became a space of religious education outside the formal structures of religious institutions, catering to a population of women hungry for (and demanding) religious knowledge.

During the moment of "perceptual breakthrough"[18] in the late 1960s, Sidqi left the safety of her discursive "home" to venture her Qurʾan interpretations to wider audiences. During this same period, Bint al-Shatiʾ turned from narratives about women in the Prophet's family to Qurʾan exegeses about the nature of the "Islamic personality." (See chapter 1.) Sidqi and Bint al-Shatiʾ can be considered Egypt's first women exegetes, even though neither is recognized as such (but rather as a preacher and a literary scholar, respectively). Both found refuge in discourses around family, domesticity, wifehood, and motherhood. Sidqi and Bint al-Shatiʾ were both mothers and public figures, preaching and lecturing widely, publishing their speeches and sermons, traveling, teaching, and writing. Their writings spoke to popular audiences that helped disseminate a revivalist idiom around women and the family. Though they published Qurʾan exegeses during the same period in the late 1960s and early 1970s, neither explicitly acknowledges the other. They must have been aware of each other's work, given the popularity and wide circulation of their respective publications and by virtue of being two women religious writers in the public scene. Instead they repeatedly draw on and cite male mentors and scholars in the introductions to the books, their dedications and epigraphs, and citations and arguments. In *Medicines of the Soul*, Fedwa Malti-Douglas interprets the predominance of male frames of reference in revivalist women's writings as a kind of protective mantle for the text itself.[19] These women situate themselves in the intellectual tradition of Islam and of predominantly male Islamic scholars, even as they reinterpret women's place in this tradition. Their utopian visions of the private sphere could be interpreted as (patriarchal) bargains with the secular state. They accept the terms of the place defined for religion (and for women in the family) and turn it into a site for the transformation of

[16] Hafez, *An Islam of Her Own*; Mahmood, *Politics of Piety*.
[17] Rida, "Sira Dhatiyya li-l-Sayyida Niʿmat Sidqi."
[18] Wickham, *Mobilizing Islam*, 34.
[19] Malti-Douglas, *Medicines of the Soul*, 16–18.

society as well as religious knowledge.[20] Their writings also articulate their belief in the pedagogical and disciplinary power of motherhood within the social institution of the family.

Both Sidqi and Bint al-Shatiʾ had backgrounds in secular education; neither had official training in religious institutions. They had very different educations: Bint al-Shatiʾ with a doctorate in Arabic literature and a close relationship with higher institutions of religious learning like al-Azhar in Cairo, the Islamic University of Omdurman in the Sudan, and the University of Qarawiyyin in Fez; Sidqi, with an education in French schools and training from one of the most important revivalist shaykhs of the twentieth century.[21] Both brought decentralized positions in Islamic thought to bear on the Qurʾan, with relatively unorthodox results. Bint al-Shatiʾ, for example, developed a theology of human freedom based on her Qurʾan exegeses; Sidqi, a theology of the female body. Sidqi calls her writings tafsīr (exegesis) in the introductions to her books, but her method clearly lies far outside the classical tradition of tafsīr. This is what makes her interpretations, her son writes in his introduction to *Muʿjizat al-Qurʾan*, "modern."[22] Similarly, Bint al-Shatiʾ's literary approach gave her a certain license in developing a new interpretive methodology. Following Sidqi's and Bint al-Shatiʾ's early lead, towering women within the revival, like Zaynab al-Ghazali and Kariman Hamza, would later venture their own Qurʾan interpretations.[23] Their works, however, follow a more orthodox, classical style of close, line-by-line readings. Sidqi and Bint al-Shatiʾ take more holistic approaches that their supporters call "literary."[24]

Sidqi's books declare themselves as Qurʾan interpretations, but she is clearly on the margins of the scholarly tradition, as a woman, a homegrown preacher, and a revivalist. She is both preacher and exegete, speaker and writer, dual modes that contribute to the power of her narrative style. Her direct voice evokes the initial context of the sermons' delivery in the intimacy of her home. The writings have the feel of sermons. Even though she is writing in impeccable *fuṣḥā* (standard, classical Arabic), her style is a clear, fluid, accessible vernacular. This feeling of directness is reinforced as she slips into the second-person at the crescendo of her arguments, addressing the reader as

[20] Deniz Kandiyoti, "Bargaining with Patriarchy," *Gender and Society* 2, no. 3 (September 1988): 274–90.

[21] Rida, "Sira Dhatiyya li-l-Sayyida Niʿmat Sidqi."

[22] Sidqi, *Muʿjizat al-Qurʾan*, 6.

[23] al-Ghazali and Faramawi, *Nazarat fi Kitab Allah*; Hamza, *al-Luʾluʾ wa-l-Marjan fi Tafsir al-Qurʾan*.

[24] ʿAbd al-Rahman ʿAbd al-Wahhab al-Wakil, "Introduction," in *Niʿmat al-Qurʾan*, by Niʿmat Sidqi (Cairo: Matbaʿat al-Sunna al-Muhammadiyya, 1968).

"you" in the singular, or sometimes in a feminine plural "you all" that suggests a female audience and the women attending the sermon in her home. Sometimes Sidqi breaks into rhyming prose, using the rhetorical flourishes of a preacher. The Salafi belief in a direct relationship with the Qurʾan, without "intermediaries," was partly what made new interpretations possible, especially by interpreters like Sidqi not formally trained in a religious institution. She condemns "worshipping tradition, blind obedience, and an inherited Islam" as a form of ignorance (*jahl*). She argues instead for education and enlightenment through a direct relationship between the heart and the Qurʾan and through "jihad of the mind for the sake of God."[25]

Just when students began mobilizing on university campuses in the late 1960s, Sidqi began circulating her teachings in print. *Al-Tabarruj* was the first of what would soon become a genre of "return to veiling" narratives. This autobiographical and confessional literature written by women spiked in the late 1970s and early 1980s, helping precipitate the return to veiling.[26] Scholarly literature describes sociopolitical, economic, and spiritual motivations behind the movement to veil, but few acknowledge the transformative potential of the discursive terrain around the hijab and tabarruj. These narratives describe similar trajectories—spiritual journeys from unveiling (*sufūr*) to veiling, from tabarruj to *ʿiffa* and *ḥayāʾ* (modesty). The repetition of these themes and motifs speaks to the adaption of a certain template for living the experience of veiling. The writings describe dramatic physical and spiritual changes in body and self but also serve as cautionary tales and pedagogical warnings. In 1982 a collective at the Centre National de Recherches Sociales et Criminologiques (CNRSC) published a two-part study on the "phenomenon of the veil," the first focusing on university students and the second on professional women.[27] In 1983 Muhammad Ibn Ismaʿil published a three-volume, 1,500-page revivalist polemic *ʿAwdat al-Hijab* (The Return of the Veil), first in Riyadh and then in Cairo.[28] Despite its immense size, the book went into five printings, was translated into English, Malay, and Indonesian, and inspired a number

[25] Sidqi, *Niʿmat al-Qurʾan*, 15.

[26] Maraʿi, *Yaqazat al-ʿIffa*; Hamza, *Rihlati*; Safinaz Kazim, *Fi Masʾalat al-Sufur wa-l-Hijab* (Cairo: Maktabat Wahba, 1982); Saʿd Siraj al-Din, *Awraq Shams al-Barudi* (Azbakiyya, Egypt: al-Rawda li-l-Nashr wa-l-Tawziʿ, 1993).

[27] Zaynab Radwan, *Bahth Zahirat al-Hijab bayn al-Jamiʿiyyat* (Cairo: al-Markaz al-Qawmi li-l-Buhuth al-Ijtimaʿiyya wa-l-Jinaʾiyya, 1982); Zaynab Radwan, *Bahth Zahirat al-Hijab bayn al-Jamiʿiyyat: al-Buʿd al-Dini li-Zahirat al-Hijab bayn al-Mihniyyat* (Cairo: al-Markaz al-Qawmi li-l-Buhuth al-Ijtimaʿiyya wa-l-Jinaʾiyya, 1984).

[28] Muhammad ibn Ahmad Ibn Ismaʿil, *ʿAwdat al-Hijab* (Riyadh: Dar Tayyiba, 1984); Muhammad ibn Ahmad Ibn Ismaʿil, *ʿAwdat al-Hijab* (Cairo: Dar al-Safwa, 1988).

of offshoots by Ibn Isma'il that also went into multiple printings.[29] One of these was a 715-page treatise on "woman between the honor of Islam and the hatred of jāhiliyya." By the mid-1980s, veiling had become a staple of both revivalist practice and revivalist discourse, with a vast body of literature on veiling and the hijab emerging where there had previously been none.[30] *Al-Tabarruj* anticipated not only the return to veiling but also the shift to an "Islamic idiom" in public discourse and in the Islamic world of letters, a literature that envisioned Muslim women's subjectivity as not only *expressed* but also *shaped* by veiling.[31] Earlier in the century, there were two other occasions of (discursive) spikes in publications around veiling, both in response to other texts on the subject. The first was the publication of Qasim Amin's *Tahrir al-Mar'a* (Liberation of Woman, 1899) and *al-Mar'a al-Jadida* (The New Woman, 1900), and the other, the publication of Nazira Zayn al-Din's

[29] Muhammad ibn Ahmad Ibn Isma'il, *Ma'rakat al-Hijab wa-l-Sufur* (Cairo: Dar al-Safwa, 1990); Muhammad ibn Ahmad ibn Isma'il Muqaddam, *al-Haya': Khuluq al-Islam* (Cairo: Dar al-Haramayn li-l-Tiba'a, 1993); Muhammad ibn Ahmad ibn Isma'il Muqaddam, *Bal al-Niqab Wajib! Al-Radd al-'Ilmi 'ala Kitab "Tadhkir al-Ashab bi-Tahrim al-Niqab"* (Alexandria: Dar al-Manar al-Salafi, 1991); Muhammad ibn Ahmad ibn Isma'il Muqaddam, *Daf' al-Sa'il 'ala Mashru'iyyat al-Hijab al-Kamil* (Alexandria: Dar al-Khulafa' al-Rashidin, 2009); Muhammad ibn Ahmad Ibn Isma'il, *al-Mar'a bayn Takrim al-Islam wa-Ihanat al-Jahiliyya* (Cairo: Dar al-Safwa, 1990).

[30] Ahmad ibn 'Abd al-Halim Ibn Taymiyya and Muhammad Nasir al-Din Albani, *Hijab al-Mar'a wa-Libasuha fi al-Salat* (Cairo: s.n., 1974); Abu al-Hasan Bani Sadr, *al-'A'ila fi al-Islam aw Makanat al-Mar'a fi al-Islam. Manhaj al-Tafakkur. Mas'alat al-Hijab* (Beirut: Dar al-Tawjih al-Islami, 1981); 'Atiyya Saqr, *al-Hijab wa-'Amal al-Mar'a* (Cairo: Jumhuriyyat Misr al-'Arabiyya, Wizarat al-Awqaf, al-Majlis al-A'la li-l-Shu'un al-Islamiyya, 1983); 'Abd Allah Jamal al-Din Afandi, *Hijab al-Mar'a: al-'Iffa wa-l-Amana wa-l-Haya'* (Cairo: Maktabat al-Turath al-Islami, 1984); 'Abd al-Wadud Shalabi and 'Ali Ahmad Khatib, *Fi Mas'alat al-Sufur wa-l-Hijab* (Cairo: Majallat al-Azhar, 1985); 'Abd al-'Aziz ibn 'Abd Allah Ibn Baz, *al-Hijab wa-l-Sufur fi al-Kitab wa-l-Sunna* (Cairo: Dar al-Kutub al-Salafiyya, 1986); Muhammad Salih Ibn 'Uthaymin, *al-Mar'a al-Muslima: Ahkam Fiqhiyya hawl al-Hijab wa-l-Dima' al-Tabi'iyya wa-Zakat al-Huli* (Cairo: Dar al-Safwa, 1987); Darwish Mustafa Hasan, *Fasl al-Khitab fi Mas'alat al-Hijab wa-l-Niqab* (Cairo: Dar al-I'tisam, 1987); 'Ali al-'Usayli 'Amili, *Ni'mat al-Hijab fi al-Islam* (Beirut: al-Dar al-Islamiyya, 1988); Sana Misri, *Khalf al-Hijab: Mawqif al-Jama'at al-Islamiyya min Qadiyyat al-Mar'a* (al-Qasr al-'Ayni, Cairo: Sina' li-l-Nashr, 1989); Shahrazad 'Arabi, *al-Bu'd al-Siyasi li-l-Hijab* (Cairo: al-Zahra' li-l-I'lam al-'Arabi, 1989); 'Abd al-'Aziz ibn 'Abd Allah Ibn Baz and Muhammad Salih 'Uthaymin, *Risalatan fi al-Hijab* (Jeddah: Dar al-Mujtama' li-l-Nashr wa-l-Tawzi', 1986); Jamal al-Banna, *al-Hijab* (Cairo: Dar al-Fikr al-Islami, 2002); Muhammad Sa'id 'Ashmawi, *Haqiqat al-Hijab wa-Hujjiyyat al-Hadith* (Cairo: Madbuli al-Saghir, 1995); Iqbal Baraka, *al-Hijab: Ru'ya 'Asriyya* (Cairo: Mu'assasat Dar al-Hilal, 2004).

[31] Wickham, *Mobilizing Islam*, 34. Wickham refers to the emergence of an "Islamic idiom" in the "beginning in the mid-1970s and accelerating in the 1980s and early 1990s," to which "print Islam" was crucial. See chapter 4 for a fuller discussion of the emergence of veiling narratives during this time.

al-Sufur wa-l-Hijab (Veiling and Unveiling, 1928).[32] Between the 1930s and the early 1960s, however, there is literally a discursive silence around veiling with the dominance of a largely secular feminism and the turn to unveiling, both in popular culture (like in films) and in public life. Only in the late 1960s does a literature on veiling begin to reemerge, a trickle that turned into a torrential flood in the 1980s with an exponential rise in writings on veiling, publications that accompanied the "return to veiling." (See chapter 4.) Not only did Niʿmat Sidqi's writings help precipitate the return to veiling; her literary production also helped formulate a revivalist culture and ethos around women's bodies.

Today there is both a worldwide return to veiling and a global revival of the term tabarruj, a concept that Sidqi's writings injected into public circulation. Like the Qurʾanic term jāhiliyya (to which tabarruj is connected in verse 33:33), public intellectuals popularized—and reinterpreted for modern times—what had been an archaic term. *Al-Tabarruj* was vastly popular, selling over ten thousand copies in its first week. Repeatedly republished by different presses, it has also been translated into Farsi, Indonesian, Malay, and Turkish.[33] Today the booklet is easily downloaded from the Internet in the original Arabic. In the wake of *al-Tabarruj*'s popularity, a satellite of new writings on adornment in Islam sprang up.[34] In the battle over veiling and unveiling, Ibn Ismaʿil writes in *ʿAwdat al-Hijab*, "Pens are the battle's weapons."[35] In the publishing world, ideas on veiling and tabarruj flowed between the Gulf and Egypt during the 1980s, through the ideas of influential

[32] Responses to Qasim Amin include (among many others) Muhammad Talʿat Harb, *Tarbiyat al-Marʾa wa-l-Hijab* (Cairo, 1899); ʿAzmi, *Fasl al-Khitab*. These writings on veiling and unveiling would also be republished later in the century.

[33] Niʿmat Sidqi, *Bersolek (Tabarruj)* (Kuala Lumpur: Dewan Pustaka Fajar, 1988); Niʿmah Rasyid Ridha, *Tabarruj* (Jakarta: Pustaka Al-Kautsar, 1990).

[34] ʿAbd al-Baqi Ramdun, *Khatar al-Tabarruj wa-l-Ikhtilat* (Beirut: Muʾassasat al-Risala, 1974); Hammud ibn ʿAbd Allah Tuwayjiri, *al-Sarim al-Mashhur ʿala Ahl al-Tabarruj wa-l-Sufur: Wa-fihi al-Radd ʿala Kitab al-Hijab li-l-Albani* (Aleppo: Maktabat al-Huda, 1974); ʿAbd al-ʿAziz ibn ʿAbd Allah Ibn Baz, *al-Tabarruj wa-Khatar Musharakat al-Marʾa li-l-Rajul fi Maydan ʿAmalihi* (Cairo: Maktabat al-Salam, 1980); Muhammad Ahmad Sibaʿi, *al-Marʾa bayn al-Tabarruj wa-l-Tahajjub* (Cairo: al-Azhar, Majmaʿ al-Buhuth al-Islamiyya, 1981); ibn ʿAbd al-ʿAziz ibn ʿUbayd al-Salmi, *al-Tabarruj wa-l-Ihtisab ʿAlayhi* (Beirut: Maktabat al-Haramayn, 1987); Muhammad Binyaʿish, *Hijab al-Marʾa wa-Khalfiyyat al-Tabarruj fi al-Fikr al-Islami* (Tetouan: Matbaʿat al-Khalij al-ʿArabi, 1993); Aba Firdaus al-Halwani, *Selamatkan Dirimu Dari Tabarruj: Pesan Buat Ukhti Muslima* (Yogyakarta: al-Mahalli Press, 1995); Ahmad Awang, *Menyembah Allah, Menghufurkan Taghut! (Tabarruj al-Jahiliyyah)* (Batu Caves: Selangor Darul Ehsan, 1996); Mikhayil Shafiq Haddad, *al-Tabarruj wa-l-Libas ʿind al-ʿArab: Dirasa fi al-Tabarruj wa-l-Libas Khilal al-ʿUsur al-Jahili, al-Umawi, al-ʿAbbasi* (Beirut: Dar al-ʿUlum al-ʿArabiyya, 2009).

[35] Ibn Ismaʿil, *ʿAwdat al-Hijab*, 1984, 198.

Islamic thinkers like ʿAbd al-ʿAziz bin ʿAbd Allah Ibn Baz, Muhammad Nasir al-Din Albani, and Muhammad Salih ʿUthaymin. With the shift from print media, these ideas are now disseminated mainly through digital media. Ibn Baz's, ʿUthaymin's, and Albani's followers have taken up the topic of tabarruj, with sermons broadcast on popular satellite television shows, posted on blogs and Islamic websites, and circulated on audiocassettes and CD-ROMs.[36] The Islamic public sphere debates the politics of seeing in Islamic cultures but also defines the parameters of how the eye should see. This is what these preachers call *naẓrat al-ʿayn*, how the eye sees or "reflects" on the world, and the ethics (or adab) of seeing. The preacher Muhammad Hassan's series of sermons on "al-Adab maʿ Allah" focuses on different kinds of tarbiya (upbringing, education, discipline) and includes a sermon on the "adab of looking." The sermon has been circulated on Facebook, is transcribed into English on jannah.org ("an online city for and about Muslims"), and is downloadable at *muslimvideo.com*. On many sites an essay by Shaykh ʿAbd Allah Ibn al-Jabrin entitled "Risala ila ʿAyni" (Letter to My Eye, 2010) accompanies Muhammad Hassan's sermon on the adab of looking. "Letter to My Eye"—also posted on different blogs, religious sites, and Facebook—reiterates arguments found in *al-Tabarruj* about the function of the eye, the connection of the eye to the heart, and the eye as portal to both virtue and vice.[37]

Sidqi describes veiling as disciplining the body and senses, performing an Islamic ethics, and producing a corporeal embodiment of the spiritual. Her writings talk about seeing as a way of being, as a means of attuning the senses to an Islamic mode of perception. Her sermons and writings develop what might be called an Islamic regime of visuality intent on distinguishing itself from the regime of visuality associated with Western, secular, colonial modernity and its culture of exposure.[38] Although polemics like Sidqi's rail against shameless indecency, they

[36] Muhammad Hasan, *al-Tabarruj*, CD-ROM; Muhammad Hasan, *Hijab al-Marʾa al-Muslima*, http://ar.islamway.com/lesson/5598.

[37] "Risala ila ʿAyni: Adab al-Nazar," *El Eman*, http://www.al-eman.com; "Risala ila ʿAyni: Adab al-Nazar," *Kalemat*, http://www.kalemat.org/sections.php?so = va&aid = 546; "Risala ila ʿAyni: Adab al-Nazar," *Musslima*, http://musslima.net/forum/showthread .php?t = 4523; "Risala ila ʿAyni: Adab al-Nazar," http://fr-fr.facebook.com/note.php?note _id = 149966085063928.

[38] Hirschkind, *Ethical Soundscape*, 153. In an excellent article probing the nature of visuality in religious media in Egypt, Yasmin Moll poses a set of questions: "How do we recuperate an understanding of visuality beyond hegemonic Western norms by exploring contemporary Islamic understandings of the faculty of seeing as a key site for reflecting certain desires and anxieties about being a believing subject in neo-liberal Egypt? . . . What visual aesthetic, or the sensuous, 'embodied experience of meaning' animates Islamic media producers? How do they conceive this aesthetic as bringing viewers close

are also concerned with constructing an Islamic imaginary that does "battle," in Ibn Isma^cil's words, with Western ways of perceiving the world.[39] In a larger polemic around the visual landscape of the modern, veiling marks off the territory of the female body as a site of the sacred unseen, challenging the value of the exposed body, displayed like a commodity in the marketplace.[40] Instead they affirm a spiritual worth augmented through limited access that translates into the sacred space of the *ḥarīm*. Sidqi's writings conceive of a spiritual interiority through graphic reference to a bodily interiority—a world not just of the soul but of organs.

The size and tone of *al-Tabarruj* are pamphlet-like, a digestible reading in an exhortatory style, drawing on (and helping forge) an already popular revivalist genre. Sidqi's second book, *Grace of the Qur'an*, is a collection of sermons on core topics like the five pillars of ritual practice in Islam, interspersed with sermons on the family. ʿAnsar al-Sunna al-Muhammadiyya published these first two books, as well as her early articles in their journal *al-Huda al-Nabawi* (some of which would be collected into the books). Sidqi published her next three works through the educational press ʿAlam al-Kutub, suggesting the expansion of her audience into the more mainstream secular publishing world. The choice of ʿAlam al-Kutub suggests that these works are pedagogical tools: the educational capacity of the Qurʾan is a frequent theme in Sidqi's writings. Her first work published with ʿAlam al-Kutub is entitled *Min Tarbiyat al-Qurʾan* (From the Qurʾan's Education, 1970). The book sits uneasily with the pedagogical treatises on educational approaches in schools that were the press's usual fare. Like the earlier *Grace of the Qurʾan, From the Qurʾan's Education* is organized as a collection of sermons, lectures, or topical articles, each on a particular virtue or vice. *From the Qurʾan's Education* develops Sidqi's tendency to interpret the world—as well as religion, society, the sexes, and nature—through binaries.[41] Her next book, *Miracle of the Qurʾan*, imagines the very structure of the universe produced through these binaries, embodied in the conjugal couple, the fruit of which is one of God's miraculous signs. *Miracle of the Qurʾan* breaks away from atomistic treatments of

to piety and religious conviction?" See Yasmin Moll, "Islamic Televangelism: Religion, Media, and Visuality in Contemporary Egypt," *Arab Media and Society*, no. 10 (2010): 19.

39 Ibn Ismaʿil, *Maʿrakat al-Hijab wa-l-Sufur*.

40 Fadwa El Guindi, *Veil: Modesty, Privacy, and Resistance* (Oxford: Berg, 1999); Kazim, *Fi Masʾalat al-Sufur wa-l-Hijab*; Sidqi, *al-Tabarruj*.

41 Niʿmat Sidqi, *Min Tarbiyat al-Qurʾan* (Cairo: ʿAlam al-Kutub, 1970). Lessons on virtues are paired with their opposite vices (such as honesty and dishonesty, ignorance and piety, heaven and hell); analogous vices are paired (gluttony and luxury, scorn and pride, tabarruj and vanity), as are opposite vices (avarice and profligacy).

single themes. Sidqi dedicates the entire book to an exegesis of two verses from the Qur'an (51:20–21) that form the basis of an Islamic cosmology in her interpretation, as well as the basis of her conception of the self and soul. Her next book, *Raʾaytu wa-Samiʿtu* (I Saw and I Heard, 1973), recycles themes from *the Qurʾan's Education,* but each sermon is now grammatically tailored to describe a feminine subject embodying different virtues and vices (as ignorant and pious, gluttonous and miserly, etc.) The feminine suggests an awareness of her audience, as her writings slip from third-person narration into a second-person form of address, especially at climactic moments. Sometimes she uses a neutral second-person "you," but other times she explicitly addresses her readers/listeners in the second-person feminine plural, recalling the oral context of the sermons' original delivery.

The stories in *I Saw and I Heard* function like parables and cautionary tales.[42] From the binaries of virtue and vice she extrapolates social binaries between the genders, with chapters on "The Two Spouses as Opposites" and "The Two Parents as Leading to Heaven or Hell." As in *From the Qurʾan's Education, I Saw and I Heard* returns to core themes like "the eye," tabarruj, and "sicknesses of the heart," echoing Ibn Taymiyya's mystical text *Amrad al-Qulub wa-Shifaʾuha* (Sicknesses of the Heart and their Cure).[43] Sidqi's last three works were all published by the Islamist press Dar al-Iʿtisam in 1975 just before her death in 1977. There is a sense of urgency, of getting her sermons into print. These publications included a new edition of *al-Tabarruj*, suggesting the extension of her audience into the larger ṣaḥwa.[44] *Al-Jihad fi Sabil Allah* (Jihad for the Sake of God, 1975) takes classic revivalist definitions of jihad as preaching ("with the pen and tongue") and adds another dimension, of jihad through religious education, childrearing, and motherhood, a jihad that she prefaces with chapters on the jihad of body and self. On the eve of her own death, her penultimate work *al-Jazaʾ: al-Janna wa-l-Nar* (Reward: Garden and Fire, 1975) deals with the nature of reward and punishment in the afterlife. Her final work *al-Shuʿaʾ min al-Qurʾan* (Rays from the Qurʾan, 1975) is a more traditional

[42] Niʿmat Sidqi, *Raʾaytu wa-Samiʿtu* (Cairo: ʿAlam al-Kutub, 1973). The vices now describe specifically female subjects, like the woman profligate and the woman miser. Other chapters describe contradictions in the female character, like the smart idiot or the cultured ignorant.

[43] Ibid.; Ahmad ibn ʿAbd al-Halim Ibn Taymiyya, *Amrad al-Qulub wa-Shifaʾuha* (Cairo: al-Matbaʿa al-Salafiyya wa-Maktabatuha, 1966).

[44] Dar al-Iʿtisam published one of Sidqi's works posthumously, a paean to Switzerland's natural beauty. Niʿmat Sidqi, *Badiʿ Sunʿ Allah fi al-Barr wa-l-Bahr* (Cairo: Dar al-Iʿtisam, 1980). Dar al-Iʿtisam would continue to issue new editions of Sidqi's writings well into the late 1980s, with republications of *al-Tabarruj, Niʿmat al-Qurʾan*, and *Muʿjizat al-Qurʾan*.

exegesis of short, mystical, Meccan suras from the Qur'an. Like the sermons, these writings suggest the context of their original oral delivery, with a question-and-answer section.

Reflections on the Eye

Sidqi develops her particular Islamic vision through what her supporters call "literary" interpretations of the Qur'an. In his introduction to *Grace of the Qur'an*, the leader of the Jama'at Ansar al-Sunna al-Muhammadiyya, 'Abd al-Rahman 'Abd al-Wahhab al-Wakil, describes Sidqi's unique contribution as a product of her literary approach to the Qur'an.

> If the foundation of literary style is soaring words, beautiful images, and purity of expression, then the style of this sublime lady exemplifies these characteristics, making you feel, when you read her, that you are in front of marvelous, unique creativity, not in front of mere imitation. . . . Clarity, radiance, the beauty of her imagery [*jamāl al-taṣwīr*], soaring ideas, words immaculate to the perception [*baṣar*], these characterize the style of the sublime lady.[45]

Like in Sidqi's own writing, the emphasis is on seeing (baṣar) and *taṣwīr* (image making), woven through her literary style. Al-Wakil cites Sidqi's literary credentials, her "insight" (baṣar) into French, Arabic, and Islamic literatures alike. He praises her Arabic, saying that it gave her "penetrating insight into the intentions and objectives of the word, and into the secrets of its rhetoric and eloquence." He chronicles her religious education in tafsīr, hadith, and the books of Ibn Taymiyya and his disciple Ibn al-Qayyim. But he also invokes her knowledge of the great modern writers like Ahmad Amin, Taha Husayn, and 'Abbas Mahmud al-'Aqqad, who all used literary license to elaborate on material from the Islamic discursive tradition. Through their "literary approaches," they deployed new genres and modes of writing toward developing new hermeneutics of classical texts. Positioned outside the traditional center of religious learning in al-Azhar, these thinkers used creative license to explore religious debates through new disciplines and genres. Al-Wakil's praise of Sidqi's literary approach situates her in this intellectual line. But he also uses the concept of literary imagery (taṣwīr) euphemistically, to justify and legitimize the development of

[45] Sidqi, *Ni'mat al-Qur'an*, 7, 9.

new techniques of Qur'an interpretations, hermeneutics that lay far outside the bounds of traditional exegeses. Sidqi was able to develop interpretations that were not just novel but radical, thanks to the testimony of revivalist leaders like al-Fiqi and al-Wakil. She innovated on the very definition of tafsīr, recentering the Qur'an not only within feminine spheres of influence, but also within the female body. Through her imagery, she describes a way of seeing and imagining God's signs that embodies the word in the self.

In the introduction to *From the Qur'an's Education,* al-Wakil again praises Sidqi's literary style and imagery. He describes her writings as vividly coming to life: her "beautiful imaginative representation (taṣwīr) makes ideas into creations that pulse with life, creations you sense that they, too, live and feel. You find her strong, pure, enchanting style illuminates expressions, sheds light on words, and stirs up in the self/soul/psyche (*nafs*) the noblest of sensations and most charitable feelings. . . . she delivers the word . . . through faith, understanding, and insight (baṣīra)."[46] The emphasis here is on literary style, creativity, beautiful words, pure expression, radiant imagery, and how this mode of representation or imagining, of taṣwīr, is able to convey an understanding of the Qur'an and insight into its mysteries. Through the polysemy of the words baṣar and baṣīra, this insight or understanding also becomes a way of perceiving the world, a way that the believer who embodies this word sees. Al-Wakil says it directly: "the education (tarbiya) of the Qur'an is a disciplining of the human soul and self until it becomes sacred (*qudsiyya*)" (5).

Sidqi's *Miracle of the Qur'an* hints at criticism of this style. Now her own son Amin Rida writes the introduction as a defense, the ʿulamaʾ who cannot accept this new kind of "modern, intellectual exegesis" (*tafsīr ʿilmī ʿaṣrī*) of the Qur'an. In order for all types of intellects to grasp the Qur'an, it must be approached through manifold dimensions, whether scientific, artistic, literary, narrative, or allegorical.[47] Rida closes with a note of warning to this ʿulamaʾ who make knowledge and religion contradictory, saying that they also make religion incompatible with the modern world. Sidqi seeks to convey a new kind of Qur'an interpretation, and through it, a new kind of knowledge. Her approach aims not just for comprehension but also for the shaping of bodily perception toward embodying God's message. By evoking the Qur'an's literary nature, Rida and al-Wakil point to the power of representation, of the image, the visual, the word, and the sign. These writings also show a preoccupation with how the images are consumed, how they enter

[46] Sidqi, *Min Tarbiyat al-Qur'an,* 4–5.
[47] Sidqi, *Muʿjizat al-Qur'an,* 6.

the body through the senses, and how they shape the soul's relationship to the cosmic order. They help to inculcate the believer through a harmonization of the body with the divine word and divine commands.

The concept of an Islamic taṣwīr developed in the 1940s, when Sidqi first began preaching. Before, taṣwīr denoted visual representation in photography and painting, as well as a certain kind of Sufi spiritual perception. With Sayyid Qutb's *al-Taswir al-Fanni fi al-Qurʾan* (Aesthetic Representation in the Qurʾan, 1947), the word came to connote a mode of both representation and perception. This conception of an Islamic and Qurʾanic worldview had far-reaching impact on the study of the Qurʾan and was connected to other terms connoting an Islamic vision like *naẓra* (reflection, contemplation, view) and *bayān* (illustration, clarity).[48] For Qutb, the aesthetic experience of the Qurʾan produces a mental image that imprints the Qurʾan on the senses, body, self, and soul. Qutb focuses on the visual aspect of representation, on taṣwīr as a mode of mental imagining and image making.

> Taṣwīr is the preferred tool in the style of the Qurʾan. Through palpable imaginative images, it expresses intellectual meanings, psychological states, perceptible events, visual scenes, human types, and human nature. It then elevates these images it draws and gives them living presence for regenerating movement, whereupon intellectual meanings become forms or motions, psychological states become spectacles or tableaux, human types become vivid and tangible, and human nature becomes visible and embodied. As for events, scenes, stories, and sights, it renders them actual and immediate, pulsating with life and movement.[49]

[48] Many Islamic thinkers would develop Qutb's concept of taṣwīr, see, for example, Sayyid Qutb, *Khasaʾis al-Tasawwur al-Islami wa-Muqawwimatuhu* (Cairo: ʿIsa al-Babi al-Halabi, 1962); Jamal Muhammad Muhriz, *al-Taswir al-Islami wa-Madarisuhu* (Cairo: al-Muʾassasa al-Misriyya al-ʿAmma, 1962); Hifni Muhammad Sharaf, *al-Taswir al-Bayani: Min al-Balagha al-ʿArabiyya* (Cairo: Maktabat al-Shabab, 1969); Tawfiq Muhammad Sabʿ, *Nufus wa-Durus fi-Itar al-Taswir al-Qurʾani* (Cairo: Majmaʿ al-Buhuth al-Islamiyya, 1971); Tharwat ʿUkasha, *al-Taswir al-Islami, al-Dini wa-l-ʿArabi* (Cairo: Dar al-Maʿarif, 1977); ʿAbd al-Hakim Barakash, *al-Qurʾan Madrasa Idariyya: Suwwar Wadiha ʿan Nizam al-Hukm fi al-Maghrib Taswir al-Qurʾan* (Beirut: Dar al-Afaq al-Jadida, 1980); Yahya Muhammad, *al-Taswir al-Islami li-l-Mujtamaʿ: Dirasa Ijtimaʿiyya li-Kull min al-Tasawwur wa-l-Manhaj wa-l-Qawanin* (Beirut: Muʾassasat Ahl al-Bayt, 1980); Muhammad Abu Musa, *al-Taswir al-Bayani: Dirasa Tahliliyya li-Masaʾil al-Bayan* (Cairo: Maktabat Wahba, 1980); Salah ʿAbd al-Fattah Khalidi, *Nazariyyat al-Taswir al-Fanni ʿind Sayyid Qutb* (Amman: Dar al-Furqan, 1983).

[49] Qutb, *al-Taswir al-Fanni fi al-Qurʾan*, 34; Hirschkind, *Ethical Soundscape*, 155.

This aesthetic representation (*al- taṣwīr al-fannī*) is how the Qur'an's tactic penetrates the senses, creating a "sensory imagination" (*al-takhayyul al-ḥissi*) that acts as an embodiment (*tajsīm*) of the Qur'an. Qutb talks about "affective logic" (*al-manṭiq al-wijdānī*), a sensory knowledge that the reader/listener grasps through the experience of the Qur'an.[50] The word that he uses to describe this logic, *wijdān* (which I translate as "affect") weaves together notions of emotional life, sensory experience, and existence, but also psyche, soul, and spirit. Wijdān encompasses what are, for Qutb, complementary aspects of feeling and spirit, "the needs of the body and the desires of the soul in a single order."[51] In *Aesthetic Representation*, he writes about wijdān as the "home (*mawṭin*) of everlasting faith," penetrating to the soul through the senses and through instinct. He builds a case for sensory knowledge in contradistinction with the mind: "The mind is only one portal among many portals, it is not in any case the widest portal, nor the truest, nor the closest path to the soul" (184). In *Reconfiguring Islamic Tradition*, Samira Haj describes how modern Islamic thought cultivated a sense of spiritual interiority through inner sentiments (wijdān), what Muhammad ʿAbduh refers to as *al-taṣdīq bi-l-wijdān*, conviction through inner feeling.[52]

The person who locks the doors of perception will be a closed, limited person, argues Qutb, because intellectual knowledge cannot represent all that is in "the world of the self/soul." Faith requires "instinct, insight (baṣīra), and opening hearts and senses to echoes and lights. . . . The Qur'an always relies on touching the instinct and awakening the senses, and through them, penetrating directly into insight and proceeding to wijdān" (185–86). This notion of *taṣwīr islāmī*, or Islamic representation, informed his later work *Khasa'is al-Tasawwur al-Islami* (The Characteristics of the Islamic Worldview), which Hamid Algar, in his translation, refuses to render as "representation" or "imagery," arguing against the anthropomorphizing of religion and of God as a "mental construct." "Most significant of all," writes Algar, "is the key word in the title *taṣawwur* ("concept"), the unmistakable lexical sense of which is an idea, something formed in the mind. . . . What is under-

[50] Embodiment, sensory imagination, and affective logic are core concepts Qutb develops in his aesthetic theory of the Qur'an. See Qutb, *al-Taswir al-Fanni fi al-Qur'an*, 62–73, 183–92.

[51] Qutb's next book *al-ʿAdala al-Ijtimaʿiyya fi al-Qur'an* (Social Justice in Islam, 1949), articulates a social vision of this Islamic worldview. In *Social Justice*, he uses wijdān in reference to "emancipation" (*taḥarrur*) as the first pillar of social justice in Islam (37).

[52] Haj, *Reconfiguring Islamic Tradition*, 114–15.

way here is clearly the construction of an Islamic ideology."[53] These writings use the mental image and the mind's eye to impart a certain vision of an Islamic self and an Islamic weltanschauung.

Critical to Qutb's—and Sidqi's—understanding of taṣwīr is baṣar, how these images are received, interpreted, understood, and imprinted on both the sight and the insight of the mind's eye. For Qutb, the aesthetic experience of the Qur'an is an embodied one (186). Imagination, imagining, and imaging are key concepts that Qutb reiterates again and again in the text, along with concepts of visualization. In *The Ethical Soundscape*, Charles Hirschkind focuses on Qutb's contributions to aesthetic appreciation of the Qur'an, noting that, etymologically, taṣwīr is not just about representation and image but also about imagining and picturing in the mind's eye.[54] Hirschkind connects taṣwīr to the mass production of the cinema, but its roots can also be traced to these new, literary interpretations of the Qur'an that emerged in the 1940s and to the expansion of print media.[55] These interpretations opened the door to new kinds of disciplinary approaches to the Qur'an and especially to reading the text as (what the romantics would call) an organic whole. Qutb's interpretation of the organic unity of the Qur'an, its tawḥīd, draws on romantic ideas about the role of sensory perception in penetrating the senses of readers (or listeners) and inspiring them to a mode of higher contemplation.[56] It was Qutb's mentor, ʿAbbas Mahmud al-ʿAqqad, who pleaded for living, breathing, sensory poetry in the world of Arabic letters, loudly lamenting how dry, conventional, and irrelevant Arabic poetry had become for modern readers. Advocating romanticism, ʿAqqad's school of thought called for passion and inspiration to infuse poetry.[57] Hirschkind emphasizes the importance of *listening* through which the "listener can undertake the ethical labor

[53] Hamid Algar, "Preface," in *Basic Principles of Islamic Worldview*, by Sayyid Qutb, trans. Rami David (North Haledon, NJ: Islamic Publications International, 2006), xi.

[54] Hirschkind, *Ethical Soundscape*, 153–56.

[55] al-Khuli, *al-Tafsir*; Khalaf Allah, *al-Fann al-Qisasi fi al-Qur'an al-Karim*; Issa J. Boullata, "Sayyid Qutb's Literary Appreciation of the Qur'an," in *Literary Structures of Religious Meaning in the Qur'ān*, ed. Issa J. Boullata (Richmond, Surrey: Curzon, 2000). Boullata writes, "There is no doubt that Sayyid Qutb hit on a powerful idea when he came upon the concept of *al-taswir al-fanni fi al-Qur'an*. Earlier Muslim writers like ʿAbd al-Qahir al-Jurjani, al-Khattabi (d. 998) . . . and a few others including Mustafa al-Rafiʿi (d. 1939) in modern times dealt with some of the literary aspects of the Qur'an that Sayyid Qutb concerned himself with. But they never conceived of them in the same forceful way as he did, nor did they see them integrated in a unitary theory in the manner that he did" (358).

[56] Qutb, *Khasa'is al-Tasawwur al-Islami*, 203–24.

[57] al-ʿAqqad and al-Mazini, *al-Diwan: Kitab fi al-Naqd wa-l-Adab*; Khatab, *The Political Thought of Sayyid Qutb*, 52–55.

involved in properly attuning his or her faculties to the word of God"; I focus on *seeing* as the mode through which the reader attunes her faculties to the word of God.[58] The literary emphasis on seeing, sight, picturing, representing, imaging, imagining, and visualizing produces its own semantics, about religion and insight, light, enlightenment, dawning, and awakening. Both listening (*samʿ*) and seeing (baṣar) are critical modes for grasping the word of God in the Qurʾan. Hirschkind quotes verse 7:179, "They have hearts wherewith they understand not, eyes wherewith they see not, and ears wherewith they hear not." But he could have just as easily quoted verses like 5:83, 7:198, 11:20–24, 20:46, or 42:51, among many others. Separating listening from seeing truncates meaning: the Qurʾan most often pairs them not just with each other but with understanding.

The Book of Healing and *The Miracle of the Qurʾan*

The Miracle of the Qurʾan can be considered Sidqi's magnum opus. It describes an Islamic cosmology through an extended exegesis of two short verses from the Qurʾan: "And on earth are signs for those who are certain / And in yourselves. Do you not see?" (51:20–21). The book is divided into two main parts: the first interprets the signs on earth (51:20), and the second, the signs in the self (51:21). Connecting the signs on earth to the signs in the self—and the Qurʾan to the believer—is the faculty of inner perception. The nexus of Sidqi's interpretation lies in the connection between the external world and the inner world of the self, between the seen and the unseen. Sidqi elucidates the spiritual dimensions of the physical earth through its hidden forces, impulses, instincts, and attractions. These are the forces that make the world function, the earth rotate, birds migrate, electricity flow, and living things reproduce. For her, these impulses and instincts express the spirituality of the physical body, the inner world of God's signs that can be perceived but not seen.

The architecture of the text—and what might be called the connective tissue of Sidqi's literary style—make startling juxtapositions. Through the organization of her materials, she articulates a vision of the female body and its place in the divine order of things. In so doing, she outlines a social vision for motherhood, through a naturalized cosmology of female reproduction. Sidqi's Qurʾan interpretations are arguably a feminine vision of the sacred text: she roots her interpretation in the female body, with the womb at its center and gestation at its

[58] Hirschkind, *Ethical Soundscape*, 39.

core, aligning the female body and its procreative capacity with God's creation of the world. These religious discourses function as a form of biopower running through the sensory plane of bodies, disciplining them toward participation in a particular kind of community or social body, and operating through reproductive and sensory power to regulate community relations. They sanctify certain kinds of gender relations—the nuclear family, a relatively monogamous couple, the role of affection and desire, the mother's role in childhood education, and the primacy of motherhood.

Miracle of the Qur'an roughly adapts the structure of Ibn Sina's great work *Kitab al-Shifa'* (Book of Healing, 1014–20) in miniature, moving (like Ibn Sina) from discussions of earth sciences to the self, the spirit, and the senses. *Miracle of the Qur'an* is Sidqi's own revivalist refutation of Ibn Sina's assertions in *The Book of Healing* about reason as the path to knowing God. For Ibn Sina, logic is the means for apprehending the divine, through rational proofs. For Sidqi, the divine is not a postulate abstractly derived or grasped through syllogisms as in Ibn Sina's formulation. For her, the proof of God's signs is material and embodied. The signs are in the Qur'an itself; they are manifest in the world ("And in the earth are signs") and in the self ("and in yourselves"). Sidqi draws on Ibn Sina's understanding of the "plant soul," which is the organic natural body that takes nourishment, grows, and reproduces as well as the "animal soul" that has sensation and movement.

The five external senses are related to the sensation and movement of the animal soul. But in Ibn Sina's philosophy, these five senses exist "in actuality," as in daily seeing or hearing, or "in potentiality," such as in infancy. Corresponding to the five external senses, Ibn Sina identifies five "internal senses" related to a "rational soul" that he says "can grasp universals." These are representation, imagination, estimation, memory, and common sense.[59] Sidqi takes this philosophical concept of the potentiality of the inner senses and transforms it into a supremely embodied and material understanding of the soul. She interprets the experience of pregnancy as an embodiment of this potentiality, rooting it in the female body and the biological experience of gestation. But she also renders the experience as not just biological, material, instinctual, and bodily but the abstract potential of a yet unrealized self, known only through imagining what is yet to come. It is spiritual as much as physical.

[59] Ibn Sina, "Kitab al-Nafs," in *Avicenna's De Anima*, ed. Fazlur Rahman (London: Oxford University Press, 1959), 4–33; Fazlur Rahman, ed., *Avicenna's Psychology* (London: Oxford University Press, 1952), 24–30, 54; Shams Inati, "Soul in Islamic Philosophy," *Philosophia Islamica*, n.d., http://www.muslimphilosophy.com/ip/rep/H010.htm.

Sidqi reinterprets Ibn Sina's inner senses for the revival, questioning, like Ibn Taymiyya, the spiritual ascendancy of the rational intellect. She replaces the rational intellect with intuition as the inner sense. In Sidqi's cosmology, this inner sense is connected to the world through the impulses that drive minerals, plants, animals, and human beings, through magnetic forces, electrical currents, migratory patterns, attractions, and repulsions. Being attuned to these forces helps in "grasping universals," if not the divine. Sidqi constructs this notion of an embodied soul in a gendered way, making the female reproductive body epitomize the natural forces that run through the world. In her weltanschauung, the child in the mother's womb epitomizes how God's creation lives and moves in the world, is perceived and felt, but exists just beyond our physical grasp. Sidqi's images of biological reproduction suggest that the developing child is the nafs, the mind/spirit/soul/self that is the very embodiment of God's signs (51:21).

Miracle of the Qurʾan is structured by the tension between Ibn Sina's philosophy and Ibn Taymiyya's critique of that philosophy, *al-Radd ʿala al-Mantiqiyyin* (Response to the Logicians, 1309). *Miracle of the Qurʾan* refutes the philosophical understanding of the soul as an essence that can exist independently of the body. In Ibn Sina's "floating man theory," the soul would still exist even without sensory input. Sidqi's vision and understanding of the soul is supremely embodied. She asserts this point explicitly but also illustrates and designs it for her reader (as she says) through the very structure and organization of the book as a whole. God's signs are manifest not only in the material world but in the mechanisms and functions of the body, and especially through the five senses. Drawing on Ibn Sina's understanding of the five "external" and five "internal" senses, Sidqi refashions his neo-Platonic understanding of inner perception (or insight, baṣīra). Her gendering of this body and of the nature of the inner eye formulates a feminine (or feminist?) theology within revivalist doctrine. Motherhood, gestation, reproduction, and nurturing the young are interpreted as God's signs in the self, as the act of creation lived and embodied in the female body. Moreover, Sidqi develops a revivalist philosophy of truth where "natural, innate knowledge (fiṭra) is sufficient for thinking and reasoning soundly, thus rendering logic superfluous."[60] Sidqi implicitly and explicitly orients her exegesis in Ibn Taymiyya's understanding of knowledge of God as natural and innate. Moreover, her interpretations

[60] Wael B. Hallaq, *Ibn Taymiyya against the Greek Logicians* (Oxford: Oxford University Press, 1993), xl.

suggest that this knowledge is a cure for bodily and spiritual illnesses, as do Ibn Taymiyya and Ibn al-Qayyim.[61]

Sidqi presents this knowledge of God's signs as a science, as knowledge of the material world that leads, like in Ibn Sina's syllogisms, to knowledge of God. Unlike Ibn Sina's syllogisms, though, this is not an arcane knowledge that can be reached only through the construction of difficult proofs. It is knowledge available to all God's creatures through the process of apprehension through the senses, instinct, and intuitive knowledge. One of Ibn Taymiyya's main critiques of the logicians was that if knowledge of God was possible only through difficult and abstract proofs, then how would all of God's creatures know God, even those without training in the discipline of logic? For Ibn Taymiyya, fiṭra, the instinct with which God created human beings, gives them intuitive knowledge of God. For Ibn Sina, the abstract intellect is the source of ethics, a higher plane of knowledge that must dominate the lower practical faculty of the body.[62] Sidqi disrupts this hierarchy by drawing on revivalist understandings of the material world's innate goodness, the "nature" (fiṭra) by which God created the human. In so doing, she challenges the philosophical formulation of intellectual hierarchies as moral hierarchies. Sidqi claims not just morality but also religious knowledge and authority for those without formal education. But she goes further: she genders this intuitive knowledge, rooting Ibn Sina's "inner senses" in a biologically female body. Even as Sidqi orients the text and its argument in a body of scientific knowledge of the material world—and the "scientific miracle of the Qurʾan"—her book aims to make this knowledge available to every Muslim and every believer, not only an elite of educated scholars. "How is every Muslim supposed to understand these obscure details and theories?" The books of the ʿulamaʾ are not for ordinary individuals, but for intellects of exceeding culture and intelligence. "Every Muslim should understand the miracle of the Qurʾan—even those heedless of the miracles that are in the Qurʾan and every ignorant illiterate that does not realize what is in the earth and in the spirit of signs. In order to understand and to grasp this miracle, there must be a clear explanation of the words with a conciseness, facility, and organization appropriate to every intellect and all levels of culture, in order to lead to the desired outcome" (13). This concept of knowledge of the message as a knowledge for all was a cornerstone not just of Ibn Taymiyya's revivalism but also of the

[61] Ibn Taymiyya, *Amrad al-Qulub wa-Shifaʾuha*; Muhammad ibn Abi Bakr Ibn Qayyim al-Jawziyya, *al-Tibb al-Nabawi* (Cairo: Dar Ihyaʾ al-Kutub al-ʿArabiyya, 1957).

[62] Mohamed Ahmed Sherif, *Ghazali's Theory of Virtue* (New York: SUNY Press, 1975), 27; Rahman, *Avicenna's Psychology*, 33; Ibn Sina, "Kitab al-Nafs," 47.

revival in Egypt. *Miracle of the Qur'an* is framed, in both Sidqi's introduction and the introduction by her son Amin Rida, as an implicit critique of those ʿulamaʾ who want to keep this knowledge for themselves, through arcane writing and complex proofs. "Scholars and researchers . . . enlightened hearts with the clear light of the scientific signs of the Qurʾan, demonstrating with the strongest proofs that the Qurʾan is from God exalted. But most regrettably, these scholars wrote and communicated without vision and without reflection" (9). This is not just a revivalist pedagogical mobilization among the masses but also Sidqi's specific targeting of her female audience at the margins of religious knowledge, with limited formal education, outside the perimeters of religious institutions but still seeking knowledge, even if to China, as the Prophet said.

Sidqi's familiarity with Ibn Taymiyya's writings came from her close relationship with her teacher and spiritual adviser Muhammad al-Fiqi. Al-Fiqi wrote and published extensively on the thirteenth-century revivalist, as well as on his disciple Ibn al-Qayyim. The first book published by al-Fiqi's press, the organ of Jamaʿat Ansar al-Sunna al-Muhammadiyya, was Ibn Taymiyya's *Kitab al-Nubuwat* (The Book of Prophecies, 1927–28). In Muhammad Dawud's *al-Jamʿiyyat al-Islamiyya fi Misr wa-Dawruha fi Nashr al-Daʿwa al-Islamiyya* (Islamic Groups in Egypt and Their Role in Spreading the Islamic Call, 1992), he describes Ansar al-Sunna's philosophy as an "extension of the Ibn Taymiyya, Ibn al-Qayyim, and Muhammad ibn ʿAbd al-Wahhab school."[63] During the period that al-Fiqi and Sidqi met in the mid-1940s, Matbaʿat al-Sunna al-Muhammadiyya published a slew of works by Ibn Taymiyya: *Response to the Logicians* in 1951 and again in 1970 (just before *Miracle of the Qurʾan*) under the title *Naqd al-Mantiq* (Critique of Logic), with two introductions, one by al-Wakil and one by al-Fiqi. Wael Hallaq describes Ibn Taymiyya's stance against the philosophers as "a realist theory of universals as an entire metaphysic."[64] Ibn Taymiyya argues that "nothing can exist outside the realm of the external world and the sphere of the mind," rejecting externally existing universals.[65] As Wael Hallaq observes of this theology: "The universal and abstract mental meaning, Ibn Taymiyya seems to be saying, is identical with the verbal utterance and the written word that stand for that meaning."[66] This is a theory not just of the sign but also of how meaning comes into being through discourse. Sidqi starts her introduction to the book, in her

[63] Dawud, *al-Jamʿiyyat al-Islamiyya fi Misr*, 177.
[64] Hallaq, *Ibn Taymiyya against the Greek Logicians*, xxii.
[65] Ibid., xx.
[66] Ibid., xxiii.

"Author's Word," with this premise. "The noble Qur'an is a book that is, without any doubt, guidance for those who are certain. It is a proof and a clear light from God exalted. With what is in it of linguistic and intellectual miraculousness, it demonstrates that it is from the intuitive knowledge of the All Wise and the All Aware" (9).

Sidqi argues for an intellectual grasp of the "clear light" of knowledge from the Qur'an, through proofs (*barāhīn*) and evidence (*dalā'il*). This intellectual grasp of "the universal and abstract mental meaning" of God's signs is consistently expressed through visual metaphors of light and through the exhortation at the end of 51:21: "And do you not see?" This acquisition, grasp, and knowledge of the divine through the sensory field of the visual is a repeated motif in Sidqi's preaching and writing. At the end of her introduction to verses 51:20–21, she quotes the revivalist writer Muhammad al-Ghazali's own interpretation of the "images, models, and stories" of the Qur'an in *Nazarat fi al-Qur'an* (Reflections on the Qur'an, 1958).[67] He writes about how God's signs—and verses (*āyāt*)—are written in the material world, on the "pages of this universe." "A searching reflection on the surfaces (*ṣafahāt*: also meaning "pages") of this universe is enough for a human to know his Lord, a look at the sky and its planets, a look at the earth and its wonders, and a look at night and day, and a look at rains and rivers, a look at trees and flowers, a look at any image of the images of life are signs for the pristine of sight."[68] Sidqi and her son garner Qur'anic corroboration for her argument, quoting the verse Fussilat 41:53 similar in meaning to 51:20–21. "Soon we will show them our signs (*āyāt*: also, "verses") on the horizons and in themselves until it becomes clear that it is the truth." Sidqi's interpretation relates tangibly to the sensory and aesthetic experience of the Qur'an. In her discussion of the meaning of *āyāt*, Sidqi asks, "Do you not see what things the Exalted created on earth, how God shaped, invented, and embellished? Do you not see what blessings God created on earth, how God organized, colored, and designed? Do you not see that God created in yourselves of limbs and organs, and how God fashioned (*ṣawwara*), beautified, and perfected??" (17). Sidqi plays on the double meaning of *āyāt*, meaning both "signs" and "verses (of the Qur'an)," making the signs in the world the Qur'an writ in the universe.

[67] Muhammad al-Ghazali, *Nazarat fi al-Qur'an* (Cairo: Mu'assasat al-Khanji, 1958). A literary interpretation of the "images and models" of the "stories" of the Qur'an, *Reflections on the Qur'an* has been enduringly popular, republished in 1961, 1970, 1993, 2004, 2005. Founder of the Muslim Brotherhood Hasan al-Banna called al-Ghazali "the literary man of the Islamic call" (*adīb al-da'wa*).

[68] Sidqi, *Mu'jizat al-Qur'an*, 18.

Through al-Ghazali, Sidqi returns to the metaphor of Islam as the cure for the sick and corrupt body, describing herself as a doctor of the Qurʾan. She has harvested the best of what the minds of the ʿulamaʾ had to offer and taken its nectar to nourish her reader, cure her heart, revive her, and heal her.[69] Al-Ghazali compares different kinds of Qurʾan exegeses to different kinds of doctors who work to cure the human body. Sidqi's positive vision of *al-jism al-salīm,* as the sound body in harmony with divine will, contrasts markedly from her depiction in *al-Tabarruj* of the sick body diseased by the dominance of human appetites. In this early work, she characterizes these appetites as "animal." In *Miracle of the Qurʾan,* she does not relegate the animal necessarily to a lower order but makes it part of God's design. Animal impulses, like human impulses, like magnetic and electric attraction, are all part of God's creation. This shift in her thinking is similar to that in Sayyid Qutb's use of the word fiṭra (human nature or instinct) in subsequent editions of *Social Justice in Islam.* Early on, fiṭra is used in its vernacular sense of natural instinct; later he uses it only in its Qurʾanic sense, as God-given nature. This nature is in no way opposed to the spiritual. On the contrary, it is the means through which the human can know, understand, and grasp the divine.

The signs, designed to cure the body from corrupt distortions, also have a pedagogical function. "I strive to teach those who do not know, and make those who are ignorant understand," she writes, "by representing (*uṣawwir*) the beauty of God's design (*ṣanʿ Allah*) on earth and in people's souls for those who perceive (*yubṣirūn*) this beauty" (15). This visual representation, this taṣwīr, acts through the body, the senses, and especially the sight to shape spiritual vision. Her repeated use of baṣar intimates not just seeing but also understanding, realization, comprehension; it is also one of the ninety-nine names of God that refer to God's capacity to see and understand. In his introduction, al-Wakil ties Sidqi's beautiful literary style to pure perception (baṣar) but also to reading and listening as modes of apprehension, aesthetic experiences that stir the self into a state of spiritual arousal. The aim of her own writings, Sidqi says, is to simplify and clarify the ʿulamaʾs complex studies of the miracle of the Qurʾan so that every Muslim can understand. She strives to teach those who do not know, to make those who are ignorant understand, and to represent the beauty of God's creation for those who are perceptive (14, 15). Her aim is to make the Qurʾan accessible to those who have been excluded from religious knowledge.

Sidqi's connection of sensory perception to (inner) spiritual, mental perception echoes Ibn Sina's philosophy in the "al-Nafs" book of

[69] Ibid., 15.

*Kitab al-Shifa*ʾ. One of the principal differences is that she emphasizes *involuntary* "impulses" as part of humans' God-given nature (fiṭra), whereas Ibn Sina emphasizes the "voluntary" aspects of the human will as leading to virtue. This was an immensely political question during Ibn Sina's time, linked to questions of free will debated among the philosophers. Sidqi explores the involuntary aspects of bodily functions, interpreting them as aspects of God's "signs," and evidence of the miracle of creation. (In other works, though, she talks more explicitly about the voluntary aspects of spiritual practice, the training of the body, the practice of virtues, *jihād bi-l-nafs* (jihad of the self), *jihād bi-l-jism* (jihad of the body), *jihād bi-l-ḥayāt* (jihad of life), and *jihād bi-l-lisān wa-l-qalam* (jihad of tongue and pen). In contrast to Ibn Sina, Sidqi grounds inner perception concretely in the physicality of the body. These signs are manifest not just in the (wondrous and miraculous) functioning of the inner organs but also in the process of gestation—in the conception, creation, formation, and development of the embryo and the fetus. Through these images, Sidqi constructs a specifically feminine—and biological—interpretation of "inner vision" as embodied through pregnancy. This is the miracle of God's creation; it is God's signs in the body and self.

Signs in the Self

*Miracle of the Qur*ʾ*an* is structured by an extended analogy between the signs in the earth and in the self, the two parts of verses 51:20–21, and the two parts of the book. The first part of the book is dedicated to "the earth," its rotation, the "attraction" of the earth and the sun, water and wind, the atmosphere, sowing, honey and milk, cattle and animals, minerals, iron, and then "instinctual" social behavior of ants, birds, bees, dogs and cats, and even of plants and minerals. The second part of the book moves to the signs in the self. Through anthropomorphic alignments, everything is created in pairs (positive and negative of electricity; male and female in people, animals, and plants). The forces of attraction (of gravity, electricity) are both "in us and around us"; instincts (*gharā*ʾ*iz*) of humans are paralleled with those in plants, insects, and animals. One of the first chapters, entitled "The Earth," epitomizes these analogies between the earth and the self (or spirit): "The earth is the origin of our existence, from her dirt and her water we were created. The earth is our mother. In her tender breast we live and from her water and fields we drink and eat. The earth is our destiny. To her we return dust disintegrating into her dust" (19). In Sidqi's earlier work, she describes Eve as coming from the (masculine) mud of Adam.

In *Miracle of the Qur'an,* though, she embraces an explicitly feminine vision of a mother earth, an analogy that becomes almost allegorical in nature, extended over the course of the entire book as an exegesis of verses 51:20–21. Her chapter on "Sowing," for example, begins with a verse from the Qur'an elaborating this analogy: "And you see that the earth is lifeless, but if we sent down water on her, she would tremble, grow, and make sprout from every mate a wonder" (22:5). Sidqi leaves out the first part of this verse, but it speaks—silently and implicitly—to her overall argument. She will return to this unspoken part of the verse, explicitly, in the second part of the book on the self and spirit. The verse encapsulates the analogy between earth and mother, suggesting the anthropomorphic alignments between earth and the female body, between sowing and conceiving. But the verse also compares the cycle of life and death to the resurrection, making the growing seeds in the earth and in the belly a taste of the next life.

> O people, if you doubt the resurrection, indeed we created you from dust, then from a drop, then from a clinging clot, then from flesh formed and unformed in order that we show you and settle in wombs what we want for a specified term, then we bring you forth a child, then the strongest of you reach maturity and among you are those who pass away and among you those who reach the most decrepit age so that he knows after knowing, nothing. And you see the earth lifeless, but if water was sent down on her, she would tremble, grow, and make sprout from every mate a wonder. (22:5)

In the chapter on "Sowing," Sidqi's exegesis focuses on the mate (*al-zawj*). Everything on earth is made of two, male and female in plants and animals, negative and positive in electricity, attraction of gravity, and so on. These binaries structure not just Sidqi's vision of gender but also the way *Miracle of the Qur'an*—and her oeuvre as a whole—is organized. Her images naturalize motherhood as part of God's miraculous design and as one of God's signs written in the world. But she also naturalizes the heterosexual couple as a union of natural opposites, like the attraction of gravity, magnetism, or electricity.

"Knowledge of God" comes through instincts, or "impulses" (*gharā'iz*). Like in Ibn Taymiyya's *Response to the Logicians,* Sidqi uses this instinctual knowledge as a way of refuting Ibn Sina's rationalist proofs of God. Instinct—or natural impulses like electricity, magnetism, gravity, and attraction—lead God's creatures to performing their "greater function" in this world. In Sidqi's worldview, this function is, most basically, propagation of the species, reproduction, and nourishing and defending the young. In the book's section on natural impulses and instincts, every example revolves around this biological function. In her chapter on *gharā'iz*, Sidqi defines "instincts" as guidance and character, using verse 20:50 from the Qur'an to illustrate her point: "Our Lord gave each thing its character then guidance." The first "instinct" Sidqi elaborates on is in a chapter on "Motherhood." "There is sexual instinct, which is a vanquishing impulse that compels every living being to reproduction. It is the will (*irāda*) of the sublime Creator on high to fill the earth with creatures" (113). This instinct is the will of the Creator; in God's creatures it is "intuitive feelings and involuntary action" (108). It is instinct that leads to "celestial wisdom—because the Exalted created every thing and then led it to its function that it was made for." That function, Sidqi says, is "preservation of the race by striving to nourish and defend oneself and one's young with the kinds of weapons and power of inner worth that the Mighty and Sublime has bestowed" (108).

Motherhood is integral to her Islamic cosmology—as God's signs written in the Qur'an, the earth, and the female body. Her vision is not just biological but also social, as she describes hens, insects, fish, and spiders as nesting, nourishing, raising, defending, guiding, and providing for their young. Though these creatures do not understand what they do, they are able to act in intelligent ways thanks to the "instinctual knowledge with which God created" his creatures (30:30). "They strive for nourishment and reproduction without will or understanding" (111). She continues to draw on her definition of *gharīza* in the previous chapter, as character (*khulq*) and guidance (*hudā*) (20:48, 114, 115). "Motherhood" is the first impulse in her cosmology of world and self, both character and guidance to the divine order of things (*niẓām*) (118, 119).

> There is the instinct of motherhood in every female. For God on high filled to overflowing the heart of the mother with love and affection for her young, and led her to her function that He created for her, and impelled her with this instinctual love to execute what he prepared her for. She dedicates her heart and soul in defending her young, devoting herself to overseeing them and suffering with them, sacrificing with her ardent love for the sake of their salvation. For in the mother living things are created and from the mother spring all kinds. (114)

Here motherhood is a universal and biological definition of the female but also one of God's signs on earth. "Indeed the mother is a sign among God's signs on earth" (118). Reproduction, for Sidqi, is the path both to survival and to salvation. The language that Sidqi employs here is of deep religious commitment—of a mother's dedication of heart and soul, devotion, and sacrifice for the sake (*fī sabīl*) of her children's salvation. Going back to the insect's instinct for reproduction and caring for its young, she reiterates that this guidance from God is involuntary—it is an innate kind of knowledge. "Every living thing in existence flowers, reproduces, and is impelled by a compelling force, performing his humble work for the order, even if stripped of will and intellect. For who induced this living being to these involuntary works in this order? And who designed this order? And gave the command in the skies and on earth? He who put instinct in every creature, that gave everything its character, then guidance" (20:48, 118–19). She reiterates this point in a subsequent chapter on "Instinct in Plants and Minerals" (137). Even while her argument is clearly situated in the nexus of the philosophical conflict between Ibn Sina and Ibn Taymiyya, between reason and instinct in apprehending the divine, Sidqi's argument is also about the primacy of reproduction, motherhood, family, and childrearing in the divine order. It is an argument for her time, formulated in the midst of controversy over the personal status laws and debates over family planning and birth control.

Sidqi begins the second section of the book on the signs in the self and spirit with a chapter on "The Embryo." Drawing on the sura from the Qurʾan by the same name (96), she calls the embryo a "miracle" of creation. Drawing on the imagery of these verses, she compares the miracle of the Qurʾan to the miracle of (reproductive) creation. Sidqi is intent on claiming this reproductive power for women, just as she emphasizes the feminine nature of the earth's creative power (versus creation coming from the "mud" of Adam). But again, she naturalizes the heterosexual reproductive union through the conjuncture of dyadic opposites. Sidqi stresses the mutuality of the act of creation; the verse does not say that the clot comes from sperm alone. Sperm alone, she says, is incapable of causing a pregnancy just as an ovum alone is incapable of causing pregnancy. It is the sperm and the egg together, the clot that attaches to the wall of the womb, that brings about the miracle of human creation. In the next chapter on the sperm, she repeats this point, emphasizing that creation is a mixture: "We created the human from a sperm drop mixture that we may try him; and we made him hearing and seeing" (76:2). This verse sets up the argument that unfolds, of a fetus that hears and sees, that is a sign inside of the self, a sign that is real and embodied but not visible to the naked eye. This argument unfolds over a series of chapters on the clot, the sperm, and the fetus. There is also a chapter on "three darknesses" from Qurʾanic verse 39:6: "He makes you in the wombs of your mothers—a creation after a creation—in three darknesses." Sidqi interprets these three darknesses as the testicle, the ovary, and the womb. In her exegesis of 51:20–21, she appears to be saying that God's sign in the self that humans literally cannot see is the developing child in the womb. Sidqi works to construct this literal physical meaning, but one that is imbued with the spiritual connotations of God's signs. Through the semantic overlap of "signs" and "verses," the procreative capacity becomes an embodiment of the Qur'an in the female body. Sidqi interprets the inner self of Islamic spirituality in starkly biological terms, as an embryo developing in the womb.

Sidqi continues to connect sensory perception to inner spiritual seeing. In the subheadings of the chapter "The Womb," the signs are the senses: the eye, ear, nose, tongue. Further down—after the brain, muscles, and skin—she includes "touch." Human sensory perception is described through the development of the child in the womb, subsumed into the chapter on "The Womb." The senses become sublimated into the darkness of the womb, making the "eye" or sight of the child in the womb the correlate of spiritual seeing that is sight without actually seeing. This neo-Platonic, allegorical image is one Sidqi almost unconsciously constructs, rendered through structural juxtapositions and parallel images. The child in the womb embodies spiritual seeing, the inner eye, and God's signs that are palpable but hidden beneath the surface. Her interpretation of "And in yourselves. Do you not see?" becomes the sign of the miracle of (pro)creation, a sign that we can see and yet not precisely see with our actual senses. Sidqi's interpretation plays on Ibn Sina's famous formulation of the five internal senses of the nafs, of the self and spirit, that correspond to the five external senses (seeing, hearing, taste, touch, and smell). Sidqi's internal sensory realm, however, emphasizes involuntary functions (like pregnancy), in contrast to Ibn Sina's emphasis on the intellect and reason—an argument that figured prominently in debates among the philosophers about free will. Sidqi ends with short chapters on the hymen as the "divine seal," the "power of the two sexes," and finally, the "comfort" that the soul and self finds in submitting to God's will.

The significance of Sidqi's argument about the embryo lies not just in revivalists' refutations of the philosophers but also in the wide campaign for family planning launched in the 1960s, in response to what was perceived as a crisis of overpopulation.[70] In the 1961 National Charter, the Nasser government articulated its intention to develop a national family planning program. After four years of planning, nearly two thousand clinics were opened to provide contraception to Egyptian

[70] Bier, *Revolutionary Womanhood*, 123.

women. Government institutions mobilized to provide the infrastructure necessary for providing these services. The Ministry of Social Affairs established the Population and Family Planning Division, and the Ministry of Public Health began providing contraception in its health centers. In 1965 Nasser established a Supreme Council for Family Planning, charged with developing a national plan for family planning services.[71] During this time there was vigorous public debate over the nature of family planning, including the publication of a number of books on Islamic (and Christian) views on family planning.[72] Stances on the permissibility of birth control in Islamic practice varied widely within both the religiously oriented literature and the policy-oriented literature. As Laura Bier observes, both secular and religious writings on the subject shared assumptions about "women's bodies as relational and reproductive." The question of choice in the matter of reproduction was not necessarily wielded by a "rational, self-aware subject acting in her own bounded self-interest. Choice instead was to be exercised within the boundaries of marital, heterosexual relations and in the interest of the health and well-being of the family and the nation."[73] Sidqi's writings raise the question of choice but subsume it within a larger design of (involuntary) impulses, instincts, and attractions and within the discipline of what she sees as God's commands. Though she does not explicitly address questions of family planning, Sidqi's writings sanctify a family structured around the nexus of two spouses (two parents) and children. She effectively makes the nuclear family a unit of God's design, largely eschewing questions of polygamy and the extended family. Her sermons repeatedly address questions of property, money, thrift, and spending within discussions of virtue, making clear that how to ethically manage money and property is among the issues confronting this Islamic family. These values reflect Sidqi's own upper-middle-class bourgeois status, as the daughter of a family of pashas, the wife of a doctor, living in the Cairo neighborhoods of Zamalek and Garden City, and summering in Alexandria.

Sidqi's theology of biological reproduction culminates in her description of an inner self epitomizing God's signs "in yourselves." Through this vision she constructs a centered interiority for the female subject,

[71] Ibid., 215n19.

[72] See, for example, Abu al-Wafa' Maraghi, *Mabadi' al-Islam fi Tanzim al-Usra* (Cairo: al-Majlis al-A'la li-l-Shu'un al-Islamiyya, 1962); Ahmad Sharabasi, *al-Din wa-Tanzim al-Usra* (Cairo: Dar wa-Matabi' al-Sha'b, 1965); Ahmad Muhammad Khalifa, *Ra'y Muwatin fi Tanzim al-Usra* (Cairo, 1966); Coptic Church, *Tanzim al-Usra: Wijhat Nazar Masihiyya* (Cairo: Lajnat al-Usra, Usqufiyyat al-Khadamat al-'Amma wa-l-Ijtima'iyya, Batriyarkiyyat al-Aqbat al-Urthuduks, 1970).

[73] Bier, *Revolutionary Womanhood*, 135.

one rooted firmly in the biological capacity for reproduction. Instead of a self split into body and soul (or self and child), Sidqi imagines a self centered and anchored in the divine order, produced through the harmonious convergence of opposites, and manifest in the sign in the self. Her biological vision of the female body is borne out by a social vision of the family in Sidqi's subsequent works, an elucidation of the family as a pillar of Islam that she first broaches in *Grace of the Qur'an*. The contours of her social ideology are elucidated most clearly in her 1975 booklet *al-Jihad fi Sabil Allah* (Jihad for the Sake of God), which she dedicates, in her "Author's Word," to "the community of jihad for the sake of God," using the word *jamāʿa* for community, suggesting not just Jamaʿat Ansar al-Sunna al-Muhammadiyya but also the range of Islamic groups (*jamāʿāt islāmiyya*) that constitute the Islamic movement as a whole. But she also dedicates the book

> to my pious believing children, grandchildren, and friends. I present to them this treatise so that we understand and we know the meanings and kinds of jihad, and we execute our duty as is wanted and we struggle in God for the truth of jihad as God commanded. I explain and clarify the greatest jihad and that is: the upbringing of children to know God and love him and obey him. For this jihad prepares an army that fights oppression and corruption and spreads the religion of Islam and summons to all goodness, makes virtue victorious, and saves society form all evil. To jihad, o you Muslim, hasten to save your brother from the evil of himself and others . . . try to awaken him from his stupor.

The final chapters of the work move from "The Upbringing of Children Is Jihad" to "Religious Upbringing," "The Danger of Childhood," and "The Wise Mother and the Criminal Mother." "Indeed, bringing up children with a religious upbringing," Sidqi writes, "is jihad for the sake of God, a sacred duty God on high imposed on every Muslim. . . . The only thing that purifies the self and your people . . . is a sound upbringing, the discipline of character with learning the ethics of the Quran, and habituating them to submitting (*ṭāʿa*) to God's commands" (23). Here she reiterates the point in the "Author's Word" that "religious upbringing prepares an army for jihad. It is wisdom, an art, and a long arduous jihad. The upbringing of children is bodily and spiritual. Every mother, whether human or animal, is skilled (*atqanat*: a loan word from the Greek techne) in the bodily upbringing, because God on high created in every female instinct" (23). Sidqi here describes wisdom, discipline, and art and also an innate, instinctual skill in every woman that prepares her for educating children. She uses instinct, or fiṭra, here like Bint al-Shatiʾ uses the same concept with respect to literature. It is an innate, specialized knowledge that gives her a special place in the techne of God's design. In the next chapter on "Religious Upbringing," she reiterates the expertise, wisdom, and art that come with "educating the child's self." Only "a wise expert of life" knows such an art, someone who "has seen life situations and from them, what awakens the child's insight, develops his acumen. Only a pious believer can succeed in this great task, one who enlightens the heart of his child with the light of the Qurʾan and disciplines him with its adab. For the basis of upbringing and discipline is religion" (26).

Family and Motherhood: A Qurʾanic Vision

Sidqi lays out her vision of the family in her first full-length book, a collection of sermons entitled *Grace of the Qurʾan*. The first part of the book is dedicated to a series of sermons on the five pillars of ritualistic practice in Islam: belief, prayer, alms, fasting, and hajj. In addition to these sermons, there are also chapters on key virtues in Islamic ethics, such as mercy and patience. Nestled within these are sermons on "the two parents," "the two spouses," "money and children," and "desire/love/and affection," sermons that situate the social construction of the family side by side with the most basic ritual practices in Islam (*ʿibādāt*). Even though the family and the *ʿibādāt* are hardly of equal weight in Islamic ethics (family being in the realm of *muʿāmalāt*), juxtaposing them has the effect of making the family, its spouses, parents, children, property, and desire parallel to Islam's core ritual practices. The themes that Sidqi explores in these chapters, of an ontological binary between the sexes and between the two "mates," forms the crux of her cosmology in *Miracle of the Qurʾan*. *Al-zawjān* (the pair, the couple, the mates) structures her entire corpus but also situates her in a genealogy of thought that raises the heterosexual couple to an ontological status, like in the work of ʿAli ʿAbd al-Wahid Wafi, Sayyid Qutb, Bint al-Shatiʾ, Muhammad ʿImara, and Muhammad Jalal Kishk. Moreover, Sidqi's writings inform a later generation of revivalists thinkers, especially her ideas on childrearing as a form of "women's jihad." Like these other Islamic thinkers, she asserts gender equality between the sexes, equivalent rights and duties, even as she asserts male guardianship over women. Her emphasis on this guardianship as guidance and discipline, as well as "leadership" (*riyāsa*), would be further taken up in the writings of Heba Raouf Ezzat as a political model of just rule (see chapter 6). This leadership, Sidqi says, is because "God on high preferred man over woman in creation, and gave him what he did not give her of strength of body and courage of heart. He is more capable in earning, protecting, and defending his people and his nation."[74] This leadership is physical, familial, communal, and political. In this argument, she draws on verse 4:34 of the Qur'an, which is the subject of an extended exegesis in her sermon/chapter on "the two mates." Like Wafi, Qutb, Bint al-Shati', Kishk, ʿImara, and other revivalist writers after her, Sidqi begins from the premise of equality between the sexes. Like these other writers, she quotes 4:1, "O people, revere your Lord that created you from one soul and created from it her mate," as evidence of an ontological equality of creation and of being. She reiterates this point by saying that Eve was made from the soul of Adam, "not from dust other than his dust. And with this she carries natural elements that he carries, and equals him with respect to her humanness and her humanity" (210). Sidqi quotes verses 30:20–21: "And among His signs are that He created you from dust and then you were humans scattered. And among His signs are that He created mates from among yourselves that you may find tranquility in them. And He made between you affection (*mawadda*) and compassion." In the later *Miracle of the Qur'an*, she moves away from Eve (and woman) as a derivative creation, instead investing the female body with the power of creation and making it one of God's signs.

Drawing on verse 4:21, which mentions a heavy covenant (*mīthāq ghalīẓ*) based on the "closing of space" (*afḍā*: "emptying") between a man and a woman,[75] Sidqi interprets this covenant as a "closing of space between two hearts." Here her emphasis is on mawadda as love (*ḥubb*) and affection. To express this, she uses the verbal form of mutual reciprocity (VIth), mutual understanding (*tafāhum*), mutual embrace (*taʿānuq*), and mutual familiarity (*ta'āluf*). This "closing of space" is an embrace between two souls, an understanding between two intellects, and harmonization between two selves, not only contact between two bodies. In her exegesis she describes this love as one heart comforting another, a "friend" sharing feelings, pains, and the secrets within his breast, "for nothing connects one heart to another, and speaks of intimate connection (*al-i'tilāf*) and love, like the closing of space between one heart and another, and one heart listening to the other." The love here becomes the locus of the "sacred covenant" between man and woman, in addition to its bodily manifestation in the sex act.

[74] Sidqi, *Niʿmat al-Qur'an*, 216.

[75] Muhammad ʿAbduh calls this closing of space between mates "an intuitive contract (*mithāq fiṭrī*) that is among the most sacred of contracts and most intensely binding." ʿImara, *al-Islam wa-l-Mar'a fi Ra'y al-Imam Muhammad ʿAbduh*, 75–76. See chapter 6 for a discussion of 4:21.

"Mawadda is love and desire together," she says, "and desire is arousal. For those who love, they must be bound to the person they love spiritually and bodily, because the human being is made of body and soul." Even though she identifies "strong instinctual attraction" between the two mates as the "first basis of the relationship between them," this attraction must be rooted in love, with tenderness, compassion, affection, and desire. Tenderness (*ḥanān*: also "piety") and desire are the "signs of love that connect each mate with the other." The body—sight, insight, and the eye, "the source of pleasure"—must be attuned to these "sacred feelings for the wisdom of God" (212). Verse 30:21 may be small in size, but it is great in meaning, she says. "The verse commands that the two spouses share the mutual compassion and understanding that befits their humanity, and it stamps spiritual significance on the sheer animal meaning between the two sexes." Its goal "is not only the body's happiness but the happiness of the mind that directs the human being to what makes the family happy. And with that, makes humanity happy" (214).

Out of these reflections on sacred love of body and soul between a husband and wife, assertions of equal origins and equal humanity, reciprocity and mutuality, comes a social vision of gendered "rights and responsibilities" in the family (214). Here Sidqi moves on to the two classic verses of inequality between the genders in the Qurʾan, 2:228 and 4:34, and makes these the structuring principle of men's leadership and guardianship over women but also, seemingly paradoxically, of "equal rights and duties." Citing verse 2:228, "They [women] have rights similar to the rights against them and men are a degree above them," she comments that

> this generous verse and compassionate word balances the rights and duties between men and women. . . . They each have rights just as each of them has duties toward the other, then the man is distinguished by a degree. And that degree of the man over the woman is the degree of guardianship (*qiwāma*), because the man and woman are equal in everything and they are equivalent, and the rights between them are reciprocal just like the duties. They are similar in rights just as the two of them are similar in their self, feelings, and intellect. But that degree of the man over the woman, it is the degree of guardianship (*wilāya*), expenditure, protection (*riʿāya*), and custodianship (*ḥiyāṭa*), not a degree of tyranny, oppression, despotism, or abuse. (215)

Sidqi ties the "degree" of 2:228 to the duty of financial maintenance and guardianship (*qiwāma*) in 4:34, reiterating the point made by Bint al-Shati''s in "The Islamic Understanding of Women's Liberation" that the degree is "guardianship" (12). Future Islamic thinkers like Heba Raouf Ezzat, still only three years old when Sidqi published these words, took these ideas and expanded them into a theory of gendered rights and responsibilities in Islamic politics. Men are responsible not just for financial maintenance (for "spending of their means" to support women as verse 4:34 says) but also for punishments (*ʿawāqib*) and surveillance (*raqāba*), guiding (*irshād*) members of the family, and disciplining (*tahdhīb*) and educating (tarbiya) them. In *From the Education of the Qurʾan*, this leadership becomes a model of compassion, fairness, and justice in politics and government, extending out of the family to the regulation of society as a whole. Sidqi also turns to the issue of the "rebellious wife," the woman who refuses to obey her husband, the subject raised in the personal status debates over *bayt al-ṭāʿa*. (See chapter 1 on legal contestations over a wife's forcible return to the household.) It is the man's duty, she says, to make the woman obey, to correct her in any way that he can, "like God commanded him to do" (220). "The weak man commanded by his wife angers God . . . the husband leads her astray with his weakness and corrupts her" (220–21). Man leads and is not led; otherwise he is not a believer. "The woman who violates the man's rights [to wifely obedience] considers herself above him and tries to be above her leader, but she also considers herself above her nature. She is like those who rebel against the earth, violating uprightness" (217).

Conclusion

Sidqi's biological, physical vision of attraction between spouses, between man and woman, is rooted in the discursive terrain of the Qurʾan. The correct embodiment of Qurʾanic righteousness depends on a proper attunement of the senses and desire itself to goodness. Desire, she says, is passion for the self and its appetite; it is the portal to both good and evil. If the self/soul of the believer is pious, then the self desires goodness and what God loves. As the Prophet said, "Not one of you believes without his desire being in accordance with what came down" (279). This final chapter of *Grace of the Qurʾan* focuses on desire leading astray, in contradistinction to the desire between the spouses that makes their bodies, minds, families, and all humanity glad. Those whose desires lead astray have not properly attuned their senses to God's message, she says. "Their ears are closed to God's message and they did not hear it; their sight blinded to his signs" (284). Sidqi's hermeneutics of the senses—of the visible and invisible world, of seeing, hearing, and understanding the divine—interpret the soul as profoundly embodied. Her interpretations grow out of the Qurʾan, the classical literature on the proper bodily execution of Islamic adab (ethics, conduct, comportment), philosophical writings on the soul and senses, and the revivalist tradition associated with Ibn Taymiyya. Her writings reorient these discursive strains around the female body, as well as feminine spheres of influence. They imagine the female body as incarnating God's signs and God's verses, constructing a profoundly gendered vision of women's Islamic subjectivity. Sidqi formulated this perspective in the late 1960s and early 1970s, when university demonstrations formed the first seeds of revivalist mobilization, an awakening that would soon spill into other domains of public life. In Sidqi's writings we see the discursive construction of a gendered Islamic self and soul, as well as an Islamic body. This discourse of gendered subjectivities drew on classical sources reinterpreted anew, accompanied by a mass return to veiling on university campuses and elsewhere in public life.[76] Moreover, Sidqi brings what Talal Asad calls "aesthetic self-invention" to develop "a new kind of subjectivity . . . a concept of 'the subject' that has a new grammar."[77] Sidqi's aesthetics have produced a new visual grammar for Islamic modernity, where the inner eye orients body and soul to God's signs.

In Sidqi's contribution, a certain literary license leads her to put the womb at the center of the divine order, draw analogies (and even allegories) between procreation and divine creation, make the couple and family a pillar of Islam, and interpret tarbiya—in its sense of both discipline and education—as a form of jihad. Through a new kind of Islamic preaching and writing, she prescribes a particular kind of Islamic sensibility and Islamic community. The intimacy with which Sidqi speaks and writes, her accessible voice and style, her address to a feminine audience, her spiritual valuation of female anatomy and biological processes, and her emphasis on an embodied Islam speak to her vast audience, which has extended to Turkey, Saudi Arabia, Iran, and Indonesia. By realizing her own spiritual vision, she saw within herself the signs of God's grace (*niʿma*), signs that she struggled to embody in both her words and her writings.

[76] Radwan, *Bahth Zahirat al-Hijab*, 1982; Arlene Elowe MacLeod, *Accommodating Protest: Working Women, the New Veiling, and Change in Cairo* (New York: Columbia University Press, 1991); Sherifa Zuhur, *Revealing Reveiling: Islamist Gender Ideology in Contemporary Egypt* (Albany: SUNY Press, 1992); Mahmood, *Politics of Piety*.

[77] Asad, *Formations of the Secular*, 225.

CHAPTER 4

Covering in the Public Eye

Visualizing the Inner I

Samah Hasan Maraʿi's book *Yaqazat al-ʿIffa: Qissat Rihlati min al-Sufur ila al-Hijab* (The Awakening of Modesty: The Story of My Journey from Unveiling to Veiling, 2004) draws on core terms and concepts from revivalist narratives about the journey to veiling. The book's title, *Yaqazat al-ʿIffa*, intimates a watchful vigilance about bodily virtue, *ʿiffa* meaning restraint, chastity, purity, and abstinence from "things that should be sacred or inviolable."[1]

Maraʿi opens with a "word of thanks" to her spiritual guide, Mahdi al-Munawwari, for "extending the hand of guidance, the hand of truth, the hand of tolerance to me at a time that I was oppressing myself, drowning in my ignorance and dissoluteness." Preaching on the tombs of martyrs in southern Lebanon during the month of ʿAshura, he delivered a sermon on "woman and the hijab" that inspired her to take the veil.[2] When Maraʿi approached him about the subject of her veiling, with the aim of thanking him ("for what he commanded me to do of right and forbade me to do of wrong"), "he insisted that I thank him by writing the story of my taking the hijab and in doing so, narrate the details of my covering and my feelings afterward" (12). The book is a testimony—through a personal account of taking the veil—of a return to Islam, "a revival of religious feelings," and "an awakening of consciousness" (24, 63). This narrative, and others of this genre, describe the experience of taking the veil through personal testimonies of feelings, emotions, and sensations, an experience that awakens both body and soul from spiritual lassitude. Like other writings of the genre, Maraʿi structures the narrative in quasi-autobiographical terms as a

[1] Lane, *Arabic-English Lexicon*, 2088. For an impressive discussion of the connection between the sacred (*ḥarām*), the forbidden (*ḥarām*), women (*ḥarīm*), and veiling (*ḥijāb, sitr*), see El Guindi, *Veil*, 82–96.

[2] Maraʿi, *Yaqazat al-ʿIffa*, 28–35.

Safinaz Kazim on the cover of her book *Rumantikiyyat,* published in 1970, just before she went on the hajj and took the veil. Photograph by Muhammad Sabri; design by Hilmi al-Tuni.

life story, beginning with her childhood and upbringing and culminating with a "reckoning"—"an accounting of the self that revived my conscience"—at the moment that she takes the hijab. Standing in front of the mirror looking at herself, she describes a "latent force" in her self awakened through her "new appearance," a flood of emotions that she calls a "passion (*ʿishq*)" for a "living Islam and an articulated Qurʾan" (57, 59).

This chapter looks at autobiographical testimonies that construct a pious self by narrating the experience of taking the veil. *Yaqazat al-ʿIffa* is a later exemplar of narratives detailing the "return to veiling." The text revisits, recycles, and reinhabits key motifs and images from earlier veiling narratives, a genre of autobiographical writing that first emerged in Egypt in the 1980s and 1990s.[3] The surge in these testimonies began with personalities working in visual cultural media like television, film, and theater, by women who began veiling in the public eye and wrote detailed accounts of their experiences. These film and television stars became known as *fannānāt islāmiyyāt* (Islamic artists), dazzling the entertainment industry with stories of their conversions. Their striking visual transformations, narrated through textual imagery, dramatized the revival of their religiosity for mass audiences eager for news about these celebrities. At the juncture of visual and print media emerged vivid images of sex symbols in their new hijabs, sometimes accompanied by photographs of the stars before and after, still in full makeup, with shaped eyebrows, ornate jewelry, and elaborate head coverings. The images of these repentant stars, with their dreamy good looks, now in veils but still camera ready, are as illustrative of their journey as the narratives themselves, encapsulating a self and a life in the sign and motif of the hijab.

I explore the life and writings of three main personalities who contributed to shaping an aesthetics of veiling in disparate but analogous ways. In their writings and their performances of a public self, these writers construct a sense of the psychic space that the outward sign of the veil helps cultivate. This psychic space, this spiritual interiority, is created by veiling but also by the words, discourses, narratives, and images of the veil in public culture and public circulation. Each writer has been profoundly invested in the politics of performance—in television (Kariman Hamza), film (Shams al-Barudi), and theater and cultural criticism (Safinaz Kazim). I focus on these three early exemplars

[3] "Return to veiling" is a stock phrase that these narratives and the accompanying religious literature repeatedly use. Muhammad Ibn Ismaʿil detailed the return to veiling in a massive, three-volume tome republished a number of times by different presses in different forms. Ibn Ismaʿil, *ʿAwdat al-Hijab*, 1984; Ibn Ismaʿil, *ʿAwdat al-Hijab*, 1988; Ibn Ismaʿil, *Maʿrakat al-Hijab wa-l-Sufur*.

that were pivotal in formulating the ideological and conceptual contours of the genre. They set down motifs and described psychic transformations that would become classic signposts on the path to veiling. Their narratives envisioned new kinds of Islamic media in which the visual signifier of the veil would become ascendant. They not only made a new kind of veiling highly visible but also gave voice to the religiosity that the veil helps cultivate, making it come alive through their vivid dramatizations. Their creative contributions revolutionized the field of Islamic cultural production as they ventured into unexplored territory (especially in forging Islamic television and film) and reenvisioned other genres like pilgrimage travelogues, narratives of Sufi spiritual transformations, prison memoirs, poetry, biography, and autobiography. At a time when women's autobiography was still a fledgling genre in Arabic literary production, they pulled a genre known for its production of a secular (male) individualism into the service of a female-centered revivalist religiosity and subjectivity. Each of these women writes Islamic scripts of veiling onto her body, reviving and reinterpreting traditional concepts through her own creative production that plays out in print, television, film, and the public sphere. The hijab becomes a stage—or a screen—on which she dramatizes her own starring role in the revival of religious sensibilities.

I examine the critical role that the "semiotic ideology" of the hijab has played in the "representational economy" of the revival.[4] Veiling narratives helped usher in an Islamic media—and an Islamic art—as tools for fostering Islamic sensibilities and lifestyles in an age of economic liberalization and for disseminating the news of these revived religious commitments. "Semiotic ideologies," Webb Keane argues in *Christian Moderns*, enable language to capture words and objects in the same frame. He describes how theological views draw lines between "animate subjects and inanimate objects" and in so doing make assumptions about the preconditions of moral action. Veiling narratives reassert the hijab as a primary indicator of Islamic morality, making it a precondition for the exercise of Islamic piety, without which a woman is nakedly vulnerable to moral exploitation and degradation. A certain class status has historically been part of the semiotic ideology of veiling and seclusion. These narratives reinterpret veiling as indicators of a new kind of class status, through new sets of images and veils

[4] Webb Keane, *Christian Moderns: Freedom and Fetish in the Mission Encounter* (Berkeley: University of California Press, 2007), 17; Jeanette S. Jouili, "Pious Practice and Secular Constraints: Women in the Islamic Revival in France and Germany" (forthcoming), 2–3. See his introduction on "Religion's Reach" and Jouili's chapter on "Learning Piety."

that intimate subjects revived by an Islamic awakening.[5] Veiling is both an expression of active piety and a tool for cultivating this piety, piety propagated through public images of private faith.

In the 1970s and 1980s, Islamic knowledge production was undergoing a radical transformation, due partly to the rise of new media but also to Anwar Sadat's political and economic liberalization, which helped foster Islamic cultural production. A proliferating series of veiling narratives accompanied the return to veiling that began in the early 1970s, paralleling an exponential rise in Islamic textual production and print Islam. Accompanying this textual production was a vast polemical literature by revivalist writers describing—and arguing for—the return to veiling.[6] Scholars trace the stirrings of the new veiling to 1974, the same year that Anwar Sadat began his campaign of economic liberalization, the *infitāḥ* (Open Door Economic Policy). One of the (perhaps unintended) consequences of Sadat's economic and political liberalization was the flourishing of Islamic cultural and intellectual production, an Islamic public sphere that gave expression to and helped precipitate the revival.[7] Both Kariman Hamza and Safinaz Kazim went on pilgrimage and took the veil in 1971 and 1972, but they would not publish their books on veiling until 1981 and 1982, respectively, when women were returning to veiling en masse and as an Islamic press began flourishing. The circulation of veiling narratives was made possible by the institutional infrastructure of an emergent Islamic publishing industry that catered an expanding market and audience for religious materials.

Scholarly analyses connect the new veiling to the rise of women in public space: in particular, the jump in the number of women enrolled in public education and working in public employment.[8] Early scholarship interprets veiling as a rejection of the growing spirit of materialism and consumerism, reflecting a negative attitude toward "secularized

[5] Soraya Hajjaji-Jarrah, "Women's Modesty in Qur'an Commentaries: The Founding Discourse," in *The Muslim Veil in North America: Issues and Debates*, ed. Sajida Sultana Alvi, Sheila McDonough, and Homa Hoodfar (Toronto: Women's Press, 2003).

[6] Saqr, *al-Hijab wa-ʿAmal al-Marʾa*; Ibn Ismaʿil, *ʿAwdat al-Hijab*, 1984; Shalabi and Khatib, *Fi Masʾalat al-Sufur wa-l-Hijab*; Ibn Baz, *al-Hijab wa-l-Sufur fi al-Kitab wa-l-Sunna*; Ibn Baz and ʿUthaymin, *Risalatan fi al-Hijab*; Ibn ʿUthaymin, *al-Marʾa al-Muslima*; ʿAmili, *Niʿmat al-Hijab fi al-Islam.*

[7] Eickelman and Anderson, "Redefining Muslim Publics"; Bayat, *Making Islam Democratic*, 137; Hirschkind, *Ethical Soundscape*, 55.

[8] El Guindi, "Veiling Infitah with Muslim Ethic"; Radwan, *Bahth Zahirat al-Hijab*, 1982; Radwan, *Bahth Zahirat al-Hijab*, 1984; MacLeod, *Accommodating Protest*; Zuhur, *Revealing Reveiling.* In the 1960s the rate of increase of female students was about 3,100 a year, but it jumped to 6,500 in 1968 and to 14,780 in 1973. The argument about the correlation between women's movement into public space and the donning of the veil is MacLeod's thesis in *Accommodating Protest.*

development and *infitāḥ*, which open the door of economic policy, but also allow moral laxity, opportunistic westernism, and capitalistic materialism to enter and disrupt Egyptian society," as Fadwa El Guindi writes in her famous article on veiling and structural adjustment.[9] Similarly, in Zaynab Radwan's massive study of veiling among university and professional women, Radwan interprets the revival as a spiritualist movement seeking an "escape from the crisis of consumerist values imposed by society" and "an awakening that tries to preserve the purity of the national body in the face of consumerism through rejection or protest."[10] But as El Guindi so eloquently argues, veiling was also a means of ethically coping with the effects of rapid development and with middle-class women's increasing circulation in public space. More recent analyses have interpreted veiling *not* as "located in a contestatory space outside circuits of capitalist consumption, but rather [as] created by such circuits."[11] Veiling became a means of visibly Islamicizing cultural production in the public sphere, cultural production that circulated the sign of the veil as indicative of new kinds of religiosity.

Veiling narratives played a catalytic role in the rise of a new Islamic visual media that acted in tandem with intellectual and cultural discursive production. So many of these testimonies talk about a "vision" of Islam—in dreams, for example—an inner experience manifest in the material object of the veil and relayed through the telling of the story behind the hijab. This new generation of veiling narratives drew on Niʿmat Sidqi's *al-Tabarruj* as a model: its autobiographical elements (a "sick" self and spirit, a transformative experience of the pilgrimage, an illuminating spiritual guide) and its focus on the faculty of seeing for cultivating an inner spirituality and an inner, sacred self. These testimonies speak of *ruʾya*, spiritual visions that inspire eruptions of affect, passion, weeping, and mystical *jouissance*. The visions awaken the women's "Islamic depths," uncover a "latent force" and a "dormant self," an "instinct" that God Himself put in the human breast.[12] Their stories—as well as their dream visions, spiritual insights, and veiling—bear witness to a true Islamic self that these narratives not only make

[9] El Guindi, "Veiling Infitah with Muslim Ethic," 476.

[10] Radwan, *Bahth Zahirat al-Hijab*, 1982, 3; Radwan, *Bahth Zahirat al-Hijab*, 1984, 8.

[11] Moll, "Islamic Televangelism," 5; Banu Gökarıksel and Anna J Secor, "New Transnational Geographies of Islamism, Capitalism and Subjectivity: The Veiling-Fashion Industry in Turkey," *Area* 41, no. 1 (2009): 6–18; Carla Jones, "Images of Desire: Creating Virtue and Value in an Indonesian Islamic Lifestyle Magazine," *Journal of Middle East Women's Studies* 6, no. 3 (Fall 2010): 91–117; Reina Lewis, "Marketing Muslim Lifestyle: A New Media Genre," *Journal of Middle East Women's Studies* 6, no. 3 (Fall 2010): 58–90.

[12] "This life that was dormant in me": Hamza, *Rihlati min al-Sufur ila al-Hijab*, 31–32; "fiṭra": Shams al-Barudi, *Rihlati min al-Zulumat ila al-Nur* (Mansura: Dar al-Wafa li-l-Tibaʿa, 1988), 22; "Islamic depth" and "latent force": Maraʿi, *Yaqazat al-ʿIffa*, 22, 57.

visible but bring into being. Through visible transformations of inward dispositions, the unseen becomes seen and in doing so enacts "a representational subject."[13] "Veiling," the sociologist Fedwa El Guindi observes, "is privacy's visual metaphor."[14]

In the 1970s and 1980s, Islamic thinkers grappled with how to deal with new media and the politics of visuality. Women's visibility played a key role in Islamicizing visual media through their own textual accounts as well as through their prominence on the screen, large and small. Eloquent spokeswomen and *duʿāt* (callers to Islam), they have been elegant models for the new Islamic fashion (*al-mūda al-islāmiyya*). Their life stories have served pedagogical ends of direction and instruction, of a path from and a path to, a "before" and an "after." Their narratives formulate an Islamic aesthetic, an Islamic art (*fann islāmī*), one that awakens religious sensibilities that help structure an ethical self. In an article on the "political economy of vision," Rey Chow writes that "the ever-expanding capacities for seeing and, with them, the infinite transmigrations and transmutations of cultures . . . into commodified electronic images are part and parcel of a dominant global regime of value making that is as utterly ruthless as it is utterly creative."[15] The hijab has been integral to a "regime of visuality" that accompanied an "epistemic 'tectonic shift' in cultural logics the world" thanks to the impact of the cinema as a new cultural realm. This visuality "sent shock waves through other cultural fields . . . altering their cultural status," transforming not just literature in this case but also religious *knowledge*.[16]

Taking the veil inspires (or is inspired by) a self-reflexivity that structures these narratives, as the writers look at their lives before the hijab and the person they have become after. They describe looking in the mirror at themselves, reflecting on their appearance, but there are also vivid moments contemplating how they are seen by others and by society, on film and in the hijab, in public and in private. ("His gaze fell on my exposed arms . . . and I felt as if a whip lashed me hard on my exposed arms.")[17] The new respect that they enjoy in

[13] Moll, "Islamic Televangelism," 22. In Moll's impressive analysis of the politics of seeing in contemporary Islamic visual culture, she writes, "The performance of representation here makes visible and present the invisible and absent and in doing so enacts it as a representation subject . . . the 'sacred event' here becomes the visible transformation of inward dispositions that is effected through these performances."

[14] El Guindi, *Veil*, 96.

[15] Rey Chow, *Sentimental Fabulations, Contemporary Chinese Films: Attachment in the Age of Global Visibility* (New York: Columbia University Press, 2007), 165.

[16] Rey Chow, *The Rey Chow Reader*, ed. Paul Bowman (New York: Columbia University Press, 2010).

[17] Hamza, *Rihlati min al-Sufur ila al-Hijab*, 158.

others' eyes becomes the source of social esteem. Even the etymology of the word respect suggests that reflexivity, of self-regard. In Arabic the word *iḥtirām* suggests the preservation of sanctity and sacredness, of that which is *ḥarām*, a word that also refers to women and wives.[18] These writers reflect on their "I" through the eye of the media—news, visual, television, film, print, and digital—where their words and images are constantly circulated, appear and reappear, are produced and reproduced, are reflected and refracted. Dramatic and emotional performances of Islamic affect—like sobbing on the pilgrimage—revive belief and renew Islamic commitments. These experiences are literally relived as their authors look back on them through their retelling.

The bodily act of veiling, and of practicing religious virtues, has been interpreted as the means of constructing an architecture of the self. "Spiritual exercises" foster belief and conviction as much as an inner self and spirit (nafs). This kind of self-cultivation entails an "entire conceptualization of the role the body plays in the making of the self," Saba Mahmood observes in her analyses of women's piety in revivalist Egypt. In this conceptualization, "the outward behavior of the body constitutes both the potentiality and the means through which interiority is realized."[19] But it is not just the "external" practice of the body that helps fashion an internal self—they are practices scripted by the Islamic discursive tradition. This tradition is prominently represented in all the writings, through Islamic authorities that underpin the narratives and act as characters and spiritual guides in the stories. Moreover, lengthy excerpts from their writings are reproduced in large chunks in the middle of the narratives; introductions and conclusions bookend the texts, serving as stamps of approval; and the opinions of authoritative reformers like Ibn Taymiyya, Hasan al-Banna, and Muhammad Albani are appended to the testimonies.[20] These authorities

[18] For an amazing discussion of the relationship between sanctity, reserve, and respect and veiling, see El Guindi, *Veil*, 82–96. El Guindi connects *ḥarām* (that which is forbidden), *al-ḥaram al-sharīf* of Mecca's Great Mosque, *iḥrām* (the state of ritual purity for pilgrims involving special dress), *ḥurma* (honor), *iḥtirām* (respect), and *harīm*, "women as sanctuary." The connection between veiling and the sanctuary in Mecca (which is "dressed like a bride") is key to veiling narratives, with pilgrimage representing the culmination of the narrators' spiritual journeys.

[19] Mahmood, *Politics of Piety*, 121–22, 159.

[20] Hamza, *Rihlati min al-Sufur ila al-Hijab*; Ilham Abu Suf, *Fannanat Mutahajjibat* (Beirut: Dar al-Qadiri, 1993); Malti-Douglas, *Medicines of the Soul*, 44–46, 68; Maraʿi, *Yaqazat al-ʿIffa*; Rida Muhammad Shaʿban, *ʿAmr Khalid Shahid ʿala Hijab al-Fannanat wa-Iʿtizal al-Nujum* (Cairo: Dar Hiwar li-l-Nashr wa-l-Tawziʿ, 2007). Of this bookending of Hamza's text, and of the interpenetration of ʿAbd al-Halim Mahmud's texts in Hamza's testimony, Malti-Douglas stresses the "importance of the external" but also of embodying textual discourses in the self. Kariman realizes that "her own behavior must be a Qurʾan," as she

also serve another function: guiding their subjects to states of blissful repose. The testimonies use the word *sakan* to describe this inner tranquility and peace, a term that connotes a kind of *habitus*, a homelike space, but also the love and compassion found between mates (30:21). Taking the veil becomes a process of de-alienation and refamiliarization as the writers take on the mantle of Islamic doctrine and slough off accretions of foreign ideological systems alien to this self. They do so by assuming the mantle of revivalist rhetoric about the importance of veiling and women's bodies to the reproduction of the Islamic body politic.

The veiling narratives draw extensively on the Islamic discursive tradition to cultivate a kind of subjective interiority: they experience mystical dream visions resonant with Sufism, transformations through ritual worship (particularly the pilgrimage), and inner journeys that lead to states of peace and enlightenment, journeys that are oftentimes at once intellectual and emotional. As Talal Asad observes in *Formations of the Secular*, modernity did not introduce subjective interiority into Islam: "Subjective interiority has always been recognized in Islamic tradition—in ritual worship (*ʿibādāt*) as well as in mysticism (*taṣawwuf*). What modernity does bring in is a new *kind* of subjectivity, one that is appropriate to ethical autonomy and aesthetic self-invention—a concept of the subject that has a new grammar."[21] I focus on this aesthetic self-invention, formulated through new veiling fashions, new kinds of visual representation in Islam, new scripts and narratives. The writers literally develop their own lexicon connected to the experience of veiling, of Islamic artists (*fannānāt islāmiyyat*) that withdraw (*inʿizāl*) from the world (*al-dunyā*) by taking the hijab, leading to feelings of internal peace and repose (sakan, *iṭmiʾnān, salām*). A more ideal existence is achieved through submission to religious disciplines but also through a certain kind of revelation realized on the affective plane of self, through the very desire (the various words used are *ighrāʾ*, *raghba, ahwāʾ, mashāʿir*) to veil. Veiling awakens what the authors variously describe as the heart, affect, instinct, an Islamic depth, a dormant self, a latent force. Drawing on older concepts about the role of heart, affect, passion, visions, and dreams, the writers simultaneously employ the disciplinary trope of self-cultivation toward the realization of piety. But they also develop an "ethics of passion" that inspires their dramatic transformations, as well as the stories they recount about

reproduces ʿAbd al-Halim Mahmud's biography of the Prophet Muhammad, who she says does not just represent the Qurʾan but *is* the Qurʾan.

[21] Asad, *Formations of the Secular*, 225.

this experience.[22] Discipline and passion are not counterposed as antithetical in these narratives but are instead intertwined—and mutually constituted—through a union of inner self and external practice, belief and discipline, heart and mind, creativity and pedagogy.

Veiling on Screen: New Islamic Media

Veiling has been one of the principal means by which revivalists have navigated the visual politics of cultural production: its narratives and storylines, its imagery and sexual politics, women's visibility and invisibility. The subject of Muslim women's visibility has so long dominated and preoccupied Orientalist—and now neo-imperialist—cultural production. These revivalist narratives perform an act of consciously reclaiming the signs and symbols of an indigenous Islamic identity.[23] They constantly frame the return to veiling as a struggle against the Western, foreign, secular, and un-Islamic through a politics of authentic cultural self-representation. They seek to control both the male gaze and the penetrating, violating gaze of an invasive and demanding West focused on the Orient and its women. The narratives resignify veiling, as these "Islamic artists" rewrite their roles on the public stage, "distancing themselves" from a certain narrative of women's bodies identified as Western, foreign, and irreligious. They reinscribe other kinds of narratives coded as Islamic, drawing on popular interpretations of the Islamic discursive tradition. The veil became a critical way that the Islamic revival made its practices and beliefs visible to a world dominated by secular images as well as a means by which it claimed public space for itself, space that secular government constantly strove to circumscribe and limit. The proliferating images of veils became a way to claim bodies and souls for the revival and to appropriate what Rey Chow calls "the drama of the ongoing cultural struggle between men and women, the drama of narrative coercions and ideological interpellations."[24]

Women's bodies, souls, minds, and sexualities have been powerful creative terrain for elucidating the ideological project of the revival,

[22] See Samira Haj's insightful discussion of the role of *wijdān* (affect) and *qalb* (heart) in the classical notions of cultivating the moral self versus modernist conceptions of the role of mind and reason. The veiling texts combine both, eschewing a mind/body split. Haj, *Reconfiguring Islamic Tradition*, 113–19; Amira Mittermaier, "Dreams from Elsewhere: Muslim Subjectivities Beyond the Trope of Self-Cultivation," *Journal of the Royal Anthropological Institute* 18, no. 2 (2012): 249.

[23] Ahmed, *Women and Gender in Islam*, 162.

[24] Chow, *Sentimental Fabulations*, 7.

its subjects, sexualities, social vision, politics, and epistemologies. The reiteration of a set of themes and motifs in veiling narratives testifies to a semiotic ideology underpinning the veil, informing the affective and corporeal experience of wearing it, and cultivating certain kinds of identities and subjectivities. The authors draw on concepts of intuitive faith from the Sufi tradition and Islamic ideas about self-cultivation, but they also formulate these selves and sexualities as a rejection of Western sexual mores, interpreted as an ethic of exposure that cheapens a woman's value. The visual may still be critical to recording (and projecting) verifiable facts and an objective reality, the knowledge production that has been so critical to the project of Orientalism. But in the age of cinematic visuality and evangelical confessionalism, the visual has also become "the terrain of subjective experience as the locus of knowledge, and power."[25]

Analyses of how the Islamic revival evolved from its embattled position in the 1970s and 1980s to its culturally dominant golden age in the 1990s and in the new millennium have focused on how Islamic ideological production has been able to capitalize on technological reproducibility to circulate its message(s).[26]

> The new ethos found institutional and discursive expression in the vast, though fragmented, "Islamic sector,' composed of Islamic media, publications, education, associations, business, *ḥalaqāt* (religious gatherings), art, entertainment, tastes, and fashion. Business quickly capitalized on this growing market for Islamic commitment and commodities. . . . these practices represented a new trend in religiosity. . . . they signified a shift from Islamism as a political project to one concerned primarily with personal salvation, ethical enhancement, and self-actualization.[27]

While some interpret this self-cultivation mainly as a struggle to embody virtue and morality,[28] others interpret it as connected to neoliberalism that sees Islamic commitment as a lifestyle choice and part of

[25] Bill Nichols, "Film Theory and the Revolt against Master Narratives," in *Reinventing Film Studies*, ed. Christine Gledhill and Linda Williams (Oxford: Oxford University Press, 2000), 42.

[26] See Wickham's discussion of "'Print Islam': Cultural Production in the Parallel Islamic Sector" in *Mobilizing Islam*, 134–49; Gonzalez-Quijano, *Les gens du livre*; Hirschkind and Larkin, "Media and the Political Forms of Religion"; Hirschkind, *Ethical Soundscape*; Moll, "Islamic Televangelism," 5. In talking about Islamic satellite channels, Yasmin Moll writes that they "are not located in a contestatory space outside of capitalist consumption, but rather are created by such circuits."

[27] Bayat, *Making Islam Democratic*, 149.

[28] Mahmood, *Politics of Piety*, 16.

the privatization of religion.[29] Yet these are not necessarily antithetical processes but different aspects or dimensions of how Islam has come to inhabit contemporary modes of technological reproducibility. This process—its effects and affects, its sense and sensibilities, its very epistemologies—is the object of Kariman Hamza's reflection in *Rihlati min al-Sufur ila al-Hijab* (My Journey from Unveiling to Veiling, 1981), a story of how she came to take the veil and became a television personality at the same time. The central drama of Hamza's *Journey* is as much about "broadcasting Islam" as her deepening Islamic commitment, two stories that she weaves together into one, bound together in her narrative about veiling. The story culminates when Kariman takes the veil and goes on the pilgrimage, a climax also punctuated by another key event: Kariman securing a position as presenter on the children's television program "Qurʾan Rabbi" (The Qurʾan of My Lord). By taking the mantle of religious knowledge and performing its ritual worship (in which veiling plays a key part), she legitimately assumes a kind of (televised) religious authority. This climax marks the beginning of her new life and her new work.

Hamza became a religious authority in her own right, a *dāʿiya* and a scholar, celebrated by both al-Azhar and the religious media. Her Qurʾan exegesis, originally intended for children, became the first commentary by a woman to be approved by al-Azhar, despite previous exegeses published by Bint al-Shatiʾ and Niʿmat Sidqi.[30] Hamza's path was partly pioneered through visible engagement with religious knowledge and practice in public. Her writings, and her presence on television, forged a place for veiled women in popular entertainment media and, most recently, on the news. In the 1990s she waged a long legal battle against the minister of information to wear the hijab on Egyptian television. Women would be allowed to wear the veil on state television only as of January 2012, in a ruling on a 2008 court case.

Hamza's *Journey* is one of the earliest examples of personal narratives describing the return to veiling, preceded only, perhaps, by Niʿmat Sidqi's autobiographical sketch in the introduction to *al-Tabarruj*. Hamza's return to veiling was closely connected with her commitment to developing Islamic knowledge through Islamic media. Kariman initiates her journey in the Institute for Islamic Studies, with a stack of

[29] Selim, "Politics of Piety." This has been known as post-Islamism and is associated with an Islamist retreat from state politics, mainly in the work of Olivier Roy and Asef Bayat, even though the latter emphasizes the interconnection between politics and cultural production.

[30] Kariman Hamza, *al-Luʾluʾ wa-l-Marjan fi Tafsir al-Qurʾan* (Cairo: Maktabat al-Shuruq al-Dawliyya, 2010).

books her father has sent her to deliver.[31] She stumbles on a lecture about the spiritual awakening of two Sufi shaykhs. The first, al-Fudayl ibn ʿIyad, hears "the divine call ringing out in the depths of the soul." ʿIyad is visiting his lover when he hears a voice from the sky reciting verses of the Qurʾan, calling for hearts to submit (57:16) and abandon the life of "amusement, diversion, and adornment" (57:20). He follows this call through a specific path: through the study of the Qurʾan, acquisition of religious knowledge, and performance of religious ritual, specifically, the pilgrimage. This *sīra*, a word for biography that also means "path," will guide Kariman's own *Journey*, as she herself hears "the divine call ringing out in the depths of the soul," turns to studying religious knowledge, and goes on pilgrimage. In *her* narrative, however, the veil gives her story a gendered dimension, both appropriating and subtly transforming the male path. The second Sufi Ibrahim Bin Adham also hears a voice reciting a Qurʾanic verse, saying, "Do you think that we created you in vain?" (23:115), reiterating the concept that life is not just for "diversion" and vanity (24). From that day, Ibrahim "wore the clothes of faithful worship for God on high, devoting himself to knowledge, studying the Qurʾan and hadith . . . and struggling in his spirit and desire." He, too, leaves a life of "amusement, frivolity, and adornment" for "the latent striving in the soul . . . toward a life of piety, virtue, spiritual and emotional purity."

Kariman returns home shaken, with the words of the Qurʾan (and the shaykh's lecture and the Sufis' stories) resounding in her heart. She spends the night restlessly reflecting on the meaninglessness of her life, on the lack of "psychological equilibrium" between its spiritual and material dimension, on her confusion, depression, and "lack of peace" (28). The word she uses for her lack of "peace" is *sakīna*, a term that also refers to the immanence of God, presence of God, and God-inspired peace of mind, as well as connoting tranquility. The morning brings a kind of spiritual awakening and illumination. "I reviewed the story of my life and was surprised by the light of day beginning to stream into my window. I was amazed at how I had spent the night." She talks about the "fatigue (*iʿyāʾ*) running through my body," as she tunes in to the Noble Qurʾan radio station while still in a half asleep, dreamlike state. *Iʿyāʾ* also refers to a kind of illness or disability and an inability to express oneself, a lack of energy for which the Qurʾan becomes the cure, religious knowledge the medicine, and religious

[31] Hamza, *Rihlati min al-Sufur ila al-Hijab*, 24. Malti-Douglas's analysis of this scene is masterful. See Malti-Douglas, *Medicines of the Soul*, 19–26.

authorities the doctors.[32] She describes this radio program as a line connecting her to religious knowledge and ultimately to God. But she does not describe the program in purely intellectual terms; rather, as inspiring love and passion for God. It was "a broadcast beloved to my spirit, one that I followed as a listener for a full seven years before I fell in love with God because of it" (28). The program, *Hadith al-Sabah* (Morning Talk), both literally and figuratively serves as a wake-up call. The voice of the shaykh began "working all that work" in her mind and soul, "putting the dots on the letters and determining the objectives and path of my future work" (28). It wakes her body from its lassitude, inspires in her a passion for God, and opens her mind and soul to the world of Islamic knowledge. After listening to yet another story about a Sufi whose "heart kept bowing in prayer until it found God," Kariman jumps from her bed and calls her father, "as if I was still dreaming." These stories become a vehicle for awakening a spiritual self lying dormant, like a vision in sleep—a motif that became dominant in veiling narratives. In Hamza's narrative, the medium is critical to the message, modern forms of technological reproducibility critical to keeping God's word alive in the age of mass media.

The shaykh speaking on the radio is ʿAbd al-Halim Mahmud, a grand shaykh of al-Azhar who helped develop religious television and radio programs in the 1970s. He is the guiding light of the narrative, partly through his connection to Kariman's father, ʿAbd al-Latif Hamza, a renowned professor of communications and media at Cairo University who authored dozens of books on the media. Mahmud wrote the introduction to ʿAbd al-Latif Hamza's posthumously published *al-Iʿlam fi Sadr al-Islam* (The Media in the Heart of Islam, 1971), mainly because Kariman pursued him to do this, a process dramatized in the opening pages of her *Journey*.[33] Mahmud was an Azhari who parlayed intellectual Islam into popular terms—through pioneering work on the radio but also through many articles published in the popular press. He contributed to the founding of the national radio station Idhaʿat al-Qurʾan al-Karim (Broadcast of the Noble Qurʾan), which specialized in religious programming. In 1970, the time that Hamza situates her narrative, Mahmud was dean at the Institute for Islamic Studies, where Kariman unwittingly walks in on his lecture. Soon thereafter Mahmud

[32] Hamza draws on Niʿmat Sidqi (who appears in the story) and her understanding of religious knowledge as a means of "nourishing, curing the heart, reviving, and healing." Sidqi is an important, if largely unacknowledged, figure in Kariman's *Journey*, speaking along with Hamza at a conference on "The Place of Woman in Islam," the moment that Kariman decides to take the hijab.

[33] ʿAbd al-Latif Hamza, *al-Iʿlam fi Sadr al-Islam* (Cairo: Dar al-Fikr al-ʿArabi, 1971); Hamza, *Rihlati min al-Sufur ila al-Hijab*, 61.

became grand shaykh of al-Azhar and later formed a planning committee to develop television programs specializing in teaching Islam to the general public.[34] By using mass media, he helped cultivate "the thriving teach-yourself cultural market, which encourages Muslims privately to acquire a knowledge of their faith without having to rely directly on authority figures."[35] Through the intervention of figures like Mahmud, religious discourse was disseminated through multiple sensory media, with the auditory and visual working in tandem with print. Radio, cassettes, video, film, television, newspapers, pamphlets, books, and testimonies repackaged material from the classical Islamic tradition (Qurʾan interpretation, stories of the early community, Sufi narratives) for a new era—for popular consumption, religious edification, and entertainment. "This discourse was propped up by the spread of audiocassettes, but was also supported by radio programmes and then by a new style of edifying entertainment on TV screens. The narrative of the awakening needed not only conceptual markers but also charismatic signposts that could be recognized by the growing audiences of electronic media, the bulk of them consisting of the middle classes. The new forms of media authority facilitated reflexive . . . processes" that cultivated faith in the age of technological reproducibility.[36] These modern modes of communication wiring Hamza's narrative draw on older stories channeled through new media, through television and radio as means of renewing and recirculating classical stories for modern sensibilities, creating an imagined Islamic community through new communicative technologies.

Reportedly, Hamza originally intended *Journey* to be a biography of ʿAbd al-Halim Mahmud. Entire chapters of his writings are reprinted verbatim in the midst of Hamza's own story, including an entire chapter from his biography of the prophet *al-Rasul: Lamahat min Hayatihi wa-Nafahat min Hadyihi* (The Prophet: Glimmers from His Life and Whiffs of His Guidance, 1965). As one scholar of ʿAbd al-Halim Mahmud observes, he was "a celebrity to whom people were eager to claim connections . . . they recognized in him the first station of their own personal *silsila*."[37] Kariman connects herself to an intellectual *silsila* (genealogy) of Sufis turning from a life of ease, vanity, and diversion to religious knowledge, piety, and devotion, partly through

[34] Hatsuki Aishima and Armando Salvatore, "Doubt, Faith, and Knowledge: The Reconfiguration of the Intellectual Field in Post-Nasserist Cairo," in *Islam, Politics, Anthropology*, ed. Filippo Osella and Benjamin Soares (Oxford: Wiley-Blackwell, 2010), 42.

[35] Ibid., 44; Raʾuf Shalabi, *Shaykh al-Islam ʿAbd al-Halim Mahmud: Siratuhu wa-Aʿmaluhu* (Kuwait: Dar al-Qalam, 1982), 535–43.

[36] Aishima and Salvatore, "Doubt, Faith, and Knowledge," 44.

[37] Ibid., 45.

the writings and words of ʿAbd al-Halim Mahmud. Through a chain of communication of religious knowledge, Kariman becomes the recipient of a hadith (in this case, *ḥadīth al-ṣabāḥ*!), becoming part of an intellectual lineage communicated through successive technologies. ʿAbd al-Halim Mahmud is a critical link in this chain, a particularly potent communicator who electrifies his listeners. Kariman literally says that this hadith ran through my being, making me submit to God. His discursive presence in the text is as a master narrative, signs that direct Kariman's path, through excerpts from his biography of the prophet, his exegesis of the Qurʾan, and his descriptions of modern daʿwa, excerpts that punctuate Hamza's own narrative.

After waking up to ʿAbd al-Halim Mahmud on the radio, Kariman calls her father to tell him what she heard. That evening he comes to pray with her, carrying a stack of books by Mahmud. Her father dies shortly thereafter, so the scene takes on an added urgency, as a final wish. As she reads ʿAbd al-Halim Mahmud's books, she begins to write her story through his:

> I read and I read, as if I am reading myself. I love these words—that I did not know how to express. I live this life that was dormant in my self. And the pen of this shaykh guided me to this self. Everything that this man says is me. Exactly me. Despite my long unruly hair, despite my naked clothes, despite my laugh and mirth, despite my immersion in colors, in the material world, in music. I found myself. My very inner nature (*fiṭratī*) agrees completely with every word this shaykh says. I feel the words and the lines; I welcome the ideas and the viewpoints. I submit and submit to every tenet and to every teaching. I love this color. I found my path. I found myself. I found God.[38]

Through these writings, she is able to awaken her dormant self and her very inner nature, a true spiritual self that exists in the material world. She is able to do this by reading the lines, the lines that lead her to her path and script her own narrative.

When Kariman's father dies, he leaves the unpublished manuscript of *The Media in the Heart of Islam*.[39] The early dramatic crux of the narrative revolves around Kariman connecting Mahmud to her father through *Media in the Heart of Islam*, as she repeatedly contacts him beseeching him to write an introduction to the book. Hamza reproduces Mahmud's introduction in its entirety, generous praise of ʿAbd

[38] Hamza, *Rihlati min al-Sufur ila al-Hijab*, 31–32.
[39] Ibid., 61; Hamza, *al-Iʿlam fi Sadr al-Islam*.

al-Latif Hamza's text, for his awakened conscience, sense of intellectual responsibility, and spiritual passion (70). Nonetheless, it is with "fear and trepidation" that the shaykh presents the work, despite the "true authenticity of the media in Islam, in Islamic culture, Islamic history, and in Islamic schools of thought. There must be in its very spirit a true authenticity to the science of communications that includes many arts." These arts—of communication, information, and media—are the work of knowledge, science, understanding, and the "preparation of the self . . . a true stimulus to the spiritual motivation of the researcher" (70). The media promises to overcome the larger problem, the "conspiracy of silence plotted against Islamic culture," especially by reaching the youth of today who have been enchanted by foreign tradition and know nothing of Islamic tradition. Mahmud remains one of Kariman's strongest advocates in the television industry and is pivotal in ushering Kariman into her new vocation. The book closes with Kariman not only taking the veil but becoming a *dāʿiya* by spreading Islamic knowledge on television. The victory is not just of religious knowledge trumping the secular in television but also the religious authority ʿAbd al-Halim Mahmud approving television for the dissemination of religious knowledge. As a veiled woman on television, Kariman Hamza defies assumptions about the secularity of visual media, as much as assumptions about the nature of veiling that place pious women outside public purview.

Mahmud's consent signals not only his approval but also the legitimacy of Hamza's vision of an Islamic media—at a time that the very concept was still in doubt. One ethnographer of Islamic media, for example, describes how preachers "routinely criticized 'media entertainment, film stars, popular singers, and television serials' while viewing categories such as *fann* (art), adab (literature), *thaqāfa* (high culture), and *mūda* (fashion) as partaking in a strictly secular-western genealogy."[40] But these very terms become the exact vocabulary and lexicon used by those mobilizing to "convert" popular media entertainment to an Islamic idiom engendering both Islamic knowledge and Islamic sensibilities. Hamza devotes much of her story to institutional resistance to Islamic media, at al-Azhar, at the Ministry of Awqaf, and in the television industry. The opposition that she faces, the trials and tribulations that meet her enthusiasm and advocacy, form the content of her drama, its *pièce de résistance.*

Kariman inevitably encounters obstacles that seem to block the flow of information, of knowledge opening the channels to the divine. It

[40] Moll, "Islamic Televangelism," 8; Hirschkind, *Ethical Soundscape*, 127. The quote is taken from Moll citing Hirschkind.

is a struggle on two fronts—against the secular biases within the entertainment industry and against biases within the religious establishment about the value of popular entertainment, and especially its role in engendering "emotions and character attributes incompatible with" Islamic piety.[41] The first obstacle is easily dispensed with through a campaign of more information that dispels the ignorance clogging people's minds and souls. The second main obstacle, a more delicate but urgently felt one for Hamza, is the resistance within the Islamic establishment (in al-Azhar and the Ministry of Waqf) to the dissemination of religious knowledge through visual media like television, film, and theater. Moreover, there is a resistance against the dissemination of this knowledge—through the popular media—to women. While these might seem like two separate but interrelated projects, they are one and the same in Kariman. When she first proposes a religious program on television for women and children, she is rebuffed: "Women have nothing to do with religious work," the producer says. "We do not have programs for children nor programs for women, that is not the domain of religious programs! Women know nothing about religion" (154). Religious knowledge must to speak to women, Hamza insists, in terms that are accessible to them and through media that are accessible to them. Throughout *Rihlati*, she emphasizes the importance of religious knowledge to women as Muslim subjects, a knowledge that Hamza herself visibly inhabits through the veil. A veiled woman is not simply "seen" as religious but also comes to embody the "epistemic sense of visibility."[42] This religious knowledge brings the subject into view, as she makes the "journey from oppression and darkness into the light," as the film star Shams al-Barudi would title her own narrative of veiling.[43] By speaking with the language and scripts of Islamic knowledge, they become visible in a way that transcends—and supersedes—secular forms of visibility, which becomes associated with an untamed, animal, and even sick self. When Hamza enters the Institute for Islamic Studies at the beginning of the narrative, she describes herself as a "strange being." The stares that greet her make clear that she has entered into territory where she does not belong. Her long hair and exposed legs, her very femininity, have transgressed certain key Islamic boundaries. Veiling becomes a means of legitimately entering into the

[41] Hirschkind, *Ethical Soundscape*, 127.

[42] Chow, *Sentimental Fabulations*, 11–12.

[43] al-Barudi, *Rihlati min al-Zulumat ila al-Nur*; Gilles Deleuze, *Foucault* (London: Continuum, 2006), 41–58. See Chow's insightful discussion of this kind of epistemic visibility and its connection to the representation of "authentic cultural identities," even if she continually reiterates that these "shimmerings" are mere images on screen. Chow, *Sentimenal Fabulations*, 12.

halls of Islamic knowledge—and literally inhabiting that knowledge—without transgressing its boundaries, a path that she forges for others.

Kariman's journey climaxes with a set of interlocking scenes that juxtapose threads from the "Islamic media" aspect of the narrative with scenes of Kariman weeping on the hajj and of a vision she has of joining the ʿulamaʾ in their circle. One of these is an encounter with a student of ʿAbd al-Halim Mahmud, whom she also hears on the radio. She gives him a copy of *The Media in the Heart of Islam*, and they plan together to distribute the book to prominent broadcasters. He becomes a point of "connection" between Kariman and "my shaykh, between me and the ʿulamaʾ of religion in general" (130). She later dreams that she is sitting with this ʿulamaʾ in heaven. Second, Kariman approaches the minister of religious endowments (*awqāf*) about making documentary films about religious subjects like mosques and "the jihad of the Prophet's family." Third, she gets a job as the host of a television show teaching the Qurʾan to children. Her meeting with the television head has the quality of a personal epiphany. As she sets out to meet him, she hears the call to prayer in a way that she had never heard it before. "It had an unusual impact on my spirit: in listening to it I fell into a special state in which I felt like I was dissolving into awe and submission, love and desire. The sound of the call to prayer transfixed my entire being. I had conflicting feelings—ultimate happiness and trust in God's support and ultimate fear and anxiety" (153). At the moment she ascends the stairs to go meet with him, she hears the call to prayer again, taking it as a sign. "I felt that God was with me, blessing the beginning of my work." The scenes of this passage juxtapose the story of Kariman's new vocation with an older communicative technology for bringing the community together in the ritual practice of Islam—the call to prayer. Her account of her spiritual awakening motivates, and coincides with, her desire to convert television into a tool for the dissemination of religion.

Hamza's text ends with an elegy to ʿAbd al-Halim Mahmud who died in 1978. The final passage is about him being "a man who believes in the message of the media and its effectiveness" (246). Only if people loyal to God and belonging to Him work with the media can it be changed, she says. This overarching tale about the means and methods of transmitting—and inhabiting—Islamic knowledge is illustrated through the very person of Kariman, who pioneers her own role as the first veiled Islamic broadcaster on Egyptian television. The story about Kariman's awakening religiosity and taking of the veil is interwoven with another story about the power of the media for promoting the message of Islam.

Kariman's journey into the world of Islamic knowledge is initiated by an Islamic media. Knowledge comes to her in cars, on the radio, by telephone, and on trains. She continually emphasizes the vehicle of the message, as information is seemingly miraculously transported to the doors of her perception, at moments of felicitous convergence in God's design. In her narrative this design appears as a grid on which electric connections are made between people, ideas, and things. Kariman's journey moves dynamically between the medium and the message, from the call to prayer to books to radio to film to television. Kariman is perpetually in motion, vacillating between these modes of sensory stimuli that awaken her religious sensibilities. They also appear to impel her religious trajectory, making it appear as inevitable progress in the realization of an Islamic self and an Islamic society.

Performing the Islamic Self

Following in the wake of Hamza's narrative about veiling was a surge of testimonies by *fannānāt islāmiyyat*, *fannānāt mutaḥajjibāt*, or *fannānāt taʾibāt* (Islamic artists, veiled artists, or repentant artists), what became a veritable genre. In the late 1980s, a wave of movie stars and belly dancers "detached themselves" (*inʿizāl*) from their roles as screen sirens and sex symbols, embraced an Islamic way of life, and took the veil. The term *inʿizāl* suggests a rejection of their former life, connoting retreat, as much as separation and segregation, even as public attention to these stars escalated in the wake of their veiling. Their covering and *inʿizāl* denotes separation from what is understood to be a Western ethic of unveiling and self-exposure but also a withdrawal from "worldly affairs" into "faith in the unseen."[44] Yet these movie stars' absence—as they slam doors in the faces of journalists, say "No . . . to journalism,"[45] and leave the blank spots where their photos should be—incites a frenzy of media attention, an incitation that has worked toward discursive production around the performance of piety. The turn of movie stars to Islam had a domino-like effect, as each of the "good friends" among these "artist sisters" influenced others—they dream about one another, call one another on the phone, and encourage one another in the renewal of and return to their faith.[46] In interviews with these repentant artists, journalists and interviewers constantly interrogate them about the origins of their transformation. The answer serves as a

[44] Siham al-Dhihni, "Hiwar maʿ Nasrin," *Sayyidati*, April 22, 1991; Abu Suf, *Fannanat Mutahajjibat*, 37.

[45] Abu Suf, *Fannanat Mutahajjibat*, 55–70.

[46] al-Dhihni, "Hiwar maʿ Nasrin"; Abu Suf, *Fannanat Mutahajjibat*, 32, 35–38; Karin van Nieuwkerk, *Performing Piety: Singers and Actors in Egypt's Islamic Revival* (Austin: University of Texas Press, 2013), 30–35.

blueprint—a model—of how to embark on veiling, as well as how to reinvigorate Islamic consciousness, piety, virtue, and modesty. These stories, and the imaginary that these Islamic artists flesh out, serve as paradigms for enacting a virtuous self, *sunna* in the age of cinematic visuality and technological reproducibility.

Despite the reiteration of a similar set of themes and motifs, and the deployment of a specific lexicon (about artists, their "detachment," repentance, journeys, and veiling), the genre is by no means fixed or even "highly rigid."[47] The writers encompass varieties of religious experience out of which the different narratives emerge—what Shams al-Barudi calls "the colors of repentance" and Kariman Hamza the "different modes of mercy" in Islam.[48] Hamza writes about different paths in service of Islam, different ways of remedying oneself: through the mind, the emotions (wijdān), or the Qurʾan, however difficult, all in the service of Islam (234). Yet there is a remarkable degree of repetition between these testimonies, with thematic echoes, identifiable motifs, and citations of similar sets of authorities.[49] This repetition is partly intertextual borrowings, but it also acts as a kind of ritualistic remembrance (*dhikr*) of the "signs" on the path to veiling.

Scores of publications, in the entertainment press, newspapers, women's magazines, pamphlets, and books, detail these stars' "conversion" to an Islamic consciousness, as the same stories were repeatedly circulated in different media and different incarnations. The turn to veiling becomes connected to the influence of popular Islamic media stars like the preachers Shaykh al-Shaʿrawi and ʿAmr Khalid.[50] One of the first of these was the Egyptian movie star Shams al-Barudi, who took the veil in 1985; she was known for roles in provocative films like *al-Mutʿa wa-l-ʿAdhab* (Pleasure and Torture, 1971), *Imraʾa Sayyiʾat al-Sumʿa* (A Woman of Bad Reputation, 1973), and *Hubb ʿala Shatiʾ Miami* (Love on Miami Beach, 1976). She seemingly withdrew from public life, taking the niqab (the face veil) even as she remained a visible public symbol of the rise in Islamic consciousness. Her testimony *Rihlati min al-Zulumat ila al-Nur* (My Journey from Darkness to Light,

[47] Judith Butler, *Gender Trouble: Feminism and the Subversion of Identity* (New York: Routledge, 1990), 25.

[48] When al-Barudi talks about the "colors of repentance," she cites the experiences of the two main mystics that began Kariman Hamza's journey, clearly drawing on Hamza. Siraj al-Din, *Awraq Shams al-Barudi*, 89.

[49] Hamza, *Rihlati min al-Sufur ila al-Hijab*, 21–26; Siraj al-Din, *Awraq Shams al-Barudi*, 89n; Malti-Douglas, *Medicines of the Soul*, 176–77.

[50] Saʿid Abu al-ʿAynayn, *al-Shaʿrawi—wa-l-Fannanat* (Cairo: Dar Akhbar al-Yawm, Qitaʿ al-Thaqafa, 1999); Shaʿban, *ʿAmr Khalid Shahid ʿala Hijab al-Fannanat*; Bayat, *Making Islam Democratic*, 153–54.

1988) reiterates the language—and many of the themes—of Hamza's *Rihlati min al-Sufur ila al-Hijab*. Her narrative differs considerably from Hamza's, but analogous elements provide conceptual milestones in the journey—material well-being and spiritual lassitude, nakedness and physical exposure, the strong family structure that supports her return to the religious fold, the "instinct" (fiṭra) leading her to religion, the religious authorities that guide her on the path of religious knowledge, a religious "vision," the transformative journey to Mecca on the hajj or the ʿumra, taking the veil, and the drive and desire to establish an "Islamic art" and promote Islamic media.

These narratives are public demonstrations of internal faith, cultivated and symbolized by the material object of the veil but also by an aesthetics that constructs a certain harmony between outer practice and inner belief, form and content. Interior belief is rendered in corporeal terms, as the "heart of the hijab" coded into the body and inhabited in the skin.[51] Repentant artists describe how their external behavior and comportment became split from their true, inner, Muslim self. They wear Western clothes, travel in Western lands, play Western roles, and study Western knowledge. Like Hamza, they talk about faith as restoring psychological equilibrium to the self, curing it of its "sicknesses," returning it to health.[52] In Shams al-Barudi's *My Journey from Darkness to Light*, she talks about the roles she accepted as an actress, describing discomfort with not just the characters she played but also her alienation from her "true personality."[53]

> Throughout my work in acting, I felt as if something inside me rejected the work. . . . The situation continued until I felt that I could not find myself in this work. . . . My work as an actor was more like a period of unconsciousness (*ghaybūba*). I felt like there was a split (*infiṣām*: schizophrenia) with my true personality. . . . I used to sit and think about my work in the cinema, the work that

[51] Maraʿi, *Yaqazat al-ʿIffa*, 101–3.

[52] The psychological illnesses and sexual complexes of the West occupy some of these revivalist writings, like that of Muhammad Jalal Kishk, *al-Hurriyya fi al-Usra al-Muslima*; Nahw Waʿy Islami (Cairo: al-Mukhtar al-Islami, 1979), 11, 15; Hamza, *Rihlati min al-Sufur ila al-Hijab* 28; Shaʿban, *ʿAmr Khalid Shahid ʿala Hijab al-Fannanat*, 16. Shaʿban writes about "faith and psychological health" as a cure for the "sicknesses" of these artists.

[53] Karim Tartoussieh, "Pious Stardom: Cinema and the Islamic Revival in Egypt," *Arab Studies Journal* 15, no. 1 (April 1, 2007): 37. Tartoussieh quotes an interview with the famous actress Shahira in *al-Mawʿid* (November 2005), who says: "When I look back on my acting career before deciding to veil, I realize that I wasn't myself. . . . I wasn't happy with myself so I returned to my true self through returning to God."

people saw. And I didn't feel that it expressed me—it was an artificial situation. I used to feel that I was outside of my own skin.[54]

This split within one's personality, as a kind of psychological sickness (a schizophrenia), is the same image that the Islamic writer Safinaz Kazim uses to describe her own self before taking the veil. In Kazim's famous essay "ʿAn al-Sijn wa-l-Hurriyya" (On Prison and Freedom, 1986), she talks of her own battle with depression, but this "split" also simultaneously refers to the political effects of secularism on the self, a conceptual secularism that divorces the spiritual self from material practice, an inside from the outside, religion from state, private from public. Taking the hijab heals this split, bringing the image of self in line with an internal reality, a Muslim subjectivity that has lain dormant but is awakened through the instinct of fiṭra. It is a Muslim self that comes into being only through Islamic practices, rituals, models, paths, and readings.

This feeling of being in a coma, split off from herself, and literally outside of her own skin, opens the section on Shams al-Barudi's life before the veil. This chapter on the jāhiliyya period of her life is structured as glimmerings (shimmerings, illuminations) of her Islamic self in the "darknesses" (*ẓulumāt*) of her "unconsciousness" (*ghaybūba*) before she emerges into the full, glorious light of Islam.[55] Each section of the chapter testifies to different instances of these glimmerings, carefully framed as a set of core domains that act as a conceptual scaffolding for constructing a pious self. She connects glimmerings with the concept of fiṭra from the Qurʾan, the intuition with which God created the human being and that leads al-Barudi back to Islam. This "instinct in the phase of unconsciousness" manifests itself through *ḥayāʾ*, a word that means modesty. While performing a rape scene on camera, she viscerally reacts. Trembling and fearful, she cannot bring her body to perform the part. The word ḥayāʾ cannot be rendered through the flat, one-dimensional term "modesty"; it literally obscures ḥayāʾ's connection to life, to motherhood, to giving birth (and to revival and awakening).[56] In al-Barudi's narrative, the instinct for ḥayāʾ is connected to sexuality's manifestation in the social institutions of marriage, the family, and childrearing. These are the main sections in this chapter on her jāhiliyya, entitled "Instinct in the Time of Unconsciousness," social

[54] Siraj al-Din, *Awraq Shams al-Barudi*, 22.

[55] Ibid., 22–52; Deleuze, *Foucault*, 50.

[56] Lane gives these definitions, among others: "A shrinking of the soul from foul conduct"; "repentance (synonym)"; "a thing that should be concealed, and of which one is ashamed to speak plainly"; "the vulva, or external portion of the female organs of generation." Lane, *Arabic-English Lexicon*, 681–82; Mahmood, *Politics of Piety*, 156–60.

institutions that provide the infrastructure of her religious awakening. In *The Politics of Piety*, Saba Mahmood defines ḥayāʾ as "feelings imprinted on your insides" and "an entire conceptualization of the role the body plays in the making of the self, one in which the outward behavior of the body constitutes both the potentiality and the means through which interiority is realized."[57]

Shams's instinct leads her to motherhood, what she calls "the most beautiful thing in life. Focusing on this great love and sacrificing for my children is the most beautiful thing in life." This, she says, is the reason that she "withdrew from the world."[58] Through a narrative of (internal) spiritual and romantic love, cultivated through her return to Islam and taking the veil, she articulates the foundation for an Islamic family. Its axis is not only marriage and children but a romanticized spiritual love that is invisible but stronger than iron.

> Love is something hidden, something you cannot see, but even so it is stronger than iron; it is like a strong backbone. It can slip from our hands like smoke even though its power is stronger than even death. Love develops from a strong connection to beautiful feelings of self-sacrifice to help the beloved. This feeling of sympathy for others is obvious even if the lover wants to hide it. The splendor of love increases the beauty of life if the lovers beautify the commitment of love by cultivating it. (29)

Shams laments that virtuous, chaste love is no longer the basis of marriage "in this age" and in "the materialist countries." These people, she says, do not have high ideals; they cannot see from the peak of "sight"; they cannot see "the true colors" of this kind of love. "I am a romantic," she says. "True love is spiritual love" (30). Sexuality is the site for cultivating "a sacred relationship that harmonizes and completes the spiritual relationship that ties the man to the woman." Otherwise sexuality is merely a vulgar animality and dissolution, something that is "inhuman," in contrast to "a sacred human relationship . . . promoting spiritual harmony and the sacred bond" (25).

This becoming more real, more true, more human is realized in spiritual love and sacred sexuality channeled through marriage and family life. Living family life "with all my feelings and all my emotions" is my true happiness, she says. Through family life, Shams says, she has become "more real" and "more true" (30). The chapter on her "path of return" begins with a 1972 interview in the entertainment magazine

[57] Mahmood, *Politics of Piety*, 157, 159.
[58] Siraj al-Din, *Awraq Shams al-Barudi*, 21.

al-Kawakib, when al-Barudi was making her most racy films (*Pleasure and Torture, Journey of Love, The Milatili Bath, Hotel of Happiness, A Woman of Bad Reputation*, etc.) When the interviewer asks what the best thing said about her is, she responds: "The best thing that I've heard about myself and that I felt was true—and that I too feel—is that I am a person really true to myself. The best that any person can be is true to himself or else he will suffer." The interviewer then asks if this is a kind of pride, to which she answers: "I consider this a sign of attuned feelings and an awakened consciousness" (53). The narrative flow switches abruptly to another interview, now in 1988, in the Muslim Brotherhood journal *al-Nur*, where al-Barudi answers a series of questions about "the beginning of the path of belief." The passage from *al-Nur* repeats the passage quoted above about how al-Barudi could not find herself in her work and "felt that she was outside her own skin," but in *al-Nur* she adds another passage about how she started looking "for roles that were close to my self." To inhabit this new role, she goes shopping to adjust her wardrobe to her "inner desire to wear the hijab" that had been awakened (56, 57).

At the core of this account of Shams's "return" is what was becoming a stock set of motifs: a physical sickness as "punishment from God," a vision of the prophet, performing the pilgrimage, and taking the veil. In Sidqi, Hamza, Kazim, and a host of other, later writings, the sickness/vision/pilgrimage/veil nexus would become a repeating trajectory on which these women modeled their spiritual transformations. These build on mystical narratives from the Islamic discursive tradition but circulate new forms of gendered, female, Muslim, revivalist religiosity, a dominant, hegemonic narrative circulated widely at the intersection of print and visual media. The physical and psychological illness suffered by those inhabiting un-Islamic roles becomes a dominant motif in the testimonies of Islamic artists as they repeatedly describe falling ill when they refuse to heed the call. Kariman's images of the shaykh healing her with his words and Sidqi's images of the abscessed, corrupted body out of tune with religion resonate in these images—with the female body as a particularly fertile (and stimulating) site for the reproduction of religious ideology. The visual and scopic power of the female body is integral to the semiotic ideology of these narratives—indicative of the power not just to promote Islamic sensibilities but also to rewrite certain scripts about the use value and ends of women's sexuality in public space.

In Mecca, Shams says "I struggled for my feelings to be true and right" (22). When Shams is in the inner sanctuary, a woman she meets recites some verses of poetry that she has composed about the hijab—"touching the inner chambers of my heart." Shams begins supplicating

> with the force of belief . . . and tears began to flow silently without stopping. I read the *fātiḥa*, the opening verse of the Qurʾan, like I had never read it before in my life, feeling all the meaning in it that I had, before, considered meaningless. God had sent down some of his mercy on me. And I felt the greatness of the opening of the book. I was crying while my very being was shaking. I continued the circumambulations and felt God's greatness like I had never felt it before in my whole life. I sensed with every word and every letter in the *fātiḥa* as if it embodied in front of me God on High's greatness. (62)

At this moment she "changes completely, even the tenor of my voice changed."[59] But it is not only the bodily performance of ritual, of veiling, of embodied ḥayāʾ that constitutes these bodily subjectivities, this psychic interiority; it is also the discursive inhabitation of the divine word, practiced with the body, grasped with the intellect, felt in the heart, and spoken with the voice.

These narratives become their own form of daʿwa, circulated widely, reproduced, republished, recirculated, and resurfacing in books and articles, on the Internet, as extended footnotes, nestled in other narratives. The multiplicity of these narratives, even as they consolidate a set of analogous motifs, is remarkable. They inhabit older scripts—Qurʾanic, ritualistic, and mystical—but also reinvent older genres like the pilgrimage travelogue and the literature of dream visions. Yet these narratives forge their own genre of testimony as well, one that is profoundly gendered and constructs a vision of the contours of the pious self. Shams al-Barudi's testimony, like so many of the testimonies of "Islamic artists" that followed, is pieced together from former interviews, cobbled from disparate sources, and reprinted from entertainment magazines. Despite—or because of—the repetition of key motifs, events, and signposts across narratives, the voice of the pious woman is depicted as an authentic expression of her true voice.

The promotion of an Islamic art, an Islamic media, and Islamic cultural production is at the crux of these transformations of self. As

[59] This physical transformation in the tenor of the voice becomes a leitmotif in testimonies about the physical transformation effected by the pilgrimage. Abu-Lughod quotes a nearly identical passage from *Repentant Artists: Unpublished Confessions*. This statement, that even "the tone of my voice changed," is repeated verbatim by the more recently veiled Islamic artist Nasrin in Abu Suf's *Fannanat Mutahajjibat*. Lila Abu-Lughod, "Movie Stars and Islamic Moralism in Egypt," *Social Text* no. 42 (April 1, 1995): 55–56; ʿImad Nasif and Amal Khudayr, *Fannanat Taʾibat: Iʿtirafat lam Tunshar* (Cairo: Dar al-Kutub wa-l-Wathaʾiq, 1991), 52–53; Abu Suf, *Fannanat Mutahajjibat*, 32. This element of the changed tone of voice is also reiterated in Maraʿi's *Awakening of Modesty*.

Shams al-Barudi's husband, Hasan Yousef, also a "repentant artist," would comment in an interview about her, "Islam respects serious art and strives toward exploiting it for the ends of Islamic daʿwa." This becomes a struggle between two kinds of imaginaries—one striving for authenticity and truth through a kind of spiritual realism, through the religious instinct of fiṭra, and the other a fabricated, inauthentic self of assumed foreign identities. "Each one of us knows in the core of his self (*nafsihi*) the limits of the permitted and the limits of the prohibited, though some try to cheat themselves and distort their own conscience. . . . they lie to themselves and betray their conscience" (75–77).

These characters in the drama of modern life switch to an Islamic script. Despite their familiarity as celebrities, as veiled women, and as mothers, they are not stock characters but fully fleshed out personalities with whom audiences clearly identify. Though they are recognizable as a type, as the number of repentant stars multiplies, each one brings a creative originality to their performances, performances that are acted out on the stage of the public sphere, especially in the media. As the feminist theorist Judith Butler observes, "The subject is neither ground nor product, but the permanent possibility of a certain resignifying process, one which gets detoured and stalled through other mechanisms of power, but which is power's own possibility of being reworked."[60] The narratives describe performing this Islamic subjectivity as a return to a more authentic, a priori, true Muslim self underlying the accretions of an imposed, hypersexualized identity associated with Western culture. Gender is resignified according to a different script with different "costumes,"[61] a process in which the material object of the hijab—and the body that inhabits it—is reconstituted through the signifying process of telling, narrating, testifying, witnessing. The shifting of roles, narratives, scripts, and performances is a motif repeated in these writings, as they abandon their "former lives" and rewrite their life stories according to Islamic codes. Study of Islamic texts and of the Qurʾan is one of the principal markers of this new life, and their texts are not only overflowing with citations from the Qurʾan and hadith but also graced by introductions by Islamic scholars that commend their newfound commitments to Islam. When Shams al-Barudi is asked what she now does with her time, she replies that she studies, and

[60] Judith Butler, "Contingent Foundations: Feminism and the Question of 'Postmodernism,'" in *Feminists Theorize the Political*, ed. Judith Butler and Joan Scott (New York: Routledge, 1992), 13.

[61] Butler, *Gender Trouble*, 25; Sara Salih, "On Judith Butler and Performativity," in *Sexualities and Communication in Everyday Life*, ed. Karen E. Lovaas and Mercilee M. Jenkins (Thousand Oaks, CA: Sage Publications, 2007), 56.

teaches her children. Ḥayāʾ is not just modesty, life-giving, or revival but also connected with putting on a show, executing a performance, giving life to a role. It is both outside and inside, body and soul, self-cultivation and an ethics of passion; product and ground; habitus and *jouissance*—in short, it is sakan. These intertwined forces are mediated by an Islamic art imagining and imaging an Islamic self, reviving Islamic senses and sensibilities.

Staging the Islamic Self

A certain psychic interiority—and inner belief—becomes essential to the cultivation of an Islamic self "in the age of global visibility." In these testimonies, the hijab, as a mode of discipline and embodiment of Islamic norms, is an ideal mode for cultivating this interiority. "The history of gradual visibility and agency accorded women in modernity, then, is in many ways a history of the molding and remolding of the abstraction of 'psychic interiority,'" writes Rey Chow in an essay on the visual production of women's inner life.[62] This belief, this psychic interiority, acts as a spiritual anchor for the material world of the body. Or, as Foucault (and Butler) might see it, this soul—this psychic interiority symbolized by the object of the hijab—is the prison of the body, requiring submission to its discipline as the very condition for its subjectivity. The process of representation, through the material object of the hijab, as much as the narratives that describe the experience of veiling, helps make visible the invisibility of psychic interiority. And in doing so, it effectively creates this space and enacts the subject that inhabits it.[63] Moreover, the resignification of the material object of the veil (through language and storytelling) aims to transform certain social structures, institutions, and knowledge formations. The politics of visibility structure the narrative arc of these writings about taking the hijab, a struggle that is part of these writers' inner battle to devote themselves fully to God and to turn away from the pleasures of a life of vanity and diversion. It is a struggle to acquire and inhabit Islamic knowledge and to keep this knowledge alive through a living Islam. As Maraʿi writes in *Awakening of Modesty*, it is a Qurʾan articulated on the tongue but literally worn on the body. The personal politics of Islamic knowledge and practice are implicit in veiling narratives, testimonies consistently framed as a rejection of the scripts of Western secular modernity—and the sexual politics of its colonialism. It is also

[62] Chow, *Sentimental Fabulations*, 85.
[63] Moll, "Islamic Televangelism," 22.

a struggle against Western, foreign, and secular modes of visuality, as much as un-Islamic modes of sensibility, subjectivity, and sociability.

Safinaz Kazim, theater critic, journalist, prolific essayist, memoirist, and public intellectual, is one of the most visible and prolific advocates of the return to veiling. She is not a film star nor a television personality but a public intellectual and cultural critic who has an acute sense of the hijab's dramatic role in staging the revival of Islamic knowledge. Kazim is a unique figure of her age—her writings combine memoir, autobiography, politics, literature, and journalism into her own distinctive style. She has published prolifically in the press, as well as putting out nearly twenty collections of essays on various topics. She identifies as a Muslim but has been connected with Arab nationalist, Marxist, feminist, and Islamist activists, though she claims absolute affiliation with none but Islam. Kazim began her career in journalism, becoming famous for a travelogue that she wrote of her experience traveling with her sister in Europe for *Akhbar al-Yawm* in 1959. Between 1964 and 1966 she studied drama at New York University, and on her return she became theater critic for *al-Musawwar* magazine. In 1971, however, she was essentially blacklisted from writing, lost her job, and was ejected from the leftist intellectual milieu in which she circulated, for reasons that she still does not understand. In her writings she agonizes over this period in her life. But it also seemed to precipitate the revival of her Islam, as she goes on the pilgrimage with her mother and takes the veil on her return. Surprisingly, she does not write about her pilgrimage experience, as so many Islamic writers would do (especially in the genre of writings by *fannānāt islāmiyyāt*), despite having written and published many travel memoirs. She writes about the pilgrimage in metaphoric terms, when she compares the experience of going to prison under Sadat to her own kind of hajj. She speaks of the experience of prison as a means of deepening her Islamic experience, devoting herself entirely to ritual worship (like prayer, fasting, and reading the Qur'an), which is its own kind of inner pilgrimage, facilitated by her solitary confinement.[64]

When Kazim returned from the pilgrimage in 1972, she took the veil and also married the Marxist vernacular poet Ahmad Fu'ad Nigm. Despite the seeming mismatch, which all her friends and her mother opposed, she seemed to marry her Islamic commitments to his leftist ones. But she also declared the union a creative one,[65] to support her husband's cultural production, even as she was forced to go underground

[64] Kazim, *'An al-Sijn wa-l-Hurriyya*, 29.

[65] Amira Howeidy, "Safynaz Kazem: Born to Be Wild," *al-Ahram Weekly*, December 23, 1999.

with her writings in the 1970s. Under Sadat she was imprisoned three times, accused of being a "communist": the first time when she was pregnant with her daughter Nawwara, the second time when Nawwara was only a year old, and the third time when she returned from exile in Iraq in 1980. The trauma of being separated from her young daughter had sent Kazim into exile in 1975. She describes her time in Iraq as a Greek tragedy, not only because of Saddam's brutality and his killings but because her mother becomes sick with cancer and dies and her husband begins sleeping with another woman. Later she likens this storm in her life to the prophet Jonah at sea, fleeing against the current of her Islamic duty and wreaking havoc in the process.[66] Jonah, commanded by God to prophesy against evil in the city in Nineveh, goes in the opposite direction by sea, seeking to escape "the presence of the Lord." When a storm arises, the sailors throw Jonah overboard, where he is swallowed by a fish. Finally, when Jonah repents in the belly of the fish, the fish spits him out, and Jonah returns to perform daʿwa. When Kazim returns to Egypt in 1980, she is imprisoned a third time under Sadat, which she compares to being in the belly of the fish. There she repents. And when she is released, she publishes a pent up flood of works, but now written in an Islamic idiom.

The 1970s mark a gap in Kazim's publications, between the "secular" period of her life (and writings) and the surge in her Islamic publications in the 1980s. After Sadat's assassination, Kazim would be released from prison and would finally begin publishing again, weaving her revived Islamic commitments into her writings. Over the next five years, she published six works, all through Islamic publishing houses (Dar al-Iʿtisam, Dar al-Zahraʾ, al-Mukhtar al-Islami, and Maktabat Wahba). After a decade of virtual eclipse from the Egyptian public sphere, she used the Islamic presses as an outlet for her pent up writings in the 1980s, facilitating her reemergence into the Egyptian cultural scene. This political and personal tumult would become fodder for her reappearance in the public sphere, as she staged her return through her revived Islam. She describes a process of struggle against the scripts of a secular society that are written on the body and a corresponding struggle to reinhabit Islamic knowledge through Islamic practice and cultural production. In her book criticizing the movement to unveil in Egypt, she calls for "a methodology of dramatic analysis that reviews the narrative threads of the script, lines, events, characters, words, and theatrical staging, in addition to the projected vision of the director," in order to expose the political and ideological motives of those seeking to strip Egypt of its Islam.[67]

[66] Kazim, *ʿAn al-Sijn wa-l-Hurriyya*, 31.
[67] Kazim, *Fi Masʾalat al-Sufur wa-l-Hijab*, 10.

Although Kazim went on the pilgrimage and took the veil in 1972, she would not begin publishing her religiously oriented writings until a decade later, just after Hamza published her own testimony. Hamza, Kazim, and al-Barudi were pioneers of the genre of veiling narratives, but Kazim belongs to an older generation that came of age during the era of Gamal ʿAbd al-Nasser and Arab nationalism. Kazim was Muhammad Jalal Kishk's colleague and friend, and like him, she moved from an Arab nationalist framework to an Islamic one, even while adapting some of the same political themes (an anti-imperialist, indigenous nationalism, the struggle against intellectual conquest, etc.). Her writings always address politics through an autobiographical, personal lens. But with the shift to an Islamic orientation, she adopts a certain set of motifs structured around the trope of the hijab. The hijab helps give her a certain wholeness and a sense of peace, which she interprets in religious terms as tawḥīd and sakan. It imparts an inner psychological repose in the face of bouts of depression that had plagued her earlier writings.

Two analogous works by Kazim from the 1980s meld the psychological experience of veiling with politics. One is her polemic on veiling, *Fi Masʾalat al-Sufur wa-l-Hijab* (On the Question of Unveiling and Veiling, 1982), published right after her release from prison (and right after Hamza's *Journey*). The second is her collection of essays *ʿAn al-Sijn wa-l-Hurriyya* (On Prison and Freedom, 1986), which combine her Islam with cultural criticism, political commentary, and memoir. Even though Kazim refutes the term Islamist for herself, her own Islamic revival is staged on the issues of the movement—on veiling and political imprisonment, the main subjects of these two texts. *On the Question of Unveiling and Veiling* is a polemic against secularism's intellectual colonialism and its targeting of women's bodies, behaviors, practices, and beliefs. Through women's bodies, she says, this colonialism aims at the heart of Islam. She characterizes the movement to unveil in Egypt as an effort to replace Islam with secularism, concluding: "I put this image in front of our eyes so that we can contemplate it together. . . . Both overtly and covertly there is a relationship between the persistent, hidden, cancerous advance of secularism—a cancer that we do not feel until after the appearance of tumors and the spread of death to the blood, body, and bones—and between the leaders proselytizing for the unveiling of Muslim women throughout the Islamic homeland" (12). Through this image of the Islamic bodily politic, the corruptions of foreign influence—symbolized by unveiling—bring on sickness and death, echoing Sidqi's imagery of the abscess-ridden, unveiled face. The political image of illness invading the umma takes on a vivid corporeality, embodied in not just the female body but a feminized nation that is "raped" (18, 25, 29). In her dramatic, allegorical images, the body gives life to these discursive forms, laying the ground for the possibility of their ideological reproduction. And the hope of the revival lies in the visible embodiment of Islamic knowledge and practice.

Kazim talks about a schizophrenia (*infiṣām*) of the self—the same image and term that Shams al-Barudi would use two years later to describe the roles she played before taking the veil. Kishk would also adopt the term to refer to the schizophrenia in Egyptian society between its secular and religious elements, epitomized by the figure of Qasim Amin.[68] Kazim takes the notion of a split between state and religion, public and private, and transposes it into her inner psychic realm as schizophrenia. She also talks about a chronological split in her life story, between the secular and religious epochs of her life, before she took the veil and after. She reflects on the time of her life before she took the veil: "I find that even though I was Muslim in belief (*al-īmān*) and conviction (*al-ʿaqīda*) in every moment of my life, I was robbed of my Islam: my Islamic conviction was split off from my actions. I suffered on the individual level from this schizophrenia between conviction and behavior, yet our society as a whole suffers from this schizophrenia."[69] This is a split between an outer and an inner self, a painful, alienating divorce carried in both body and soul. It is also a temporal and political split in Egypt between the era of Arab nationalism and that of the return to Islam. Secularism waged a malicious war, Kazim says, to strip Egypt of its Islam and to strip the nahḍa (*baʿth al-nahḍa al-miṣriyya*) from its true origins in Islam. The secularists succeeded in this war and in separating religion from the state, making Egyptians "butt naked without defense" (*ʿarāyā al-ẓahr bi-lā difāʿ*), "our backs exposed" (34). The aim of this stripping naked, she says, was an obscene rape, precipitated by the desire for and infatuation with all that is Western. It was a great *fitna*, she says. Tawḥīd, the unity of God, heals the split between practice and faith and the rift that secularism promotes with religion.

In *On the Question of Veiling and Unveiling*, Kazim describes the Islamic Awakening through the imagery of "birthing pains: the preparation, readiness, training, determination, and endurance to anchor the promised beginnings of the revival. The awakening of the people of the region from their long slumber prepares the way for the healthy birth of the fetus . . . the duration of her secret pregnancy nourished directly from the heart of Islam" (17). The true aim of the movement to unveil, however, is what she calls the "abortion" of the revival and the "rape"

[68] Kishk, *Jahalat ʿAsr al-Tanwir*, 54.
[69] Kazim, *ʿAn al-Sijn wa-l-Hurriyya*, 33.

of Islam. Her 1970 work *Rumantikiyyat*, written before her religious turn, has analogous images of abortion. Describing her bouts with depression, she talks about silence and eclipses (Do you remember the eclipse, Safinaz? Do you remember the eclipse, Safinaz? she asks repetitively). "I fade, wane, and shrink," she says, "until I become an embryo that dwindles until it becomes a seed again, falls, and disappears" (75). This melancholic fear of disappearance and silencing is likened to a reverse kind of pregnancy, a sterility, a sapping of life, an abortion or miscarriage. In *On the Question of Unveiling and Veiling*, though, she reverses these images of depression, silence, and eclipse. Some, she says, think that veiling makes girls depressed as they fade behind "the refuge of their veils." But no, it is a "public declaration," she repeats, a public demonstration of the teachings of religion, its merits, injunctions, and aspects. Rather than a silencing, it is a declaration; rather than a disappearance, a demonstration; rather than depression, a celebration. On the stage of the hijab, Safinaz performs her self; with the script of the revival, she writes her voice. In these essays Kazim expresses her politics and religion with intensely personal, private, interior reflections on her faith. Through these ruminations she constructs a bounded, interior world that she describes as giving her refuge, safety, and peace. Veiling is one of the ways she creates this sacred space, a place safe from the predations of secular tyranny, predations she consistently describes in terms of rape.

On Prison and Freedom elaborates Kazim's vision of a bounded, safe world in the bosom of an invasive secularism. At the beginning of the essay, she reflects on the "split" that secularism effects in the self and soul. For her, not only Islam but the experience of prison—as a pilgrimage—becomes a way of healing that split, by embarking on a spiritual journey into the self, through ritual practice. By comparing her prison experience to Jonah in the belly of the whale, she makes herself into a kind of prophet and *dāʿiya*, but there is also a sense of a rebirth into her sacred mission, as she is ejected back into society. Part of this prophecy is proclaiming the evils of the state, like Jonah, warning people of God's retribution, and urging penance. In other places she compares her exile in Iraq to Jonah fleeing his duty to spread God's word, and the prison, the "fish," becomes her salvation from the storm, as she pledges herself again to spreading God's word. Safinaz likens her emergence from the belly of the fish to the sun's rising. "For the tyrannized the sun always rises, even at night, in prison, or in the grave" (29). This light—of awakening, emancipation, or salvation—is *raḥmat* Allah, she says, evoking God's mercy. She also evokes, through *raḥma*, connected to *raḥm* (womb), her allegorical imagery of a nascent Islamic awakening. Kazim constructs intensely gendered images of a bounded self—bound by walls of prison, by solitary confinement, by the protective contours of the hijab.

Through a set of disparate mediations on a variety of themes (suicide bombing, political incarceration, prison literature, cultural imperialism, discourses of human rights and democracy) in *On Prison and Freedom*, Kazim develops, through a mosaic-like set of pieces, her own theory of an Islamic art. But she also tells the political history of Egypt through fragments of her own story. In one essay, "Tanwiʿat ʿala Masʾalat al-Hijab" (Variations on the Question of the Hijab, 1983), she reflects on the relationship between veiling and Islamic knowledge and cultural expression. The essay begins on the beach, where she observes the victory of Islamic ideology on the bodies of women: there is not a single woman in a bathing suit. The children are playing and mothers are watching them; girls wade out in their pants and shirts or in a long *jilbāb*. "Despite everything, an Islamic conscience has been victorious in Egypt the land of God, opening consciousness of essential conviction (*al-ʿaqīda al-huwiyya*) little by little."[70] The passage connects the veiled body to Egypt through language of identity and its scripts; ideology and conviction mediated through practice. The term that she uses for "essential conviction" (*al-ʿaqīda al-huwiyya*) connotes conviction of an "essential identity," what Kazim calls her own "deep-rooted (*mutaʾaṣṣil*: authentic), permanent belief. She decries the "imitation" of Europe, using a word (*muḥākāa*) etymologically connected to the concept of "narration." Instead she calls for an Arabic letters of the *salaf* that "are Qurʾanic certainty and unity; they are Arab letters that became the pillar of Islamic art for over 1,400 years of surging vitality" (50). The title of the essay echoes the language of Kazim's earlier booklet on veiling, but now the "question" is linked not just to Islamic letters but also to Islamic art. The subjects of the different essays in this volume are wildly diverse, but in their entirety she suggests her own vision of an Islamic art, of an Islamic cultural life framed as variations on musical themes, fantasias, string compositions, mosaics, theater, poetry, novels, and "Islamic artists."

Kazim is not an Islamist, she repeatedly insists. She is not a feminist. She is a Muslim. This is sufficient for encompassing all these identities. "I'm a Muslim, always was," she says. "Islam sums it all up." This is the ontological Islam, she seems to be saying, not some Islamism that is Islamic-like; this is the ontological me, not some Islamic-like self. The autobiographical "I" has been interpreted as a sign of the enlightenment subject—unified, rational, coherent, autonomous, free,

[70] Ibid., 49.

but also white, male, Western.[71] Here we see a very different self unified through tawḥīd, a self that is also distinctly feminine and Muslim. Julia Kristeva refers to the self as a fiction sustained by representation, but here we see a Muslim self sustained and inspired by ritual practice and bodily performativity.[72] I think it is helpful to think about Foucault's sense of the process of subjection, or *assujetissement*, as a mode of subject formation. It was through the very image of the prison that Foucault theorized the production of the self and of the soul. Kazim resignifies that prison, turning it into a sacred space for the production of an Islamic self. Here we see submission to Islam not just producing the Muslim subject but authoring a particular kind of body, self, and psyche. Rather than subjugation, darkness, and oppression (*ẓulm*), she sees liberation and the dawning of a new day.

Conclusion

These testimonies revolve around the particularly rich symbolism of the veil: in the Islamic tradition, orientalist and colonial discourses, secular modernity, and the nationalist imaginary. In her classic analysis of the return to veiling, Fedwa El Guindi refers to the "complexity and rich symbolism in the institution of veiling," as she talks about the Islamic movement as a "creative alternative (from within and below) to institutional channels, be they political, legal, social or religious. It is . . . a domain rich in symbolism and ritual which serves as a dynamic storage area, as it were, for indigenous premises meaningful to culture bearers."[73] The testimonies give veiling new life through new stories, as well as describing their own minds and spirits as "revived" by the act of veiling. They emulate Islamic stories that they weave into their own stories, using them to guide their own paths to religiosity, narratives that are in turn disseminated and circulated among ever-wider publics, spreading the word in the age of technological reproducibility.[74] Veiling is one way of cultivating piety, but it also becomes connected to other kinds of embodied discursive practices: weeping by the Kaʿba, submitting to a religious authority's intellectual guidance, engaging in

[71] Sidonie A. Smith and Julia Watson, "Situating Subjectivity in Women's Autobiographical Practices," in *Women, Autobiography, Theory: A Reader*, ed. Sidonie A. Smith and Julia Watson (Madison: University of Wisconsin Press, 1998), 27.

[72] Ibid., 19.

[73] El Guindi, "Veiling Infitah with Muslim Ethic," 466, 475.

[74] Saba Mahmood, "Preface to the 2012 Edition," in *Politics of Piety: The Islamic Revival and the Feminist Subject* (Princeton, NJ: Princeton University Press, 2012), xi.

the daʿwa of writing about one's spiritual transformation, and "broadcasting Islam."

In the 1980s religion was something to be "managed" and "controlled," "containing and neutralizing a domestic Islamic threat."[75] By the mid-1990s new Islamic satellite channels like Iqraa and al-Risala began producing popular Islamic programming that was also entertaining in nature, with the aim of attracting viewers. Veiled (former) movie stars and television announcers became integral to this programming. "Film actresses and drama stars are brought in, now in Islamic attire, to preach a moral message of repentance to an audience which tunes in as much for spiritual uplift as to take pleasure in seeing their favorite celebrity speaking 'From the Heart'—as the title of [the wildly popular Islamic televangelist] Amr Khaled's first show puts it."[76] Although Saudi capital and consumer demand helped precipitate this shift to popular Islamic television channels,[77] the stories of Islamic media stars paved the way for the Islamicization of popular entertainment media. Their narratives pioneered new models of righteous living for women, using new pulpits for proselytization, and developing new modes of daʿwa rooted in Islamic practice coded as specifically feminine. Their *siyar dhātiyya* (autobiographies) are modern *tarājim* (biographies of the early Muslim community) forged for a new era through new communicative technologies.[78] The first-person personal testimony imagines the realization of self as a spiritual journey, drawing on classical stories, paradigms, texts, and rituals from the Islamic tradition rendered in a popular idiom.

These stories demonstrate the power of visuality to transform other cultural fields and alter their cultural status, not just of literature in this case but also of religious knowledge, now embodied in (and inhabited by) these "repentant stars." Their "morally impassioned rebuke of images goes hand in hand with the massive production and circulation of more images."[79] Even as they denounce the male gaze, they reify it by flagging it, signaling its significance, calling attention to its power. The testimonies deploy the trope of the veil to narrate life stories, a self that

[75] Lila Abu-Lughod, *Dramas of Nationhood: The Politics of Television in Egypt* (Chicago: University of Chicago Press, 2004), 163–92; Moll, "Islamic Televangelism," 14.

[76] Moll, "Islamic Televangelism," 9.

[77] Naomi Sakr, *Satellite Realms: Transnational Television, Globalization and the Middle East* (London: I. B. Tauris, 2002).

[78] Interestingly, Hamza titles a later work, a collection of disparate essays, an "autobiography." See Hamza, *Li-llah Ya Zamri.*

[79] Chow, *Rey Chow Reader*, xiv. In his introduction, Bowman writes, "The impact of the cinematic apparatus as an epochal modern field in its own right and as a new cultural realm sent shock waves through other cultural fields (such as literature), challenging them, altering their cultural status and their forms."

the material object of the hijab helps delineate and define. The narratives develop a semiotics of the veil that intimates active religious commitments, stirs up a range of feelings, connotes certain kinds of experience, and defines the type of person that inhabits the veil—her moral quality, virtue, and allegiances. The hijab is used as a weapon against a master narrative about Western visuality—and female sexuality—but it is also a visual marker of cultural authenticity, Islamic identity, and Arab ethnicity. In these texts, the hijab signifies a revival of religious knowledge, knowledge that the pious self inhabits, through practice as much as through conviction (*ʿaqīda*) and belief (*īmān*), desire (*raghba*) and instinct (fiṭra).

This chapter, however, is concerned not just with the rise of an Islamicized cinema, television, satellite, and Internet but also with how "the performance of representation" helps enact "a representational subject." The "sacred event" of taking the veil "becomes the visible transformation of inward dispositions that is effected through these performances." This is what Yasmin Moll, an anthropologist of Islamic media, calls "visual daʿwa" where the hijab becomes a "walking symbol of Islam." She calls for analyzing public spheres both as "sites of disembodied debate" and as "arenas for the formation and enactment of embodied social identities."[80] This chapter analyzes how this new media draws on older forms of Islamic knowledge, from the Qurʾan, from scholars of al-Azhar, and from the Sufi tradition, reinventing and reviving key elements of the Islamic tradition through modern forms of technological reproducibility. This new media develops a new kind of aesthetics, what this literature calls an "Islamic art," for the promotion of Islamic sensibilities. The visual screen of the hijab is critical for imagining, creating, and cultivating Islamic selves and citizens in the age of mechanical reproduction, through modern techniques of self. It takes on new meanings as emblem not just of religiosity but also of a deep interiority, an authentic inwardness, and a "real" self where faith is both embodied and performed. Moreover, the "private" realm of home and family becomes the sphere proper for the cultivation of these selves, where Islamic knowledge is lived and reproduced in ordinary, daily life. This private life, publicly proclaimed, develops a political economy of the Islamic family for the Islamic revival, as well as an aesthetics of a properly cultivated Islamic self.

[80] Moll, "Islamic Televangelism," 22.

CHAPTER 5

The Islamic Homeland

Iman Mustafa on Women's Work

Criticizing "the working woman" in the mainstream economic journal *al-Ahram al-Iqtisadi*, the journalist Iman Muhammad Mustafa published a ten-part series of articles in 1989, in the midst of economic crisis and Egypt's contentious negotiations with the International Monetary Fund (IMF). Flowing from—and in response to—a tide of reports published in the 1980s on women in development, the articles identify women as a great, untapped resource of human capital in Egypt. Using the statistics, charts, arguments, and language of development reports, Mustafa critiques Western, secular, feminist valorization of remunerated labor through a celebration of the economic and social worth of women's work in the household economy. Women's efforts are better spent investing in the human resources of the household economy, she argues, rather than being exploited by the economic and moral predations of wage labor. In 1991, just when Egypt came to an agreement with the IMF, Mustafa published a version of the articles as a book entitled *Imbaraturiyyat al-Nisa' al-ʿAmilat* (Empire of the Working Women). Reframing her argument as an Islamic one, the book—published by the Islamist press al-Zahra' li-l-Iʿlam al-ʿArabi—opens with a verse from the Qur'an (41:33) about "good words and righteous work."[1] The first chapter, "Islam . . . and Woman's Work," states the book's aim: "to rectify all that resists conforming and harmonizing with the nature that God created in us (*faṭaranā Allah*), rather than being mere vehicles for the proselytizing call to emancipation."[2]

This chapter traces the rhizome-like proliferation of debates over women's work—tangled dialectics among development experts, femi-

[1] "And who is better of speech than he who calls to God and works righteousness and says I am among the Muslims" (41:33).

[2] Mustafa, *al-Nisa' al-ʿAmilat*, 57. The language is taken from verse 30:30 from the Qur'an: "the nature with which God made people."

Cover of the September 4, 1989, issue of *al-Ahram al-Iqtisadi* (no. 1077) featuring the first of series of articles by Iman Mustafa "Empire of the Working Women!" and a photo essay by Sherif Sonbol. Photograph courtesy of Sherif Sonbol.

nists, academics, politicians, Marxists, Azharis, Islamists, and journalists like Mustafa. Mustafa charts a specific chronological timeline of these debates, from 1974 to 1989, a period of intense economic and political liberalization in Egypt. In the midst of dominant discourses about the liberating potential of paid labor emerged an Islamic narrative about the economic worth of women's work in the home and family. Raising questions about the "price" that society pays for neglecting the bonds of children, family, and community, this narrative emphasized the social and economic value of work in the "informal economy" of the family. Though these Islamic writers situate themselves in opposition to the imperialism of a global neoliberalism, they employ development language of economic crisis, progress, and productivity, as well as of rights, choice, equality, freedom, and independence. These appear as two narrative strands: the secular, foreign, and neoliberal, on one hand, and the Islamic, Egyptian, and indigenous, on the other. But both narrative strands have similar aims: to harness the productive power of women's labor to the social and economic progress of an Egypt intent on competing on a global scale. One side of this discourse—associated with international development organizations, global capitalism, secular liberalism, and Western feminism—sees women engaged in the paid workforce of the formal economy as the means to total development.[3] The other side—seen as an indigenous Islamic discourse—calls for women's commitment to nurturing the family "as the core of society, its first cell, and the key to true change."[4] In development reports, this discourse of the family is implicitly understood as antifeminist and attributed to culture, religion, and custom. But it is also strangely familiar. In the United States this type of narrative of the family is associated with the neoconservative movement and public figures like Phyllis Schlafly, Anita Bryant, and Sarah Palin. Some thinkers interpret neoconservatism as developing in tandem with neoliberalism, emphasizing religion, community, and family as absorbing the shocks of economic developments that increasingly disconnect traditional affective ties.[5] A neoconservative Islamic family is conceptualized as the locus of community and of social discipline that helps promote an Islamic modernity, sociability, and politics for future generations. This family, "a haven in a heartless world," is the sacred interior of a capitalism that emphasizes materialist desires, consumption, and individualism.[6] The family, a utopian sphere of self-

[3] Lajnat al-Khidmat, *Tanmiyat al-Marʾa*.
[4] Mustafa, *al-Nisaʾ al-ʿAmilat*, 15.
[5] Brown, "American Nightmare."
[6] Lasch, *Haven in a Heartless World*; Raouf Ezzat, *al-Marʾa wa-l-ʿAmal al-Siyasi*, 173–81.

less relations, becomes a reaction against the mercenary relationships of a capitalist society, as much as one of its products.

Family, the mother, women, and children, Mustafa argues, are the interior of society: its depth, soul, kernel, nucleus, center, and starting point. With vivid, evocative imagery, Mustafa identifies motherhood and family as the very core of society, as the lifeblood connecting its scattered parts. She begins the book by describing how a minority discourse about women's work outside the family has come to dominate public consciousness, partly through manipulation of the media. She talks about this dominant discourse in terms of an ideological authoritarianism, an undemocratic suppression of the desires, opinions, and beliefs of the majority. But she also writes of this dominant discourse in psychological terms, as a form of repression of "the hopes and desires of the majority." This discourse perpetrates a lie, suppressing the truth at the heart of the majority. A Westernized elite has been able to consolidate a unified image, speaking with "a loud voice capable of obliterating other opinions." "It appears as a truth personified," she writes, "as if she [truth is feminine] is a body moving everywhere. . . . Though the minority opinion has gained preeminence, the buried hopes and desires of the majority remain in the silenced and repressed breasts" (12–13). The dominant (minority) discourse is epitomized through the feminine figure—in the very "body"—of the working woman. The liberating potential of this woman, of this body, is a lie. It is a false image of women, the intellectual invasion of a dominant image of modern womanhood that does not reflect the truth of women's experiences—not their beliefs, their practices, their desires, or their reality. The truth of women's work, she says, is a "truth buried deep in ourselves"; it is the truth that children speak about, the pain of disconnection. Using vivid bodily imagery of desires buried in the chest, of an interior space of self where truth lies, of heart and soul, Mustafa calls for the liberation of truth. Superimposed on these images of the true heart and soul of society are images of the social body, with the family, mother, women, and children at its center. There, she says, "the scattered, dispersed majority collects its unified desires and its shared hopes." Employing psychological language of an inner psyche and self, she also calls for a liberation of the collective desires of the majority. This liberation is also an economic liberation from the imperialism of a free market economy, an economy that values monetary remuneration over all other forms of labor. But it is also a liberation of a body politic so long dominated by an undemocratic elite imposing itself on the desires of the majority. She acknowledges mirroring discourses—of a modernity that defines itself against tradition, but also of an Islamic, indigenous discourse that defends itself against the "intellectual invasion" (*hujūm*) of the West. Her aim, she says, is not to return women to the home but to speak the "plain honest truth among ourselves," "the truth that we realize in the insides of selves, souls, and psyches (*anfusinā*)."

Telling the "truth" about the logistical difficulties faced by women working outside the home is an issue that has also erupted in American public discourse, with claims about the "lies" told about the emancipating power of wage labor.[7] "What have we collectively traded?" Mustafa asks, using the word for commerce (*tijāra*). What do we desire? What is the relationship between current economic pressures and the task of raising generations of the future? Is the social cost of women's work worth the economic return of that work? Where is the conscience of the world? The beginning of reform lies with women. "If we want true reform," she writes, "let's begin with a social organization in which the family is the kernel of society and its primary unit, the key to true change" (12–15).

The Context: Economic Liberalization

Public debates over the nature of women's work (inside the home and outside the home) first erupted in the late nineteenth- and early twentieth-century awakening known as the *nahḍa*. With increased educational opportunities and literacy for women, debates erupted—many in the women's press—about whether education should prepare women for work in the home or in wage labor. Though there was an acknowledged need for women in professions like midwifery and education, discussions of women's work tended to focus on women's labor in the family and the domestic sphere, reflecting the class biases of the people writing about women's work—middle-class women who were not forced by economic exigency to work outside the home. As historians acknowledge, one of the most striking developments in debates over women's work was the crystallization of a discourse about the domestic sphere.[8] Domestic work became professionalized, "with its own schools, texts, journals, and a jargon. Phrases like *tadbīr al-manzil* (household management) and *rabbat al-dār* (mistress of the house) fre-

[7] Anne-Marie Slaughter, "Why Women Still Can't Have It All," *Atlantic*, August 2012; Sindhu Hirani Blume, "Lies I Was Told: Women, Work, and 'Having It All,'" Pricewater houseCoopers International Limited, *The Gender Agenda*, July 19, 2012, http://pwc.blogs.com/gender_agenda/2012/07/lies-i-was-told-women-work-and-having-it-all.html.

[8] Badran, *Feminists, Islam, and Nation*, 61; Beth Baron, *The Women's Awakening in Egypt: Culture, Society, and the Press* (New Haven, CT: Yale University Press, 1997), 146; Shakry, "Schooled Mothers and Structured Play."

quently appeared in the press."[9] In Beth Baron's seminal work *Women's Awakening in Egypt*, she discusses the emergence of a modern household in conjunction with the capitalist economy. Women's writings played a critical role in reimagining and restructuring the domestic sphere. With the transition to a capitalist economy, Baron observes, men worked with fixed wages and longer, more regular hours away from home.

> This may have left a vacuum of authority in the home, into which women willingly stepped. By elaborating woman's role as manager of the home and as wife and mother, intellectuals did not see themselves as reaffirming a customary gender division of labor prescribed by religion. They sought to revalue women's domestic work and invest it with greater meaning. At the same time, they strove to restructure family roles and relations, placing the couple at the center of the family, shifting some authority from the husband to the wife, and turning more attention to childhood. (146)

Modern literature shifted attention to the mother, her pedagogical role in raising children, and the importance of proper household management and, especially, economy.[10] "Household management placed a special stress on productivity," Baron writes. "The new emphasis placed on productivity and order was linked to 'real savings' in the household budget. Although their work in the home went unremunerated, it had economic value in the eyes of authors, some of whom suggested that the housewife be paid a monthly allowance. Housewives managed money; urged to be careful in spending, they wanted concrete advice on budgeting" (156). The household became a critical domain for the management of an economy invested in the hands of an educated, modern middle class in which women, mothers, and wives played key roles. "The values associated with the ideology of domesticity were greater efficiency and economy in the home, appealing to the middle class, raising the value of housework and of women in the eyes of society" (156). These older discourses of women's work would be reconfigured in the era of neoliberal expansion, in which the household and family were interpreted as not only one of the most critical units of economic development but also an indigenous economy cultivating Egypt's most sacred natural resources.

Mustafa's timeline of debates over women's work begins only fifteen years earlier, in 1974, the year Anwar Sadat initiated his free

[9] Baron, *Women's Awakening in Egypt*, 156.

[10] Also see Badran, *Feminists, Islam, and Nation*, 63.

market economic reforms known as the infitāḥ.[11] It was also the year that American president Richard Nixon visited Egypt and pledged aid, money that began to flow into Egypt only after Sadat's "journey to Jerusalem" in 1977. For a loan of $146 million from the IMF, Egypt agreed to a set of structural adjustment policies that included cutting state subsidies on basic goods like flour, sugar, rice, and gas. But when riots erupted in all of Egypt's major cities, the state reversed its policy.[12] On the eve of the Camp David Accords the following year, the IMF approved a loan of $700 million.[13] During this period, international organizations focused not only on privatizing the economy but also on harnessing women's labor to the project of economic development, partly through reform of the family and the "informal economy" (what some reports call the "traditional economy"). Centers, studies, reports, conferences, and projects all targeted women's work as "the entryway to total development."

The United States Agency for International Development (USAID) documents of the 1970s show great concern with the "human resource setting in Egypt" and especially with developing a "comprehensive planning system" for cultivating Egyptian "manpower."[14] Women—identified as a source of untapped human capital—are of paramount concern to these development reports, as they fret over the low productivity of Egypt's labor force. Studies bemoan "the significant problem of underutilization" and the high "degree of nonproductive labor" or "nonproductives" in Egypt—urban women, the unemployed, agricultural workers, and those contributing to the informal economy.[15]

[11] Saad Eddin Ibrahim, Said Abdel-Messih, and Hans Lofgren, *Governance and Structural Adjustment: The Egyptian Case* (Cairo: Ibn Khaldoun Center for Development Studies, 1994), 7.

[12] Mervat F. Hatem, "Privatization and the Demise of State Feminism in Egypt," in *Mortgaging Women's Lives: Feminist Critiques of Structural Adjustment*, ed. Pamela Sparr (New York: Palgrave Macmillan, United Nations, 1994), 40.

[13] Bessma Momani, *IMF-Egyptian Debt Negotiations*, Cairo Paper in Social Science (Cairo: American University in Cairo Press, 2005), 1; Margaret Garritsen de Vries, *IMF History (1972–1978), Volume 1: Narrative and Analysis* (Washington, DC: International Monetary Fund, 1985). Egypt would default on the conditions of the 1978 loan, even after spending $87 million.

[14] David Evans and United States Department of Labor, *The Development of a Human Resource Information Planning and Policy System for Egypt: A Feasibility Study* (Advisory Council on Technical Education and Manpower Development and the National Committee on Manpower and Training, United States Agency for International Development, June 23, 1978), 28. For a discussion of the production of national developmentalist discourse in Egypt, see Timothy Mitchell, *Rule of Experts: Egypt, Techno-Politics, Modernity* (Berkeley: University of California Press, 2002), 209–43.

[15] Jerome M. Segal, *The Employment Problem in Egypt: The Extent of Non-Productive Labor Force* (Washington, DC: Bureau for Program and Policy Coordination, United States

Women's labor became the site of intense scrutiny and the object of reform, identified as a primary source of underutilized economic potential that could be drawn into development. Initiatives targeted women for training and education but also the family as potentially impinging on economic productivity. Population control was a critical pillar of the development agenda, with millions of dollars in US aid allocated for family planning immediately after Egypt's negotiations with the IMF in 1977: $87 million in funds was pledged between 1977 and 1983, and an additional $117 million between 1983 and 1992.[16] The United States, the World Bank, USAID, the United Nations, and the IMF heavily invested in women's productive labor in the formal economy, an issue closely connected to the management of reproductive labor within the family.[17] Economic development projects in Egypt envisioned a well-planned, well-managed modern family as facilitating women's participation in the broader economic activities of society and as promoting the overall economic development of the nation.

New legislation, government reports, development projects, and policy initiatives focused on how to facilitate women's participation in the "productive labor" of the formal economy. Productive labor is understood as that which contributes to national growth in "productive/expansionary sectors" like industry, finance, commerce, and services. In contrast, these reports emphasize the "belief that additions to the informal sector are not productive uses of labor."[18] Despite the wide use of the term "informal sector" in these documents, it remains largely undefined (or "unclassified") but is vaguely associated with earnings not monitored or taxed by the government. The World Bank gives two main (and very limited) definitions of the informal sector, of subsistence-level and criminal or corrupt-type economic activities that evade regulation. Development writings on women's labor in Egypt constantly voice frustration at the difficulty of accounting for and measuring women's (informal) work, leading to gross underestimations of women's economic contributions, productivity, and labor. The "invisibility" of this work is a constant motif. How to make the work "visible" to the economy becomes one of the biggest challenges for economic development in the region.[19] "A comprehensive human resource

Agency for International Development, September 1981), 10; Lajnat al-Khidmat, *Tanmiyat al-Marʾa*, 11–12, 26; Mustafa, *al-Nisaʾ al-ʿAmilat*, 79–85.

[16] Kamran Asdar Ali, *Planning the Family in Egypt: New Bodies, New Selves* (Austin: University of Texas Press, 2002), 32.

[17] Ibid., 31–32.

[18] Segal, *Employment Problem in Egypt*, 3.

[19] Lajnat al-Khidmat, *Tanmiyat al-Marʾa*, 24–25; Camillia Fawzi Solh, *al-Marʾa wa-l-Faqr fi Mintaqat ESCWA: Qadaya wa-Ihtimamat*, Studies of the Arab Woman in Development

information system," one report states, is the "cornerstone of any economic development strategy."[20]

Development documents continually worry about the difficulty of accounting for work in the household, gauging the productivity of women's labor in the informal economy, and measuring it in statistics and numbers. They seek to formalize this labor, through a systematization of women's work, training and education, "family planning," and the reformulation of the family as a crucial economic unit. But it is precisely the hidden quality of this work that makes the family the site of potential mobilization, frustratingly outside the reach of these international organizations, an economy whose worth cannot necessarily be measured by the same gauges. In this way, a spiritual economy of the Islamic family was reinvented for the neoliberal age, as an alternative value system and a "politics of informality."[21]

By beginning her timeline in 1974, Mustafa connects contentious debates over women's work to the context of economic liberalization, reforms that directly and aggressively targeted women's labor. These discourses of economic development are consistently framed as a means to securing women's right to work, their economic independence (from men), and gender equality. Development projects, studies, reports, and conferences connect themselves to the goals of the United Nations Decade for Women, whose first objective—development—was later taken up by the Arab Human Development Reports (focusing on women, freedom, knowledge production, etc.)[22] Women's labor is cloaked in a positive ideology of liberation from the traditional constraints of the "patriarchal family system,"[23] even while obscuring the harsh logistical realities faced by working women—realities that Mustafa's articles set out to expose.

(New York: Economic and Social Commission for Western Asia, United Nations, 1995); Valentine M. Moghadam, *Women, Work, and Economic Reform in the Middle East and North Africa* (Boulder, CO: Lynne Rienner Publishers, 1998); Bier, *Revolutionary Womanhood*, 62. Bier writes: "The focus on formal waged labor consistently underestimates the productive capacity of Egypt's women by ignoring their participation in the 'informal economy.'"

[20] Evans and United States Department of Labor, *Human Resource Information Planning*, 3, 15.

[21] Raouf Ezzat, "Politics of Informality."

[22] For a critique of the Arab Human Development Reports, see Frances S. Hasso, "Empowering Governmentalities Rather than Women: The Arab Human Development Report 2005 and Western Development Logics," *International Journal of Middle East Studies* 41, no. 1 (2009): 73. Hasso discusses how the ADHR "treats Arab societies as exceptionally patriarchal" but ignores "how colonial, imperial, and capitalist styles of intervention . . . have empowered modern patriarchies."

[23] Julinda Abu Nasr, Nabil F. Khoury, and Henry Azzam, eds., *Women, Employment, and Development in the Arab World* (Berlin: Mouton, 1985), 131.

A dual-wage household becomes primarily a means of boosting the family to a middle-class status, through the acquisition of commodities associated with the modern, bourgeois household. Development reports confirm this, showing that lower-middle-class women mainly work outside the home because they want to "raise their standard of living," not for survival or subsistence.[24] The additional income envisioned from women's work helps support the services and products required to produce such a family, one dependent on modern modes of food preparation, childcare and childrearing, appliances, household maintenance, and other forms of domestic labor.[25] In her book on working women and the new veiling in Cairo, Arlene MacLeod describes "the specific economic ideology of this transitional group, trying to edge their way up from lower to middle-class status. This ideology emphasizes gaining a higher status and a level of household goods commensurate with middle-class standing."[26] The testimony of MacLeod's interviewees echoes Mustafa's portrait of the tired and harried mother working to bring home extra income for appliances (refrigerator, fan, washing machine, tape deck, cassettes), clothes, a bigger apartment, and children's education. "Despite their anger and increasing cynicism," MacLeod writes, "these women accept the idea of ever expanding need and the goal of getting ahead—of consumerism and mobility."[27] Appliances help transform the family into a unit of consumption (rather than production) but also integrate this family into an international consumer class connected by communications technology. Media like televisions, cassette players, video machines, Internet, satellites, and so forth help channel global images of a normative middle-class home and its models of consumption. One of Mustafa's most vivid images is of the working woman racing home to prepare dinner and straighten the house while her husband and children sit in front of the television or watch the latest rented videos. "She victimizes herself," Mustafa writes, "in keeping with the characteristics of progress in this era."[28] Mustafa challenges this consumerist ethic by imagining an "alternative economy," with women as cultivators of household resources and

[24] Lajnat al-Khidmat, *Tanmiyat al-Mar'a*, 25–26; Radwan, *Bahth Zahirat al-Hijab*, 1984.

[25] The emphasis in many of these initiatives is on the availability of appliances to ease the burden of housework. International Labour Office, *Employment and Conditions of Work of African Women: Second African Regional Conference Addis Ababa 1964* (Geneva: International Labour Office, 1964); Lajnat al-Khidmat, *Tanmiyat al-Mar'a*, 41; Bier, *Revolutionary Womanhood*, 81–89. As Bier observes, "In addition to day care, the other social policy solution posed to the problem of female worker productivity was to increase the availability of labor-saving domestic technology" (81).

[26] MacLeod, *Accommodating Protest*, 85–86.

[27] Ibid., 89–90.

[28] Mustafa, *al-Nisa' al-'Amilat*, 25.

family values. Yet this unit reproduces some of the assumptions about the economic functions of the family, women's labor, and household management for the value system of a neoliberal economy.

Neoliberal Expansion and the Development of Women's Work

A proliferation of writings connected women to the problem of economic development during the Sadat years, addressed through a satellite of concerns about birth control, family structure and organization, and gender relations. The reports treat these concerns as problems and accordingly cultivate a certain recognition among subject populations about the need for reform (and restructuring) for the good of progress and the good of the national and global economy.[29] This biopolitics intensely focuses specifically on Arab women as a subgroup that has been particularly (frustratingly) outside the reach of a globally conceived regime of rights. Later development reports constantly express aggravation with the low rate of employment among Arab women, equating it with social, political, and economic repression (slow progress and backwardness). The socialist government of Gamal ʿAbd al-Nasser had also focused on women's participation in the workforce. Under Sadat, foreign capital would become inordinately invested in the question of women's labor. Not only were vast amounts of money spent, but a staggering amount of technocratic skill and human effort was devoted to researching and reporting on the issue.

The onslaught of development discourses around Arab women began soon after Sadat took power. In 1972 UNICEF, the League of Arab Nations, and the International Center for Adult Employment Education organized a conference on "The Arab Woman and Human Development" that focused largely on women's employment and its role in economic progress. As in the development writings that would proliferate later on, the conference primarily concentrated on how to reform the family so that women's labor could become more economically productive. The most critical aspect of this reform was family-planning initiatives and awareness.[30] In the midst of Sadat's overtures to Israel

[29] Hasso observes that "the major task of intervention is to have Arab and other oppressed women 'recognize' this global subject-position, which requires them to gain a universalized understanding of womanhood." Hasso, "Empowering Governmentalities," 69.

[30] League of Arab States, UNICEF, and Markaz al-Dawli li-l-Taʿlim al-Wazifi li-l-Kitab fi al-ʿAlam al-ʿArabi, *al-Marʾa al-ʿArabiyya wa-l-Tanmiya al-Qawmiyya*. The term *al-Tanmiya al-Qawmiyya* is not exactly "human development" but more accurately "development of

in 1977—and his negotiations with the IMF—aid began pouring into Egypt. Early development projects targeted privatization, the promotion of foreign investment and trade, and "business procurement," but millions of dollars were also devoted to family planning and population control—known as the Women in Development projects. These reports generally address the shape and nature of the family structure, its organization and values, and how these might impinge on—or facilitate—economic development.[31]

With the influx of money from international aid and the IMF loan in 1977, UNICEF helped set up a Center for Women and Development at al-Azhar's Women's Faculty. The center's aims dovetailed with, and followed up on, the objectives of the 1975 International Women's Year (IWY)—development, equality, and peace. Sadat's wife Jihan had led an Egyptian delegation to the IWY conference in Mexico City, a group that included development expert Nadia Youssef and family-planning activist Aziza Hussein.[32] On the first lady's return, she presided over

---

the people." It notably suggests "people" as a gens of the region rather than all "humans" or even nations.

[31] See, for example, Andrea Rugh, *Women in Development Projects in Egypt: Final Report* (Washington, DC: USAID, May 31, 1979); Andrea Rugh, *Family in Contemporary Egypt* (Syracuse, NY: Syracuse University Press, 1984); USAID/Cairo Development Information Center, *Women in Development: Special Bibliography* (Washington, DC: USAID, May 1980); Heba El Kholy, *Women in Development: Assessment of Selected USAID-Financed Projects* (Washington, DC: USAID Office of Women in Development, March 9, 1987); Jean C. Weidemann and Zohra Merabet, *Egyptian Women and Microenterprise: The Invisible Entrepreneurs*, Development Alternatives, Inc., Growth and Equity through Microenterprise Investment (Washington, DC: USAID Office of Women in Development, March 1992); Soraya Altorki and Huda Zurayq, *Taghayyur al-Qiyam fi al-ʿAʾila al-ʿArabiyya*, Studies of the Arab Woman and Development (New York: United Nations, Economic and Social Commission for Western Asia, 1994).

[32] Nadia Haggag Youssef, "Women Workers and Economic Development: A Comparative Study of Latin America and the Middle East" (PhD diss., University of California, 1970); Nadia Haggag Youssef, *Women and Work in Developing Societies*, Population Monograph Series (Berkeley: Berkeley Institute of International Studies, University of California, 1974); Nadia Youssef, "The Interrelationship between the Division of Labour in the Household, Women's Roles, and Their Impact on Fertility," in *Women's Roles and Population Trends in the Third World*, ed. Richard Anker and Mayra Buvinic (London: Routledge, 1982); Nadia Haggag Youssef and Carol B. Hetler, *Rural Households Headed by Women: A Priority Concern for Development*, World Employment Programme Research, Working Paper (Geneva: International Labour Office, 1984). Youssef now works at the National Center for Population and Development in Cairo. Hussein was Egypt's first woman representative to the UN General Assembly (in 1954), was a UN expert on the role of women in development, and led an Egyptian delegation to the UN's World Population Year Conference in Addis Abba. Between 1977 and 1983, Hussein was president of the International Planned Parenthood Federation. She also founded the Cairo Family Planning Association. See Irene Tinker and Arvonne Fraser, eds., *Developing Power: How Women Transformed International Development* (New York: Feminist Press at CUNY, 2004).

another conference, *Makanat al-Marʾa fi al-Usra al-Islamiyya* (The Place of Woman in the Islamic Family, 1975), at al-Azhar's International Islamic Center for Population Studies and Research—another center established in the aftermath of the IWY. This was the inaugural conference of the center, established in 1975 with assistance from the United Nations Population Council. The conference reiterated the family as a "fundamental unit for building society; a microcosmic image of society itself; society takes from the family its means of government, organization, and modes of nation building."[33] One of the lectures, by the Islamic thinker Bint al-Shatiʾ, proposed an interpretation of the Islamic family—and particularly of men's guardianship—as purely economic, an interpretation that has become widely embraced in new feminist interpretations of verse 4:34 from the Qurʾan.[34] It is an economic vision that understands the reciprocal rights and duties in the family as connected to men's obligation (duty) to provide for women financially, which is their "right."[35] Although the Center for Women and Development would be short lived, shut down in 1981, only a few years after its establishment, its work would be conceptually carried on by the al-Azhar International Islamic Center for Population Studies and Research. The latter organization has played a critical role in development, with a number of high-profile projects undertaken with—and funded by—USAID, UNICEF, and the Ford Foundation.[36]

The Egyptian state and international organizations jointly worked to situate initiatives around women and development in indigenous Islamic institutions, thinkers, and intellectual production. These efforts targeted the family as a social institution, promoting Islamic knowledge around the issue of the family and around the regulation of women's reproductive powers. The language and academic style of the

[33] International Islamic Center for Population Studies and Research, al-Azhar, *Makanat al-Marʾa fi al-Usra al-Islamiyya* (Cairo: International Islamic Center for Population Studies and Research, al-Azhar, 1975), 69.

[34] Barbara Stowasser, "Gender Issues in Contemporary Qurʾan Interpretation," in *Islam, Gender, and Social Change*, ed. Yvonne Haddad and John Esposito (Oxford: Oxford University Press, 1998), 40; Amina Wadud, *Qurʾan and Woman: Rereading the Sacred Text from a Woman's Perspective* (New York: Oxford University Press, 1999), 69.

[35] Bint al-Shatiʾ, "Shakhsiyyat al-Marʾa fi al-Qurʾan al-Karim," in *Makanat al-Marʾa fi al-Usra al-Islamiyya* (Cairo: International Islamic Center for Population Studies and Research, al-Azhar, 1975), 140–44.

[36] F. Hefnawi, "The Role of Research and Training in Family Planning Programmes," *Population Sciences* no. 4 (1983): 7–15; Abdel R. Omran, *Family Planning in the Legacy of Islam* (London: Routledge, United Nations Population Fund, 1992). The United Nations Population Fund supported the preparation of the report by Omran, founder of the World Association of Muslim Scholars for Population, Health, and Development and a consultant to the International Islamic Center for Population Studies and Research at al-Azhar.

publications associated with the al-Azhar Center for Women and Development differ markedly from those of their more secular counterparts in the development world.[37] The al-Azhar reports begin from an Islamic intellectual perspective, citing Qur'an, hadith, and Islamic thinkers to support arguments that focus on religion's role and capacity in social development and social cohesion. Rather than disparaging the Islamic family as a barrier to development, they locate development within the family and see the Islamic family as the key to development. These reports appear as diametrically opposite the discourse of international aid organizations, but they adopt some their key assumptions. The writings represent the emergence of parallel, or perhaps interlocking, discourses connecting the (religiously) enlightened and educated mother in the home as the counterpart of the enlightened and educated woman working outside the home. The two discourses developed as deeply contingent narratives of modern womanhood in private and public, in the religious and secular spheres.

The Azhari "woman and development" publications identify religion as the source of social solidarity, beginning with the mother-child bond and extending through the family and out into the community. They see religion simultaneously as a tool of communal cohesion and a means of promoting good management of the family. This work ethic in the family promoted "the traditional patriarchal nuclear family [as] fundamental to economic success."[38] The Azhari writings envision an intimately defined religious ethic as a blueprint for larger social development. This ethic is a means of fostering ethics and values at a microcosmic level, with the aim of extending out to the larger body politic of the nation, the region, and the umma.

Even as a grassroots religious discourse vied with developmentalist visions of social and economic progress, this religious discourse adapted and transformed developmentalist terminology and its conceptual infrastructure. Similarly, more secular development reports were

[37] Mahmud Abu Zayd, *al-Din wa-l-Tamasuk al-Ijtimaʿi* (Cairo: Jamiʿat al-Azhar, Kulliyyat al-Banat al-Islamiyya, Markaz Dirasat al-Marʾa wa-l-Tanmiya, 1977); Muhammad Shihata Rabiʿ, *Dawr al-Umm fi ʿAmaliyyat al-Tatbiʿ al-Ijtimaʿi* (Cairo: Jamiʿat al-Azhar, Kulliyyat al-Banat al-Islamiyya, Markaz Dirasat al-Marʾa wa-l-Tanmiya, 1977); ʿAblah Muhammad Kahlawi, *al-ʿAmal fi al-Islam wa-Hukm ʿAmal al-Marʾa wa-l-Hadath* (Cairo: Jamiʿat al-Azhar, Kulliyyat al-Banat al-Islamiyya, Markaz Dirasat al-Marʾa wa-l-Tanmiya, 1979).

[38] For critiques of how neoliberal discourses connect the traditional patriarchal nuclear family to wider economic development, see Kathi Weeks, *The Problem with Work: Feminism, Marxism, Antiwork Politics, and Postwork Imaginaries* (Durham, NC: Duke University Press, 2011), 64; Anne R. Roschelle, "Gender, Family Structure, and Social Structure: Racial Ethnic Families in the United States," in *Revisioning Gender* ed. Myra Marx Ferree, Judith Lorber, and Beth B. Hess (Thousand Oaks, CA: Sage, 1999), 316.

forced to contend with how religion and culture effectively permeate the substance of family and community relations, something that the reports constantly voice frustration with. The two spheres are implicitly understood in religious versus secular terms, governed by different sets of laws. On one hand, home and family (and women inside) are governed and protected by religious laws, customs, and knowledge; on the other hand, women working outside the home operate under the auspices of a different set of laws, in a world governed by the logic of secular capitalism. These competing governmentalities are the focus of much anxiety in both the religious writings and the aid reports. Religious writers fret over relinquished morals in the public sphere, just as aid reports agonize over the iron grip of "tradition, religion, and custom" on women and the family. These divergent narratives hover around conceptual antitheses of spiritual and material, private and public, but also around differentially defined knowledge systems, one religious and the other secular. The discourses of motherhood and of the working woman cannot be considered as precisely antithetical but rather as two dimensions of a developmentalist understanding of social and economic progress, mapped and coded onto two overlapping, imbricated spheres that the modern woman is expected to navigate. Mustafa's writings testify to how religious intellectual production took up the logic of economic development, just as international organizations were forced to contend with religion as a potent barrier—or potential conduit—to development.

In the conferences and reports associated with the International Women's Year and the ensuing Decade for Women, development experts wrung their hands over Arab women's low rate of participation in the "modern work sector." These reports consistently see *employment* as the primary means of securing gender equality and economic independence.[39] The Egyptian Ministry of Information published a booklet commemorating the IWY, entitled *al-Marʾa al-Misriyya: Mishwar Tawil min al-Hijab ila ʿAsr al-ʿUbur* (The Egyptian Woman: A Long Trajectory from the Hijab to the Age of the October War, 1976). Emblazoned with the IWY symbol—the dove with the woman sign and the equal sign—the booklet stresses women's "public work" as the solution to "increasing the general economic progress in the nation." The document equates a rise in the number of women working outside the home with "a parallel increase in the nation's general economic progress," especially in industry, economics, and business. Photographs of Jihan Sadat appear on nearly every page. Her official portrait adorns the book's opening

[39] International Center for Research on Women, *Keeping Women Out: A Structural Analysis of Women's Employment in Developing Countries* (Washington, DC: USAID, 1980).

pages, and she is pictured meeting veterans wounded in Egypt's October War with Israel, addressing Parliament, leading the Arab and African Women's Congress in Cairo, commemorating Huda al-Shaʿrawi, and shaking the hand of "the working woman." The booklet extols women's work in the public sphere, epitomized by the figure of Jihan Sadat, the public figure engaging in public politics, representing the Egyptian nation (and Egyptian society) to a watchful international community eager to pull a backward Egypt into the community of developed nations. *The Egyptian Woman* testifies to how larger international initiatives came to operate through states and through other privileged, elite actors.

The image of the enlightened, educated, and progressive modern working woman depended on an analogous (or antithetical) image of women's reproductive labor in the home as emblematic of underdevelopment—of poor planning, overpopulation, illiteracy, and mismanaged economic resources. Motherhood and the family were targets of reform not only to support women's move into the formal economy; these projects also sought to organize the Egyptian family according to liberal understandings of an upwardly mobile, dual-wage, nuclear family based on individual rights to economic self-determination—middle-class values for the age of economic liberalization. *The Egyptian Woman*'s advocacy of women's work outside the home is coupled with a seemingly contradictory hymn to women's roles as mothers in the family. In Anwar Sadat's introduction, he sings women's praises as "the maker of men and mother of heroes. . . . Her sons restored honor to the Arab umma. . . . The Arab woman makes those men by suckling them on nationalism. . . . I salute you O great mother!" But he also draws extensively on the language of rights and democracy, saying that the Arab woman was given her rights with the coming of Islam, not by the International Year of the Woman. She has the right to "full political participation in the democratic life of her country . . . and in this new society, the mother has the right to the noble work of her responsibilities as mother and as mistress of the house."[40] Within the text, the chapter "Focus on the Family" (*al-Ihtimām bi-l-Usra*) immediately precedes the chapter "Women's Work" (outside the home). *The Egyptian Woman* reiterates official language about the nature of the family as a repository of "religion, morals, and nationalism" but also conceives of the family as an economic unit. It reproduces nearly verbatim the 1971 constitution's language emphasizing the family as a place for the "protection" of motherhood and childhood, as well as a

[40] Ministry of Information, *al-Marʾa al-Misriyya: Mishwar Tawil min al-Hijab ila ʿAsr al-ʿUbur* (Cairo: Public Information Council, 1976), n.p.

place for the cultivation of property. This stands in stark contrast to the 1956 (socialist) constitution that defined property as public.[41]

The Egyptian Woman goes further in its description of the economy of the national family. It describes this family as built on the economic principles of (1) good management and (2) good balance between consumption and income. This would become Mustafa's very definition of the concept "economy" nearly thirteen years later, in the midst of another round of Egypt's negotiations with the IMF. Critical to the discourse of the working woman was a corresponding vision of the family—a place that must be brought, through good management, under the auspices of the formal economy so it can contribute to national progress. Public debates over the "working woman" were nearly always predicated on concerns about the organization of the family—about family planning, childcare and child rearing, education, and training. These proliferating studies, reports, and discussions sought to make the household's organization transparent and open to the intervention of experts and technocrats, so it could be organized for optimal economic productivity.

Islamic Ethics and the Spirit of Economic Development

In the midst of both new negotiations with the IMF and the Camp David Accords in 1978, the Sadat government promulgated a set of labor laws designed to facilitate women's entry into the paid workforce. The laws were intended to "apply the principle of women's right to work" and to help women "to reconcile their duties to their families with their responsibilities to their place of employment."[42] These laws, guaranteeing paid maternity leave and the possibility of working half

[41] Al-Dustur al-Misri, 1971. Article 9 says, "The family is the basis of society, her support is religion, morals, and nationalism. The state is vigilant to preserve the original nature of the Egyptian family and what it represents of values and traditions, assuring that this character is developed within the relationships of Egyptian society." Article 10 asserts the state's role in "protecting motherhood and childhood, as well as children and offspring, and increasing the necessary circumstances for the development of its property." Article 11 asserts the state's role in promoting harmony between "women's duties toward the family and her work in society and her equality with men in the fields of social, political, cultural, and economic life, without infringing on the dictates of the Islamic shariʿa." Articles 10 and 11 are nearly identical to Articles 18 and 19 of the 1956 constitution, except the 1971 constitution under Sadat shifts to a protection of private property in the family (in contradistinction to the 1956 constitution's emphasis on public property).

[42] Azza M. Karam, *Women, Islamisms and State: Contemporary Feminisms in Egypt* (New York: Palgrave Macmillan, 1997), 159.

time for half pay, were designed to help ease women's entry into wage labor. Yet the laws also acknowledged women as primary caretakers in the family by making legal accommodations for these tasks. A flurry of Islamic publications responded to the new laws by connecting them to colonial feminism. In the immediate aftermath of the legislation, the Islamic thinker Muhammad ʿAtiyya Khamis collected the opinions of different Islamic groups on the question of women's work into a book entitled *al-Marʾa wa-l-Huquq al-Siyasiyya wa-l-Aʿmal al-ʿAmma: Raʾy al-Hayat wa-l-Jamʿiyyat al-Islamiyya fi Misr* (Woman, Political Rights, and Public Employment: The Opinion of Islamic Organizations and Groups in Egypt, 1978).[43] Khamis was a leader of the (more radical) Muslim Brotherhood offshoot Shabab Sayyidina Muhammad. But the volume represents an ideological range of Islamic groups: shaykhs and thinkers of al-Azhar, radicals associated with Shabab Sayyidina Muhammad and al-ʿAshira al-Muhammadiyya, representatives of preaching and welfare organizations like al-Jamʿiyya al-Sharʿiyya, and more mainstream Islamic activists from the Muslim Brotherhood. These writings express an unmistakable consensus about the primary place of women in Islam as in the family and home. Nearly all the essays acknowledge women's *legal* right to work outside the home and to participate in politics, but there is a constant reiteration of women's "celestial mission" in motherhood, caring for the household, and raising children.[44] These Islamic thinkers appear to have a conflictual relationship with development initiatives like the labor laws, as they consistently position themselves in opposition to new forms of imperial dominance and as advocates of indigenous cultural forms like the family. But they also deploy development concepts toward defining a modern Islamic family conducive to economic and social progress. They not only use the language of rights, equality, and freedom but also understand the family as a critical economic unit in which the umma's most sacred resources are cultivated.

[43] Muhammad ʿAtiyya Khamis, *al-Marʾa wa-l-Huquq al-Siyasiyya wa-l-Aʿmal al-ʿAmma: Raʾy al-Hayat wa-l-Jamʿiyyat al-Islamiyya fi Misr* (Cairo: Dar al-Ansar, 1978). The book was also published under another title connecting "the women's movement in the East" with "colonialism and global Zionism" through the issue of women's public empoloyment. See Muhammad Fahmi ʿAbd al-Wahhab, *al-Harakat al-Nisaʾiyya fi al-Sharq wa-Silatuha bi-l-Istiʿmar wa-l-Sihyuniyya al-ʿAlamiyya: Raʾy al-Jamiʿat wa-l-Hayʾat al-Islamiyya wa-Kibar al-ʿUlamaʾ fi Misr fi Ishtighal al-Marʾa bi-l-Siyasa wa-l-Aʿmal al-ʿAmma* (Cairo: Dar al-Iʿtisam, 1979). The topic became fervently debated in a number of publications, among them Kamal Judah Abu al-Maʿati Mustafa, *Wazifat al-Marʾa fi Nazar al-Islam* (Cairo: Dar al-Huda li-l-Tibaʿa, 1980) and Muhammad ʿAli al-Barr, *ʿAmal al-Marʾa fi al-Mizan* (Jeddah: al-Dar al-Saʿudiyya, 1981).

[44] Khamis, *al-Marʾa wa-l-Huquq al-Siyasiyya*, 48.

Woman, Political Rights, and Public Employment bemoans the "catastrophe of imitating the West." The Muslim Brother Muhammad Hilmi Nur al-Din observes that "the Eastern woman has become inflamed with the traditions of Western women—how they go out into the market vulgarly exposed, nakedly deviant from virtue, disdaining tradition, mocking chastity and purity, resentful of the hijab and modesty" (17). God, he warns, "will curb their recalcitrance" (18). This rhetoric of "going out into the market" is a metaphor often used during this time. It suggests the selling of women's bodies in a free market economy that has allowed foreign influence to penetrate Egypt both economically and culturally. This is what Safinaz Kazim, in her 1982 book on veiling and unveiling, calls a "new jāhiliyya," a new, un-Islamic era characterized by a "materialist, business mentality that has gone to extremes to exploit women's femininity to sell products, attract tourists, and incite desire, make the female public property that is circulated and presented as a course of pleasure of the master man.[45] Islamic thinkers were not alone in decrying the commercialization of women's bodies under Sadat's infitāḥ—it was a motif that characterized feminist literature of the 1970s.[46] In Egyptian intellectual production, the selling of women's labor came to be understood as a kind of prostitution to foreign interests, where bodies and labor were exploited cheaply and left without much value.

The title of *Woman, Political Rights, and Public Employment* comes from one of the essays, by another leader of Shabab Sayyidina, Muhammad Hussein Muhammad Youssef. He begins his critique with colonial feminism under the British in the late nineteenth century, a movement that aimed to "overturn the pillars of the Islamic order . . . attacking it through the family" (71). He calls for retrenchment within the family as a means of protecting an Islamic society at its very core. Women are critical to fostering the household as a sphere of Islamic values, through their piety, "passion for the household work," and training and discipline of new Islamic citizens. They are, another writer asserts, the first page of the child's first book, before the child can read. These writings continually repeat a line of poetry taken from the Egyptian nahḍa poet Ahmad Shawqi: "A woman is like a school, train her and you train an entire nation." This line of poetry is reiterated in Egyptian government publications, by Islamic groups and Azharis, by Mustafa in *Empire of the Working Women*, and by Bint al-Shatiʾ in her lecture "Islam

[45] Kazim, *Fi Masʾalat al-Sufur wa-l-Hijab*, 45.

[46] Nawal El Saadawi, *al-Wajh al-ʿAri li-l-Marʾa al-ʿArabiyya* (Beirut: al-Muʾassasa al-ʿArabiyya li-l-Dirasat wa-l-Nashr, 1977), 182; Nawal El Saadawi, *Imraʾa ʿind Nuqtat al-Sifr* (Beirut: Dar al-Adab, 1977); Ellen McLarney, "The Socialist Romance of the Postcolonial Arabic Novel," *Research in African Literatures* 40, no. 3 (2009): 198–200.

and the New Woman."[47] The household in these writings becomes a site of Islamic training, discipline, and adab.

The essays in this volume carve out both a physical and a psychological space for the mother/wife in the family and home. They consistently understand the household as under the "protection" and "care" of the mother/wife. The essays repeatedly and pointedly draw on the hadith: "The man is the shepherd of his people and is responsible for his flock. The woman is a shepherd in the house of her husband and is responsible for her flock" (47, 51, 56). They use this hadith in the same way the nineteenth-century Islamic reformer and jurist Muhammad ʿAbduh did—to emphasize that the sphere of women's authority is in the home—ideas revived for the awakening.[48] (See chapter 6.) They highlight a division of labor between women and men inside and outside the home. Critiques of development and colonial discourses in the 1990s refer to this as a conceptual "feminization of the household," as the sphere of the family and household in interpreted as "under the auspices of" (*riʿāya*) the mother/wife.[49] This gendered division of labor became an ideological lens through which Islamic sources like the Qurʾan and hadith are reinterpreted for a new age. In *Empire of the Working Women*, Mustafa draws on this same language of *riʿāya*, advocating the "protection of the mother from the burdens of modern life—work that has prohibited her from nourishing and caring for [shepherding] her children" (65).

In the first essay of the book, the Muslim Brother Muhammad Hilmi Nur al-Din interprets verse 30:21 from the Qurʾan through this gendered lens. "Among his signs is that he created mates from yourselves that you may live in tranquility with them. And he put love and compassion between you. In that are truly signs for people who reflect." This verse of love, compassion, and tranquility has been a virtual axis of women's revivalist writings. It was used by Bint al-Shatiʾ in the Place of Woman in the Islamic Family conference, by Niʿmat Sidqi in *Grace*

[47] Khamis, *al-Marʾa wa-l-Huquq al-Siyasiyya*, 13; Jumhuriyyat Misr al-ʿArabiyya, *al-Marʾa al-Misriyya* (Cairo: Wizarat al-Iʿlam, al-Hayʾa al-ʿAmma li-l-Istiʿlamat, 1985), 39; Mustafa, *al-Nisaʾ al-ʿAmilat*, 50; Bint al-Shatiʾ, "Islam and the New Woman," 198.

[48] ʿImara, *al-Islam wa-l-Marʾa fi Raʾy al-Imam Muhammad ʿAbduh*, 63; Raouf Ezzat, *al-Marʾa wa-l-ʿAmal al-Siyasi*, 201.

[49] Altorki and Zurayq, *Taghayyur al-Qiyam*, 16; Shakry, "Schooled Mothers and Structured Play"; Afsaneh Najmabadi, "Crafting an Educated Housewife in Iran," in *Remaking Women: Feminism and Modernity in the Middle East*, ed. Lila Abu-Lughod (Princeton, NJ: Princeton University Press, 1998). Shakry and Najmabadi discuss the modern shift to a mother-headed household in the different contexts of Egypt and Iran, respectively. Both analyze an ideology of women's domesticity that emerged with colonial modernity.

of the Qur'an, and by Heba Raouf Ezzat in *Woman and Political Work.*[50] Bint al-Shati' calls the affective foundations of mutual love the conceptual underpinnings of the Islamic family, the spirit of the law.[51] In Nur al-Din's interpretation, the mutuality and reciprocity of the verse are elided in his assertion that "the wife is an abode for the husband." Taking the word for "rest," *sakan*, he draws on its other meaning—"home"—and synecdochically equates the wife with a physical space in which the husband finds rest. Heavy burdens weigh down the husband in his work outside the home, and he comes home seeking refuge. Using vocabulary that associates wives with the physical space of the home, he writes: "Woman is a pillar of man's authority, a stake holding down his home, companion of his life, storehouse of his secrets, fielding his complaints, cradle of his confidences, and abode of his self (*sakan nafsihi*: tranquility for his spirit)" (9).

A striking consensus exists between the Azhari shaykhs and the Islamists in the different essays in the volume. Muhammad Youssef Musa, from the Front of the Azhari ʿUlama', asserts that a woman's first job is in "the affairs of the house, the family, and the children. In that there is enough work to keep her busy. If she has truly devoted herself to her special work inside the home, there might be a remote possibility that she has time for another kind of work outside the home" (47). It is the woman's good fortune, he goes on, that she has this "celestial mission . . . of caring for the affairs of the home," even as he still recognizes the woman's right to work and hold public office in Islamic law (48).

The essays repeatedly return to the question of women's "rights, freedom, and equality," even as they criticize Western conceptions of rights, freedom, and equality. Each of the essays addresses the question of rights—women's rights to financial maintenance, their rights to perform their "celestial mission," the right to not have to suffer the drudgery of wage labor, and the falseness of the "alleged rights" presumed by Western feminism (8, 25, 43, 47, 53, 60–67). The Azharhi shaykh Muhammad Youssef Musa reiterates verbatim a passage from the Islamic activist Sayyid Qutb's *al-ʿAdala al-Ijtimaʿiyya fi al-Islam* (Social Justice in Islam, 1949) that talks about women's equality with men in Islam. The only difference—or discrimination—in these rights, Qutb and Musa assert, is in each citizen's individual nature, aptitude, and talents. Musa's essay develops this argument specifically for the debate

[50] International Islamic Center for Population Studies and Research, al-Azhar, *Makanat al-Mar'a fi al-Usra al-Islamiyya*, 140–44; Sidqi, *Niʿmat al-Qur'an*, 214; Raouf Ezzat, *al-Mar'a wa-l-ʿAmal al-Siyasi*, 185.

[51] Bint al-Shati', "Shakhsiyyat al-Mar'a fi al-Qur'an al-Karim," 140.

over women's work: "and each citizen should earn recompense for the work suited to him through nature, aptitude, and talents" (49).

Closely connected to these discourses around women's work was an emergent discourse of veiling.[52] If a woman must work/go outside the home, she must wear the hijab to "protect her status and character." Musa, using the word "*manzila*" to refer to women's status or position, plays on the word "*manzil*" (house, as in woman's "celestial mission . . . in caring for the affairs of the house.") The hijab becomes a way of protecting this celestial mission, even when a woman leaves the sacred space of the home and goes out into public. The early 1980s witnessed a surge in veiling, primarily among university women and women working outside the home.[53] In Arlene MacLeod's *Accommodating Protest: Working Women, the New Veiling, and Change in Cairo*, she argues that veiling was a way of making women's work outside the home Islamically legitimate, conforming to norms of "appropriate female behavior" even while women forge new paths in the professions. During this same time there was an exponential rise in the publication of veiling narratives. Muhammad ʿAtiyya Khamis would write the introduction to one of the most famous of these writings, the television personality Kariman Hamza's *Rihlati min al-Sufur ila al-Hijab* (My Journey from Unveiling to Veiling, 1981), just after publishing *Woman, Political Rights, and Public Employment*. Hamza epitomizes the pious working woman, wearing the legal hijab and exercising her legal right to work outside the home. Another work written at this time, *al-Hijab wa-ʿAmal al-Marʾa* (The Hijab and Woman's Work, 1983), by the Azhari shaykh ʿAtiyya Saqr, reflects at length on how women should stay at home and that if they do work outside the home, they must wear the hijab and refrain from mixing, making eye contact, and shaking men's hands—an assertion that blew up in public debate. *The Hijab and Woman's Work* was published in the High Council of Islamic Affairs journal *al-Dirasat al-Islamiyya*, a series of booklets usually on a single topic by a single author. Saqr, however, combined two topics, the hijab and women's work. He had previously published a six-volume study entitled *Mawsuʿat al-Usra Taht Riʿayat al-Islam* (Encyclopedia of the Family under the Protection of Islam, 1980), using the same term *riʿāya* to refer to the Islamic family as a haven. First published in Kuwait, it would be reissued in Egypt in 1990, in the midst of renewed debates over women's work, when Mustafa was publishing her own

[52] See chapters 3 and 4 for a fuller discussion of the return to veiling and its connection to women's visibility in public space.

[53] El Guindi, "Veiling Infitah with Muslim Ethic"; Radwan, *Bahth Zahirat al-Hijab*, 1984.

writings and Raouf Ezzat was formulating her master's thesis on women's work in Islam.

In the dialectic between international discourses of economic and social development and indigenous or local conceptions of the Egyptian family, there are clear echoes of an older colonial rhetoric seeking to co-opt women into the project of the ideological reproduction of modernity. In these discourses women and the family are indicators of a nation's degree of civilization, now called development. Economic development projects envision a well-planned, well-managed modern family as key to the management of the larger national and transnational economy. They urgently call for the effective management of the family as a form of biopower, so that its human resources can be shaped toward the ends of economic productivity. Even as these discourses target Egyptian, Muslim, third-world, developing, and African women, some of these writings—and their authors—clearly resist cooptation into the global economy. In a conference in Kuwait on Women and Development in the 1980s, for example, one participant calls for adherence to "traditional socioeconomic systems that work, like the Arab family," systems that are "slowly fading away without really being replaced by others."[54] But rather than a fading away, the Arab family is strengthened by these development projects, which gird it for a new age of global socioeconomic relationships. Elite actors—like Mustafa and Khamis—question material factors as the primary gauge of development, criticizing the "spirit of consumerism" sweeping the region, even as they call for cultivating the human resources in the family.[55] These thinkers envision the human capital of the family as one of the most precious resources of an Islamic society.

Women's Work as the "Entryway to Total Development"

When Hosni Mubarak assumed power in October 1981, one of the first acts of Parliament (in November) was revisiting of the issue of women's role in development. Earlier that year Sadat had enacted a second set of labor laws, this time facilitating women's work in the private (versus the public) sector. Sadat's assassination afforded a kind of mandate to completely review his policies of rapid economic, political, and social change. The Labor Committee of the Majlis al-Shura (the upper house of the Egyptian Parliament) issued a report on *Tanmiyat al-Marʾa*

[54] Nadia Hijab, *Womanpower: The Arab Debate on Women at Work* (Cambridge: Cambridge University Press, 1988), 63–65.

[55] Ibid.

ka-Madkhal li-l-Tanmiya al-Shamila (The Development of Woman as a Key to Total Development, 1984). The editor describes the publication as making the analyses of "men of knowledge" available to "the people" and "the public at large."[56] The report appears as a rumination on the structural difficulties impeding women's movement into public employment, but it focuses more on the family as the site of women's (economic) labor. Listing a formidable set of social conditions, the report talks about problems of illiteracy, birth control, transportation, currently existing laws, productivity, childcare, health, and public perception. It also talks about women's low productivity (in comparison to men) in the paid labor force, attributing this to "physical and psychological makeup and endurance, her biological and social role, and the social conditions under which she labors" (26–27).

In the introduction to the report, the president of the Majlis al-Shura, ʿAli Lutfi, lists a set of critical points related to women's role in development, nearly all of them related to women's roles in the family. He begins by saying that "the point of origin of human development is the family" in which the mother plays the "biggest part," especially through "the education of offspring." "She gives the child the first milk in the formation of the personality, infusing it with the original values, ideals, and traditions of society, deepening the Egyptian personality that is distinguished by religiosity and deepening the sense of belonging to family, land, and nation" (11). It is thus, he says, that the past is joined to the future. His next points are about "Woman and Productivity" and "Woman and the Economics of the Family and Guidance of Consumption." He calls the housewife's productivity as "invisible, unacknowledged as work. But this falls within the framework of woman's natural employment. . . . In addition to this, she manages the income and expenditures, making her indirectly responsible for 85% of the national income" (12). Her job—in the family, the economy, and the nation—is "managing consumption." Part of this job entails limiting population growth, fostering economic resources, and cultivating the value of human capital. Lutfi acknowledges this intimate connection between larger questions of economic development and what he calls

> a new conception of development . . . extending into the fields of social, human, and cultural development. This new understanding is an important factor in the dialogue circulating between different states about how to agree to a new global economic order. If development is—according this understanding—a total and complete ongoing process in different sectors and activities,

[56] Lajnat al-Khidmat, *Tanmiyat al-Marʾa*, 3, 5.

> then there is no doubt that the crux of this total development is concentrated in human development. The human is a fundamental element in any socioeconomic activity, the principal pillar in the struggle for development, which is—also—its objective and goal. (10)

This human capital is most important in the case of Egypt, with its limited natural resources and invested capital. Lutfi speaks in the language of development—of not just investment, profit, earnings, income, consumption, capital, productivity, and resources but also birth control and the central importance of women and the family to realizing this process of economic, social, and cultural development. The emphasis on the family as an economic unit is more than a patriarchal ruse to keep women in the home; it is also an economic strategy to subsume all life into the aims of "complete and total" economic development, to leave no domain of economic life untouched, to make the informal economy formal, and the "invisible" work of the home (and fields) visible.

Development efforts strive toward integrating the household economy into the global economy, by rescuing it from backward (local, indigenous) methods. But there is also a canny, implicit recognition of the effective economic units that already function locally, without the management, interference, or co-optation of the global economy or of the state. Development initiatives have been concerned with how local economic units might be reconfigured so that they are compatible with the circulation of products and technology "revolutionizing" the household, making families into consumers rather than local manufacturers, a movement from a household based on production to one based on consumption. In several places the report talks about the importance of making household appliances available to women in the home. This "frees" women for other, more important work, either in the paid labor force or in intensified childrearing practices cultivating the "human capital" of the future. The well-organized bourgeois nuclear family is the disciplinary force that connects Egyptian traditions to an economically flourishing future.

After three years of meetings and research, the Labor Committee issued its report in 1984. The following year Lutfi, a Swiss-educated economist specializing in development, would become prime minister. The minister of economics during Sadat's infitāḥ, he was seen as the IMF's choice for prime minister and as "speaking for the IMF."[57] Lutfi's

[57] Thierry Lalevée, "Egypt and the IMF: Is a Break Coming?" *Executive Intelligence Review* 12, no. 39 (October 4, 1985): 11.

most famous publications were *La technique élevée à la suprême puissance: la planification de l'économie* (Technique Raised to a Supreme Power: Planning the Economy, 1964) and *al-Tatawwur al-Iqtisadi* (Economic Progress, 1965), the latter published ten times over three decades, three times by Dar al-Qur'an. By the 1980s, the title had been changed to *al-Tanmiya al-Iqtisadiyya* (Economic Development). In 1985 the Egyptian government renegotiated with the IMF to try to break its debt crisis, with a promised $1.5 billion dollar loan.[58] Lutfi was also a prominent face in the midst of the 2011 revolution, advocating in the press, on television programs, in interviews, and on Twitter for a continued relationship with the IMF.

In 1985—nearly ten years after the Sadat government's publication of *The Egyptian Woman*—the Mubarak government would release its own *The Egyptian Woman*, which reads as a companion piece to the prior book. The two publications bookend the United Nations' Decade for Women but also stake out women's important roles in the interrelated projects of economic development and family planning. Both are similar in format, interspersed with celebratory photographs of Egyptian women, but now the family has become a more explicitly articulated site of economic development, even as the sacred importance of women's role continues to be emphasized. The 1976 publication barely mentions religion, except in Anwar Sadat's opening address and in the section on the family. In fact, the subtitle emphasizes that the Egyptian woman's path to liberation is *from* the hijab. The modern photographs exclude any veiled women—except one peasant woman in the countryside wearing a headscarf. On the cover and inside the book, women soldiers shoot guns, women scientists look through microscopes and x-ray peasant men, and women politicians (Jihan Sadat) address Parliament. In contrast, two veiled women adorn the cover of the 1985 version: one with a folklore-type head covering (a made-up model with an embroidered veil suggesting indigenous handicrafts); the other of a university student in hijab with two unveiled students. The women are looking through a surveying camera whose lens points directly out at the reader. (The image echoes the 1976 cover depicting the unveiled woman looking through a microscope.) The dialectic of the two images of the microscope and the surveying camera reifies the sense of mirroring realms of microcosmic and a macrocosmic, mediated through the image of the "modern Egyptian woman." Instead of the earlier text's narrative of teleological progress *from* veiling, the 1985 text shows a

[58] Gaye Muderrisoglu and Jonathan Hanson, "Authoritarian States and IMF Conditionality" (presented at the Midwest Political Science Association, Chicago, April 22, 2010), 22.

past that is part of the present, heritage compatible with knowledge, Egyptian girls that are educated, pious, and immersed in indigenous culture.

The 1976 publication takes the IWY as its point of reference, while the 1985 document begins with "Women's Place in Islam" and with the Qur'an, stating that "under the protection of Islam, woman obtained legal rights without precedent in any constitution or human laws, restoring her honor and humanity."[59] The following two sections deal with "The Mother's Place in Islam" and "Mothers of Prophets in the Qur'an." After a celebration of women in different fields of Egyptian society (health, industry, agriculture, business and economics, the legal profession, journalism, scientific research, media, sports, and other "public employment" like driving buses and delivery trucks), the book moves to an ideologically charged section on "The Mother in Egyptian Society" that invests in the mother and the family vast duties of material, spiritual, ethical, moral, cultural, intellectual, and educational training. This section discusses three interlocking roles: the education of children, family planning, and economic development. Drawing directly from ʿAli Lutfi's introduction to *The Development of Woman as the Key to Total Development*, it describes the mother as giving the child "the first milk that forms his personality, infusing it with the original values of society, its ideals and its traditions, deepening his Egyptian personality distinguished by religiosity and belonging to the family, the land, and the nation, imparting him with the cultural heritage, connecting his past to his future" (39). In this section on "the mother's role in bringing up offspring," the document uses the line of poetry from Ahmad Shawqi from *Woman, Political Rights, and Public Employment*, a verse later reiterated by Mustafa, Bint al-Shatiʾ, and Heba Raouf Ezzat: "A mother is a school, if you prepare her you prepare a people of good roots." In *The Egyptian Woman*, an official discourse around the Islamic family intensifies, where the family becomes the site of an intense effort to preserve, utilize, and channel the powers of religion. It is also a place where women's labor is naturalized as the space of her optimal productivity and of inculcation of certain disciplines. These disciplinary practices—of not only childrearing and education but also managing family resources and balancing income with consumption—become the hope for exploiting the human capital seen as the path to Egypt's economic salvation. These discourses recognize the roles already played by women in the informal economy and in local networks but also shift the burden of labor and self-sacrifice onto women working in the home. The book uses capitalist language of

[59] Jumhuriyyat Misr al-ʿArabiyya, *al-Marʾa al-Misriyya*.

(spiritual) reward for hard work, work that is understood as women's "natural employment" synchronized with her God-given nature, her fiṭra.

During this period in the 1980s, the government also published a series of books and pamphlets on motherhood and family planning in Islam. The section of *The Egyptian Woman* on women's role in educating children ends by emphasizing the mother's role in family planning. The section begins with religion, with a hadith that stresses the mother's role as a shepherd of her husband's house and children. The report goes on to detail her role in their physical, spiritual, and intellectual preparation, emphasizing women's job of inculcating "a clear vision of both religion and the world." The book describes how the interlocking spiritual and material aspects of childrearing work "to refine society and promote its material, spiritual, and ethical growth" (40). These government narratives of the Islamic family emphasize mothers' role in the "total development of the resources and potential of society," and especially the importance of their work in managing the economy of the family (44). They fuse the family's importance to national cultural identity with its function as an economic unit, citing studies and experiments conducted by vocational institutes that affirm the importance of women's labor in the home. "A woman does not need to leave her house to work; her work within the context of the home should be considered productive work." As in *The Egyptian Woman* (1976) and in Mustafa's *Empire of the Working Women* (1989), a mother's job is said to be managing consumption and spending, contributing not just to the economy of the family but to the "progress of the nation's economy" (44).

Empire of the Working Women

In the midst of intense international pressures—from lending agencies and developmental organizations—Iman Muhammad Mustafa published her articles on working women in *al-Ahram al-Iqtisadi*.[60] She does

[60] The articles were first published at the same time as an ESCWA conference on "progress of indicators and amelioration of statistics" with respect to the "Arab woman." The conference, held in the midst of Egypt's negotiations with the IMF, followed up on two other, similar conferences also held at key moments in Egypt's path to economic liberalization. These other two conferences were both entitled Woman and Development, the first held in 1972 and the second in 1984. United Nations, *Ijtimaʿ Majmuʿat al-ʿAmal hawl Tatwir al-Muʾashshirat wa-Tahsin al-Ihsaʾat al-Khassa bi-Wadʿ al-Marʾa al-ʿArabiyya: 15–19 Uktubir 1989* (Cairo: al-Markaz al-Qawmi li-l-Buhuth al-Ijtimaʿiyya wa-l-Jinaʾiyya, 1990).

not initially, or primarily, frame her indictment of working women in Islamic terms but rather in economic ones. Lamenting women's low productivity in wage labor, she simultaneously valorizes their roles in managing the household economy. Interpreting the family as a unit of economic development, she uses a vocabulary of productivity, informal economy, marginal yields, and balanced budgets. She asks questions about balancing the economic return of women's work outside the home with the social cost—the "price"—that society must pay (14, 101). Published just as Egypt came to an agreement with the IMF, the book positions itself as a protest against an economic imperialism that entails women's work outside the home. Using language similar to Islamist books published in the wake of Sadat's 1978 labor laws, Mustafa associates women's work outside the home with a Western economic imperialism connected to, and masquerading as, a feminist agenda. Her writings question women's work outside the home as a form of liberation, characterizing it as a new kind of colonial enslavement masked as the path to "freedom" and "equality." Mustafa makes the family the site for the development of an alternative economy rooted in nature, the sacred, and the indigenous. Yet this opposition discourse carries within it elements of the secular-liberal-materialist-capitalist vision of the role of the nuclear family and its stewardship of community.

Empire of the Working Women develops an Islamic economy of women's work in the family. In the second chapter, "The Economy Is . . . a Woman," Mustafa begins with a disclaimer: she is not an expert in economics, but she understands the basic meaning of "economy" to be "good management that balances between spending and saving." "The development of the family depends on the wife mother's power and ability of good management and proper utilization of the husband's resources." The wife mother needs to be "worthy" of this job and should do it with "aptitude," "to be a good resource first for her husband and for her nation after that" (27). Mustafa qualifies the informal labor of the household as "falling under the modern economic concept of underdeveloped productive labor" such as handicrafts, artisanal arts, weaving, embroidery, agriculture, raising pigeons, and other manual labor (as well as the marketing of these products). These, she asserts, occupy an important place in the "economic and financial capacity of the family."

In one of the book's introductory chapters, an expansion of one of the articles in *al-Ahram al-Iqtisadi*, Mustafa profiles three seemingly unrelated public figures—Qasim Amin, ʿAbbas Mahmud al-ʿAqqad, and Mikhail Gorbachev—and discusses their perspectives on women's work. With respect to Amin, she reiterates his assertion of women's key role in cultivating a "nation living among civilized nations" through their work in the home and the family. She deploys the literary scholar and Islamic writer ʿAbbas Mahmud al-ʿAqqad to corroborate this argument, through his vision of the "ideal society," not one that "compels women to a life of drudgery by force, nor one of broken motherhood or a stifled self, where women's desires and demands go unfulfilled. Nor is it a society raised without motherhood, fatherhood, or family. . . . There is no dispute that woman's ideal function in the jihad of life is protecting the house under the guard of marital harmony, nurturing future generations by preparing them for that jihad with a proper education" (41). This function, this "employment" (*waẓīfa*), is the work of a political jihad carving out a future politics, a discourse of political jihad in the family that had been key to Niʿmat Sidqi's writings and would become the core of Heba Raouf Ezzat's thought. This political role in the family, Mustafa and ʿAqqad assert, is a claiming of rights that have been denied. "The demand for woman's rights is a new demand that she deserves for all her strenuous effort. But this time the eternal right that she struggles and fights for is the right to motherhood and to femininity. . . . peace in the little world—the world of the house and the family—is peace in the larger world" (42–43).

Mustafa twice quotes a long passage from Mikhail Gorbachev's *Perestroika*, which was published in 1987 amid the implementation of economic reforms in the Soviet Union permitting privatization. The word *perestroika* is nearly identical to the term infitāḥ used under Sadat for his Open Door Economic Policy. Both connote "openness" or "opening." Like the Soviet Union, Egypt had also turned from a socialist economy, albeit fifteen years earlier (the start of Mustafa's timeline). In the mid-1980s both countries were facing escalating debt and intensifying pressures from the IMF. The passage, taken from Gorbachev's chapter entitled "Women and Family," begins by acknowledging how women have managed to penetrate all fields of public life—like so many of these paeans to women's work in the family, such as the two books on *The Egyptian Woman* and Bint al-Shatiʾ's lectures. Gorbachev frames the importance of women's work in the family in liberal terms, as a *right* that women have been denied and as a *freedom* of which they have been deprived. "We have failed," Gorbachev writes, "to pay attention to women's special [*al-khāṣṣa*: also, private] rights and their needs stemming from their role as mother and as housewife and pertaining to their educational function that children cannot do without." Even though women now work in every field of public life, he laments that they "do not have time for their daily duties in the home, in housework, in educating their children, in creating a good family environment." Our problems—in the behavior of our children and youth, in our culture and productivity—"partially returns to the decimation of family relationships and neglect of family responsibilities, a contradictory consequence of our desire for women's equality with men in all things." This has led to a public conversation about the relationship between work and home—"especially what we should do about the situation and how to facilitate women's return to her pure womanly mission. . . . in all fields of production we have begun to remedy this problem . . . through improving the health of the family and strengthening its role in society" (45–46). This pure womanly mission becomes the lifeblood sustaining the affective economy that is the family.

Mustafa, via Gorbachev, inverts developmentalist logic that equates women's liberation with work outside the home. This passage echoes Bint al-Shatiʾ's denunciation of the principle of exact equivalence with men in "The Islamic Understanding of Women's Liberation." Rather than liberating, women's work outside the home is, according to Mustafa, "imprisoning women with chains softened by freedom and equality" (25). She ends her first chapter with an ironic exclamation, written in bold: "**Let her enjoy her freedom!!!**" The passage preceding this revolves around a home bereft of good meals and conviviality, as the working woman "victimizes herself" racing home to prepare a quick (cold) bite of leftovers for her family ("the same thing she prepared the night before"). Time is short, so she cannot tidy up either the house or herself to be presentable for her children and husband. The portrait of overburdened working mothers, racing from place to place, unable to tend to domestic tasks, is a familiar one from Western literature on the "mommy wars," as are the nostalgia and romance of a time, if ever, when women's loyalties were not divided between home and workplace.

The book closes with an epigraph on the "burden of freedom that is robbed and stripped of all that is rich, sweet, and important in it and of what is in it of free will and choice. What is the value of a freedom that shackles and fetters us? What is a freedom that is forced on us with compulsion even if it was only for a morsel of bread?!" (159). The words' connotations, connected to welcome (into the home: *ahlān bihā*) and to the sweetness of food (*hanīʾān*), make it seem as if the working woman is welcome to "eat" her freedom, if that's what pleases her. Mustafa also uses language that connotes being "shackled" (*tukabbilunā*) with debt, robbed of freedom, and "compelled" to "convert" to a religion of capitalism in a way that sells the very values of Islam. Among these values is the actual freedom to practice religion. Throughout her writings, Mustafa continues to suggest that women are being stripped of their choice to be mothers, forced by economic necessity—and by ideology—into the workforce. The ideology is not just "women's liberation" but also the seductions of all the latest trends, products, and television shows. These create certain desires and pleasures in the working woman, as she lingers in front of shop windows, avoiding her real work, the hard responsibilities and duties of home, children, and family. The reality of the situation, Mustafa writes in *al-Ahram al-Iqtisadi,* is completely incommensurate with what the "pioneers of the call to liberation" had envisioned (78). Though woman is born free, she is everywhere in chains.

Women's ontological right to freedom—and how to recoup this freedom—is Mustafa's preoccupation, as it is in so many of the revivalist writings of this period. Mustafa critiques "the burden of freedom" imposed by a capitalist society that enslaves women in the workplace and prevents them from the richness of their "womanly mission in life." Yet she begins with an assertion of the primacy of rights and freedoms in Islam, valorizing those (the freedom to work and freedom of opinion) that closely echo the rights and freedoms of the Universal Declaration of Human Rights, even though she asserts that they were granted "fourteen centuries ago." Women's work is only a partial vision of a system "that grants freedom of opinion and freedom to work to all humanity in its entirety, in a way that moves this freedom from a mere right to a sacred duty incumbent on every Muslim man and Muslim woman that is led to the face of God who rewards them for the work they have performed" (17). Women's work outside the home is depicted in *Empire of the Working Women* as fleeing her sacred duty (and right to work) as a mother, "claiming a few hours of rest from the responsibility of the home and children, spending these hours in some kind of work, or in mere chatter, or in window shopping" (or in plant dusting or in sleeping on a typewriter) (24). This is not freedom but chains of a different kind, Mustafa says, chains preventing the full realization of women's worth in a sacred economy—and a sacred labor—that transcends idle pursuits in the marketplace. Her argument reproduces the contradictions inherent in the capitalist work ethic, a chain that makes you free (from penury, idleness, dependence), a sacred obligation that leads to (spiritual) rewards. Mustafa's writings function as a critique of a materialist capitalism fetishizing work as the path to liberation, but she also formulates what might be called an Islamist economy of the home that sanctifies a "family ethic" as the counterpart to a capitalist "work ethic."[61]

This freedom, much like the freedom to work, is strangely unfree. As in *The Egyptian Woman* (1985), inordinate burdens are placed on women's function in the family, as an economic manager, caregiver, moral guide, teacher, and shaper of society, in addition to whatever

[61] Weeks, *The Problem with Work*, 164–67.

work in the fields or on handicrafts that she might do (and market) in addition to cooking and housework. This sacred role frees women from the burden of working outside the home but also promises to liberate Egyptian society from economic dependence and Islam from foreign dominance. A heavy load for women to bear, it also invests power in the economy of the Islamic family as a place where indigenous ideologies can be cultivated and disseminated, without parceling them out to institutions connected to the service economy. Protecting women from the commodification of the market appears as an important aspect of this ideology, even as these writers construct their own alternative—and analogous—economy. The assertions of "the burden of freedom" and the repression of Egyptian and Muslim society by foreign powers function as an incitation to discourse around women's subjugation in the marketplace. Yet this "alternative economy" of the family and home subjected women's bodies and work to another set of demands.

Women's right to work becomes contingent on the rights of other family members: first the child, then the husband, then the grandparents (mother of the father and mother of the mother), and finally "the wife." Even though rights and freedoms are always contingent on the rights and freedoms of others (and the contract *not* to infringe on one another's rights), women's rights here appear as profoundly embedded in a matrix of interlocking rights and duties. These rights are also subordinate to the demands of family life and to a reproductive model of the nuclear family. Mustafa's family is enmeshed in a vision of liberal citizenship, with its rights, duties, freedoms, and models of "consultative" (democratic) leadership. But she also reproduces a patriarchal conjugal bourgeois family structure premised on a monogamous couple (wife and husband) conjoined by love and affection, with children primarily nurtured by the mother (or the grandmother), and the father as the primary provider.[62] Mustafa both acknowledges the critical importance of this family's economic function (in the chapter "Economy . . . Woman") and simultaneously asserts the family's transcendent spiritual function as a repository of affect, intimacy, and communal identification. It is this, she says, that is the "capital" of the family as a "corporation." Quoting the verse from the Qur᾽an 30:21 (discussed above), she argues that affection, compassion, and tranquility (as well as affect) are the "capital of the marital corporation" (21). Men, she says, are in charge of the "burdens of the expenses of life,"

[62] For analyses of the patriarchal conjugal bourgeois family in revivalist discourse, see Haddad, "The Case of the Feminist Movement"; Stowasser, "Religious Ideology"; Hatem, "Secularist and Islamist Discourses"; Abu-Lughod, "Marriage of Feminism and Islamism."

but women manage the affective capital of the family, a role that is "of sacred importance" (23).

Mustafa's vision of family life also develops a particular model of childhood in which the mother is not only the primary caretaker and educator but also the locus of affect, emotion, and bonding. Intriguingly, she situates this affective model of family, motherhood, and childhood in a discourse of rights. Children are described as having rights to

> tenderness, warmth, and love, with nourishment that only a mother can provide no matter who she is. . . . This is the literal meaning of a nursery in all that the word means of closeness, protection, and affect. This nursing is at the head of a mother's duties throughout the years of the child's life that gradually emerges from her being as a nursery for the child, connected to his education, to directing him, and to guiding him. How many peerless individuals that history mentions have come from women who grasped this sacred duty.

This, Mustafa says, is "the most important thing among all the factors affecting women's work. . . . Islam sees woman's natural function, and the nature with which God created her (30:30), as her first place. The place of woman as mother cannot be equaled by any other position in society" (20–21).

The ambivalence toward (or love/hate relationship with) women's emancipation and its accompanying discourses of freedom and rights are also reproduced in these writings' ambivalence toward the figure of Qasim Amin and his famous book *Tahrir al-Marʾa* (The Liberation of Woman, 1899). As in manifold texts written during this time, Amin haunts discourses of women's liberation in a double incarnation—as a stooge of Western powers and as a pioneer of women's liberation in Islam. (See chapter 2.) Mustafa begins *Empire of Working Women* by citing a long quote from *Liberation of Woman* warning that Egypt will have no place among civilized nations "before its homes and families provide a sound environment that prepare men . . . for success" (9). Even though she disparages Amin's call to "women's emancipation" as a foreign ideology, the understanding of the family as reflective a nation's level of civilization—itself partly a response to colonial discourses—becomes the "core" or "pith" of Mustafa's argument. Her writings embrace Amin's vision of the importance of the family and the importance of women's roles as domestic managers and loving companions, connecting these "enlightened, educated, and modern" roles to their "emancipation."

Conclusion: The Work of Motherhood

Mustafa's articles were published in the midst of an avalanche of reports on "Arab Woman and Development" issued by the United Nations Economic and Social Commission for Western Asia (ESCWA), whose members are the Arab states. Written in Arabic, many of these focused on the reform of women's labor. Why, asks sociologist Maria Mies, did international capital suddenly rediscover women, and poor, Third World women in particular? "If one were to believe the many official statement on the need to 'integrate women into development' made in the 1970s, particularly following the International Women's Conference in Mexico in 1975, one might think that there was a real change in the heart of the centers of capitalist patriarchy." She advocates looking at the "deeper reasons for the attention given to women in the colonies today." In the early stages of colonialism, she writes, women had already been discovered as an important "natural resource" to be exploited. She describes new forms of "colonization and housewifization" in the 1970s and 1980s, as development projects sought to "integrate poor women's supposedly underutilized productivity into the global capital accumulation process." Part of this process, she argues, is obscuring women's work as producers for capital, mainly by defining them as housewives, not workers, and by emphasizing their "reproductive" rather than "productive" roles.[63]

This is what Islamic thinker Heba Raouf Ezzat would call—in 1992, just after Mustafa published her book—"the new colonialism" that took the place of the "the old colonialism," seeking "to not only leave behind—but to terminate—the social units of the Islamic umma: the family extending out to neighborhoods, unions, groups, and brotherhoods." The institutions of the Islamic umma, including the family, Raouf Ezzat argues, are the *real* work of development. Women have political responsibilities of great importance in these social units, "units that attract individuals on a daily basis to the milk of political efficacy."[64] Raouf Ezzat trenchantly criticizes secularist understandings of women's work "outside her home with material compensation as the measure of her economic independence, the path to her social equality,

[63] Mies, *Patriarchy and Accumulation*, 116, 122–23.

[64] Raouf Ezzat, *al-Marʾa wa-l-ʿAmal al-Siyasi*, 161. Again, this discourse emerges at precisely the time that Egypt came to an agreement with the IMF about structural adjustment policies, when Raouf Ezzat finished her master's thesis that would become the book.

and the basis of her political participation."[65] Raouf Ezzat's book on women's work, *al-Mar'a wa-l-ʿAmal al-Siyasi: Ru'ya Islamiyya* (Woman and Political Work: An Islamic Vision, 1995) aims to "shape a new discourse that surpasses the reigning debate over the issue of women's work," a debate caught between the poles of foreign, secular development and an indigenous Islamic alternative. She calls for "investment in 'human capital,' meaning education in the family, a labor of cultivation [*tanammū* derived from the word for development *tanmiya*] of no less importance than the work of public employment. This social labor without material recompense has its own material rewards irrespective of money . . . social work that similarly aims to develop society" (161). She contrasts this with development discourses that see work outside the home as a form of liberation from the constricted domain of housework. The home and family, Raouf Ezzat argues, is a vast domain that speaks to the reality of a large swath of women (Mustafa's "truth in the heart of the majority") and leaves room for what she calls a "wider freedom" for women's movements. Using "movements" in its double sense of physical and social movement—and recalling Mustafa's image of the body of truth moving everywhere—Raouf Ezzat allows for the reinterpretation of family and home as an expansive (rather than restrictive) domain, as liberating rather than confining, as a biopolitics "from below."[66]

Islamic thinkers, historical research, and ethnographic scholarship all dispute that Muslim women are socially and economically subordinate in the extended family structure, instead stressing their political power within the informal economy.[67] The scholarship of historian Judith Tucker in particular emphasizes how the capitalist economy around the turn of the century disenfranchised women from their economic

[65] Ibid., 160.

[66] Mark LeVine, "The UN Arab Human Development Report: A Critique," *Middle East Research and Information Project* (July 26, 2002); Aradhana Sharma, *Logics of Empowerment: Development, Gender, and Governance in Neoliberal India* (Minneapolis: University of Minnesota Press, 2008), 11–16. See especially Sharma's discussion of the ethics of self-rule at the local level.

[67] See Lawrence Rosen, *Bargaining for Reality: The Construction of Social Relations in a Muslim Community* (Chicago: University of Chicago Press, 1984); Lila Abu-Lughod, *Veiled Sentiments: Honor and Poetry in a Bedouin Society,* (Berkeley, CA: University of California Press, 1986); Mona Abaza, *Feminist Debates and "Traditional Feminism" of the Fallaha in Rural Egypt* (Bielefeld: Sociology of Development Research Centre, University of Bielefeld, 1987); Homa Hoodfar, "Survival Strategies and the Political Economy of Low-Income Households in Cairo," in *Development, Change, and Gender in Cairo: A View from the Household,* ed. Diane Singerman and Homa Hoodfar (Bloomington: Indiana University Press, 1996); Singerman, *Avenues of Participation,* 173–243; El-Kholy, *Defiance and Compliance.*

activities—in agriculture, animal husbandry, and small businesses in the traditional quarters of Cairo.[68] In her book on working women in Cairo, Arlene MacLeod criticizes Western characterizations of Muslim women as oppressed:

> From the Western vantage point, women in the Middle East have been pitied as the victims of a difficult and oppressive cultural milieu, usually mechanically equated with the Islamic religion. They are perceived as downtrodden, repressed, and severely constrained victims, and the ultimate symbol of their oppression is the veil. Yet, as anyone who has known Middle Eastern women quickly realizes, this picture is impossible to reconcile with the assertive behavior and influential position of women in many Middle Eastern settings. In Cairo, for instance, women manage the household budgets, conduct marriage arrangements, and coordinate extensive and very important economic and social networks. . . . The literature on Middle Eastern women in recent years has offered a proliferation of examples of women's informal powers.[69]

In the 1980s, development writings calling for women's emancipation in wage labor and the paid workforce met with an opposition discourse valorizing women's work in the informal economy, a narrative that had both reactionary and revolutionary potential. It sought to reinvest women's work in the family with economic worth, as well as infusing these roles with sacred value. This "politics of informality" focused primarily on community-building institutions like the family as a center of democratic mobilization.[70] Religion, conceptually associated with this informal economic and political space within the secular state, flourished as

[68] Judith E. Tucker, "Problems in the Historiography of Women in the Middle East: The Case of Nineteenth-Century Egypt," *International Journal of Middle East Studies* 15, no. 3 (1983): 321–36; Judith E. Tucker, "Decline of the Family Economy in Mid-Nineteenth Century Egypt," in *The Modern Middle East*, ed. Albert Hourani, Phillip Khoury, and Mary Wilson (Berkeley: University of California Press, 1993); Judith E. Tucker, *Women in Nineteenth-Century Egypt* (Cambridge: Cambridge University Press, 2002).

[69] MacLeod, *Accommodating Protest*, 17. MacLeod's research was conducted between 1983 and 1988 and published in 1991, precisely in the period chronicled in Mustafa's timeline of economic reform targeting women's labor.

[70] Raouf Ezzat, "Politics of Informality"; Raouf Ezzat, *al-Marʾa wa-l-ʿAmal al-Siyasi*, 205–28; al-Majlis al-Qawmi li-l-Marʾa, *al-Marʾa wa-Suq al-ʿAmal: al-Qitaʿ al-Rasmi wa-Ghayr al-Rasmi* (Cairo: al-Majlis al-Qawmi li-l-Marʾa, 2001).

it took root in new institutions. One of the most important of these was the middle-class family.[71]

During this same period of structural adjustment, when Mustafa and Heba Raouf Ezzat were formulating their critiques of women's work, the Islamic thinker and Arabic literary scholar Bint al-Shatiʾ presented a lecture on "Islam and the New Woman" at a conference in Padua, Italy. Speaking a year before her death in 1998, she talks about how Muslim women "have made the journey from inside the walls of the harem to the farthest horizons of public life, from the dark depths of illiteracy to the hallowed halls of academia. In a single generation we entered into three different but interconnected battles: to discard the veil, to be educated, and to go out to work. And we have paid a huge price for these achievements."[72] At this point in her argument, Bint al-Shatiʾ turns to motherhood. She disparages an "inferiority complex of belonging to humble mothers . . . which cultural colonialism and intellectual invasion implanted firmly in the consciousness and mentality of the East" (200). Echoing Raouf Ezzat, her own intellectual "daughter," she talks about motherhood as a leadership role, about women's "natural" capacity for leadership, both inside and outside the home. Bint al-Shatiʾ criticizes wage labor as either a mode of liberation or giving women leadership roles. The lecture is a plaintive cry against the devaluation of mothers and their work and productivity.

Western feminism has coped with women's marginalization from the formal economy in two main ways. One strategy has focused on integrating women into waged labor by emphasizing their "right to work," an approach that reflects what political scientist Kathi Weeks calls "'the labor market bias' of US feminism [that] continues to characterize broad segments of mainstream feminism." A "second response to the characterization of women as nonproductive citizens . . . insisted instead on the status of domestic work as real work—that is, on its standing as a comparably worthy form of socially necessary and dignified labor . . . insisting that household labor requires a level of discipline, efficiency, and systematic effort."[73] Yet this, Weeks observes in her book *The Problem with Work*, revives the "ghost of dead

[71] A number of excellent sources discuss the centrality of the middle-class family in modern Islamic thought. On the rise of this discourse during the nahḍa, see Shakry, "Schooled Mothers and Structured Play"; Stowasser, "Religious Ideology"; Abu-Lughod, "Marriage of Feminism and Islamism," 253; Abugideiri, "On Gender and the Family." Abu-Lughod writes about "the ideals of domesticity that seem to be part of being pious in Egypt today" (253).

[72] Bint al-Shatiʾ, "Islam and the New Woman," 194.

[73] Weeks, *The Problem with Work*, 66–67.

family values," where the free enterprise system and the modern family are mutually dependent on each other for survival. Family is "the engine of democratic capitalism."[74] Development sought to engineer this kind of family in Egypt, a family that Islamic writers claimed as their own territory and as the motor for the progress of a properly Islamic society.

[74] White House Working Group on the Family, *The Family: Preserving America's Future: A Report to the President* (Washington, DC: U.S. Department of Education, 1986); Mimi Abramovitz, *Regulating the Lives of Women: Social Welfare Policy from Colonial Times to the Present* (Cambridge, MA: South End Press, 1996), 350–51; Weeks, *The Problem with Work*, 64.

CHAPTER 6

Soft Force

Heba Raouf Ezzat's Politics of the Islamic Family

In the introduction to Heba Raouf Ezzat's *al-Mar'a wa-l-ʿAmal al-Siyasi: Ru'ya Islamiyya* (Woman and Political Work: An Islamic Vision, 1995), Tariq al-Bishri, a leading thinker associated with the Islamic awakening, describes Raouf Ezzat as a promising scholar of the awakening (*nāhiḍ*) generation. She is one of the "stimulants of catalytic change," he writes, "working to bring about an awakening [nahḍa] of Islamic knowledge."[1] A bright star in the Islamic movement, Heba Raouf Ezzat (Hiba Ra'uf ʿIzzat) has assumed a place of leadership in Islamic politics, both intellectually and politically. Like other Islamic thinkers associated with the revival, she has successfully translated her scholarly work into popular parlance, disseminating her ideas among intellectual elites and popular audiences alike. Ranked the thirty-ninth most influential Arab on Twitter, with over 100,000 followers, voted one of the hundred most powerful Arab women by ArabianBusiness.com, and elected a Youth Global Leader by the World Economic Forum, Raouf Ezzat has articulated and disseminated her Islamic politics in a global public sphere.[2] She is one of the founders of the

[1] Raouf Ezzat, *al-Mar'a wa-l-ʿAmal al-Siyasi*, 16, 29.

[2] Khaled El Ahmad, "The 100 Most Influential Arabs on Twitter," *Wamda*, http://www.wamda.com/2012/01/the-100-most-influential-arabs-on-twitter; "100 Most Powerful Arab Women 2011," *ArabianBusiness*, http://www.arabianbusiness.com/100-most-powerful-arab-women-2011–384182.html?view=profile&itemid=384141, both accessed March 21, 2012; Riham Ashraf Bahi, "Networking for Power and Change: Muslim Women Activism and the Transformation of Muslim Public Sphere" (Department of Political Science, Northeastern University, 2008). A "public figure" on Facebook with nearly 50,000 admirers, she also has her own YouTube channel that dates from the immediate aftermath of the 2011 uprisings. Her website is a comprehensive mine of her books, lectures, interviews, presentations on satellite television, speeches on the 2011 revolution, scholarly essays, popular articles, debates in online magazines, blog posts, and research for the United Nations Development Programme. See "Heba Raouf Ezzat," *Facebook*, http://www.facebook.com/Heba.Raouf.Ezzat; Heba Raouf Ezzat, "DrHRaouf's Channel—YouTube,"

From Raouf Ezzat's essay "al-Quwwa al-Nāʿima" (Soft Force), published by al-Jazeera Center for Studies in October 2011. Image courtesy of Evandro Monteiro.

influential website *IslamOnline*, along with Yusuf al-Qaradawi, the Islamic intellectual who is the star of the popular al-Jazeera television show *al-Shariʿa wa-l-Hayat* (Islamic Law and Life). Al-Qaradawi, like Raouf Ezzat, envisions that women's "special leadership talents and abilities" will play a key role in the Islamic movement and in the democratization of the Muslim world.[3] For both thinkers, the media have been a means of rallying for "a civil state with a religious background" through the grassroots mobilization of the umma as an imagined community.[4] Raouf Ezzat's writings and lectures develop an Islamic theory

---

http://www.youtube.com/user/DrHRaouf?ob=0&feature=results_main; "Heba-Ezzat," http://www.heba-ezzat.com/, all accessed March 21, 2012.

[3] Yusuf al-Qaradawi, "Fatwa hawl Musharakat al-Nisaʾ fi al-ʿAmaliyyat al-Istishhadiyya," *Filastin al-Muslima*, March 2002. Though the Islamic movement in Egypt is a diverse set of strands, parties, associations, sensibilities, and political agendas, I use the term "Islamic movement" (*al-ḥaraka al-islāmiyya*) as Raouf Ezzat and al-Qaradawi do. In line with a recent tendency, Raouf Ezzat and al-Qaradawi deny participation in a single party (such as the Muslim Brotherhood), preferring identification with the broader notion of Islamic politics and reform. This more unified notion of the Islamic movement blurs contradictory agendas in favor of broader political solidarity.

[4] Muhammad Abu Musa and Abdel Hadi Abu Taleb, "Govt Pressures Ban Qaradawi from Egypt TV," February 22, 2011, http://www.onislam.net/english/news/africa/451164-govt-pressures-ban-qaradawi-from-egypt-tv.html. Al-Qaradawi made this call for "a civil state with a religious background" after the fall of Hosni Mubarak. Returning to Egypt after decades in exile, he led prayers in Tahrir Square before nearly five million on Friday, February 18, just one week after Mubarak was forced out of office. His scheduled appearance on Egyptian state television was abruptly canceled after the prayers.

of women's political participation but simultaneously address other contested questions about women's leadership, women's work, and women's participation in the public sphere. Heba Raouf Ezzat is one of the most visible public figures in the Arab and Islamic world today, visibility that began with her book on the question of women's political work in Islam.

Published when she was only twenty-nine and the mother of young children, *Woman and Political Work* was originally written as Raouf Ezzat's master's thesis at Cairo University. Its translation into Indonesian, Malay, Farsi, and Kurdish and republication in Algeria bears witness to the power and reach of her "Islamic vision" (*ruʾya islāmiyya*). The book's main thesis is that the family is the basic political unit of the Islamic community or nation (the umma). The thesis has both feminist and Islamist resonance, as she argues that the "private is political."[5] An Islamic family is a powerful locus for the transformation of sociopolitical institutions; it is a politics of the microcosmic with macrocosmic ramifications, effected through the very embodiment and practice of an Islamic ethos at a grassroots, capillary level. By breaking down the dichotomy between family and umma, personal and political, private and public, Raouf Ezzat seeks to dismantle the oppositions of secular society, to challenge the "increasing division of society into discrete spheres." This challenge strives "to imbue each of the various spheres of contemporary life with a regulative sensibility that takes its cue from the Islamic theological corpus rather than from modern secular ethics."[6] Women identifying with the Islamic revival in Egypt testify that the movement emerged as a response to "modern structures of secular governance" that have alienated religion from everyday life. What they refer to as " 'secularization' (*ʿalmana* or *ʿalmāniyya*) or 'westernization' (*tagharrub*)" has transformed both religious knowledge and religious conduct (adab), corroding "the sensibilities and habits of a certain kind of religious life."[7] Raouf Ezzat's project seeks to reinvest Islamic religiosity and conduct into the everyday life of the umma by mobilizing Islamic knowledge (adab) toward an Islamic sociopolitical order.

[5] Raouf Ezzat, *al-Marʾa wa-l-ʿAmal al-Siyasi*, 27. *Woman and Political Work* draws on (and quotes) Western feminist scholarship from the 1980s that critiqued and analyzed the relationship between public and private spheres. See, for example, Pateman, *Sexual Contract*; Linda Nicholson, *Gender and History* (New York: Columbia University Press, 1986); and Susan Moller Okin, *Justice, Gender, and the Family* (New York: Basic Books, 1991).

[6] Mahmood, *Politics of Piety*, 47.

[7] Ibid., 44. See Talal Asad's etymological history of the neologism *ʿalmāniyya* in *Formations of the Secular*, 206–7.

Raouf Ezzat contrasts the theological notion of tawḥīd, "the crux of Islamic faith," with secularism's presumed split between church and state, religion and politics, faith and science (47). Tawḥīd, or the unity of God, is a classical theological concept referring to the oneness of God and to the monotheistic nature of Islam and the Muslim community, but it has assumed new connotations in the modern period. Contemporary Islamist thought, for example, defines it polemically against secularism's split between religion and politics, a split that Islam "heals" by bringing the two together. "Tawḥīd rejects secularism's dualisms," Raouf Ezzat writes, "just as it rejects the split of the human into body and soul, and the material world into religion and state" (48). These understandings of secularism have contributed to defining political Islam as the "solution" (*ḥall*) to modern problems and as a "complete way of life" as opposed to the merely private belief of religion in secular societies. Raouf Ezzat develops the notion of the umma as family writ large, or the family as a unit or cell of the umma—morals and ethics fostered on a microcosmic scale that form the basis of an ethical and moral politics. In emphasizing the family as the political unit of the umma, Raouf Ezzat stresses the family as the site of women's political participation in the Islamic community, playing on the feminine connotations of the word *umma* and its etymological connections to the word "mother" (*umm*). In *Woman and Political Work*, Raouf Ezzat also imparts tawḥīd with a sense of gender unity, as healing "the division of social labor on the basis of sex" (52). She applies tawḥīd to the relationship between man and woman, because "the link between them is one of unity and completion, affirming the harmony of this link through mutual instinct (fiṭra)" (188).

Raouf Ezzat conceptualizes the family as not only the site of political change but also the source of the Islamic movement's political power.[8] Her writings and lectures articulate a concept of "nonviolent jihad" and "soft force" that is performed in the private sphere, in the family, in social institutions, and by women.[9] Women's work

[8] Heba Raouf Ezzat, *Hawl Mawaqif al-Quwa al-Siyasiyya, Khassatan al-Harakat al-Islamiyya wa-l-Harakat al-Diniyya, Min Tamkin al-Nisa' fi al-Buldan al-ʿArabiyya*, Background Paper, Arab Human Development Report: Toward the Rise of Women in the Arab World, 2005; Heba Raouf Ezzat, "al-Usra wa-l-Taghyir al-Siyasi: Ru'ya Islamiyya," *Islamiyyat al-Maʿrifa* 2 (2007), http://www.eiiit.org/resources/eiiit/eiiit/eiiit_article_read.asp?articleID=804.

[9] Raouf Ezzat, *al-Mar'a wa-l-ʿAmal al-Siyasi*, 156–58; Raouf Ezzat, "al-Quwwa al-Naʿima." The Waqf Foundation's polemic against US infiltration of Muslim society through "soft force" is a veritable reiteration of Raouf Ezzat's thesis about the power of institutions to effect political change, an idea that was parodied in television comedy after the 2011 revolution. The people interviewed on the street unanimously see "soft power" as women's. See *al-Quwwa al-Naʿima* (Waqf Foundation, 2011), http://www

in the family, Raouf Ezzat argues, is a form of nonviolent political action that she calls "women's jihad." Through the labor of *tarbiya* (discipline, childrearing, education, pedagogy), women train and educate new generations of Islamic citizens, "cultivating the human capital" of Islamic society and "reviving the social units of the Islamic umma."[10] Through this approach, Raouf Ezzat reorients politics around women's spheres of influence, in "informal networks and informal institutions [that] seek to avoid the notice of the state," networks ignored by "reigning typologies of politics."[11] Raouf Ezzat does for Islamic thought what Nancy Fraser has done for theories of the public sphere: she politicizes the social institution of family by arguing for the recognition of the worth of women's labor, interpreting women's daily lives as a form of political struggle. Like Fraser, she argues that women's labor in the informal economy constitutes a critical unit of civil society and cannot, in good conscience, be regulated to a domain isolated from public influence.[12] Raouf Ezzat's thesis also speaks specifically to the political context of Egypt, as she calls for nurturing and strengthening Islamic civil society as a means of combating authoritarian secularism. For her, the institutions of civil Islam are not just the foundations but the very manifestation of "a democratic and progressive Islam . . . a radical democracy" that constitutes the best hope for Egypt's future.[13] Raouf Ezzat calls for the

.youtube.com/watch?v=UGcNTE1T1jo&feature=youtube_gdata_player and "al-Quwwa al-Naʿima: Siyasat Sitt al-Hajja," *TheRamadanComedy*, August 2, 2011.

[10] Raouf Ezzat, *al-Marʾa wa-l-ʿAmal al-Siyasi*, 156–58. This understanding of the education of children as a form of women's jihad in the family echoes Niʿmat Sidqi's writings. Especially see the latter's third chapter, "Tarbiyat al-Awlad Jihad" (Bringing Up Children Is Jihad), in Sidqi, *al-Jihad fi Sabil Allah*, 23.

[11] Singerman, *Avenues of Participation*, 4. Singerman observes that many ethnographic and anthropological studies "depict women as important community figures who exert influence over the management of the household and wider society networks, yet the classic works on Egyptian politics and political economy barely allude to them. Where does all that power go? Does it dissipate at the 'higher' levels of power and authority in Egypt? Despite the recent proliferation of research on women in Egypt and their participation in political and economic life, the macro analysis of 'high politics' remains androcentric and gender blind" (6).

[12] See especially her lecture "Politics of Informality"; Nancy Fraser, *Unruly Practices: Power, Discourse and Gender in Contemporary Social Theory* (Cambridge: Polity Press, 1989); Fraser, "Rethinking the Public Sphere."

[13] Heba Raouf Ezzat and Ahmed Mohamed Abdallah, "Towards an Islamically Democratic Secularism," in *Faith and Secularism*, ed. Rosemary Bechler (London: British Council, 2004), 50; Heba Raouf Ezzat, "Toward a Culture of Shura: Citizenship and Democracy Reform from a Muslim Woman's Perspective," *Arab Reform Initiative*, Critical Dialogue between Different Intellectual Movements: The Experience in the Arab World (July 2010), http://www.arab-reform.net/.

"democratization of the man-woman relationship inside the family structure," proposing an Islamic politics based on fair, just, and democratic gender relations within the family.[14] Her articulate elucidation of such a politics before the 2011 revolution metamorphosed into an urgent campaign after President Hosni Mubarak's fall, as she traveled widely, lecturing on the power of democratic change in Egypt and its relationship to "civil Islam."[15] For her, the family and women fortify nascent democratic forms against the "hard force" of continued military rule, nonviolent jihad against the "thug state."[16]

Raouf Ezzat's work belongs to a body of revivalist writings that have used increasingly liberal language of women's emancipation in Islam, human rights in Islam, and equality in Islam. This is partly due to the political conditions of the Islamic opposition in Egypt, whose efforts at grassroots mobilization have been concentrated in social institutions associated with a "civil Islam." The movement was largely barred from political participation in the state, but the Egyptian state allowed social mobilization through a policy of "partial liberalization," a policy intermittently rescinded when Islamic groups seem to gain too much power (such as at the end of the 1970s under Sadat and at the beginning of the 1990s under Mubarak). This dual policy of partial liberalization and authoritarian crackdown produced a thriving Islamic movement entrenched in civil society, a movement that retained its oppositional character in the face of the authoritarianism of the secular state.[17]

[14] Karim El-Gawhary and Heba Raouf Ezzat, "An Islamic Women's Liberation Movement: An Interview with Heba Raouf Ezzat," *Middle East Report* no. 191 (December 1994): 26.

[15] Raouf Ezzat, "al-Marʾa wa-Mustaqbal al-ʿAmal al-Siyasi" (al-Maktaba al-ʿAmma, al-Mahalla al-Kubra, April 20, 2011); Heba Raouf Ezzat, "Hawl al-Dawla wa-l-Mujtamaʿ wa-l-Umma" (Center for Civilization Studies and Dialogue of Cultures, Faculty of Economics and Political Science, Cairo University, May 16, 2011); Heba Raouf Ezzat, "al-Dawla al-Diniyya wa-l-Dawla al-Madaniyya" (presented at the Barnamaj al-Tathqif al-Siyasi, Bibliotheca Alexandrina, May 19, 2011); Heba Raouf Ezzat, "al-Siyasi wa-l-Insani wa-l-Ghayr Rasmi" (presented at the Peaceful Revolution in Egypt: Lessons Learned, Center for Civilization Studies and Dialogue of Cultures, Faculty of Economics and Political Science, Cairo University, June 6, 2011).

[16] Amar, "Turning the Gendered Politics of the Security State Inside Out?"; Amar, *Security Archipelago*, 210–13.

[17] Theories of secularism in general, and in Egypt in particular, analyze the central role of religion in secular modernity (and of secularism in religious modernity), theories that Raouf Ezzat acknowledges. But maintaining the sense of binary opposition is critical to the Islamic nature of Raouf Ezzat's political vision. The state in Egypt continually deploys religious rhetoric, just as Islamic groups employ secular concepts. Asad, *Formations of the Secular*; José Casanova, *Public Religions in the Modern World* (Chicago: University of Chicago Press, 1994); Bayat, *Making Islam Democratic*, 48, 138, 166, 173, 181, 192; Raouf Ezzat and Abdallah, "Towards an Islamically Democratic Secularism";

These political conditions set the stage for the emergence of a liberal discourse calling for freedom of speech, the right to political participation, and the right to congregate, as the Islamic revival used public discourse to criticize what it characterizes as an unjust and tyrannical secular state.

My analysis focuses on Raouf Ezzat's exegeses of key verses from the Qur'an (mainly 2:228, 4:21, 4:34, 30:21, and 30:30). Her hermeneutic produces a liberal interpretation of Islamic politics, taking democracy, freedom, equality, and rights as political ideals. But she simultaneously asserts a gendered division of labor where men are leaders and women are led; men are authorities and women are obedient. These deep contradictions—of the equalities and hierarchies, rights and duties, freedoms and disciplines associated with the public and private spheres—have long been the target of liberalism's critics.[18] Even as Raouf Ezzat presumes to transcend liberalism's gendered division of labor, she reproduces some of its most basic assumptions. She envisions the Islamic family as the site of revolutionary change, social justice, and democratic politics but also perpetrates liberal concepts about male leadership, natural roles in the family, and women's vocation in life. Liberal discourse has been garnered in service of Islamist political aims in the quest for equal representation, free speech, a robust civil society (of religious institutions), and freedom of political participation. For Raouf Ezzat, revolutionary democratic change begins in the family, but some of liberalism's deepest paradoxes materialize within this site of political transformation. My aim is not to depict liberal Islam's view of gender relations as merely a derivative discourse but to contextualize its relationship to liberalism and secularism. In Partha Chatterjee's words, this political-ideological discourse is a kind of "political contest, a struggle for power . . . a struggle with an entire body of systematic knowledge, a struggle that is political at the same time as it is intellectual. Its politics impels it to open up that framework of knowledge

Hatem, "Secularist and Islamist Discourses on Modernity"; Abu-Lughod, "Marriage of Feminism and Islamism."

[18] Pateman, *Sexual Contract*; Brown, "Liberalism's Family Values"; Hatem, "Secularist and Islamist Discourses on Modernity"; Scott, *Only Paradoxes to Offer*. For the case of Egypt, Mervat Hatem observes the overlap between "modern/Western and traditional/Islamic cultures in their attitudes toward women and the position women occupy in society." "Feminist discussion of the liberal emphasis on gender inequality in the family as the basis for women's unequal incorporation into the political arena bears a striking resemblance to some of the assumptions and definitions offered by the Islamist discourse." Hatem, like Raouf Ezzat, uses Pateman's *Sexual Contract* to interpret the adaption of liberal (and neoliberal) discourses in Egypt. Motherhood and domesticity, Hatem observes, grants "women a special" status and an "indirect means of political participation." See Hatem, "Egyptian Discourses on Gender and Political Liberalization," 663–64.

which presumes to dominate it, to displace that framework, to subvert its authority, to challenge its morality."[19]

Raouf Ezzat's thesis, developed within the strictures of an authoritarian state, carves out a sacrosanct space for Islamic thought and practice seemingly beyond the reach of secularism. One of the most integral elements of this politics has been an Islamic family, a core institution for the expression of an Islamic politics. For Raouf Ezzat, the Islamic family has been critical to the maintenance and cultivation of an "Islamic sociopolitical contract,"[20] one based on the sunna of the early community as much as modern, liberal understandings of the family as a unit of politics and as a repository for religious conviction, gendered difference, and communal identification. Women, in this formulation, are made to shoulder an inordinate burden of communal identification, through the attachments of childbearing and childrearing, but also as keepers of the home. Raouf Ezzat essentially sacralizes the affective bonds of intimate relations, making the family the domain of religion. In political scientist Wendy Brown's essay "Liberalism's Family Values," she describes how "the *family* or *personal life* is *natural* to *woman* and in some formulations *divinely ordained*; it is a domain governed by needs and affective ties, hence a domain of *collectivity*; and the hierarchy within it also constitutes the domain of 'real political life' for feminists. . . . 'Woman has her substantial vocation in the family, and her ethical disposition consists in this piety.' "[21] For Raouf Ezzat, family and women's work are expressions of the affective ties of belief in its most intimate instantiation. Even though her scholarship draws widely on feminist theory, Raouf Ezzat rejects feminism as a political agenda.[22] The family is the domain of "real political life" for the Islamic movement, of which "women's liberation—an Islamic one" is an integral part.[23]

[19] Chatterjee, *Nationalist Thought and the Colonial World*, 42.

[20] Heba Raouf Ezzat and Emran Qureshi, "Are Sharia Laws and Human Rights Compatible?" *Qantara.de*, October 4, 2004, 52, http://en.qantara.de/Are-Sharia-Laws-and-Human-Rights-Compatible/7606c43/index.html.

[21] Brown, "Liberalism's Family Values," 147. The emphasis is hers. The quote "Woman has her substantial vocation in the family, and her ethical disposition consists in this piety" is from Friedrich Hegel, *Philosophy of Right*, trans. T. M. Knox (Oxford: Oxford University Press, 1957), 114.

[22] Nawal El Saadawi and Heba Raouf Ezzat, *al-Mar'a wa-l-Din wa-l-Akhlaq* (Damascus: Dar al-Fikr, 2000), 134–35; El-Gawhary and Ezzat, "Interview with Heba Ra'uf Ezzat," 26; Heba Raouf Ezzat, "Rethinking Secularism . . . Rethinking Feminism," *SuhaibWebb.com Your Virtual Mosque* (December 11, 2008), http://www.suhaibwebb.com/islam-studies/rethinking-secularism-%E2%80%A6-rethinking-feminism-by-dr-heba-raouf-ezzat/.

[23] El-Gawhary and Ezzat, "Interview with Heba Ra'uf Ezzat."

Civil Jihad

Woman and Political Work catapulted Raouf Ezzat into international renown, a platform that she has used to rally vocally for democracy in Egypt. For Raouf Ezzat, the cultivation of a robust public sphere is critical to the realization of a democratic politics, a public sphere to which she has exuberantly and tirelessly contributed.[24] Because she advocates jihad against the "tyranny" of the secular state, the book has never been published in Egypt, despite (or most likely because of) Raouf Ezzat's popularity. Instead, it was published by the International Institute of Islamic Thought in Herndon, Virginia (near Washington, DC), an Islamic think tank whose motto is "The Islamization of Knowledge and Reform of Islamic Thought." Not long afterward, the Center for Democracy at the University of Westminster invited Raouf Ezzat to be a visiting researcher. In 2003 she organized a conference at Cairo University on "al-Muwatana al-Misriyya wa-Mustaqbal al-Dimuqratiyya: Ruʾa Jadida li-ʿAlam Mutaghayyir" (Egyptian Citizenship and the Future of Democracy: New Visions for a Changing World) and edited a 1,300-page volume of the proceedings with her colleague ʿUla Abu Zayd (Ola Abou Zeid).[25] Like Raouf Ezzat, Abu Zayd has written widely on the role of civil society in democratic change in Egypt, although from a more secular perspective.[26] These scholar-activists represent an ideological cross section of women working for democratic change in Egypt through the question of women's political participation.

[24] Raouf Ezzat and Abdallah, "Towards an Islamically Democratic Secularism," 53; Raouf Ezzat, "Politics of Informality."

[25] Heba Raouf Ezzat and ʿUla Abu Zayd, *al-Muwatana al-Misriyya wa-Mustaqbal al-Dimuqratiyya: Ruʾa Jadida li-ʿAlam Mutaghayyir: Aʿmal al-Muʾtamar al-Sanawi al-Sabiʿ ʿAshar li-l-Buhuth al-Siyasiyya, 21–23 Disimbir 2003* (Giza: Jamiʿat al-Qahira, Kulliyyat al-Iqtisad wa-l-ʿUlum al-Siyasiyya, Markaz al-Buhuth wa-l-Dirasat al-Siyasiyya, 2005).

[26] Amani Qindil and ʿUla Abu Zayd, *al-Marʾa al-Misriyya wa-l-ʿAmal al-ʿAmm: Ruʾya Mustaqbaliyya* (Cairo: Jamiʿat al-Qahira, Kulliyyat al-Iqtisad wa-l-ʿUlum al-Siyasiyya, Markaz al-Buhuth wa-l-Dirasat al-Siyasiyya, 1995); Jan Aart Scholte, *Democratizing the Global Economy: The Role of Civil Society*, trans. Ola Abou Zeid (Coventry: Centre for the Study of Globalisation and Regionalisation, University of Warwick, 2004). Just after the publication of *Woman and Political Work*, Abu Zayd and Qindil organized a conference with the title "al-Marʾa al-Misriyya wa-l-ʿAmal al-ʿAmm: Ruʾya Mustaqbaliyya" (Egyptian Woman and Public Work: Vision for the Future, 1995) that was almost identical to Raouf Ezzat's book. The conference, sponsored by Cairo University's Center for Political Research and Studies, focused on women's participation in formal governmental institutions like parliament, political parties, and government ministries, as well as in trade unions and the media. Qindil, executive director of the Arab Network for NGOs (a division of the League of Arab States), has written prolifically on civil society in the Arab world.

In conjunction with theorizing Islamic democracy, Raouf Ezzat has built on Islamic conceptions of human rights, criticizing what she calls a "secularist weltanschauung" that fails to recognize religion's capacity to secure human rights for its citizen-believers.[27] In a section of *Woman and Political Work* on the "Analytical Concepts," "rights" occupy a central place, as she criticizes how Western, secular documents have become the "background" against which Islamic conceptions of human rights have emerged.[28] In 1997, just after the publication of *Woman and Political Work*, Raouf Ezzat participated in a conference on "Islam and Equality" organized by the Lawyers' Committee for Human Rights in New York. Raouf Ezzat locates religion and family as the sites where Egyptian women mobilize for their rights, both economic and political. Muslim women, she says, turn to "the liberating potential of their religious traditions" and choose to "participate in the wider Islamic resurgence" as a form of protest against the "restrictions and sometimes rigid discrimination and violations of their human rights by political regimes. . . . They demand respect, they already participate in economic and political life, but they are also proud of their motherhood as a value. They believe in the family as a social institution and regard themselves as the guardians of their culture." Raouf Ezzat cites "the household economy as an informal sector that women use for their benefit," as they draw on rich kinship ties to battle economic inequality. In the shadow of an oppressive secular dictatorship, family and religion become means of securing basic human rights, economic equality, and political freedom.[29]

[27] Heba Raouf Ezzat, "Islam and Equality," in *Islam and Equality: Debating the Future of Women's and Minority Rights in the Middle East and North Africa* (New York: Lawyers Committee for Human Rights, 1998), 182; Raouf Ezzat and Qureshi, "Are Sharia Laws and Human Rights Compatible?"; Heba Raouf Ezzat, "Islamic Media in a Secular Environment" (presented at the Deutsche Welle Global Media Forum 2011: Human Rights in a Globalized World, Challenges for the Media, Bonn, Germany, June 20, 2011).

[28] Raouf Ezzat, *al-Marʾa wa-l-ʿAmal al-Siyasi*, 80–87; Qutb, *al-ʿAdala al-Ijtimaʿiyya fi al-Islam*; Wafi, *Huquq al-Insan fi al-Islam*; Muhammad al-Ghazali, *Huquq al-Insan bayn Taʿalim al-Islam wa-Iʿlan al-Umam al-Muttahida* (Cairo: al-Maktaba al-Tijariyya, 1963). Qutb's, Wafi's (see chapter 1), and al-Ghazali's texts are classic Islamic responses to the principles outlined in the Universal Declaration of Human Rights, an Islamic discourse of rights that has come to govern discussions of Islamic politics. Some of these have been clearly inflected by Raouf Ezzat. See, for example, ʿUmar Saʿid Muhammad Fariʿ ʿAhami, *al-Huquq al-Siyasiyya li-l-Marʾa fi al-Fiqh al-Islami: Maʿ Tahlil li-Baʿd al-Duwal al-ʿArabiyya* (Alexandria: al-Maktab al-Jamiʿi al-Hadith, 2011).

[29] Raouf Ezzat and Lawyers Committee for Human Rights, "Islam and Equality," 182; Heba Raouf Ezzat, "Secularism, the State and the Social Bond: The Withering Away of the Family," in *Islam and Secularism in the Middle East*, ed. Azzam Tamimi and John L. Esposito (New York: New York University Press, 2000), 136–37. Kinship and community

Raouf Ezzat calls for religious rights within the context of a secular state that has consistently denied religious groups freedom of expression, opinion, congregation, belief, and political participation. A debate over human rights in Islam was orchestrated between Raouf Ezzat and Emran Qureshi (then a scholar at Harvard University's Carr Center for Human Rights Policy). In the online magazine *Qantara*, the dialogue was set up as a false opposition between Islamic and secular perspectives on human rights, making them appear as antithetical, even as both thinkers affirm rights as the path to justice. Human rights violations in Muslim countries, Raouf Ezzat notes, are "mainly exercised by the state" and have been an extension of human rights violations practiced under the colonial state. Secular regimes based their legal systems on colonial models, judicial reform that became the basis for modernizing the state. "However," Raouf Ezzat states, "these new secular and socialist regimes were totalitarian." Shariʿa law, she says, "is not only compatible with human rights but also the most effective way to achieve human rights. . . . Shariʿa is a progressive platform which empowers the people and protects their rights against totalitarianism and utilitarian ultra-capitalism. It can be an egalitarian force for democratic social justice, in the Muslim countries and globally. Islam's central values are justice and personal freedom."[30] Raouf Ezzat sets up her argument in opposition to secular forms of knowledge, but her ideas about democracy and rights have been formed both within and against the strictures of state secularism, reflecting the specific historical circumstances of Islamic political mobilization in the region.

To combat the tyranny of the secular state in the Muslim world, Raouf Ezzat calls for "a pacifist struggle for civil jihad . . . by expanding and empowering religion in a more civilized public sphere." She envisions an Islamic sociopolitical contract that starts "by building an open and strong civil society that cherishes human integrity and dignity, a commitment that we see deeply rooted in the Qurʾan and the hadith, the traditions of the Prophet Muhammad. This is the basis, she says, of "a democratic sociopolitical contract that aims to be as inspiring as the bond underlying the early city state of Islam, bearing in mind all the differences, but recapturing its humanist egalitarian logic." Through local politics and civil activism, Islam can be "a major source of liberation, equality and justice, not a heap of false legacies and authoritarian policies."[31] What is at stake in these authoritarian states is "the right

networks as political economies in which women play pivotal roles are the subject of Diane Singerman's *Avenues of Participation*.

[30] Raouf Ezzat and Qureshi, "Are Sharia Laws and Human Rights Compatible?"

[31] Raouf Ezzat and Abdallah, "Towards an Islamically Democratic Secularism," 52–53.

to belief and expressing one's religious devotion in the sociopolitical sphere, advocating social justice by employing religious rhetoric." It is the "freedom of people to turn Islam into a liberation theology against despotic regimes. When they do, even in the most pacifist way, they are accused of being terrorists and are subject to harassment, human rights violations, imprisonment and even death sentences by military courts. This was the case in Syria and Iraq, and still is the case in Egypt and Tunisia. . . . the most brutal regimes that the region has witnessed were secular: the Baʿth in Syria and Iraq" (41). These governments, she says, have abused religion and religious institutions. But "social movements attempted to recapture the liberating, egalitarian and democratic role of faith. . . . Such movements are engaged in a protracted struggle with these non-democratic regimes over matters of human rights, power-sharing and social justice" (35). This essay, written with her husband, Ahmad Muhammad ʿAbd Allah (Ahmed Mohammed Abdalla), and published by the British Council, pleads for Islamic democracy as an antidote to secular authoritarianism, an argument she first formulated in *Woman and Political Work*. Raouf Ezzat envisions the family as a unit of civil society critical to realizing a rights-based polity.

In the wake of the 2008 al-Mahalla al-Kubra demonstrations said to set the ground for the 2011 revolution, Raouf Ezzat published writings in the opposition press about the human "price" of living under authoritarian government and calling for "soft force" against the "strong force" of the "weak state." Her works aim to formulate a blueprint for a politics of the "future," through "transformative visions" of democratic society and women's participation, in a "changing" world, terms that appear repeatedly in these writings and in their titles.[32] Just before the revolution, Raouf Ezzat participated in two democracy workshops: one on "Building Global Democracy" in Cairo in 2009 and one on "Citizen Learning for Global Democracy" in New Delhi in 2010. In the immediate aftermath of the 2011 revolution, she presented a lecture in al-Mahalla al-Kubra to commemorate the demonstrations there that had led up to the revolution. Her talk, "Woman and the Future of Political Participation," riffed on her book's themes. The notion of "soft force" (*al-quwwa al-nāʿima*), developed in her book and a number of subse-

[32] Raouf Ezzat, *al-Marʾa wa-l-ʿAmal al-Siyasi*; Qindil and Abu Zayd, *al-Marʾa al-Misriyya wa-l-ʿAmal al-ʿAmm*; Heba Raouf Ezzat, "Ruʾa Mughayira: Nahw ʿAlam Akthar ʿAdlan wa-Dimuqratiyyan; al-Mawsim al-Thaqafi 2000–2001," in *al-ʿAwlama Nahw Ruʾa Mughayira*, ed. Hasan Hanafi and Heba Raouf Ezzat (Giza: Jamiʿat al-Qahira, Kulliyyat al-Iqtisad wa-l-ʿUlum al-Siyasiyya, 2001); Raouf Ezzat and Abu Zayd, *al-Muwatana al-Misriya wa-Mustaqbal al-Dimuqratiyya*; Raouf Ezzat, "al-Usra wa-l-Taghyir al-Siyasi: Ruʾya Islamiyya"; Raouf Ezzat, "al-Marʾa wa-Mustaqbal al-ʿAmal al-Siyasi."

quent publications, would become the eleventh and final principle of the (short-lived) 2012 constitution under the Islamist government.[33]

Democratic Family

In al-Bishri's introduction to *Woman and Political Work*, he calls the issue of gender relations the "pinnacle" of "the intellectual battle between Islamists and secularists" (17). Scholarly work on gender and the family in the Muslim world, and in Egypt specifically, has tended to reinforce the perception of secular and religious practices as diametrically opposing, a perspective partly propagated by revivalist intellectuals. But Raouf Ezzat's ideas lie at what she calls the intersection of ideas.[34] Though she grounds her scholarship in religious knowledge, her training was at the more secular Cairo University, where she received her bachelor's, master's, and doctoral degrees in the department of political science (and where she is now a professor). *Woman and Political Work* begins by challenging the exclusion of religious knowledge from the field of political science, calling for a critique of "the secularism of the sciences" and "a return to religion as the source of values and as the point of departure for knowledge" (45). Raouf Ezzat deploys academic conventions and literature connected with the discipline of political science, but her "point of departure is faith connected to revelation" (44). She masterfully combines Islamic scholarship with "Western/secular/modern" (44) disciplines, drawing expertly on the foundational texts of Islamic jurisprudence, Western feminism, political science works in both English and Arabic, and contemporary Islamic theorizations of politics, gender, and the family. Her vantage point in the political science department has given her a certain creative license outside the formal disciplinary constraints of Islamic scholarship, enabling her to perhaps more easily adapt political concepts from the Islamic intellectual tradition to modern models of governmentality. This approach has made her arguments readily intelligible to contemporary audiences, as she has harnessed the language of revolutionary democracy to Islamic politics.[35] She has revitalized Islamic scholarship, even though such creative reinterpretations of the Islamic intellectual tradition have a long history in the region. Her most radical contribution may be her injection of ideas

[33] Raouf Ezzat, "al-Quwwa al-Naʿima"; Jumhuriyyat Misr, "al-Dustur," December 26, 2012.

[34] Heba Raouf Ezzat, "Tanazuʿ al-Afkar . . . al-Dawla al-Madaniyya (Contending Ideas . . . The Civil State)," accessed April 5, 2012, http://www.heba-ezzat.com.

[35] Raouf Ezzat and Abdallah, "Towards an Islamically Democratic Secularism"; Raouf Ezzat, "Citizenship and Democracy Reform."

culled from the Islamic intellectual tradition (and the Islamic movement) into the discipline of political science. In doing so, she destabilizes the occidental, secular biases that structure such imported fields of inquiry, reimagining standard political typologies for the discipline of political science, as much as for the Islamic resurgence.[36]

For Raouf Ezzat, a just and democratic Islamic politics stands in contrast to what she calls "extremist secularism," "autocratic leadership," and "totalitarianism."[37] The family is a microcosm of good Islamic governance, fostering—as a "natural nursery"—such governance on a larger social and political scale. Raouf Ezzat understands consultation and authority, *shūrā* and *qiwāma*, as the two main principles governing an Islamic politics.[38] Shūrā, consultation or counsel, has been widely interpreted—and widely contested—as an Islamic version of democracy.[39] In an interview with *Middle East Reports*, Raouf Ezzat defines shūrā as democracy. "We have shūrā like the West has democracy. The

[36] In Diane Singerman's *Avenues of Participation*, she recognizes that "constituencies that are intentionally excluded from formal political participation by a ruling power are not only repressed by their governments but discounted and ignored by reigning typologies of politics." Singerman proposes new typologies that recognize "nonviolent extralegal protest activities as political participation in authoritarian or nondemocratic nations . . . an interactive notion of the political process captures the participation of less visible members of the community" (4).

[37] El-Gawhary and Ezzat, "Interview with Heba Raouf Ezzat," 27; Raouf Ezzat, *al-Marʾa wa-l-ʿAmal al-Siyasi*, 157, 192, 200; Raouf Ezzat and Qureshi, "Are Sharia Laws and Human Rights Compatible?".

[38] Raouf Ezzat, *al-Marʾa wa-l-ʿAmal al-Siyasi*, 196, 204; Raouf Ezzat, "Toward a Culture of Shura." Raouf Ezzat's mentor, the Islamic thinker Tariq al-Bishri, similarly identifies shūrā and riyāsa, consultation and leadership, as the main principles of an Islamic politics. But Raouf Ezzat's formulation slightly differs from al-Bishri's, in that she uses the word *qiwāma*, which connotes male authority over a wife (based on verse 4:34 from the Qurʾan) instead of riyāsa (which more closely connotes political leadership). Al-Bishri wrote the introduction to *Woman and Political Work* and participated in her democracy conference at Cairo University. See Tariq al-Bishri, *al-Muslimun wa-l-Aqbat fi Itar al-Jamaʿa al-Wataniyya* (Cairo: al-Hayaʾ al-Misriyya al-ʿAmma li-l-Kitab, 1980), 693–96. See also Leonard Binder's discussion of al-Bishri's thought in his chapter "Nationalism, Liberalism, and the Islamic Heritage: The Political Thought of Tariq al-Bishri," in Binder, *Islamic Liberalism*, 243–92.

[39] Khaled Abou El Fadl, "Islam and the Challenge of Democracy," *Boston Review*, May 2003, http://bostonreview.net/BR28.2/abou.html; ʿAbd al-Hamid Ismaʿil Ansari, *al-Shura wa-Atharuha fi al-Dimuqratiyya* (Cairo: al-Matbaʿa al-Salafiyya wa-Maktabatuha, 1980); Salim ʿAli Bahnasawi, *al-Khilafa wa-l-Khulafaʾ al-Rashidun bayn al-Shura wa-l-Dimuqratiyya* (Madinat Nasr, Cairo: al-Zahraʾ li-l-Iʿlam al-ʿArabi, 1991); Farid ʿAbd al-Khaliq, *Fi al-Fiqh al-Siyasi al-Islami: Mabadiʾ Dusturiyya: al-Shura, al-ʿAdl, al-Musawaa* (Cairo: Dar al-Shuruq, 1998); ʿAbd al-Hamid Ismaʿil Ansari, *al-ʿAlam al-Islami al-Muʿasir bayn al-Shura wa-l-Dimuqratiyya: Ruʾya Naqdiyya* (Madinat Nasr, Cairo: Dar al-Fikr al-ʿArabi, 2001); Muhammad ibn ʿAli Hirfi, *Bayn al-Shura al-Islamiyya wa-l-Dimuqratiyya al-Gharbiyya* (Cairo: Muʾassasat al-Mukhtar, 2005); Muhammad ʿAbd al-Fattah Fattuh,

same value is dominant in family relations. You can't have a totalitarian patriarchal system in Islam. The family should be run by shūrā. The same values and laws count in the public and the private arenas. Marriage is like voting for or choosing the caliph. We do have a family head, but he is like the caliph and should be chosen freely."[40] Raouf Ezzat is referring to the two different "levels" of shūrā, the microcosmic and macrocosmic, as consultation within the family and within the political community. These are the two main senses in which it occurs in the Qur'an: consultation between two spouses about when to wean a child (2:233) and consultation between a leader and his followers (3:159). Shūrā in verse 42:38 contrasts with tyranny, injustice, and oppression in subsequent verses. In *Woman and Political Work*, Raouf Ezzat initially defines shūrā as a political idea. "The umma," she says, "is in its totality 'a people of consultation' . . . and a means of administrating society."[41] Only later in her argument does she strengthen the sense of shūrā in the family, as consultation between husband and wife over family affairs. Similarly, in her later book *al-Mar'a wa-l-Din wa-l-Akhlaq* (Woman, Religion, and Morality, 2000), she focuses her argument on the democratic nature of family relations in Islam and accordingly, the democratic nature of Islamic government.

Raouf Ezzat's second principle of Islamic government, qiwāma, is usually understood as "guardianship," but Raouf Ezzat defines it as "leadership" (riyāsa) that refers to the leadership of the head of state. This leadership, which she defines as "administration of the house," must be (1) consultative (*shūrī*) and (2) just. "The administration is consultative (*shūrī*) within this small social structure. It is not desirable that one part autocratically rules the whole by command, but that it takes the opinions of all parts in respect for the limits of the shariʿa. . . . For the leadership (riyāsa) of the family is a consultative, not autocratic, form of leadership; this resembles to a great extent the imamate or the caliphate at the level of the state" (200–201). Based on two verses from the Qur'an (4:135, 5:8) referring to believers as "guardians of justice," she argues that this leadership, or guardianship, is inherently just (197), an argument repeated in her later writing.[42]

In *Woman and Political Work*, Raouf Ezzat interprets core terms from classical Islamic thought within a matrix of democratic concepts. An overlapping set of political ideals govern both the umma and the family,

---

al-Dimuqratiyya wa-l-Shura fi al-Fikr al-Siyasi al-Islami al-Muʿasir: Dirasa fi Fikr al-Shaykh Muhammad al-Ghazali (Cairo: Maktabat al-Shuruq al-Dawliyya, 2006).

[40] El-Gawhary and Ezzat, "Interview with Heba Raouf Ezzat," 27.

[41] Raouf Ezzat, *al-Mar'a wa-l-ʿAmal al-Siyasi*, 146.

[42] El Saadawi and Raouf Ezzat, *al-Mar'a wa-l-Din wa-l-Akhlaq*.

what Raouf Ezzat calls the "sphere of the umma" and the "sphere of the family," the titles of the book's two main sections. In "The Sphere of the Umma," she outlines four main political principles from the Islamic intellectual tradition. The first is *bayʿa*, "election of the Caliph" through a "contractual agreement" between the elected and the electorate.[43] The second is *al-wilāya al-ʿāmma*, or "public leadership." The third is shūrā, "consultation representing the umma's participation in political administration."[44] And the fourth is jihad. Like other thinkers who espouse forms of Islamic democracy, Raouf Ezzat understands leaders as elected through *bayʿa* and as ruling through consultation (shūrā) with citizens and religious scholars (ʿulamaʾ). Jihad, or political struggle, becomes a means of resistance against unjust forms of government where leaders have violated the terms of this sociopolitical contract by transgressing the law (here shariʿa, not the more secular *qānūn*). Jihad, usually understood as armed force or warfare (especially against nonbelievers), is interpreted in *Woman and Political Work* as a struggle against injustice and the infringement of rights. Raouf Ezzat develops an understanding of jihad as a means of bringing down a tyrannical government through nonviolent tactics like civil disobedience and social, economic, and political noncooperation (156–57). These are means of "liberating different social structures from subjection, a liberation that necessitates the participation of the masses in the efforts (*juhūd*) of effectively developing . . . disparate underlying social forms." Such "social forces," she argues, are one of "the most effective tools for resisting the tyranny of dominant regimes from within . . . solidarity that also supports society's ability to persist in jihad" (157). In the context of this discussion of what she calls "civil defense," she turns, in a timely way, to the issue of "women's jihad." Jihad is incumbent not just on the community (as a *farḍ kifāya*) but on every believer (*farḍ ʿayn*), including every competent woman. Jihad "represents an underlying legal framework for women's mobilization, making her socially and politically responsible for effectively executing a required duty." Moreover, this framework for jihad "permits women's mobilization within the actual social context of numerous Islamic societies," giving her flexibility and wide latitude to perform this duty under ordinary conditions. "In the shelter of the abode of jihad" (*fī ẓill al-manākh al-jihādī*), Raouf Ezzat writes, "women can change their circumstances in the shelter of the Islamic shariʿa" (160). With the expression "in the shelter of the abode of jihad," she plays on the traditional expression of the duty of jihad as "in the path of God/for the sake of God" (*fī sabīl*

[43] E. Tyan, "Bayʿa," *Encyclopaedia of Islam*, 2nd ed. (Leiden: Brill Online, n.d.).
[44] Raouf Ezzat, *al-Marʾa wa-l-ʿAmal al-Siyasi*, 149.

Allah), imparting a more sedentary expression for the cultivation of nonviolent social jihad. Such conceptions of jihad give women a point of participation in the political affairs of the umma, she further argues, something that both the discourse of "development" and the discourse of "good citizenship" have failed to do in modern times. Raouf Ezzat simultaneously operates on two registers, interpreting jihad as not just struggle against tyrannical leaders and the "new colonialism" of secular authoritarianism but a means of women's mobilization against tyrannical governance within the social units of the umma. Because she identifies secularism as the source of political injustice at the state level, she similarly understands secularization as the source of injustice within the Islamic family.

Raouf Ezzat's definition of the family as the microcosm of the umma has a long history in the region, going back to colonial and missionary discourses that interpreted women's roles in the family as indicative of the level of civilization in Muslim societies. Egyptian nationalist writings at the turn of the century deployed this conception of the family, equating household reform with reform of the nation, progress in household management with progress in the nation, and liberated women with a liberated nation.[45] These tropes were revived during (or persisted through) the ṣaḥwa, partly via the resuscitation of nahḍa works during the revival. Deploying the nahḍa's sense of intellectual mobilization coupled with political reform, Raouf Ezzat continued to draw on these ideas for the era of the Arab Spring.[46] Muhammad ʿImara, an Islamic public intellectual associated with the Islamic awakening, has been instrumental in collecting, redacting, and republishing works by the principal thinkers of the nahḍa, recycling their ideas for a new generation. (See chapter 2.) One of these books, *al-Islam wa-l-Marʾa fi Raʾy al-Imam Muhammad ʿAbduh* (Woman and Islam in the Opinion of the Imam Muhammad ʿAbduh, 1975), emphasizes the family as a

[45] Ibid., 196, 204; Amin, *The Liberation of Woman*; ʿImara, *al-Islam wa-l-Marʾa fi Raʾy al-Imam Muhammad ʿAbduh*; Shakry, "Schooled Mothers and Structured Play"; Abugideiri, "On Gender and the Family." The introduction to Qasim Amin's *Tahrir al-Marʾa* (Liberation of Woman, 1899), "The Status of Women in Society: A Reflection of the Nation's Moral Standards," argues that the shariʿa stipulates women's equality, freedom, emancipation, and human rights, a nahḍa discourse that has proved enduringly resilient (7). (See chapter 2.)

[46] Heba Raouf Ezzat, "al-Nahda wa Usturat al-Tahakkum al-Kamil," *al-Wasat*, April 21, 2009; Heba Raouf Ezzat, "Hiwarat fi-l-Nahda: Nahw Idrak Jadid li-l-Marhala" (Yaqazat al-Fikr and al-Markaz al-Thaqafi al-ʿArabi bi-Ittihad al-Atbaʾ al-ʿArab, July 20, 2012). *Al-Wasat* is a Bahrain newspaper known for the exercise of free speech and critiques of regional governments, but it was closed down in the midst of the 2011 protests in Bahrain. "A call to awakening the soul and putting the mind to work" is the motto of Yaqaẓat al-Fikr (Intellectual Awakening), the institute where Raouf Ezzat presented her lecture.

model for national and civilizational progress. The epigraph, a quotation from ʿAbduh, is written on the book's cover: "The umma is made up of families. The reform of one is the reform of the other. Whoever does not have a home does not have an umma" (6). ʿImara dedicates the volume to the "Egyptian, Muslim, and Eastern family," arguing that the only way to cure the social ills plaguing the region is to cure the ills plaguing the family (4). The solution for both, he says, is the Islamic shariʿa. In an article on conceptions of the family in contemporary Islamic thought, Hibba Abugideiri describes the family as the "building block, the very core, of the larger unified Muslim *umma*. Whatever affects the microcosmic unit certainly and necessarily impacts on the macrocosmic one. . . . Few Muslims, if any, deny the centrality of the family as the bedrock of Islamic society, and therefore Islamic law."[47] The enduring popularity of these concepts is attested to by the publishing history of ʿImara's compilation of ʿAbduh's writings on women and Islam. These writings were first published in the late nineteenth century and were reissued, with ʿImara's commentary and editing, in 1979, 1980, 1997, and 2004.

Like Raouf Ezzat, nahḍa thinkers interpreted the Islamic family as "consultative" rather than "dictatorial." And like her, these writers envisioned the family as a site of reform for Egyptian politics. This conception of the family was developed as much under secular modernity as under the encroaching pressures of colonial and missionary discourses. But it also grew out of the Islamic intellectual tradition, especially out of ideas about adab, or the cultivation of the self and its connection with the larger body politic.[48] The Islamist thinker Rashid Rida, a disciple of the nahḍa mufti, jurist, and reformer Muhammad ʿAbduh, made a similar argument in *Nidaʾ li-l-Jins al-Latif* (Call to the Gentle Sex, 1932). Rida asserts that men's leadership in the family is consultative (*shūrī*), rather than dictatorial (*istibdādī*).[49] The text deals almost exclusively with women's roles in the family but also identifies the family as the source of women's rights. The book's subtitle, *Huquq al-Nisaʾ fi al-Islam wa Hazzuhunna min al-Islah al-Muhammadi al-ʿAmm* (The Rights of Women in Islam and Their Fortune in Muhammad's Public Reform), emphasizes that those rights will be secured through Islamic (public) reform. The content of *Nidaʾ li-l-Jins al-Latif*, about a woman's (and a wife's) rights and duties within the family, has continued to resonate well into the twenty-first century as the book has been republished, reedited, and

[47] Abugideiri, "On Gender and the Family," 232.

[48] Shakry, "Schooled Mothers and Structured Play"; Asad, *Formations of the Secular*; Moosa, *Ghazali and the Poetics of Imagination*; Haj, *Reconfiguring Islamic Tradition*.

[49] Rashid Rida, *Nidaʾ li-l-Jins al-Latif* (Cairo: Matbaʿat al-Manar, 1932). The book was published among new formulations of the personal status laws after independence. (See chapter 2.)

redacted, reincarnating nahḍa discourse for Raouf Ezzat's generation.[50] Analyzing Rida's and ʿAbduh's writings in the Islamic journal *al-Manar*, Omnia El Shakry describes how these reformers drew on intellectual "resources indigenous to the Islamic discursive tradition" that emphasized moral education in the family "as essential for the constitution of a rightly guided Islamic community. Such norms of pedagogy were complementary, and not antithetical to the modernist disciplining of the body and rationalization of the household." The inculcation of such virtues, Shakry observes, "was intended explicitly to serve the renaissance of the *umma*."[51] Reviving the umma through the family is Raouf Ezzat's project for the ṣaḥwa, as she harnesses intellectual trends from earlier in the century for new forms of social mobilization.

Raouf Ezzat describes the family as "withering" under the secular, imported political form of the Western state, as colonial rule organized the Arab and Islamic world into states, forcing them to undergo processes of secularization analogous to the West.[52] These nations were "constructed with the tools of the Western state" and subjected to what Raouf Ezzat calls an "extremist secularism" that has attacked the core institutions of Islamic society, notably the family. She describes "the extension of the power of the enormous apparatus of the secular state and the corresponding shrinkage of the functions of family, mosque, and community group (*jamāʿa*) . . . institutions that are independent of the control of the state and its power" (190). She pinpoints a specific constellation of institutions: the family as the preserve of Islamic law, the mosque as sacred space, and the Islamic community group (the *jamāʿa islāmiyya*). These are "natural nurseries for confronting the expansion of the power of the state, representing lines of defense of the umma and its individuals. We must invest in them in order to protect the shariʿa, which is to protect religion" (191). Drawing on political theory in both English and Arabic, Raouf Ezzat charts how, in secular societies, the family ceased to function as a unit of social solidarity. Drawing extensively on Christopher Lasch's *Haven in a Heartless World*, she discusses how the family's responsibility for social education was parceled out to other social institutions, with consumer relationships supplanting familial ones. In the process, she describes how "the civil" became the sphere of secular (Western, modern) sociability. At the same time, religion lost its function as connecting an "imagined

[50] The book was republished in 1947 with the same title, but when it was republished in 1956, 1975, 1985, 1989, 1992, 2003, 2005, and 2007 (after the United Nations Declaration of Human Rights), the subtitle *Huquq al-Nisaʾ fi al-Islam* (Women's Rights in Islam) became the main title.

[51] Shakry, "Schooled Mothers and Structured Play," 128, 153.

[52] Raouf Ezzat, "Secularism, the State and the Social Bond."

community" of believers, becoming separate from public life and invested in a separate sphere of private belief (173). While Raouf Ezzat aims to show how the family became divested of its role in social education, for her, the most critical part of this process is how *religion* became stripped of its function in social education, consigned to an artificially depoliticized domain of private relations. The "removal of religion from society was one of the last steps of secularization. Despite this, the family and relationships of human love and understanding connected to religion despite all that had befallen it" (175). As secularism began to dominate, the family "as a value and an ideal" should have resisted this "vicious attack. . . . Secularism can be summarized as a 'stripping of sacredness.' In the West, this coincided with a call to revive the institution of the family . . . with the tendency to return to religion in the West after realizing the disadvantages of an extremist secularism. . . . The linking of family and religion was the only way to save both" (175, 178). Raouf Ezzat's writings grow organically out of the intellectual soil of an Islamic liberalism that extends back to the nahḍa of the late nineteenth century, another protest movement mobilizing concepts of freedom and rights against the illiberalism of colonial government. Both revolted against what Raouf Ezzat calls "traditional colonialism" and "new colonialism," dictatorial secularism "erected on the annihilation of the social units of Islamic civilization like the family."[53]

Soft Revolution

Social scientists have interpreted the Islamic movements' mobilization in Egypt as a soft (or passive) revolution, a war of persuasion rather than armed struggle, what Raouf Ezzat calls "soft force" and the "battle of the private." In *Making Islam Democratic*, Asef Bayat describes a powerful grassroots social movement made up of Islamic institutions, religious welfare and professional associations, neighborhood groups, student organizations, and media. Egyptian Islamism at its height in the late 1980s was

> a complex web of dispersed and heterogeneous organizations, activities, and sympathies around a distinct core embodied in the reformist Muslim Brotherhood, which aimed to Islamize the society at the grassroots, ultimately establishing an Islamic state, and in the revolutionary Islamists who combined social agitation and

[53] Raouf Ezzat, *al-Marʾa wa-l-ʿAmal al-Siyasi*, 161.

Peace Machine mural by graffiti artist El-Zeft, sprayed on a Cairo wall after the 2011 revolution. Image courtesy of Mia Gröndahl.

> armed struggle. . . . Along the political core stood the vast sector of "civil Islam" with its large religious welfare and professional associations, Muslim youth and women's groups, and Islamic activism in universities, schools, and neighborhoods. [54]

This mobilization is less concerned with the transformation of the state and more concerned with how an Islamic sensibility and ethos transform daily practices, bodily discipline, social networks, and modes of expression. These scholars argue that the real power of the Islamic revival lies in its social character, giving it political leverage, without taking state power as its overt aim.[55] This approach has long been a tactic of Islamic groups in Egypt, going back to the Islamic preaching and welfare organizations first established under the monarchy in the 1920s. In *Mobilizing Islam*, Carrie Rosefsky Wickham describes the development of

[54] Bayat, *Making Islam Democratic*, 136–37.

[55] Wickham, *Mobilizing Islam*; Mahmood, *Politics of Piety*, 3. In her book on the women's mosque movement in Egypt, Saba Mahmood defines the Islamic revival as a "term that refers not only to the activities of state-oriented political groups but more broadly to a religious ethos or sensibility that has developed within contemporary Muslim societies. This sensibility has a palpable public presence in Egypt, manifest in the vast proliferation of neighborhood mosques and other institutions of Islamic learning and social welfare . . . a brisk consumption and production of religious media and literature, and a growing circle of intellectuals who write and comment upon contemporary affairs in the popular press from a self-described Islamic point of view" (3).

a "parallel Islamic sector," as the "dynamic periphery" of Egyptian politics, made up of preaching and welfare organizations, private mosques, Islamic schools, institutes, study groups, Islamic banks, NGOs, publishing houses, and media. "During the 1980s and early 1990s"—when Raouf Ezzat published *Woman and Political Work*—"these ostensibly 'nonpolitical' institutions became important sites of Islamist outreach to educated youth. . . . In authoritarian settings, in which opposition groups' access to formal political institutions and elites is typically restricted, we must also consider the space available to opposition actors in ostensibly 'nonpolitical' arenas less subject to state control." At the periphery of the state are many "potential arenas for collective action, including religious institutions, local community and youth centers, schools, and even private households. . . . When regular party channels are blocked, other institutional arenas can become important sites of political contestation 'by default.' The Egyptian case indicates that these 'substitute' sites can also permit formally excluded opposition groups to reach out to the mass public." Even when state repression is high, she observes, the state "may permit—or may be unable to prevent—the emergence of 'autonomous zones' in which mobilization is possible."[56] Raouf Ezzat understands the family as one such autonomous zone and as one of the most fertile sites for the revitalization of the Islamic umma at a grassroots level.

Cultural production has been one of the most critical institutions of "the parallel Islamic sector."[57] Islamic publishing houses, bookstores, periodicals, books, pamphlets, journals, and the "dissemination of the Islamist daʿwa [call] through print and audio technologies at the microlevel was intricately related to institutional developments at the macrolevel."[58] Since the mid-1970s, there has been a huge rise in the production of religiously oriented literature, a phenomenon that has continued through the present in print as well as in visual, auditory, digital, satellite, and social media. In addition to the growth of religious institutions like private mosques and Islamic associations, Bayat describes the flourishing in Islamic books, pamphlets, and religious cassettes. "In 1994, more than a quarter of all books published were religious, a 25 percent increase since 1985, and Islamic books constituted 85 percent of those sold during the 1995 Cairo book fair. Recordings of Islamic figures such as Shaykh Kishk, which numbered over a thousand, sold in the millions. Dozens of Islamic newspapers, weeklies, and monthlies were in high circulation. Radio Qurʾan, devoted entirely

[56] Wickham, *Mobilizing Islam*, 93–94.
[57] Ibid., 95.
[58] Ibid., 134.

to religious matters, maintained its highest rating during this period."[59] Emerging out of this cultural and intellectual ferment are modern public spheres that serve as a "locus in which rational views are elaborated that should guide government."[60] Raouf Ezzat describes this public sphere in idealistic, almost utopian terms, as building a fair and just society through public deliberation and debate. This public sphere also serves as a site for challenging the nation-state as a political form, with the aim of constructing new kinds of communities bound by the "sociopolitical contract" of Islam. The rise of a "global civil society," "network society," and informational technology, Raouf Ezzat writes, "can empower us . . . to build communities and defend the politics of presence, along with a new mapping of the spheres of influence of the *umma* and the different sphere of Shariʿa."[61] In the aftermath of the 2011 revolution, Raouf Ezzat has been instrumental in setting up, in conjunction with the Global Media Forum, a media watchdog group called al-Khabar al-Yaqin, applying the Qurʾanic concept of *yaqīn* (2:2) (certainty) to truth telling in media reporting after the 2011 revolution.

Raouf Ezzat's writing is the fruit of a boom in Islamic publishing that began in the mid-1970s. During this time, Islamic activism went from a clandestine opposition movement into the "wider arenas of public life, in which the Islamists established independent religious, cultural, and service organizations; acquired their own independent press and publishing houses; and gained control of the country's leading professional organizations. . . . Islamic activism assumed the form of gradual institution building and persuasion."[62] The movement's success in Egypt was due to this gradual institution building and persuasion—it succeeded in its war of position. *Woman and Political Work* was written precisely when the Mubarak government came to an agreement with the International Monetary Fund to implement structural adjustment policies. Women were an important part of these policies, as international aid organizations focused on reforming the family, economically and otherwise. The 1980s were marked by an escalating discourse on the question of women's work both in the family and in "public work," with hundreds of publications by United Nations agencies on questions of women and development. (See chapter 5.) In these writings, women are identified as an important source of untapped capital. Raouf Ezzat situates her argument in *Woman and Political Work* against these development discourses, reclaiming women's labor for the informal economy

[59] Bayat, *Making Islam Democratic*, 33.
[60] Taylor, *Modern Social Imaginaries*, 189–90.
[61] Raouf Ezzat and Abdallah, "Towards an Islamically Democratic Secularism," 52.
[62] Wickham, *Mobilizing Islam*, 34.

and the political economy of Islamic mobilization. Women have the capacity of "cultivating human capital through education in the family," what Raouf Ezzat calls "development work of no less significance than the work of public employment. This social labor without material recompense has equivalent weight as institutional labor with its own material rewards irrespective of money" (161). At the same time, writers like Bint al-Shatiʾ and Iman Muhammad Mustafa would expand on Raouf Ezzat's argument, pleading for the recognition of women's labor in the family and informal economy, articulating their argument as an Islamic one.[63]

In the aftermath of 9/11, Raouf Ezzat contributed to the UN's Arab Human Development Reports. Traces of her thought are clear in the first paragraphs of the fourth report, "Towards the Rise of Women in the Arab World" (2005). These passages address how Islamic movements might reconcile (women's) freedom with faith. She characterizes certain Islamic currents as forging a "creative marriage between freedom in its contemporary, comprehensive definition and the ultimate intent of Islamic law (Sharia) that is required for a society of freedom and good governance."[64] These Islamist currents, the report asserts, "have experienced important developments over the past five decades with regard to their stance on certain societal issues, such as respect for human rights and good governance or democracy." The report characterizes the "enlightened" leadership of these social movements as cultivating "growing activity from the grassroots demanding greater internal democracy." In 2005, the year of the report's publication, Raouf Ezzat was invited to become a Young Global Leader at the World Economic Forum.

Raouf Ezzat's work belongs to a body of revivalist writings espousing women's emancipation in Islam, human rights in Islam, and Islamic democracy. Bayat describes a "handful of 'Islamic liberals' . . . all of whom appeared to speak the language of *tanwīr* (enlightenment) integrating notions of democracy, civil society, and human rights into their doctrines. . . . Some critics argued that these intellectuals used such modern concepts to counter secularists with their own idioms and to

[63] Mustafa, *al-Nisaʾ al-ʿAmilat*; Bint al-Shatiʾ, "Islam and the New Woman." For a fuller analysis of these works, see chapter 5.

[64] United Nations Development Programme, *Arab Human Development Report 2005*, 2. A powerful critique of the report can be found in Lila Abu-Lughod, Fida Adely, and Frances Hasso's special issue of the *International Journal of Middle East Studies*. Lila Abu-Lughod, Fida Adely, and Frances Hasso, "Overview: Engaging the Arab Human Development Report 2005 on Women," *International Journal of Middle East Studies* 41, no. 1 (February 2009): 59–60.

secure recognition for the Islamic camp."[65] Bayat himself argues that the Islamicization of the secular intelligentsia helped legitimize the Islamic revival but also "helped produce a somewhat 'secularized' religion," what he calls the "secularization of religious symbols" in Egyptian Islam.[66] Gender rights—especially in the family—have been a core part of this liberal discourse. Women and the family are understood as bastions against the increasing encroachment of secular society. Yet Raouf Ezzat's own arguments simultaneously privatize religion as the realm of the family, as she simultaneously asserts women's primary role in this religious politics. Far from a circumscription, it is an intensification of religion.

"Liberalism's Family Values"

Raouf Ezzat sees the family as the site of an Islamically democratic politics, but its relationships are structured by gendered hierarchies, mediated by economics. Raouf Ezzat's understanding of leadership, qiwāma, derives from verse 4:34 of the Qur'an. Because of its assertion of God's "preference" for some over others, the verse has a long exegetical history.[67] Translations of the verse into English reflect the contested nature of the words for "guardians" and "preferred." Different renderings include: "Husbands are the protectors and maintainers of their wives because Allah has given the one more (strength) than the other" (Abdullah Yusuf Ali); "Men are the supporters of the women, by what God has given one more than the other" (Thomas Cleary); "Men are the support of women as God gives some more means than others" (Ahmed Ali); "Men are the managers of the affairs of women because Allah has made the one superior to the other" (Mawdudi).[68] The debate has revolved around whether guardianship and God's preference are signs of men's absolute superiority over women, or whether these are restricted to the particular conditions set down by the verse, namely, by what men provide of their means, wealth, or property in the material support of women. Contemporary feminist exegeses favor the latter interpretation, arguing that if men do not provide for women, the conditions of their guardianship (and their preference) are null and void.[69]

[65] Bayat, *Making Islam Democratic*, 178.

[66] Ibid., 41.

[67] Stowasser, "Gender Issues in Contemporary Qur'an Interpretation."

[68] See Amina Wadud's discussion of different interpretations of the verse in Wadud, *Qur'an and Woman*, 69–74.

[69] Bint al-Shati', *al-Mafhum al-Islami li-Tahrir al-Mar'a*; Wadud, *Qur'an and Woman*.

Based on another Qur᾽anic verse, Raouf Ezzat, like others, argues that piety "is the only gauge of preference."[70] She ultimately concludes by arguing for an intrinsic hierarchy in men's guardianship over women. The degree men have over women is "the degree of guardianship. This is not based on an essential lack in woman. . . . What is intended by preference is the greater amount of competence of the man over the competence of the woman with respect to leadership of the family. She is competent, but he is more competent" (199). The word Raouf Ezzat uses for "competence" (*ṣalāḥ*) is actually closer in meaning to piety, goodness, or righteousness, suggesting an inherent superiority on the part of men that is both spiritual and material. Even in the face of this assertion of the superiority of male competence and leadership, Raouf Ezzat continues to argue for a certain equality between men and women. The reference to "degree" in the quote above refers to another Qur᾽anic verse: "Women have rights like the rights against them according to what is fair, but men have a degree over them" (2:228). Raouf Ezzat argues that this "degree" is not absolute; it does not mean that "one is raised over the other," or that men are superior biologically, emotionally, and intellectually.

The valorization of equality while asserting male leadership has become a consistent motif in modernist Islam and one of the staples of the Islamic awakening, interpretations that also have their roots in the nahḍa. Raouf Ezzat's interpretations of key Qur᾽anic verses (4:34 and 2:228) echo those of Muhammad ʿAbduh, which were republished by ʿImara during the 1970s and 1980s.[71] Like ʿAbduh, she combines guardianship (qiwāma of verse 4:34), leadership (riyāsa), and men's degree (of verse 2:228), arguing that men's role in the family is one of governance thanks to the "law of nature."[72] The "degree" of the husband over the wife is the degree of leadership (riyāsa), the same terminology Raouf Ezzat uses. Raouf Ezzat also uses a hadith on the idea of shepherding to support her argument about male leadership, just as ʿAbduh does in the same context. "The man is a shepherd of his people and is responsible for his flock. The woman is a shepherd in the house of her husband and is responsible for her flock."[73] This means the man's

[70] Raouf Ezzat, *al-Mar᾽a wa-l-ʿAmal al-Siyasi*, 199.

[71] These were initially presented as a series of lectures in 1900–1901. ʿAbduh's disciple Rashid Rida wrote them up and published them as a Qur᾽an commentary known as *Tafsir al-Manar*. Many suspect that Rida contributed his own ideas to the work, adding another layer of complexity to the question of authorship and Islamic authenticity. It reads like a modernist *isnād*: ʿImara representing the writings of Rida representing the writings of ʿAbduh interpreting the Qur᾽an.

[72] ʿImara, *al-Islam wa-l-Mar᾽a*, 58.

[73] Ibid., 63; Raouf Ezzat, *al-Mar᾽a wa-l-ʿAmal al-Siyasi*, 201.

right to force obedience in the case of rebellion, "like a leader of the army and the president of a nation in the interest of the whole." This "execution of authority" is like the leadership of society:

> Marital life is like social life and every society needs a leader. . . . The man is more entitled to leadership (riyāsa) because he is more knowledgeable about what is beneficial (*maṣlaḥa*), and more capable of executing it with his strength and his wealth. . . . She is accountable for obedience (*ṭāʿa*) to him in all fairness. If she rebels from obedience to him, then he must discipline her with a warning, a separation, and a painless hit, if she deserves disciplining. This is appropriate for the leader of a household, working in the interest of the welfare of the extended family and the well-being of the couple, just as it is appropriate for an army commander or the president of a nation for the sake of the well-being of the whole.[74]

Raouf Ezzat's understanding of men as "more competent" with respect to leadership in the family echoes ʿAbduh's understanding of men as "more knowledgeable about what is beneficial" for the family.[75] They use analogous words of *ṣalāḥ* and *maṣlaḥa*, indicating men's fitness or rightness for the job of this leadership. But both words have added denotation: Raouf Ezzat's *ṣalāḥ* as a moral righteousness and ʿAbduh's *maṣlaḥa* as government authority and administration. Neither uses language carelessly; both indicate men's spiritual right to leadership over women. In doing so, they assert not only the political nature of the husband's power in the home but also the gendered nature of political power in government.

Raouf Ezzat's exegeses focus on key verses from the Qurʾan (mainly 2:228, 4:21, 4:34, 30:21, and 30:30). Her hermeneutic produces a liberal interpretation of Islamic politics, taking democracy and equality as ideals but asserting a gendered division of labor where men are leaders and women led; where men are the authorities and women obey. These contradictions inherent in liberalism have long been observed by its critics.[76] ʿImara groups ʿAbduh's writings on male leadership and female obedience under a chapter entitled "Equality between Man and Woman." Both ʿAbduh's and Raouf Ezzat's exegeses of verse 2:228 epitomize the equality/hierarchy paradox. ("They have rights

[74] ʿImara, *al-Islam wa-l-Marʾa*, 62–63.
[75] Raouf Ezzat, *al-Marʾa wa-l-ʿAmal al-Siyasi*, 199
[76] Pateman, *Sexual Contract*; Scott, *Only Paradoxes to Offer*; Hatem, "Egyptian Discourses on Gender"; Brown, "Liberalism's Family Values."

like those rights fairly demanded of them, and men have a degree over them.") The first part of the verse indicates equality between husband and wife, men and women:

> It is desirable that the rights between them are mutual and they are equal. . . . They are equivalent in rights and deeds, just as they are equivalent in essence and in the senses, in feelings and intellect. Each of the two of them is a complete human being that has an intellect . . . and a heart with which to love. . . . It is unjust if one of the two sexes dominates the other, taking the other as a slave that he oppresses and uses for his own interest, especially after the marriage contract and a shared life that cannot be happy except with mutual respect and mutual rights. (56)

The second part of the verse refers to a "division of labor" between husband and wife. ʿAbduh cites a hadith in which the Prophet says that Fatima's work is in the home, whereas ʿAli's work is outside the home. This is the division of labor between the two spouses: the woman's task is to manage the house and perform the work inside it, and the man's task is to strive and earn outside it. This is the "equivalence" between them (61). The relationship of the ruler to the ruled, of the leader and the led, of guardianship and the guarded, is the "division of labor" between them. The second part of the hadith emphasizes women's obedience in stark terms, using religious imagery of the ritual practice of kneeling in prayer to describe women's duty and obedience to men. "If there was any situation in which I commanded a person to prostrate themselves to another, then I would command the woman to prostrate herself to her husband" (61).

The legitimizing claim of equality and the simultaneous assertion of gendered hierarchies (or "difference") are characteristic of liberal discourse, argues Wendy Brown in an essay on "Liberalism's Family Values." Liberal discourses obscure the "sexual division of labor" that it "presumes to transcend" (143). Brown, like Raouf Ezzat, draws on Carole Pateman to support her critique of liberalism's contradictions. On the one hand, the social contract of the public sphere is depicted as premised on equality between (male) citizens; on the other, the sexual contract of the private sphere is based on "natural relationships existing in the family where a woman's submission to her husband is natural because he is stronger."[77] Even as Raouf Ezzat makes the radical move toward declaring the private as political, she reproduces what Brown calls the "constitutive dualisms of liberalism"—theoretical

[77] Raouf Ezzat, *al-Marʾa wa-l-ʿAmal al-Siyasi*, 180; Pateman, *Sexual Contract*, 283–84.

equality coupled with gendered hierarchies.[78] This dualism has become a hallmark of contemporary theologies of gender relations in Islam. (See chapters 1 and 2.) "What is striking about this body of literature," observes Hibba Abugideiri in an essay on twentieth-century Islamic thought, "is that it premises its interpretive view of gender and the family on the notion of spiritual equality. Man and woman are created from the same 'divine breath,' invested with inherent dignity . . . and endowed with the same moral duties and responsibilities as God's appointed vicegerents."[79] But Abugideiri demonstrates that women's primary spiritual and legal rights have been sacrificed to a certain thinking about women's roles in the family, an "Islamic view of gender based on biological difference that ultimately institutionalizes a gender hierarchy within the family." While these appear as eternal and everlasting Islamic dictates, they are actually "interpretive acts that are necessarily subjective and context-specific."[80] A particular hermeneutics of the Qurʾan has been harnessed to legitimize the sacredness of the family and assert divine sanction of male leadership. This has come to be seen as an authentic and indigenous expression of true Islam. Yet the sociopolitical contexts out of which these discourses emerged suggest a complex call-and-response, a mirroring of sorts. The Islamic opposition discourse accepts the basic coordinates of liberal democracy, setting up a framework that nonetheless continues to be contested and renegotiated.

The Sexual Contract and the Sacred

Raouf Ezzat's understanding of the family as the basic political unit of the Islamic umma echoes, in some ways, Wendy Brown's understanding of the family as the basic unit of political analysis in liberalism (along with, and in contradistinction to, the individual). In liberalism the family is seen as both natural and divinely ordained, as "outside history."[81] Raouf Ezzat and ʿImara (relying on ʿAbduh) draw on the Qurʾanic concept of fiṭra to assert both the "natural" and "divinely ordered" aspects of the Islamic family. Fiṭra connotes both the creation

[78] Brown, "Liberalism's Family Values," 140–52.

[79] Abugideiri, "On Gender and the Family," 232. "Divine breath" refers to verse 4:1 from the Qurʾan: "O people, revere your lord that created you from a single spirit [*nafs* can also mean "breath"] and created from her her mate." The word *nafs* (spirit, soul, self) is feminine, despite lacking a feminine ending, so the original soul is syntactically referred to with the feminine pronoun in the Qurʾan.

[80] Ibid., 253.

[81] Brown, "Liberalism's Family Values," 145, 147.

of God and human nature but also can mean instinct or intuition when referring to the human being's innate character or natural disposition. "Raise your face truly toward religion the creation of God [*fiṭrat Allah*] according to which he created [*faṭara*] people" (Qurʾan 30:30). Both texts use fiṭra to express the relationship between husband and wife. Raouf Ezzat draws on Qurʾanic language nearly verbatim (rendered in italics): "The foundation of the family is connected *to the creation of God according to which he created people*, from the desire of each of the sexes for the other. And this drive is what makes the family one of the social models (*sunan*). The importance of legislation is in its preservation of *love, mercy, and tranquility*. This is a trait at the core of human nature [fiṭra] according to God's creation" (187).

"Love, mercy, and tranquility" refers to another, earlier verse from the same chapter: "Among his signs is that he created for you mates from among yourselves so that you may live in tranquility with them. And he put love and mercy between you" (30:21). ʿAbduh's text similarly draws on these two verses to refer to the "order of the instinct" (*niẓām al-fiṭra*). He describes the organization of the family as a system along the lines of both human instinct and divine creation. This instinctual order is structured by male authority, leadership, and guardianship; if the wife steps outside of this order, through rebellion (*nushūz*), she is trying to be "above her master, but she also tries to raise herself above her own nature and what the order of creation (*niẓām al-fiṭra*) requires of mutual cooperation."[82] But a woman does not have any power of discipline over the male. The "order of the instinct" is a "gentle reminder of women's place" (68). This order becomes the basis of the Islamic sexual contract described by ʿAbduh, the "inviolable covenant" or "sacred contract" (*mīthāq ghalīẓ*) between man and woman mentioned in verse 4:21 in the Qurʾan. This intimacy, desire, appetite, or "closing of space" is both divine (*al-fiṭra al-ilāhiyya*) and instinctual (74).

> This is an intuitive contract (*mīthāq fiṭrī*) that is among the most sacred of contracts and most intensely binding. Indeed the human being grasps this meaning through the human senses, contemplating this state that God established between man and his woman, finding that the woman is weaker than the man and that she dedicates herself to him and submits to him with the knowledge that he is capable of violating her rights. On what does this dedication and this submission rely? What guarantee does she have, what is the contract that she enters into? . . . What, beyond

[82] ʿImara, *al-Islam wa-l-Marʾa*, 67.

> desire, settles into her nature? That thing is a divine knowledge and an intuitive knowledge laying down in her the inclination to a special bond she had not promised before, a special trust she did not have with her own family, and a special affection who has no other place but in the husband, the lord (*al-baʿl*). All of that is the sacred contract that she enters into with the man in accordance with the order of creation that closely binds what the contract does not bind with words, promises, or belief. . . . This is centered in the depths of our souls—with God's utterance that with marriage, women entered into a sacred contract with men. (75–76)

Through this contract, this treaty, this pact, this covenant, women and men are bound, by desire, mercy, and affection, but also by a hierarchy of gender rooted in both human nature and divine creation. What is this contract? It is one freely entered into, but not of equal status. The man is the lord, *al-baʿl*; he is stronger; she submits to him. Again, however contradictorily, this exegesis, like the sections on guardianship and leadership, is included in ʿImara's chapter on "Equality between Men and Women in the Opinion of the Imam Muhammad ʿAbduh."

The meaning of fiṭra is expanded on in both texts to encompass a range of social roles, including the division of labor between the head of the family and its body, the ruler and the ruled. They interpret these relations through a reformist hermeneutic model and draw conclusions about the nature of the family as a social and a political institution. Raouf Ezzat extensively develops the connection among divine creation, human instinct, and social laws, mainly through her concept of religious social models (*sunan ijtimāʿiyya*). Sunan is the plural of sunna, the model of the Prophet Muhammad, articulated through his sayings (hadith) and reports about his example. Raouf Ezzat does not use sunan in its conventional sense of a collection of traditions and legal pronouncements but in a novel way to refer to a kind of ontological model, path, or understanding of how to behave.[83] She uses the words sunna, shariʿa, and *fiqh*, which mean model, path, and understanding but also have more technical (and popular) meanings related to Islamic law. Raouf Ezzat defines sunan as the "group of laws prescribed by God in the soul and throughout the world," connecting it to fiṭra (67). She describes levels of sunna: the first is cosmic; the second, the sunna of fiṭra, has two levels, the existential and the social; and the last is the sunna of legal obligation (66). The sunna of fiṭra is clearly the most important to her argument, as the connective tissue holding together the hidden and the manifest, the mystical and the practical, belief and

[83] G. H. A. Juynboll, "Sunan" and "Sunna," *Encyclopaedia of Islam.*

practice, the cosmic and the law, the individual and the group. Fiṭra is the basis of this, and Raouf Ezzat defines human intuition about the "right path" as ultimately leading to the realization and safeguarding of political society. The "greater shariʿa" is the "divine shariʿa in harmony with the nature of fiṭra," in contradistinction to the legal positivism of secularism that is divorced from these ontological sources, from belief, and from ethics (67).

Weaving a tight scriptural argument around the figure of the family, Raouf Ezzat connects divine creation to human nature to the sunna of the Prophet Muhammad to the shariʿa, the "path" of Islamic law. The family structured by primal human nature and social mores, by intuition and legal dictates, is an institution that is simultaneously sacred and immanent. As Abugideiri observes in her analysis of contemporary Islamic texts on gender, "The family in Islam is believed to be a divinely-inspired and ordained institution, characterized by a necessary sexual division of labor. . . . The self-identifying Islamic framework employed essentially constructs an impermeable template of the Muslim family that renders the Islamic values of family commensurate with traditional gender roles."[84] Abugideiri attributes the reification of and consolidation of this thinking about the Islamic family—"paradoxically," she says—to social and global change (224). The family has become a discourse of cultural authenticity resisting foreign influence in political discourses in the Muslim world, a phenomenon that a number of important scholars have observed in Egypt.[85] This has led to a "stubborn adherence to this longstanding paradigm of the Muslim family, *as a form of active resistance to such change*. . . . In sum, modernity, postcoloniality, globalization and Western cultural hegemony have all served as pretexts for the reinscribing of traditional notions of the family, and thus women's roles, within Islamic thought."[86] The explanation of resistance to change is a common paradigm in interpreting the rise of "traditional" values, especially with respect to the persistence of particular gender roles within the family. Yet scholarship in Middle Eastern studies shows how the normative bourgeois family structure is a product of recent historical processes—of the encroachment of colonial modernity, of eugenics discourses of imperial nationalism, of capitalist modes of production, and of the influence of the discourses of liberal secularism.[87] This is not a "reversion" to traditional values but their

[84] Abugideiri, "On Gender and the Family," 232.

[85] Badran, "Competing Agendas," 219; Abugideiri, "On Gender and the Family"; Haddad, "Case of the Feminist Movement"; Stowasser, "Religious Ideology."

[86] Abugideiri, "On Gender and the Family," 246–47. Emphasis in the original.

[87] Najmabadi, "Crafting an Educated Housewife in Iran"; Shakry, "Schooled Mothers and Structured Play"; Tucker, *Women in Nineteenth-Century Egypt.*

reinvention within the sphere of Islamic thought. Abugideiri theorizes that the discourse of cultural authenticity around the family developed in reaction to the encroachment of globalization and the pressures of Western secularism. Raouf Ezzat argues as much, observing that the family as a bastion of Islamic values is the umma's "line of defense" against the encroachment of Western secularism, whether in the form of statecraft, knowledge production, or social institutions.

At the crux of Raouf Ezzat's argument is one of feminism's principal axioms from the 1990s: that the personal is political. Raouf Ezzat asserts political agency for women within the framework of the family and motherhood but simultaneously reinforces the most basic assumptions of liberalism: that the family is (1) divinely ordained, (2) the sphere proper of religion, (3) structured by a natural (and instinctual) division of labor, (4) women's principal realm of activity, (5) headed by the husband, and (6) the "basic unit of political analysis." She aims to politicize—and hence reinforce the value of—family life but also reinscribes the primacy of women's connection to the family and to the sphere of affective relations. Raouf Ezzat's analysis is attuned to the power of the family, the power of the social, and the power of a religious ethos and religious sensibilities. Even so, the secular state partly created the conditions for Islam as a social movement, by banning Islamic activists from political participation and defining the family as the sphere proper of religious law. As Foucault observes in *The History of Sexuality*, the "deployment of alliance" secures the law "even in the new mechanics of power" that constitutes the secular state. This structure of alliance "is built around a system of rules defining the permitted and the forbidden, the licit and the illicit. . . . The deployment of alliance has as one of its chief objectives to reproduce the interplay of relations and maintain the law that governs them. . . . The deployment of alliance is attuned to a homeostasis of the social body, which it has the function of maintaining; whence its privileged link with the law; whence too the fact that the important phase for it is 'reproduction.' "[88] The secular state in Egypt enshrined religious law in the family, making it the site of reproduction of spiritual, affective, and juridical-political relations that are critical to regulating the social body as a whole and to maintaining this governing law. Even while taking religious knowledge as her point of departure, Raouf Ezzat frames her arguments by a secular governmentality that disburses ethical burdens and responsibilities onto the affective realm of private relations.[89] Articulated within

[88] Foucault, *History of Sexuality, Vol. 1*, 107–9.

[89] Hasso, *Consuming Desires*, 24–61, especially the chapter on "Legal Governmentality and the National Family."

the parameters of the Islamic discursive tradition, this liberalism uses the family as a model of democratic politics, a model of religious government, and a model of male leadership.

Conclusion

In the 2011 revolution, women were one of the most visible components of the demonstrations, in both the public square and the public sphere, as they rallied vocally and visibly alongside men. Raouf Ezzat, who grew up on Tahrir Square, positioned herself at the center of the uprisings, reiterating her own conceptions of Islamic democracy and the special role that women play in cultivating nonviolent resistance against the military state. Raouf Ezzat's own activism may appear as a contradiction in terms: with her advocacy of the family as the site of women's political action, even as she herself is everywhere visible in the public sphere—on television, Twitter, Facebook, the media, the web. But this is precisely Raouf Ezzat's point: that there is not necessarily a contradiction between this public space and the private institution building that is the infrastructure of an Islamic ethics, as much as an Islamic politics. It is a biopolitical cultivation of power at its source, as the individual citizen willingly submits to a nonsecular disciplining of body and soul with the aim of participating in a different kind of polity. Many see Islamist women's embrace of the family and of women's roles in the family as contradictory, especially when these women so visibly participate in public discourse. Raouf Ezzat has been central to formulating new definitions of human identity through a public discourse around Islam, just as she has been instrumental in creating a new kind of public sphere through her discussions of these intimate politics. Scholarly analyses of Islamic liberalism suggest that this political ideology is being cultivated for its compatibility with neoimperial designs in the region.[90] This may be indisputable. Yet the creative and subversive potential of Islamic democracy within the region cannot be denied. There is widespread public fear in the West of Islamic government, even if (or perhaps even especially if) it is democratically inclined. Islamic democracy has a powerful ability to destabilize liberalism's founding myths (about a secular public sphere), as much as the West's self-righteous monopoly of this political form for itself, despite

[90] Mahmood, "Questioning Liberalism, Too"; Mahmood, "Secularism, Hermeneutics, Empire."

claims of its universalism. And despite liberalism's coerciveness as a political ideology, it also has a certain revolutionary potential.[91]

Even as Raouf Ezzat reproduces some of liberalism's assumptions about the family, she does so to challenge the nation-state as the center of politics, hypocritical assumptions about secularism's neutrality, and the devaluation of women's labor in the home. Moreover, Raouf Ezzat and other Islamist activists embrace the contradictions of liberalism as productive of a different kind of politics and a different kind of subjectivity. After all, difference continues to be the counterpart of liberal equality, just as subjection (*assujetissement*) produces the subject, chains make us free, and obligations give us rights. This liberal politics, produced in the shade of a secular dictatorship, contains an emancipatory promise within its own disciplinary dimensions.

[91] Rose, *Powers of Freedom*, 63; Michel Foucault, "What Is Enlightenment?" in *The Foucault Reader*, ed. Paul Rabinow (New York: Pantheon, 1984).

Fann wa-Fiṭra: Art and Instinct

In her Omdurman lecture "The Arab Literary Woman Yesterday and Today," Bint al-Shatiʾ reflects at length on women's literary and intellectual participation in public life. Women, she says, have been "cut off from the life of the public" throughout Islamic history. She uses the word *ʿuzla,* which denotes not just seclusion and segregation but also isolation, insulation, and "privacy." To describe this isolation, she uses images of veils, harems, darknesses, and burials. But then she abruptly counters this imagery with countless examples of illustrious women who have contributed to Arab and Islamic literary and religious history. Citing examples from women in the Prophet's family, she writes that women have always "seriously participated in the religious, literary, and political life of the Islamic umma."[1] Arab women, assumed to be outside the discursive production of the Islamic literary tradition, she argues, have actually been central actors in religious history. They have been narrators of the details of the Prophet's life and deeds, important transmitters of hadith, and key links in the chain of authority. "The idea spread among us—that the Islamic veil cuts woman off from the public life of Muslims—is not true. Historical reality testifies that she was always in every vital public domain. This *is* true."

Knowledge, Bint al-Shatiʾ argues, enables women's participation in the public life of letters. It is a means of liberation from "the darkest ages of her trial of slavery and metaphoric suffocation . . . hidden from sight behind a curtain, shackled in fetters." But this liberation is not just intellectual; she also argues for a liberation of emotion and desire through a passion for God. She begins her lecture with verses of mystical poetry from the Sufi poet Rabiʿa al-ʿAdawiyya. She draws on Rabiʿa as an illustrious example of women's literary production from the early Islamic community but also for the devotion that inspired her own literary production. Bint al-Shatiʾ recites Rabiʿa's most famous poem, "I Love You with Two Loves," about two different kinds of passion for God: one that is profane and the other that is "more worthy" of God. To describe the first kind of love, Rabiʿa uses the word *al-hawā,*

[1] Bint al-Shatiʾ, *al-Adiba al-ʿArabiyya,* 4–5.

intimating desire, passion, and pleasure. The other kind of sacred love is an erotic image of mystical union with the divine: "You lift the veil so that I can see you." As a slave who resisted her master's advances because she said she belonged to God alone, her desire to see the unseen is manifest in both a sacred love and a corporeal, sensory passion (al-hawā) that she feels for the divine. This love is what leads Rabiʿa to praise God with her words, to create a language for this devotion, a "testimony" (*shahāda*) that bears witness to the power of the unseen, a ritualistic mentioning and remembering and repeating (*dhikr*) that keeps the spirit alive in the human body.

Drawing on powerful lexical concepts from the Islamic discursive tradition exemplified in Rabiʿa's poetic language, Bint al-Shatiʾ reinvigorates, reinterprets, and reinvents an Islamic poetics for the age of secularism. In doing so, she creates new vocabularies that draw on older ones and formulates new grammars of the self through processes of aesthetic self-invention.[2] Rabiʿa al-ʿAdawiyya's words resonate through time and space, Bint al-Shatiʾ says, singing of a living, breathing, passionate faith across twelve centuries and across the Islamic community. These words "liberate" both devotion and poetry from "fear and base desire (*al-khawf wa-l-ṭamaʿ*) into sheer eternal love . . . filling the horizons throughout the expanse of time with her heart's affective hymns, the intimate soliloquy of her living feeling, realizing her literary existence with authenticity and ability" (3).[3] The story of Rabiʿa's life is about liberation through devotion: she is emancipated when her master hears her supplicating God to free her so that she can devote herself to God day and night. Bint al-Shatiʾ interprets her poetry about her love for God as Rabiʿa's own kind of liberation in the Islamic world of letters, through her own poetics of Islamic affect for God. Her "living feeling," or "feeling for life," liberated Rabiʿa from her earthly master into the pure passion for God but also inspired her devotional love poetry.

"The Arab literary woman of yesterday" lives on through "the Arab literary woman of today"—Bint al-Shatiʾ herself, but also the myriad other women literati she invokes in these lectures. These literati reinvent keywords from the Islamic discursive tradition for an Islamic modernity: fiṭra (instinct), wijdān (affect), hawā (desire), taṣwīr (represen-

[2] Talal Asad writes about how "new vocabularies . . . are acquired and linked to older ones. Would-be reformers, as well as those who oppose them, imagine and inhabit multiple temporalities." Modernity, he argues, brings in a "new *kind* of subjectivity, one that is appropriate to ethical autonomy and aesthetic self-invention—a concept of 'the subject' that has a new grammar." Asad, *Formations of the Secular*, 222, 225.

[3] Bint al-Shatiʾ uses the phrase "*khawf wa-ṭamaʿ* " (fear and base desire), alluding to verse 30:24 of the Qurʾan.

tation, perception), baṣīra (insight), *badāha* (intuition), and *fann* (art, aesthetics). They infuse these words with new significance through the regenerative process of artistic creation, creation that draws on modernist concepts of renewal, reform, and revival, as well as Qur'anic concepts of the cyclical nature of (God's) creation from Surat al-Rum (30).

Bodily and spiritual desire is at the crux of Bint al-Shati''s own theory—and method—of Islamic literary production. This desire informs a mode of representation that both cultivates and expresses an Islamic mode of perception (*al-taṣwīr al-islāmī*). The word that Bint al-Shati' uses to describe bodily and spiritual desire, wijdān, weaves together notions of emotional life, sensory experience, and existence but also of psyche, soul, and spirit. Wijdān encompasses complementary aspects of feeling and spirit, "the needs of the body and the desires of the soul in a single order."[4] "Art" in all its different modes of representation, she says, "is an affective (*wijdānī*) grasp of—and receptivity to—life. Without affect (*al-wijdāniyya*), literature would not be art" (3). I am interested in Bint al-Shati''s theory of the role of affect in creating an Islamic art. For these Islamic literary women, emotion and sensation are critical to envisioning and imagining an Islamic art, as well as expressing the gendered selves so central to this cultural production. But Bint al-Shati' is more concerned with how religion, the divine, and Islam orchestrates this relationship between sensation and representation, between the world and the word, between the material and spiritual. For Bint al-Shati', an Islamic aesthetics mediates between the otherworldly word of God and its embodied incarnation in the Qur'an, the creation of God and the creation of human beings, religion and art. Islam is the cure healing the split, or the disjuncture, between these worlds, bringing them together in the divine harmony of tawḥīd. This aesthetics is also a means of maximizing the sensory experience of the world and the perception of its wonders, a sensory awakening that hints of the splendor of the sublime.

Romantic notions of divine inspiration and the role of emotion in artistic creation run through Bint al-Shati''s theory of art. This theory however, should not be *reduced* to romantic influences—it would be a grave disservice to her training and orientation in the Islamic intellectual tradition. Her lecture "The Arab Literary Woman Yesterday and Today" is not just on literature; it is on women's contributions to an Islamic poetics. It is a companion to an analogous essay, "al-Mar'a al-Muslima

[4] Sayyid Qutb, *al-ʿAdala al-Ijtimaʿiyya fi al-Islam*, 37; Masʿud, *al-Ra'id*, 1595. *Al-Ra'id* gives the definition as "faithful personal feeling" and "genuine spiritual/psychological representation."

Ams wa-l-Yawm" (The Muslim Woman Yesterday and Today, 1965), published in a volume entitled *Islam: Today and Tomorrow*.[5] She talks not just about (romantic) affect but about an *instinct* for the divine—two concepts, wijdān and fiṭra, that she weaves together. She connects affect to the "law of instinct and the model (the sunna) of nature"—what has been fertile ground, she declares, for woman's "literary existence" in Arab and Islamic history. She has left her marks on the Arabo-Islamic literary tradition through her "living emotion," even if literary history has obscured their traces in "a region of darkness" (5).

Bint al-Shatiʾ's argument in her lecture revolves around this natural instinct (fiṭra), a Qurʾanic term referring to the process of God's creation. "Affect (*al-wijdāniyya*) is an originary element in the instinct (fiṭra) of the female," she says, "so it is intuitive that she would excel in a field instinctually made for her by virtue of her sympathetic nature" (3). Her theory of an Islamic art and its relationship describes women's natural "preparation" for the "discursive arts" (*fann al-qawl*). The concept of fiṭra comes from verse 30:30 in the Qurʾan, "*fiṭrat Allah* with which God created (*faṭara*) people," simultaneously connoting both creation and the instinct for the divine that God put in the human breast. Fiṭra appears in all the texts discussed here, as the instinct to embody, live, and sense the divine, through God's signs and verses (*āyāt*), the guidance of Islamic knowledge, and spreading the word (daʿwa).

The language and imagery of the Qurʾan structures Bint al-Shatiʾ's argument. Fiṭra (30:30) is a *hawā bi-l-ʿilm* (desire with knowledge) that turns the human face toward righteous religion, instinct that God implanted in the human heart. Desire without knowledge (*ahwāʾ bi-ghayr ʿilm*, 30:29), in contrast, is the capricious, profane passion and pleasure referred to by Rabiʿa in her poem, the life of vanity and diversion described by Kariman Hamza in her *Journey* (57:20).[6] It is the fiṭra that leads Kariman Hamza and Shams al-Barudi on the journeys to their revived Islamic commitments and to veiling. For Bint al-Shatiʾ, fiṭra is the instinct that informs the devotional literary production of an Islamic art.[7] God creates human beings with the word and uses words to teach human beings; through the word humans relive and re-create the divine by continually mentioning Him, praising Him, and bearing witness to Him (as

[5] Bint al-Shatiʾ, "al-Marʾa al-Muslima Ams wa-l-Yawm," in *al-Islam al-Yawm wa-Ghadan* (Cairo: Dar Ihyaʾ al-Kutub al-ʿArabiyya, 1965).

[6] Hamza, *Rihlati min al-Sufur ila al-Hijab*, 24.

[7] On "the strong bond between art and Islam," and especially its relationship to the spirit's grasp of truth, see Siraj al-Din, *Awraq Shams al-Barudi*, 75–77. Later Islamic artists would refer to *al-fann al-hādif* (purposeful art), transforming earlier socialist concepts of political commitment in art, now understood as religious commitment in art. Tartoussieh, "Pious Stardom," 33–34.

Rabiʿa says in her poem). It is through clear words and signs, through eloquence and articulation (the "al-bayān" that Bint al-Shatiʾ uses so frequently in her own writings) that the believer testifies to the effect of the divine on the self.[8] This is how God's creation proliferates, as Surat al-Rum repeatedly reiterates: "God begins creation and then repeats it" (30:11, 27).

Women, Bint al-Shatiʾ argues, are particularly equipped for "the discursive arts" by virtue of their "authentic instinctual preparation" and their affective nature. She deploys these words and concepts—fiṭra and wijdān—to elucidate a modern conception of belief (*īmān*), cultivated through Islamic knowledge, inspired by Islamic art, and fostering an Islamic mode of perception through an Islamic mode of representation (*al-taṣwīr al-islāmī*). Even as Bint al-Shatiʾ essentializes women's affective nature, this essentialization justifies—and privileges—women's role in the art of Islamic literary production. She paves the way for a new mode of literary production in which women are key players, discursively situating women's voices as authentic expressions of an Islamic worldview, destabilizing the idea of a male monopoly on religious knowledge and authority, and legitimizing her own literary production. She also performs a certain feminine religious authority through her recourse to authoritative Islamic texts and language. Furthermore, she stages a new role for women through her own creative reinterpretation of the scripts of the Islamic intellectual tradition.

Bint al-Shatiʾ weaves romantic notions of wijdān as emotion inspiring literary creation into classical Islamic terminology and concepts. She and the other writers discussed here draw deeply on Sufi (and classical) notions of the limits of reason and intellect in grasping the nature of the divine.[9] The Sufi understanding of intuitive knowledge of God, an understanding that goes beyond intellectual knowledge, is key to this connection among emotion, instinct, and the divine. In reformist and revivalist writings, fiṭra is "sufficient for thinking and reasoning soundly, thus rendering logic superfluous."[10] Bint al-Shatiʾ's sense of the importance of emotion (wijdān) to Islamic literary production is directly influenced by Sayyid Qutb's understanding of the role of wijdān in the human understanding of, grasp of, and feeling for the divine. Qutb's own writings emerged out of the movement to reinvigorate the

[8] Bint al-Shatiʾ, *al-Tafsir al-Bayani li-l-Qurʾan al-Karim*; Bint al-Shatiʾ, *al-Mafhum al-Islami li-Tahrir al-Marʾa*; Bint al-Shatiʾ, *al-Tafsir al-Bayani li-l-Qurʾan al-Karim*; Bint al-Shatiʾ, *al-Iʿjaz al-Bayani li-l-Qurʾan wa-Masaʾil Ibn al-Azraq*.

[9] See, for example, Hamza, *Rihlati min al-Sufur ila al-Hijab*, 235–40; Fedwa Malti-Douglas, *A Woman and Her Sufis* (Washington, DC: Georgetown University Center for Contemporary Arab Studies, 1995).

[10] Hallaq, *Ibn Taymiyya Against the Greek Logicians*, xl.

conventions of Arabic poetry with emotion, a school that also called for elevating women as muses inspiring this emotion.[11] Qutb was closely mentored by the founder of this movement for an Arab romanticism, ʿAbbas Mahmud al-ʿAqqad, a thinker who, like Qutb, would turn his literary energies and talents toward religion and the Qurʾan. Qutb's *al-Taswir al-Fanni fi al-Qurʾan* (Artistic Representation in the Qurʾan, 1946) develops a theory of Qurʾanic aesthetics, arguing that its taṣwīr, its mode of representation (or "imaging"), touches the senses, which in turn awakens the emotions, leading to "the enlightened insight that righteous fiṭra grasps."[12] "A pillar of the Qurʾan has always been its simple touch of intuition (badāha), awakening the senses, penetrating through intuition and the senses directly to insight, leading intuition and the senses to emotion (al-wijdān). Its material is eternal instinctual truths opened up by enlightened insight that righteous instinct (fiṭra) grasps" (175–76). This is what Qutb calls the "affective logic" (*al-manṭiq al-wijdānī*) of the Qurʾan, a mode of artistic representation that penetrates through to the senses, creating a visual image of itself on the mind and heart of those who listen and of those who see. Intellect and logic, he argues, are not sufficient for understanding or grasping the divine, nor for "widening spiritual horizons or for opening the portals of knowledge." "The mind," he says, "is only one window among the many windows of the self (nafs: also, spirit). A person should not close these portals of the self unless the person wants to become narrow." Qutb argues against those who see the mind "as the highest horizon above all horizons." Conviction (*ʿaqīda*), he argues, is the highest horizon. Intuition refines the path to this horizon, leading with the guidance of insight, opening the heart and the senses to "echoes and lights" (185). These lights and echoes illuminate the Qurʾan, through the very seeing and hearing that the Qurʾan itself repeatedly stresses are critical to grasping its message.

The sensory impact of visual imagery is a key element of this emotional awakening. Qutb talks about visual images that travel through the senses, to emotion, and to insight and instinct. Taṣwīr, in Qutb's writings, *is not just a mode of representation, but also a mode of perception.* The aesthetic experience of the Qurʾan produces a mental image that imprints the Qurʾan on the senses, body, self, and soul. Qutb focuses on the visual aspect of representation, on taṣwīr as a mode of mental imagining and image-making. This aesthetic representation (*al-taṣwīr al-fannī*) is the Qurʾan's tactic for penetrating through to the senses and creating what Qutb describes as sensory imagination (*al-*

[11] al-ʿAqqad and al-Mazini, *al-Diwan*; Sayed Khatab, *The Political Thought of Sayyid Qutb: The Theory of Jahiliyyah* (London: Routledge, 2006), 52–55.

[12] Qutb, *al-Taswir al-Fanni fi al-Qurʾan*, 185–86.

takhayyul al-ḥissī) that functions as an embodiment (*tajsīm*) of the Qurʾan. In *The Ethical Soundscape*, Charles Hirschkind interprets Qutb's sense of imagining and picturing with the mind's eye as the influence of the cinematic on the literary field.[13] In classical literary interpretations of the Qurʾan, theorists focused on the relationship between the "*ẓahr*" (form, style, factual denotation) and the "*baṭn*" (belly, content, meaning). Qutb takes this classical approach and transforms it with new interpretations of how the Qurʾan's artistic style translates into the human sensorium and inspires a living Qurʾan and a "living Islam." For Qutb, the aesthetic experience of the Qurʾan is an embodied one (186). He focuses on the importance of the visual for an Islamic worldview, a concept of an Islamic weltanschauung, a *taṣwīr islāmī*, that would have far-reaching impact on interpretations of the Qurʾan. Moreover, *taṣwīr islāmī* also became understood as a political and social vision for contemporary Islam. This mode of Islamic seeing would be deeply connected to Islamic modes of representation, a mutually constitutive experience of creating a living Islam both in the world and in the hearts and minds of Muslims.

This kind of visual representation within Islamic cultural production has been critical to new kinds of Qurʾan interpretation, as well as a social vision of an Islamic worldview. Wijdān is central to Qutb's conception of the pillars of social justice in Islam. The first of these pillars, *al-taḥarrur al-wijdānī*, argues that the freedom at the heart of Islam is affective. It is intrinsic, affective, emotional, psychic freedom from submission to any master except God. Submission to God and to God's word led to spiritual and psychological freedom from earthly masters (and secular governments), so that no person could stand over another as his or her authority. The only kind of difference between men and women in this regard, he argued, was (purely) socially constructed, through a kind of training that came from the performance of different biological functions in child bearing and childrearing. In *Social Justice* he defines wijdān as "*shuʿūr nafsī bāṭin*," a phrase that can be interpreted as either "personal gut feeling" or "inner spiritual consciousness"—both definitions corresponding to

[13] "While *taswir* involves more than the strictly visual—Qutb frequently mentions the contribution of Quranic rhythm and musicality and their ability to engage sense of hearing, touch, and taste—it is nonetheless the visual sense that dominates and gives unity to the overall sensory experience. . . . The Quran's power to influence the hearts of sensitive listeners lies in its presentation of 'scenes' that in their sensual intensity, their movement and sequential flow, transcend mere images to become life itself. . . . The visual imagination that Qutb locates at the heart of the Quran's aesthetic procedures constantly gestures to the cinematic." Hirschkind, *Ethical Soundscape*, 154–56.

Qutb's understanding of the transcendent materiality, or the immanence, of the Qur^ʾan.[14]

These writings for the age of Islamic awakening reinvent classical concepts of the seen and unseen, manifest and intrinsic, literal and metaphoric, inner and outer. Fiṭra plays a central role in understandings of an inner self and of inner belief. In the veiling narrative of Kariman Hamza, her "inner nature" (*fiṭratī al-dākhiliyya*) synchronizes with the words of the shaykh ʿAbd al-Halim Mahmud, as he guides her to her true self, speaking words that she did not know how to express. He awakens a life that was dormant in her self, through his writings and his words. She describes herself as immersed in the material world, a world of colors, a world of her bare, exposed body and hair. He shows her another "color" of the world, one that synchronizes with her very inner nature. "I love this color," she says. "I found my path. I found myself. I found God."[15] This Islamic knowledge awakening her fiṭra will lead her to her own mode of Islamic expression—first through veiling, then through Islamic television, then through her narrative describing her path to veiling, guiding her on the path of Islamic knowledge, and to Islamic forms of expression. These entwined forms—Islamic knowledge, Islamic cultural production, and Islamic practice—are colors among colors in the world that she calls the varieties of God's mercy. These "colors" and "languages" are part of God's signs in the world (30:22). For Shams al-Barudi, fiṭra would be the glimmers of an Islamic self in a netherworld of a virtual coma, the "darknesses" and "oppressions" (*ẓulumāt*) that stand in stark contrast to the liberating potential of enlightened insight in Qutb's *Aesthetic Representation* and the power of the inner eye in Sidqi's writings. It is an a priori self that has already been created by the word but (in the words of Kariman Hamza and Shams al-Barudi) lays dormant and buried in the human spirit.

Fiṭra is profoundly gendered in the writings analyzed in this book. For Bint al-Shatiʾ, it is emotion that equips women with the instinct for literary composition, for devotional literature, for praise of the divine through speaking of love for Him. Yet in some of her other writings, it is the fiṭra of sexual attraction and for motherhood; fiṭra also equips women with a sense of the limits of the licit and an instinct

[14] Samira Haj, in *Reconfiguring Islamic Tradition*, 114–15, describes how modernist thought in Islam cultivated a sense of spiritual interiority, through inner sentiments (wijdān) that are brought under the control of the intellect or mind. Muhammad ʿAbduh refers to this interiority as *al-taṣdīq bi-l-wijdān*, or conviction through inner feeling.

[15] Hamza, *Rihlati min al-Sufur ila al-Hijab*, 31–32.

for restraint, chastity, and modesty; it is also the instinct that makes a woman submit to a man, a "law" that renders any "complete equality" between men and women impossible.[16] For Niʿmat Sidqi, fiṭra becomes the means by which women repeat the process of God's creation, through reproduction, literally embodying the process of God's material creation through the instinct of sexual attraction. Instinct also gives women the skills, training, and knowledge for childrearing, what Sidqi calls the "technique for bodily education, because God on high created in every female instinct" and Bint al-Shatiʾ calls "her natural training."[17] Childrearing is one of the most important aspects of women's jihad, Sidqi argues, a notion that Heba Raouf Ezzat took up in the 1990s, reinterpreting this jihad as a form of nonviolent struggle in Islam. For Raouf Ezzat, the jihad of childrearing is the struggle to invest religious discipline in the unruly (raw) material of human life. In Raouf Ezzat's "Islamic vision" of women's work, she writes about the natural division of labor between and man and woman, an "instinctual order" and an "instinctual contract" between man and woman. These writers' own discursive production helps to create and imagine the gendered subjectivities that give expression to this instinctual order. They also position women as primary authorities in the social labor of childrearing, as guardians over the home and its inhabitants, what Raouf Ezzat (and other contemporary Islamic thinkers) identify as the first cell of the Islamic umma.[18]

In these texts, fiṭra structures the relationship between mates, bringing them together in natural harmony.[19] Verse 30:30 of the Qurʾan is the culmination of a series of verses about God's signs and God's verses in the world. It is especially about God's creation ("*fiṭrat Allah*") and the repetition of this creation through the cycle of the seasons and the propagation of humanity (30:19–20). These texts link the fiṭra

[16] Bint al-Shatiʾ, *al-Mafhum al-Islami li-Tahrir al-Marʾa*, 13; Bint al-Shatiʾ, *al-Adiba al-ʿArabiyya*, 20.

[17] Bint al-Shatiʾ, *al-Adiba al-ʿArabiyya*, 3; Sidqi, *al-Jihad fi Sabil Allah*, 23.

[18] Scholars and historians observe that women's primacy to childrearing emerged with the shift to capitalist and colonial modernity. See Baron, *The Women's Awakening in Egypt*, 158–59; Najmabadi, "Crafting an Educated Housewife in Iran," 95; Shakry, "Schooled Mothers and Structured Play," 135. Almost all the works discussed here cite the hadith saying that a woman is "a shepherd in the house of her husband and is responsible for her flock." See Khamis, *al-Marʾa wa-l-Huquq al-Siyasiyya wa-l-Aʿmal al-ʿAmma*, 47, 51, 56; Jumhuriyyat Misr al-ʿArabiyya, *al-Marʾa al-Misriyya*, 40; Mustafa, *Imbaraturiyyat al-Nisaʾ al-ʿAmilat*, 65; Siraj al-Din, *Awraq Shams al-Barudi*, 55; Raouf Ezzat, *al-Marʾa wa-l-ʿAmal al-Siyasi*, 201.

[19] Bint al-Shatiʾ, *al-Mafhum al-Islami li-Tahrir al-Marʾa*, 11–13; Siraj al-Din, *Awraq Shams al-Barudi*, 20; Raouf Ezzat, *al-Marʾa wa-l-ʿAmal al-Siyasi*, 188.

of 30:30 to the relationship between the mates in 30:21.[20] "Among the signs that God created for you are that from yourselves are mates in which you find tranquility (*li-taskunū*). And he put between you love and compassion. In that are signs for people who think" (30:21). This love, affection, and desire are the very expression of a gendered fiṭra, the very habitus (*sakan*) that reproduces God's signs and God's creation. Even though the texts discussed here root this sakan in a heteronormative couple, the verse itself does not assert a heteronormative pair but actually is followed by another verse about the diversity of the languages and colors of humanity as another of God's signs of creation. The sakan, the peace, tranquility, and repose of marital life, is the proper channeling of fiṭra into love and compassion, as a reflection of God's mercy. Verse 30:21 figures centrally in all the writings discussed here: they all use the concept of sakan to talk about family life as a spiritual abode but also about the emotional connection between mates.

Verse 30:21 may be small in size, Niʿmat Sidqi writes, but it is great in meaning. "The verse commands of the two spouses the mutual compassion and understanding that befits their humanity and stamps spiritual meaning on the sheer animal meaning between the two sexes." Its goal, she goes on to say, "is not only the body's happiness but the happiness of the mind that directs the human being to what makes the family happy. And with that, it makes humanity happy" (214). "*Mawadda* is love and desire together," she says, "and desire is arousal. For those who love, they must be bound to the person they love spiritually and bodily, because the human being is made of body and soul." Even though she identifies "strong instinctual attraction" between the two mates as the "first basis of the relationship between them," this attraction must be rooted in love, with tenderness, compassion, affection, and desire. Tenderness (*ḥanān*: also "piety") and desire are the "signs of love that connect each mate with the other." The body—sight, insight, and the eye, "the source of pleasure"—must be attuned to these "sacred feelings for the wisdom of God" (212, 214). Responding to the debates over the nature of women's work, Heba Raouf Ezzat directly connects fiṭra to the desire of the sexes for each other, a drive that structures the family. Drawing on 30:21, she connects fiṭra to the inclination toward love, mercy, and tranquility (mawadda, *raḥma*, sakan). These are the fruit of desire, love, and the sexual contract be-

[20] Sidqi, *Niʿmat al-Qurʾan*, 214; Bint al-Shatiʾ, "Shakhsiyyat al-Marʾa fi al-Qurʾan al-Karim," 140; Khamis, *al-Marʾa wa-l-Huquq al-Siyasiyya*, 91; Mustafa, *al-Nisaʾ al-ʿAmilat*, 21; Raouf Ezzat, *al-Marʾa wa-l-ʿAmal al-Siyasi*, 68.

tween mates. This intimacy, she says, this sexual appetite, is both divine (*al-fiṭra al-ilāhiyya*) and instinctual. It is what these authors refer to as the heavy covenant (*mīthāq ghalīẓ*) based on the "closing of space" (*afḍā*: "emptying") between a man and a woman, the instinctual order (*al-niẓām al-fiṭrī*) that is the basis of the sexual contract.[21] This contract becomes what both Bint al-Shatiʾ and Heba Raouf Ezzat refer to as the "sunna of fiṭra," a fiṭra that has both an affective and a social manifestation. Raouf Ezzat defines human intuition about the "right path" as safeguarding political society, harmonizing "greater shariʿa and divine shariʿa with the nature of fiṭra."[22]

Even as these concepts refract (and reinterpret) certain modern notions of an idealized middle-class family with two loving mates, they are projected back into the Qurʾan, legitimizing and authorizing the modern bourgeois family for the Islamic revival.[23] In the wake of the International Women's Year conference in Mexico City, to which Egypt sent a delegation of high-profile women, al-Azhar convened its own conference on "the place of woman in the Islamic family." At this conference Bint al-Shatiʾ presented a lecture on "the personality of woman in Islam," arguing that men's guardianship of women is (only) an economic—not an ontological—arrangement. Drawing on Surat al-Rum, she argues for an Islamic family bound by love and affection, not by hierarchies of dominance. But even as such discourses assert an ontological equality of spirit, self, and soul of women and men, they continue to posit an economic and social hierarchy based on assumptions of male (economic) guardianship of women. A bourgeois Islamic family is conceived of as an economic—and a spiritual—unit. This family is structured by reciprocal rights and duties, with a mother/wife as the angel in the household, and a conjugal couple connected by love and consent. This suggests that women's sacred duty is in the cultivation of a private domesticity, where free labor is lovingly and consensually performed.[24] In *Empire of the Working Women*, Iman Mustafa acknowledges the critical importance of this family's economic function (in the

[21] This closing of space between the mates is what Muhammad ʿAbduh referred to as "an intuitive contract (*mīthāq fiṭrī*) that is among the most sacred of contracts and most intensely binding." Sidqi, *Niʿmat al-Qurʾan*, 212, 214; ʿImara, *al-Islam wa-l-Marʾa fi Raʾy al-Imam Muhammad ʿAbduh*, 75–76.

[22] Bint al-Shatiʾ, *al-Adiba al-ʿArabiyya*, 5; Raouf Ezzat, *al-Marʾa wa-l-ʿAmal al-Siyasi*, 67.

[23] Haddad, "Case of the Feminist Movement," 56; Stowasser, "Religious Ideology"; Hatem, "Secularist and Islamist Discourses on Modernity," 93; Abu-Lughod, "Feminist Longings and Postcolonial Conditions," 8–12; Abu-Lughod, "Marriage of Feminism and Islamism," 252–55.

[24] Khamis, *al-Marʾa wa-l-Huquq al-Siyasiyya*. Verse 30:21 reappears repeatedly in this collection of essays by Islamic intellectuals, a response to initiatives to increase women's

chapter "Economy . . . Woman") but also asserts the family's transcendent spiritual function as a repository of affect, intimacy, and communal identification. Quoting verse 30:21, she argues that affection, compassion, and tranquility (and wijdān, she adds) are the "capital of the marital corporation" (21). Men, she says, are in charge of the "burdens of the expenses of life," but women manage the affective capital of the family, a role that is "of sacred importance" (23).

Along with the physical attraction between mates are certain forms of intellectual attraction that permeate these writings. The intellectual attraction to others' ideas helps generate a public discourse for the Islamic community, the circulation, dissemination, and indeed the propagation of an intellectual lineage in which women now become key producers. But they also became visual signifiers of the circulation of new kinds of Islamic discourses in the public sphere, new kinds of belief, new kinds of bodies and selves. They became integral to the semiotic ideology of the revival—its practices, beliefs, cultural production, and social infrastructure. Bint al-Shatiʾ consummated her intellectual attraction to Amin al-Khuli through a public partnership in the life of Islamic letters. But she also engaged publicly with a number of other public intellectuals, even while staying well within disciplinary parameters. She literally derived her pen name from Sayyid Qutb, from a public exchange of poems and stories: he writing a famous poem that became the title of his first *diwan* of poetry, *al-Shatiʾ al-Majhul* (The Unknown Shore), and she responding with her own short stories *Sirr al-Shatiʾ* (Secret of the Shore); he published a semiautobiographical story of unrequited love, *Ashwak* (Thorns), and then later quarreled with al-Khuli in print over literary interpretations of the Qurʾan. They moved in the same intellectual circles connected with the public sphere: they worked together at the Ministry of Education and the newspaper *al-Ahram*. Bint al-Shatiʾ would not publish her own theories of the liberating nature of Islam until after her husband al-Khuli's death, paying tribute to the first principle and pillar of Qutb's *Social Justice in Islam*—even if, by that time, Qutb, too, would be dead. As Bint al-Shatiʾ publicly mourned al-Khuli with her own *rithāʾ*, paying intellectual tribute to him, she also mourned Qutb with a different kind of tribute—in a flood of writings on freedom in Islam, referencing his thought, ideas, and language in ways she never would have while al-Khuli was alive. Wooed by the Islamic thinker ʿAli ʿAbd al-Wahid Wafi at the Islamic University of Omdurman, she politely declined his overtures in her public lectures, thanking him

work outside the home, one aspect of the structural adjustment policies that Anwar Sadat implemented after agreements with the International Monetary Fund.

for welcoming her into his metaphoric home but talking about her continued grief and mourning for al-Khuli. Even so, the following year she would pay tribute to Wafi's ideas about "human rights in Islam," ideas that Wafi himself had derived directly from Qutb.

The spiritual guidance found by writers like Sidqi, Hamza, and Maraʿi bore fruit in their literary creations. These spiritual relationships ran alongside these women's relationships to their husbands, complementing and completing them. Sidqi met Muhammad Hamid al-Fiqi, the founder and leader of Ansar al-Sunna al-Muhammadiyya, while on the hajj with her husband. Though she maintained a close relationship with al-Fiqi and he visited her house nearly every Friday, there is never any hint of jealousy, rivalry, or interdictions from her husband. On the contrary, these spiritual relationships enhance their positions as wives and mothers, giving them meaning and imparting them with sacredness. Hamza's narrative, for example, begins with her unhappiness despite marriage to a husband who loves her and who gives her complete freedom. Something is missing, she says. She finds that something in Shaykh ʿAbd al-Halim Mahmud, who wakes her up in the morning with his voice, who "burns" her with his looks at her naked arms, and whom she pursues with the doggedness of a lover—or a disciple. After she dreams of ʿAbd al-Halim Mahmud, she runs to her husband, throws her arms around him, kisses him, and exclaims: "I am going to be resurrected with ʿAbd al-Halim Mahmud!" This attraction to the world of religious letters, the magnetism of spiritual guides, and the public exchange of intimate ideas form the substance and crux of these narratives. This public world of Islamic letters is hardly separate from the intimate domain. On the contrary, "desire with knowledge" (30:29) permeates human lives and human bodies, directs their trajectories, and becomes a mode of perception and expression. As Hamza says, these women *feel* and instinctually seek words and lines, ideas and perspectives, ideologies and teachings. These become the colors and languages of being (30:22), signs on the path not just to God but to an Islamic self.[25] For these writers, a feminized domain of compassion and affection is at the heart of knowledge of God, the umma, and Islam. It is knowledge inspired by righteous love, emotion, attraction, and sensation, structuring the very habitus of Islamic belief: self, mates, children, family, home, umma.

Why then, Bint al-Shatiʾ asks, has the Arab woman disappeared from literary history? "Has her emotional life become barren? Is this because of some lack of the law of instinct and the sunna of nature? No. The

[25] Hamza, *Rihlati min al-Sufur ila al-Hijab*, 31–32.

emotional life of the Arab literary woman is not barren. She has realized her literary presence and left her mark, expressing her sensitive, living emotional life. But for the most part our historians have left these contributions in a region of darkness."[26] Bint al-Shatiʾ points to a paradox: that women have always contributed to the public life of the Islamic umma but have remained contradictorily obscured from view. She describes marks, signs, works (*āthār*) left on the literary field, traces of a vital presence in the public sphere but also intimating the history of women's marginalization. She compares this "region of darkness" to the burial of infant girls in the pre-Islamic age of jāhiliyya and to the "emotional burial" of the harem, seclusion, and "the veil of ignorance"—not a piece of cloth but a state of mind. Women must break out and sing their desires, she says, through literature, knowledge, poetry, and religion.

Analyses of women in the revival have focused on concepts like *ʿawra* and *fitna*, emphasizing the shameful and disruptive potentiality of women's sexuality and of women's public presence.[27] Such concepts could have little appeal for women and fail to account for what attracts women to Islamic ideology. Even though concepts such as fiṭra and wijdān inscribe an affective nature into women's spirituality, literary vocations, and social roles, they also give women privileged position in the expression of new forms of Islamic knowledge and (discursively) give them access to the insight that sensory knowledge inspires. They also put women and family at the center of not just an Islamic society but Islamic politics. Women may carry a heavy burden in embodying religion in this way—in epitomizing intimate relations, reproducing the social body, and representing the body politic. Many criticize and reject these roles as confining; others, however, interpret them as expansive expressions of different "colors" of Islamic womanhood. The home and family, Raouf Ezzat argues, is a vast domain: it speaks to the reality of a large swath of women (Mustafa's "truth in the heart of the majority") and leaves room for what she calls a "wider freedom" for women's movements, one that does not just see money as a measure of value.[28] Like Mustafa's image of the body of truth moving everywhere, Raouf Ezzat leaves room for the reinterpretation of family and home as an expansive (rather than a restrictive) domain, as liberating rather than confining, as biopower in its microcosmic instantiations. These thinkers see an Islamic worldview embodied in the microcosmic

[26] Bint al-Shatiʾ, *al-Adiba al-ʿArabiyya*, 5.

[27] Hoffman-Ladd, "Polemics on the Modesty and Segregation of Women," 28. Malti-Douglas, "Faces of Sin," 70.

[28] Mustafa, *al-Nisaʾ al-ʿAmilat*, 12–13; Raouf Ezzat, *al-Marʾa wa-l-ʿAmal al-Siyasi*, 161.

as much as the macrocosmic, in the home as much as the polity, in the body as much as the umma. They stage starring roles for themselves in the revival of Islamic knowledge. By creating new modes of Islamic representation, they cultivate new modes of perception, envisioned through new kinds of Islamic subjectivities and selves, toward the realization of an Islamic society and politics of the future.

Bibliography

Abaza, Mona. *Feminist Debates and "Traditional Feminism" of the Fallaha in Rural Egypt*. Bielefeld: Sociology of Development Research Centre, University of Bielefeld, 1987.

ʿAbd al-Khaliq, Farid. *Fi al-Fiqh al-Siyasi al-Islami: Mabadiʾ Dusturiyya: al-Shura, al-ʿAdl, al-Musawaa*. Cairo: Dar al-Shuruq, 1998.

ʿAbd al-Wahhab, Muhammad Fahmi. *al-Harakat al-Nisaʾiyya fi al-Sharq wa-Silatuha bi-l-Istiʿmar wa-l-Sihyuniyya al-ʿAlamiyya: Raʾy al-Jamiʿat wa-l-Hayʾat al-Islamiyya wa-Kibar al-ʿUlamaʾ fi Misr fi Ishtighal al-Marʾa bi-l-Siyasa wa-l-Aʿmal al-ʿAmma*. Cairo: Dar al-Iʿtisam, 1979.

Abou El Fadl, Khaled. "Islam and the Challenge of Democracy." *Boston Review*, May 2003. http://bostonreview.net/BR28.2/abou.html.

Abramovitz, Mimi. *Regulating the Lives of Women: Social Welfare Policy from Colonial Times to the Present*. Cambridge, MA: South End Press, 1996.

Abu al-ʿAynayn, Saʿid. *al-Shaʿrawi—wa-l-Fannanat*. Cairo: Dar Akhbar al-Yawm, Qitaʿ al-Thaqafa, 1999.

Abugideiri, Hibba. "On Gender and the Family." In *Islamic Thought in the Twentieth Century*, edited by Suha Taji-Farouki and Basheer M. Nafi. London: I.B. Tauris, 2004.

Abu-Lughod, Lila. "Against Universality: Dialects of (Women's) Human Rights and Capabilities." In *Rethinking the Human*, edited by J. Michelle Molina and Donald K. Swearer. Cambridge, MA: Harvard University Press, 2010.

———. "Do Muslim Women Really Need Saving? Anthropological Reflection on Cultural Relativism and Its Others." *American Anthropologist* 104, no. 3 (September 2002): 783–90.

———. *Do Muslim Women Need Saving?* Cambridge, MA: Harvard University Press, 2013.

———. *Dramas of Nationhood: The Politics of Television in Egypt*. Chicago: University of Chicago Press, 2004.

———. "Feminist Longings and Postcolonial Conditions." In *Remaking Women: Feminism and Modernity in the Middle East*. Princeton, NJ: Princeton University Press, 1998.

———. "The Marriage of Feminism and Islamism in Egypt: Selective Repudiation as a Dynamic of Postcolonial Cultural Politics." In *Remaking Women: Feminism and Modernity in the Middle East*, edited by Lila Abu-Lughod. Princeton, NJ: Princeton University Press, 1998.

———. "Movie Stars and Islamic Moralism in Egypt." *Social Text* no. 42 (April 1, 1995): 53–67.

———, ed. *Remaking Women: Feminism and Modernity in the Middle East*. Princeton, NJ: Princeton University Press, 1998.

———. *Veiled Sentiments: Honor and Poetry in a Bedouin Society*. Berkeley: University of California Press, 1986.

Abu-Lughod, Lila, Fida Adely, and Frances Susan Hasso. "Overview: Engaging the Arab Human Development Report 2005 on Women." *International Journal of Middle East Studies* 41, no. 1 (February 2009): 59–60.

Abu Musa, Muhammad. *al-Taswir al-Bayani: Dirasa Tahliliyya li-Masaʾil al-Bayan*. Cairo: Maktabat Wahba, 1980.

Abu Musa, Muhammad, and Abdel Hadi Abu Taleb. "Govt Pressures Ban Qaradawi from Egypt TV," February 22, 2011. http://www.onislam.net/english/news/africa/451164-govt-pressures-ban-qaradawi-from-egypt-tv.html.

Abu Nasr, Julinda, Nabil F. Khoury, and Henry Azzam, eds. *Women, Employment, and Development in the Arab World*. Berlin: Mouton, 1985.

Abu-Odeh, Lama. "Modernizing Muslim Family Law: The Case of Egypt." *Oxford University Comparative Law Forum* (2004).

Abu Shuqqa, ʿAbd al-Halim Muhammad. *Tahrir al-Marʾa fi ʿAsr al-Risala: Dirasa ʿan al-Marʾa Jamiʿa li-Nusus al-Qurʾan al-Karim wa-Sahihay al-Bukhari wa-Muslim*. Kuwait: Dar al-Qalam, 1990.

Abu Suf, Ilham. *Fannanat Mutahajjibat*. Beirut: Dar al-Qadiri, 1993.

Abu Zayd, Mahmud. *al-Din wa-l-Tamasuk al-Ijtimaʿi*. Cairo: Jamiʿat al-Azhar, Kulliyyat al-Banat al-Islamiyya, Markaz Dirasat al-Marʾa wa-l-Tanmiya, 1977.

Abu-Zayd, Nasr. "The Dilemma of the Literary Approach to the Qurʾan." *Alif: Journal of Comparative Poetics* 23, no. Literature and the Sacred (2003): 22–34.

Adelkhah, Fariba. "Framing the Public Sphere: Iranian Women in the Islamic Republic." In *Public Islam and the Common Good*, edited by Dale Eickelman and Armando Salvatore, 227–41. Leiden: Brill, 2006.

Afandi, ʿAbd Allah Jamal al-Din. *Hijab al-Marʾa: al-ʿIffa wa-l-Amana wa-l-Hayaʾ*. Cairo: Maktabat al-Turath al-Islami, 1984.

Agamben, Giorgio. *Homo Sacer: Sovereign Power and Bare Life*. Translated by Daniel Heller-Roazen. Stanford, CA: Stanford University Press, 1998.

ʿAhami, ʿUmar Saʿid Muhammad Fariʿ. *al-Huquq al-Siyasiyya li-l-Marʾa fi al-Fiqh al-Islami: Maʿ Tahlil li-Baʿd al-Duwal al-ʿArabiyya*. Alexandria: al-Maktab al-Jamiʿi al-Hadith, 2011.

El Ahmad, Khaled. "The 100 Most Influential Arabs on Twitter." *Wamda*. Accessed March 21, 2012. http://www.wamda.com/2012/01/the-100-most-influential-arabs-on-twitter.

Ahmed, Leila. *Women and Gender in Islam: Historical Roots of a Modern Debate*. Cairo: American University in Cairo Press, 1993.

Aishima, Hatsuki, and Armando Salvatore. "Doubt, Faith, and Knowledge: The Reconfiguration of the Intellectual Field in Post-Nasserist Cairo." In *Islam, Politics, Anthropology*, edited by Filippo Osella and Benjamin Soares. Oxford: Wiley-Blackwell, 2010.

Algar, Hamid. "Preface." In *Basic Principles of Islamic Worldview*, by Sayyid Qutb, translated by Rami David. North Haledon, NJ: Islamic Publications International, 2006.

Ali, Kamran Asdar. *Planning the Family in Egypt: New Bodies, New Selves*. Austin: University of Texas Press, 2002.

Ali, Kecia. "Progressive Muslims and Islamic Jurisprudence: The Necessity for Critical Engagement with Marriage and Divorce Laws." In *Progressive Mus-*

lims: On Gender, Justice, and Pluralism, edited by Omid Safi. Oxford: One World, 2003.

Altorki, Soraya, and Huda Zurayq. *Taghayyur al-Qiyam fi al-ʿAʾila al-ʿArabiyya.* Studies of the Arab Woman and Development. New York: United Nations, Economic and Social Commission for Western Asia, 1994.

Amar, Paul. *The Security Archipelago: Human-Security States, Sexuality Politics, and the End of Neoliberalism.* Durham, NC: Duke University Press, 2013.

———. "Turning the Gendered Politics of the Security State Inside Out?" *International Feminist Journal of Politics* 13, no. 3 (2011): 299–328.

ʿAmili, ʿAli al-ʿUsayli. *Niʿmat al-Hijab fi al-Islam.* Beirut: al-Dar al-Islamiyya, 1988.

Amin, Muhammad. "A Study of Bint al-Shati's Exegesis." MA thesis, McGill University, 1992.

Amin, Qasim. *Les Égyptiens: reponse à Duc d'Harcourt.* Cairo: Jules Barbier, 1894.

———. *The Liberation of Woman and the New Woman.* Translated by Samiha Sidhom Peterson. Cairo: American University in Cairo Press, 2000.

———. *Tahrir al-Marʾa wa-l-Marʾa al-Jadida.* Cairo: al-Markaz al-ʿArabi li-l-Bahth wa-l-Nashr, 1984.Anderson, Benedict. *Imagined Communities: Reflections on the Origin and Spread of Nationalism.* New York: Verso, 2006.

Ansari, ʿAbd al-Hamid Ismaʿil. *al-ʿAlam al-Islami al-Muʿasir bayn al-Shura wa-l-Dimuqratiyya: Ruʾya Naqdiyya.* Madinat Nasr, Cairo: Dar al-Fikr al-ʿArabi, 2001.

———. *al-Shura wa-Atharuha fi al-Dimuqratiyya.* Cairo: al-Matbaʿa al-Salafiyya wa-Maktabatuha, 1980.

al-ʿAqqad, ʿAbbas Mahmud. *ʿAbqariyyat al-Imam.* Cairo: Dar al-Maʿarif, 1943.

———. *ʿAbqariyyat al-Siddiq.* Cairo: Matbaʿat al-Maʿarif wa-Maktabatuha, 1943.

———. *ʿAbqariyyat Muhammad.* Cairo: Matbaʿat al-Istiqama, 1942.

———. *ʿAbqariyyat ʿUmar.* Cairo: Matba'at al-Istiqama, 1942.

———. *Rajʿat Abi al-ʿAlaʾ.* Cairo: Dar al-Kutub al-Haditha, 1939.

al-ʿAqqad, ʿAbbas Mahmud, and Ibrahim al-Mazini. *al-Diwan: Kitab fi al-Naqd wa-l-Adab.* Cairo: Maktabat al-Saʿada, 1921.

ʿArabi, Shahrazad. *al-Buʿd al-Siyasi li-l-Hijab.* Cairo: al-Zahraʾ li-l-Iʿlam al-ʿArabi, 1989.

Arendt, Hannah. *The Origins of Totalitarianism.* New York: Harcourt, Brace, Jovanovich, 1973.

———. "What Is Freedom?" In *Between Past and Future: Eight Exercises in Political Thought.* New York: Penguin Books, 1993.

Asad, Talal. *Formations of the Secular: Christianity, Islam, Modernity.* Stanford, CA: Stanford University Press, 2003.

ʿAshmawi, Muhammad Saʿid. *Haqiqat al-Hijab wa-Hujjiyyat al-Hadith.* Cairo: Madbuli al-Saghir, 1995.

Awang, Ahmad. *Menyembah Allah, Menghufurkan Taghut! (Tabarruj al-Jahiliyya).* Batu Caves: Selangor Darul Ehsan, 1996.

ʿAzmi, Mukhtar ibn Ahmad Muʿayyid. *Fasl al-Khitab aw Taflis Iblis min Tahrir al-Marʾa wa-Rafʿ al-Hijab.* Beirut: al-Matbaʿa al-Adabiyya, 1901.

Badran, Margot. "Competing Agendas: Feminists, Islam, and the State in Nineteenth- and Twentieth-Century Egypt." In *Women, Islam and the State*, edited by Deniz Kandiyoti. Philadelphia: Temple University Press, 1991.

———. *Feminism in Islam: Secular and Religious Convergences*. Oxford: Oneworld, 2009.

———. *Feminists, Islam, and Nation: Gender and the Making of Modern Egypt*. Princeton, NJ: Princeton University Press, 1996.

———. "Gender Activism: Feminists and Islamists in Egypt." In *Identity Politics and Women: Cultural Reassertions and Feminisms in International Perspective*, edited by Valentine M. Moghadam. Boulder, CO: Westview Press, 1994.

———. "Islamic Feminism: What's in a Name?" *al-Ahram Weekly Online*, January 17, 2002.

Bahi, Riham Ashraf. "Networking for Power and Change: Muslim Women Activism and the Transformation of Muslim Public Sphere." Ms., Department of Political Science, Northeastern University, 2008.

Bahnasawi, Salim ʿAli. *al-Khilafa wa-l-Khulafaʾ al-Rashidun bayn al-Shura wa-l-Dimuqratiyya*. Madinat Nasr, Cairo: al-Zahra li-l-Iʿlam al-ʿArabi, 1991.

Bani Sadr, Abu al-Hasan. *al-ʿAʾila fi al-Islam aw Makanat al-Marʾa fi al-Islam. Manhaj al-Tafakkur. Masʾalat al-Hijab*. Beirut: Dar al-Tawjih al-Islami, 1981.

al-Banna, Jamal. *al-Hijab*. Cairo: Dar al-Fikr al-Islami, 2002.

———. *al-Hurriyya fi al-Islam*. Beirut: Muʾassasat al-Intishar al-ʿArabi, 2011.

———. *Qadiyyat al-Hurriyya fi al-Islam*. Cairo: al-Ittihad al-Islami al-Dawli li-l-ʿAmal, 1985.

Baraka, Iqbal. *al-Hijab: Ruʾya ʿAsriyya*. Cairo: Muʾassasat Dar al-Hilal, 2004.

Barakash, ʿAbd al-Hakim. *al-Qurʾan Madrasa Idariyya: Suwar Wadiha ʿan Nizam al-Hukm fi al-Maghrib Taswir al-Qurʾan*. Beirut: Dar al-Afaq al-Jadida, 1980.

Baron, Beth. *Egypt as a Woman: Nationalism, Gender, and Politics*. Berkeley: University of California Press, 2005.

———. *The Women's Awakening in Egypt: Culture, Society, and the Press*. New Haven, CT: Yale University Press, 1997.

al-Barr, Muhammad ʿAli. *ʿAmal al-Marʾa fi al-Mizan*. Jeddah: al-Dar al-Saʿudiyya, 1981.

al-Barudi, Shams. *Rihlati min al-Zulumat ila al-Nur*. Mansura: Dar al-Wafa li-l-Tibaʿa, 1988.

Bayat, Asef. *Making Islam Democratic: Social Movements and the Post-Islamist Turn*. Stanford, CA: Stanford University Press, 2007.

Benhabib, Seyla. "Autonomy, Modernity, and Community: Communitarianism and Critical Social Theory in Dialogue." In *Cultural-Political Interventions in the Unfinished Project of Enlightenment*, edited by Axel Honneth. Cambridge, MA: MIT Press, 1992.

———. *Situating the Self: Gender, Community, and Postmodernism in Contemporary Ethics*. New York: Routledge, 1992.

Benzine, Rachid. *Les nouveaux penseurs de l'Islam*. Paris: Albin Michel, 2004.

Bier, Laura. *Revolutionary Womanhood: Feminisms, Modernity, and the State in Nasser's Egypt*. Stanford, CA: Stanford University Press, 2011.

Binder, Leonard. *Islamic Liberalism: A Critique of Development Ideologies*. Chicago: University of Chicago Press, 1988.

Bint al-Shati'. *al-Adiba al-ʿArabiyya Ams wa-l-Yawm: Muhadara ʿAmma*. Cairo: Matbaʿat Mukhaymir, 1967.

———. *ʿAla al-Jisr: "Usturat al-Zaman."* Cairo: Dar al-Hilal, 1967.

———. *Ard al-Muʿjizat: Rihla fi Jazirat al-ʿArab*. Cairo: Dar al-Maʿarif, 1956.

———. *Banat al-Nabi ʿalayhi al-Salaa wa-l-Salam*. Cairo: Dar al-Hilal, 1956.

———. *Batalat Karbala: Zaynab Bint Al-Zahra*. Beirut: Maktabat al-Andalus, 1956.

———. "Fi al-Ahwal al-Shakhsiyya." *al-Ahram*, December 3, 1959.

———. *al-Hayat al-Insaniyya ʿind Abi al-ʿAlaʾ al-Maʿarri*. Cairo: Matbaʿat al-Maʿarif, 1939.

———. *al-Iʿjaz al-Bayani li-l-Qurʾan wa-Masaʾil Ibn al-Azraq*. Cairo: Dar al-Maʿarif, 1971.

———. "Islam and the New Woman." Translated by Anthony Calderbank. *Alif: Journal of Comparative Poetics* 19 (1997): 194–202.

———. *al-Mafhum al-Islami li-Tahrir al-Marʾa: Muhadara ʿAmma*. Cairo: Matbaʿat Mukhaymir, 1967.

———. *Maqal fi al-Insan: Dirasa Qurʾaniyya*. Cairo: Dar al-Maʿarif, 1969.

———. "al-Marʾa al-Muslima Ams wa-l-Yawm." In *al-Islam al-Yawm wa-Ghadan*. Cairo: Dar Ihyaʾ al-Kutub al-ʿArabiyya, 1965.

———. *Muqaddima fi al-Manhaj*. Cairo: Maʿhad al-Buhuth wa-l-Dirasat al-ʿArabiyya, 1971.

———. *Nisaʾ al-Nabi ʿalayhi al-Salaa wa-l-Salam*. Cairo: Dar al-Hilal, 1961.

———. *al-Qurʾan wa-Huquq al-Insan: Muhadara ʿAmma*. Cairo: Matbaʿat Mukhaymir, 1968.

———. *al-Qurʾan wa-Qadaya al-Insan*. Beirut: Dar al-ʿIlm li-l-Malayin, 1972.

———. *al-Qurʾan wa-l-Tafsir al-ʿAsri "Hadha Balagh li-l-Nas"*. Iqraʾ. Cairo: Dar al-Maʿarif, 1970.

———. *al-Shakhsiyya al-Islamiyya*. Beirut: Jamiʿat Bayrut al-ʿArabiyya, 1972.

———. "Shakhsiyyat al-Marʾa fi al-Qurʾan al-Karim." In *Makanat al-Marʾa fi al-Usra al-Islamiyya*. Cairo: International Islamic Center for Population Studies and Research, al-Azhar, 1975.

———. *Sirr al-Shatiʾ*. Cairo: Dar Ruz al-Yusuf, 1952.

———. *Sukayna Bint al-Husayn*. Cairo: Dar al-Hilal, 1958.

———. *al-Tafsir al-Bayani li-l-Qurʾan al-Karim*. Maktabat al-Dirasat al-Adabiyya. Cairo: Dar al-Maʿarif, 1962.

———. *al-Tafsir al-Bayani li-l-Qurʾan al-Karim*. 2 vols. 2nd ed. Cairo: Dar al-Maʿarif, 1966, 1968.

———. *Umm al-Nabi*. Cairo: al-Sharika al-ʿArabiyya li-l-Tibaʿa wa-l-Nashr, 1958.

———. *Wives of the Prophet*. Translated by Matti Moosa and D. Nicholas Ranson. Lahore: Sh. Muhammad Ashraf, 1971.

———. *Zaynab Banu-yi Qahraman-i Karbala*. Translated by Naini (Hisan) Ayat Allah'zadah and Habib Chaychiyan. Tehran: Amir Kabir, 1979.

Binyaʿish, Muhammad. *Hijab al-Marʾa wa-Khalfiyyat al-Tabarruj fi al-Fikr al-Islami*. Tetouan: Matbaʿat al-Khalij al-ʿArabi, 1993.

al-Bishri, Tariq. *al-Muslimun wa-l-Aqbat fi Itar al-Jamaʿa al-Wataniyya*. Cairo: al-Hayaʾ al-Misriyya al-ʿAmma li-l-Kitab, 1980.

Blume, Sindhu Hirani. "Lies I Was Told: Women, Work, and 'Having It All.' " PricewaterhouseCoopers International Limited. *The Gender Agenda*, July 19, 2012. http://pwc.blogs.com/gender_agenda/2012/07/lies-i-was-told-women-work-and-having-it-all.html.

Bohn, Lauren E. "Tunisia's Forgotten Revolutionaries." *Foreign Policy*, July 14, 2011.

Bonebakker, S. A. "Adab and the Concept of Belles-Lettres." In *Cambridge History of Arabic Literature: ʿAbbasid Belles-Lettres*, edited by Julia Ashtiany. Cambridge: Cambridge University Press, 1990.

Booth, Marilyn. *May Her Likes Be Multiplied: Biography and Gender Politics in Egypt*. Berkeley: University of California Press, 2001.

———. "Prison, Gender, Praxis: Women's Prison Memoirs in Egypt and Elsewhere." *MERIP* 149, Human Rights in the Middle East (1987): 35–41.

Boullata, Issa J. "Modern Qurʾan Exegesis: A Study of Bint al-Shatiʾ's Method." *Muslim World* 64 (1974): 103–13.

———. "Sayyid Qutb's Literary Appreciation of the Qurʾān." In *Literary Structures of Religious Meaning in the Qurʾān*, edited by Issa J. Boullata. Richmond, Surrey: Curzon, 2000.

Brown, Wendy. "American Nightmare: Neoliberalism, Neoconservatism, and De-Democratization." *Political Theory* 34, no. 6 (2006): 690–714.

———. "Liberalism's Family Values." In *States of Injury: Power and Freedom in Late Modernity*. Princeton, NJ: Princeton University Press, 1995.

Butler, Judith. "Contingent Foundations: Feminism and the Question of 'Postmodernism'." In *Feminists Theorize the Political*, edited by Judith Butler and Joan Scott. New York: Routledge, 1992.

———. *Gender Trouble: Feminism and the Subversion of Identity*. New York: Routledge, 1990.

———. *Precarious Life: The Powers of Mourning and Violence*. New York: Verso, 2006.

Casanova, José. *Public Religions in the Modern World*. Chicago: University of Chicago Press, 1994.

Casanova, Pascale. *The World Republic of Letters*. Cambridge, MA: Harvard University Press, 2007.

Chakrabarty, Dipesh. *Provincializing Europe: Postcolonial Thought and Historical Difference*. Princeton, NJ: Princeton University Press, 2007.

Chatterjee, Partha. *Nationalist Thought and the Colonial World: A Derivative Discourse*. Minneapolis: University of Minnesota Press, 1993.

———. *Texts of Power: Emerging Disciplines in Colonial Bengal*. Minneapolis: University of Minnesota Press, 1995.

Chow, Rey. *The Rey Chow Reader*. Edited by Paul Bowman. New York: Columbia University Press, 2010.

———. *Sentimental Fabulations, Contemporary Chinese Films: Attachment in the Age of Global Visibility*. New York: Columbia University Press, 2007.

Cole, Juan Ricardo. "Feminism, Class, and Islam in Turn-of-the-Century Egypt." *International Journal of Middle East Studies* 13, no. 4 (November 1, 1981): 387–407.

Collins, Patricia Hill. "Shifting the Center: Race, Class, and Feminism Theorizing about Motherhood." In *Motherhood: Ideology, Experience, and Agency*, edited by Evelyn Nakano Glenn, Grace Chang, and Linda Rennie Forcey. New York: Routledge, 1994.
cooke, miriam. "Prisons: Egyptian Women Writers on Islam." *Religion and Literature* 20 (1988): 139–53.
———. *Women Claim Islam: Creating Islamic Feminism through Literature*. New York: Routledge, 2001.
Coptic Church. *Tanzim al-Usra: Wijhat Nazar Masihiyya*. Cairo: Lajnat al-Usra, Usqufiyyat al-Khadamat al-ʿAmma wa-l-Ijtimaʿiyya, Batriyarkiyyat al-Aqbat al-Urthuduks, 1970.
Dabashi, Hamid. *Islamic Liberation Theology: Resisting the Empire*. New York: Routledge, 2008.
Dawud, Muhammad ʿAbd al-ʿAziz. *al-Jamʿiyyat al-Islamiyya fi Misr wa-Dawruha fi Nashr al-Daʿwa al-Islamiyya*. Cairo: al-Zahraʾ li-l-Iʿlam al-ʿArabi, 1992.
Dean, Jodi. *Zizek's Politics*. New York: Routledge, 2006.
Dean, Mitchell. *Governmentality: Power and Rule in Modern Society*. New York: Sage Publications, 1999.
Deleuze, Gilles. *Foucault*. London: Continuum, 2006.
De Vries, Margaret Garritsen. *IMF History (1972–1978), Volume 1: Narrative and Analysis*. Washington, DC: International Monetary Fund, 1985.
al-Dhihni, Siham. "Hiwar maʿ Nasrin." *Sayyidati*, April 22, 1991.
Eickelman, Dale, and Jon Anderson, eds. *New Media in the Muslim World: The Emerging Public Sphere*. Bloomington: Indiana University Press, 2003.
———. "Redefining Muslim Publics." In *New Media in the Muslim World: The Emerging Public Sphere*. Bloomington: Indiana University Press, 2003.
Engineer, Asgharali. *Islam and Liberation Theology: Essays on Liberative Elements in Islam*. New Delhi: New Delhi Sterling Publishers, 1990.
Euben, Roxanne L. *Enemy in the Mirror: Islamic Fundamentalism and the Limits of Modern Rationalism*. Princeton, NJ: Princeton University Press, 1999.
Evans, David, and United States Department of Labor. *The Development of a Human Resource Information Planning and Policy System for Egypt: A Feasibility Study*. Washington, DC: Advisory Council on Technical Education and Manpower Development and the National Committee on Manpower and Training, United States Agency for International Development, June 23, 1978.
Farag, Iman. "Private Lives, Public Affairs: The Uses of Adab." In *Public Islam and the Common Good*, edited by Armando Salvatore and Dale F. Eickelman. Leiden: Brill, 2004.
Fattuh, Muhammad ʿAbd al-Fattah. *al-Dimuqratiyya wa-l-Shura fi al-Fikr al-Siyasi al-Islami al-Muʿasir: Dirasa fi Fikr al-Shaykh Muhammad al-Ghazali*. Cairo: Maktabat al-Shuruq al-Dawliyya, 2006.
Fernando, Mayanthi L. "Reconfiguring Freedom: Muslim Piety and the Limits of Secular Law and Public Discourse in France." *American Ethnologist* 37, no. 1 (2010): 19–35.
Foucault, Michel. *Discipline and Punish: The Birth of the Prison*. Translated by Alan Sheridan. London: Allen Lane, 1977.

———. "Governmentality." In *The Foucault Effect: Studies in Governmentality*, edited by Graham Burchell, Colin Gordon, and Peter Miller, 87–104. Chicago: University of Chicago Press, 1991.

———. *Histoire de la sexualité I: la volonté de savoir*. Paris: Gallimard, 1976.

———. *The History of Sexuality, Vol. 1: An Introduction*. New York: Vintage, 1990.

———. *Security, Territory, Population: Lectures at the Collège de France 1977–1978*. Edited by Michel Senellart. Translated by Graham Burchell. New York: Picador, 2009.

———. "What Is Enlightenment?" In *The Foucault Reader*, edited by Paul Rabinow. New York: Pantheon, 1984.

Fraser, Nancy. "Rethinking the Public Sphere: A Contribution to the Critique of Actually Existing Democracy." In *Habermas and the Public Sphere*, edited by Craig Calhoun, 109–42. Cambridge, MA: MIT Press, 1992.

———. *Unruly Practices: Power, Discourse and Gender in Contemporary Social Theory*. Cambridge: Polity Press, 1989.

———. "What's Critical about Critical Theory? The Case of Habermas and Gender." In *Unruly Practices: Power, Discourse and Gender in Contemporary Social Theory*. Cambridge: Polity Press, 1989.

El-Gawhary, Karim, and Heba Ra'uf Ezzat. "An Islamic Women's Liberation Movement: An Interview with Heba Ra'uf Ezzat." *Middle East Report* no. 191 (December 1994): 26–27.

Gershoni, Israel, and James P. Jankowski. "Print Culture, Social Change, and the Process of Redefining Imagined Communities in Egypt." *International Journal of Middle Eastern Studies* 31 (1999): 81–94.

———. *Redefining the Egyptian Nation, 1930–1945*. Cambridge: Cambridge University Press, 2002.

al-Ghazali, Muhammad. *Huquq al-Insan bayn Taʿalim al-Islam wa-Iʿlan al-Umam al-Muttahida*. Cairo: al-Maktaba al-Tijariyya, 1963.

———. *Nazarat fi al-Qur'an*. Cairo: Mu'assasat al-Khanji, 1958.

al-Ghazali, Zaynab, and ʿAbd al-Hayy Faramawi. *Nazarat fi Kitab Allah*. Cairo: Dar al-Shuruq, 1994.

Gökarıksel, Banu, and Anna J Secor. "New Transnational Geographies of Islamism, Capitalism and Subjectivity: The Veiling-Fashion Industry in Turkey." *Area* 41, no. 1 (2009): 6–18.

Gonzalez-Quijano, Yves. *Les gens du livre: édition et champ intellectuel dans l'Égypte républicaine*. Paris: CNRS Éditions, 1998.

Gramsci, Antonio. *Selections from the Prison Notebooks*. Translated by Quintin Hoare and Geoffrey Nowell Smith. London: Lawrence & Wishart, 1971.

Grosz, Elizabeth A. *Volatile Bodies: Toward a Corporeal Feminism*. Bloomington: Indiana University Press, 1994.

El Guindi, Fadwa. *Veil: Modesty, Privacy, and Resistance*. Oxford: Berg, 1999.

———. "Veiling Infitah with Muslim Ethic: Egypt's Contemporary Islamic Movement." *Social Problems* 28, no. 4 (April 1, 1981): 465–85.

Habermas, Jürgen. *The Structural Transformation of the Public Sphere: An Inquiry into a Category of Bourgeois Society*. Translated by Thomas Burger. Cambridge, MA: MIT Press, 1991.

Haddad, Mikhayil Shafiq. *al-Tabarruj wa-l-Libas ʿind al-ʿArab: Dirasa fi al-Tabarruj wa-l-Libas Khilal al-ʿUsur al-Jahili, al-Umawi, al-ʿAbbasi*. Beirut: Dar al-ʿUlum al-ʿArabiyya, 2009.

Haddad, Yvonne Yazbeck. "The Case of the Feminist Movement." In *Contemporary Islam and the Challenge of History*. Albany: State University of New York Press, 1982.

Hafez, Sabry. *The Genesis of Arabic Narrative Discourse*. London: Saqi Books, 2001.

Hafez, Sherine. *An Islam of Her Own: Reconsidering Religion and Secularism in Women's Islamic Movements*. New York: NYU Press, 2011.

Haj, Samira. *Reconfiguring Islamic Tradition: Reform, Rationality, and Modernity*. Stanford, CA: Stanford University Press, 2008.

Hajjaji-Jarrah, Soraya. "Women's Modesty in Qurʾanic Commentaries: The Founding Discourse." In *The Muslim Veil in North America: Issues and Debates*, edited by Sajida Sultana Alvi, Sheila McDonough, and Homa Hoodfar. Toronto: Women's Press, 2003.

Hallaq, Wael B. *An Introduction to Islamic Law*. Cambridge: Cambridge University Press, 2009.

———. *Ibn Taymiyya against the Greek Logicians*. Oxford: Oxford University Press, 1993.

al-Halwani, Aba Firdaus. *Selamatkan Dirimu Dari Tabarruj: Pesan Buat Ukhti Muslima*. Yogyakarta: al-Mahalli Press, 1995.

Hamza, ʿAbd al-Latif. *al-Iʿlam fi Sadr al-Islam*. Cairo: Dar al-Fikr al-ʿArabi, 1971.

Hamza, Kariman. *Li-llah Ya Zamri: Min Adab al-Sira al-Dhatiyya*. Cairo: Matabiʿ al-Shuruq, 1999.

———. *al-Luʾluʾ wa-l-Marjan fi Tafsir al-Qurʾan*. Cairo: Maktabat al-Shuruq al-Dawliyya, 2010.

———. *Rihlati min al-Sufur ila al-Hijab*. Cairo: Dar al-Iʿtisam, 1981.

Hanafi, Hasan. *al-Din wa-l-Thawra fi Misr*. Cairo: Maktabat Madbuli, 1988.

Hanafi, Hasan, and Heba Raouf Ezzat, eds. "Ruʾa Mughayira: Nahw ʿAlam Akthar ʿAdlan wa-Dimuqratiyyan; al-Mawsim al-Thaqafi 2000–2001." In *al-ʿAwlama Nahw Ruʾa Mughayira*. Giza: Jamiʿat al-Qahira, Kulliyyat al-Iqtisad wa-l-ʿUlum al-Siyasiyya, Qism al-ʿUlum al-Siyasiyya, 2001.

Harb, Muhammad Talʿat. *Tarbiyat al-Marʾa wa-l-Hijab*. Cairo, 1899.

Hasan, Darwish Mustafa. *Fasl al-Khitab fi Masʾalat al-Hijab wa-l-Niqab*. Cairo: Dar al-Iʿtisam, 1987.

Hasan, Muhammad. *Hijab al-Marʾa al-Muslima*, n.d. http://ar.islamway.com/lesson/5598.

———. *al-Tabarruj*. CD-ROM, n.d.Hassan, Fayza. "Women's Destiny, Men's Voices." *Al-Ahram Weekly*. February 3, 2000, 467 edition.

Hasso, Frances S. *Consuming Desires: Family Crisis and the State in the Middle East*. Stanford, CA: Stanford University Press, 2010.

———. "Empowering Governmentalities Rather than Women: The Arab Human Development Report 2005 and Western Development Logics." *International Journal of Middle East Studies* 41, no. 1 (2009): 63–82.

Hatem, Mervat. "Egyptian Discourses on Gender and Political Liberalization: Do Secularist and Islamist Views Really Differ?" *Middle East Journal* 48, no. 4 (1994): 661–76.

———. "Gender and Islamism in the 1990s." *Middle East Report* no. 222 (2002): 44–47.

———. "Privatization and the Demise of State Feminism in Egypt." In *Mortgaging Women's Lives: Feminist Critiques of Structural Adjustment*, edited by Pamela Sparr. New York: Palgrave Macmillan, United Nations, 1994.

———. "Secularist and Islamist Discourses on Modernity in Egypt and the Evolution of the Postcolonial Nation-State." In *Islam, Gender, and Social Change*, edited by Yvonne Yazbeck Haddad and John L. Esposito. Oxford: Oxford University Press, 1997.

Haykal, Muhammad Husayn. *Hayat Muhammad*. Cairo: Matbaʿat Misr, 1935.

"Heba-Ezzat." Accessed March 21, 2012. http://www.heba-ezzat.com/.

"Heba Raouf Ezzat." *Facebook*. Accessed March 21, 2012. http://www.facebook.com/Heba.Raouf.Ezzat.

Hefnawi, F. "The Role of Research and Training in Family Planning Programmes." *Population Sciences* no. 4 (1983): 7–15.

Hegel, Friedrich. *Philosophy of Right*. Translated by T.M. Knox. Oxford: Oxford University Press, 1957.

Hijab, Nadia. *Womanpower: The Arab Debate on Women at Work*. Cambridge: Cambridge University Press, 1988.

Hirfi, Muhammad ibn ʿAli. *Bayn al-Shura al-Islamiyya wa-l-Dimuqratiyya al-Gharbiyya*. Cairo: Muʾassasat al-Mukhtar, 2005.

Hirschkind, Charles. *The Ethical Soundscape: Cassette Sermons and Islamic Counterpublics*. New York: Columbia University Press, 2009.

———. "Heresy or Hermeneutics: The Case of Nasr Hamid Abu Zayd." *Stanford Electronic Humanities Review* 5, no. 1. Contested Polities (February 26, 1996).

Hirschkind, Charles, and Brian Larkin. "Media and the Political Forms of Religion." *Social Text* 26, no. 3 (2008): 1–15.

Hizb al-ʿAdala wa-l-Hurriyya. "General Features of the Nahda (Renaissance) Project." *IkhwanWeb*, April 28, 2012. http://www.ikhwanweb.com/article.php?id=29932.

———. "Ihtimam Khass bi-l-Marʾa fi Mashruʿ al-Nahda." *IkhwanOnline*, April 28, 2012. http://www.ikhwanonline.com/new/president/Article.aspx?ArtID=107305&SecID=470.

Hizb al-ʿAdala wa-l-Tanmiya. "Qiyada bi-l-Nahda al-Tunisiyya: Tahrir al-Marʾa wa-Taʿziz Huquqiha Juzʾ min Risalat al-Islah wa-Binaʾ li-Harakatina." *Harakat al-Nahda*. March 7, 2013.

Hoffman-Ladd, Valerie J. "Polemics on the Modesty and Segregation of Women in Contemporary Egypt." *International Journal of Middle East Studies* 19, no. 1 (1987): 23–50.

Hoodfar, Homa. "Survival Strategies and the Political Economy of Low-Income Households in Cairo." In *Development, Change, and Gender in Cairo: A View from the Household*, edited by Diane Singerman and Homa Hoodfar. Bloomington: Indiana University Press, 1996.

hooks, bell. "Homeplace: A Site of Resistance." In *Yearning: Race, Gender, and Cultural Politics*. Boston: South End Press, 1990.

Hourani, Albert Habib. *Arabic Thought in the Liberal Age, 1798–1939*. Cambridge: Cambridge University Press, 1962.

Howeidy, Amira. "Safynaz Kazem: Born to Be Wild." *al-Ahram Weekly*. December 23, 1999.
Husayn, Muhammad al-Khidr. *al-Hurriyya fi al-Islam*. Cairo: Dar al-Iʿtisam, 1982.
Husayn, Taha. *Fi al-Shiʿr al-Jahili*. Cairo: Matbaʿat Dar al-Kutub al-Misriyya, 1926.
———. *Tajdid Dhikrat Abi al-ʿAlaʾ*. Cairo: Matbaʿat al-Maʿarif, 1937.
Ibn Baz, ʿAbd al-ʿAziz ibn ʿAbd Allah. *al-Hijab wa-l-Sufur fi al-Kitab wa-l-Sunna*. Cairo: Dar al-Kutub al-Salafiyya, 1986.
———. *al-Tabarruj wa-Khatar Musharakat al-Marʾa li-l-Rajul fi Maydan ʿAmalihi*. Cairo: Maktabat al-Salam, 1980.
Ibn Baz, ʿAbd al-ʿAziz ibn ʿAbd Allah, and Muhammad Salih ʿUthaymin. *Risalatan fi al-Hijab*. Jeddah: Dar al-Mujtamaʿ li-l-Nashr wa-l-Tawziʿ, 1986.
Ibn Ismaʿil, Muhammad ibn Ahmad. *ʿAwdat al-Hijab*. Riyadh: Dar Tayyiba, 1984.
———. *ʿAwdat al-Hijab*. Cairo: Dar al-Safwa, 1988.
———. *al-Marʾa bayn Takrim al-Islam wa-Ihanat al-Jahiliyya*. Cairo: Dar al-Safwa, 1990.
———. *Maʿrakat al-Hijab wa-l-Sufur*. Cairo: Dar al-Safwa, 1990.
Ibn Qayyim al-Jawziyya, Muhammad ibn Abi Bakr. *al-Tibb al-Nabawi*. Cairo: Dar Ihyaʾ al-Kutub al-ʿArabiyya, 1957.
Ibn Sina. "Kitab al-Nafs." In *Avicenna's De Anima*, edited by Fazlur Rahman. London: Oxford University Press, 1959.
Ibn Taymiyya, Ahmad ibn ʿAbd al-Halim. *Amrad al-Qulub wa-Shifaʾuha*. Cairo: al-Matbaʿa al-Salafiyya wa-Maktabatuha, 1966.
Ibn Taymiyya, Ahmad ibn ʿAbd al-Halim, and Muhammad Nasir al-Din Albani. *Hijab al-Marʾa wa-Libasuha fi al-Salat*. Cairo: s.n., 1974.
Ibn ʿUthaymin, Muhammad Salih. *al-Marʾa al-Muslima: Ahkam Fiqhiyya hawl al-Hijab wa-l-Dimaʾ al-Tabiʿiyya wa-Zakat al-Huli*. Cairo: Dar al-Safwa, 1987.
Ibrahim, Saad Eddin, Said Abdel-Messih, and Hans Lofgren. *Governance and Structural Adjustment: The Egyptian Case*. Cairo: Ibn Khaldoun Center for Development Studies, 1994.
Ilhami, Muhammad. "Muhammad Jalal Kishk." *Majallat al-Mujtamaʿ al-Kuwaytiyya*, August 26, 2009.
ʿImara, Muhammad. *al-Aʿmal al-Kamila li-l-Imam Muhammad ʿAbduh: Dirasa wa-Tahqiq*. Beirut: al-Muʾassasa al-ʿArabiyya li-l-Dirasat wa-l-Nashr, 1972–1974.
———. *al-Aʿmal al-Kamila li-Qasim Amin: Dirasa wa-Tahqiq*. Beirut: al-Muʾassasa al-ʿArabiyya li-l-Dirasat wa-l-Nashr, 1976.
———. *Fajr al-Yaqaza al-Qawmiyya*. Cairo: Dar al-Katib al-ʿArabi, 1967.
———. *Fi al-Tanwir al-Islami*. Cairo: Dar Nahdat Misr, 1997.
———. *al-Islam bayn al-Tanwir wa-l-Tazwir*. Cairo: Dar al-Shuruq, 1995.
———. *al-Islam wa-l-Marʾa fi Raʾy al-Imam Muhammad ʿAbduh*. Cairo: al-Qahira li-l-Thaqafa al-ʿArabiyya, 1975.
———. *al-Islam wa-l-Marʾa fi Raʾy al-Imam Muhammad ʿAbduh*. Cairo: Dar al-Hilal, 1979.
———. *Qasim Amin wa-Tahrir al-Marʾa*. Cairo: Dar al-Hilal, 1980.

———. *Qasim Amin wa-Tahrir al-Mar'a wa-l-Tamaddun al-Islami*. Beirut: Dar al-Wahda, 1985.
———. *Rifaʿa al-Tahtawi: Ra'id al-Tanwir fi al-ʿAsr al-Hadith*. Cairo: Dar al-Mustaqbal al-ʿArabi, 1984.
———. *Shubuhat wa-Ijabat hawl Makanat al-Mar'a fi al-Islam*. Cairo: al-Majlis al-Aʿla li-l-Shu'un al-Islamiyya, 2001.
———. *al-Tahrir al-Islami li-l-Mar'a*. Cairo: Dar al-Shuruq, 2002.
———. *al-Tariq ila al-Yaqaza al-Islamiyya*. Cairo: Dar al-Shuruq, 1990.
———. *Tayyarat al-Yaqaza al-Islamiyya al-Haditha*. Cairo: Dar al-Hilal, 1982.
———. *al-Umma al-ʿArabiyya wa Qadiyyat al-Tawhid: Dirasat fi al-Qawmiyya wa-l-Umma*. Cairo: al-Dar al-Misriyya li-l-Ta'lif wa-l-Tarjama, 1966.
———. *al-ʿUruba fi al-ʿAsr al-Hadith: Dirasat fi al-Qawmiyya wa-l-Umma*. Cairo: Dar al-Katib al-ʿArabi, 1967.
Inati, Shams. "Soul in Islamic Philosophy." *Philosophia Islamica*, n.d. http://www.muslimphilosophy.com/ip/rep/H010.htm.
International Center for Research on Women. *Keeping Women Out: A Structural Analysis of Women's Employment in Developing Countries*. Washington, DC: USAID, 1980.
International Islamic Center for Population Studies and Research, al-Azhar. *Makanat al-Mar'a fi al-Usra al-Islamiyya*. Cairo: International Islamic Center for Population Studies and Research, al-Azhar, 1975.
International Labour Office. *Employment and Conditions of Work of African Women: Second African Regional Conference Addis Ababa 1964*. Geneva: International Labour Office, 1964.
Jamal, Ahmad. "Manal Abu al-Hassan: The Security of Woman in the Freedom and Justice Party Focuses on All Groups of Women." *IkhwanOnline*. Accessed October 12, 2012. http://www.ikhwanonline.com/new/Article.aspx?ArtID=123235&SecID=323.
Jawad, Haifaa. "Islamic Feminism: Leadership Roles and Public Representation." *Hawwa* 7, no. 1 (2009): 1–24.
Jawish, ʿAbd al-ʿAziz. *al-Islam Din al-Fitra wa-l-Hurriyya*. Cairo: Dar al-Maʿarif, 1968.
———. *Athar al-Qur'an fi Tahrir al-Fikr al-Bashari*. Edited by Muhammad ʿImara. Cairo: Majallat al-Azhar, 2012.
Jones, Carla. "Images of Desire: Creating Virtue and Value in an Indonesian Islamic Lifestyle Magazine." *Journal of Middle East Women's Studies* 6, no. 3 (Fall 2010): 91–117.
Jouili, Jeanette S. "Beyond Emancipation: Subjectivities and Ethics among Women in Europe's Islamic Revival Communities." *Feminist Review* 98, no. 1 (July 2011): 47–64.
———. "Pious Practice and Secular Constraints: Women in the Islamic Revival in France and Germany." Ms., forthcoming, n.d.
Jouili, Jeanette S., and Schirin Amir-Moazami. "Knowledge, Empowerment and Religious Authority among Pious Muslim Women in France and Germany." *Muslim World* 96, no. 4 (2006): 617–42.
Jumhuriyyat Misr al-ʿArabiyya. "al-Dustur," 1956.
———. "al-Dustur," December 26, 2012.

———. *al-Marʾa al-Misriyya*. Cairo: Wizarat al-Iʿlam, al-Hayʾa al-ʿAmma li-l-Istiʿlamat, 1985.

Juynboll, G.H.A. "Sunan." *Encyclopaedia of Islam*, 2nd ed. Leiden: Brill Online, n.d.

———. "Sunna." *Encyclopaedia of Islam*, 2nd ed. Leiden: Brill Online, n.d.

Kahlawi, ʿAblah Muhammad. *al-ʿAmal fi al-Islam wa-Hukm ʿAmal al-Marʾa wa-l-Hadath*. Cairo: Jamiʿat al-Azhar, Kulliyyat al-Banat al-Islamiyya, Markaz Dirasat al-Marʾa wa-l-Tanmiya, 1979.

Kandiyoti, Deniz. "Bargaining with Patriarchy." *Gender and Society* 2, no. 3 (September 1988): 274–90.

Karam, Azza M. *Women, Islamisms and State: Contemporary Feminisms in Egypt*. New York: Palgrave Macmillan, 1997.

Kawakibi, ʿAbd al-Rahman. *Tabaʾiʿ al-Istibdad wa-Masariʿ al-Istiʿbad*. Edited by Muhammad ʿImara. Cairo: Matabiʿ Ruz al-Yusuf, 2011.

Kazim, Safinaz. *ʿAn al-Sijn wa-l-Hurriyya*. Madinat Nasr, Cairo: al-Zahraʾ li-l-Iʿlam al-ʿArabi, 1986.

———. *Fi Masʾalat al-Sufur wa-l-Hijab*. Cairo: Maktabat Wahba, 1982.

———. "al-Fiminizm: Harakat al-Ghetto al-Nisaʾi." *al-Muqattam*, June 24, 1994, 45.

———. *al-Haqiqa wa-Ghasil al-Mukh fi Qadaya Muʿasira*. Madinat Nasr, Cairo: al-Zahraʾ li-l-Iʿlam al-ʿArabi, 1985.

———. *al-Khadiʿa al-Nasiriyya: Min Awraq Shaʿb Misr al-Sirriyya, Shahadat Muwatina Misriyya ʿala Sanawat ʿAshatha*. Cairo: Dar al-Iʿtisam, 1984.

———. *Kitabat Ruʾa wa-Dhat*. Cairo: al-Hayʾa al-Misriyya al-ʿAmma li-l-Kitab, 2003.

———. *Risaliyyat fi al-Bayt al-Nabawi*. Cairo: Dar al-Mukhtar al-Islami, 1984.

———. *Rumantikiyyat*. Cairo: Dar al-Hilal, 1970.

———. *Sanʿat Latafa*. Cairo: Dar al-ʿAin li-l-Nashr, 2007.

———. *Talabib al-Kitaba*. Cairo: Dar al-Hilal, 1994.

———. *Yawmiyyat Baghdad: 1975–1980*. London: Open Press, 1984.

Keane, Webb. *Christian Moderns: Freedom and Fetish in the Mission Encounter*. Berkeley: University of California Press, 2007.

Khalaf Allah, Muhammad Ahmad. *al-Fann al-Qisasi fi al-Qurʾan al-Karim*. Cairo: Maktabat al-Nahda al-Misriyya, 1950.

Khalidi, Salah ʿAbd al-Fattah. *Nazariyyat al-Taswir al-Fanni ʿind Sayyid Qutb*. Amman: Dar al-Furqan, 1983.

Khalifa, Ahmad Muhammad. *Raʾy Muwatin Fi Tanzim al-Usra*. Cairo, 1966.

Khamis, Muhammad ʿAtiyya. *al-Marʾa wa-l-Huquq al-Siyasiyya wa-l-Aʿmal al-ʿAmma: Raʾy al-Hayat wa-l-Jamʿiyyat al-Islamiyya fi Misr*. Cairo: Dar al-Ansar, 1978.

Khatab, Sayed. *The Political Thought of Sayyid Qutb: The Theory of Jahiliyyah*. London: Routledge, 2006.

El-Kholy, Heba Aziz. *Defiance and Compliance: Negotiating Gender in Low-Income Cairo*. New York: Berghahn Books, 2002.

———. *Women in Development: Assessment of Selected USAID-Financed Projects*. Washington, DC: USAID Office of Women in Development, March 9, 1987.

al-Khuli, Amin. *Manahij Tajdid fi al-Nahw wa-l-Balagha wa-l-Tafsir wa-l-Adab*. Cairo: Dar al-Maʿarif, 1961.

———. *Ra'y fi Abi al-ʿAla'*. Cairo: Jamaʿat al-Kuttab, 1945.
———. *al-Tafsir: Maʿalim Hayatihi, Manhajuhu al-Yawm*. Cairo: Jamaʿat al-Kitab, 1944.
Kishk, Muhammad Jalal. *al-Ghazw al-Fikri*. Mafahim Islamiyya. Cairo: Maktabat Dar al-ʿUruba, 1964.
———. *al-Hurriyya fi al-Usra al-Muslima*. Nahw Waʿy Islami. Cairo: al-Mukhtar al-Islami, 1979.
———. *Jahalat ʿAsr al-Tanwir: Qira'a fi Fikr Qasim Amin wa-ʿAli ʿAbd al-Raziq*. Cairo: Maktabat al-Turath al-Islami, 1990.
———. *al-Jihad: Thawratuna al-Da'ima*. Beirut: Dar al-Irshad, 1970.
———. *Khawatir Muslim fi al-Mas'ala al-Jinsiyya*. Cairo: M.J. Kishk, 1984.
———. *al-Naksa wa-l-Ghazw al-Fikri*. Beirut: Dar al-Katib al-ʿArabi, 1969.
———. *al-Qawmiyya wa-l-Ghazw al-Fikri*. Beirut: Dar al-Irshad, 1970.
———. *Rusi wa-Amriki fi al-Yaman*. Cairo: Wakalat al-Sihafa al-Afriqiyya, 1957.
———. *Tahrir al-Mar'a al-Muharrara*. Nahw Waʿy Islami. Cairo: al-Mukhtar al-Islami, 1979.
Kishk, Muhammad Jalal, and Nasr Hamid Abu Zayd. "Akhir Ma Nutiqa bihi Jalal Kishk." *al-Shaʿb*, December 17, 1993.
Kooij, C. "Bint al-Shati': A Suitable Case for Biography?" in *The Challenge of the Middle East*, edited by Ibrahim El-Sheikh, C. Aart van de Koppel, and Rudolph Peters. Amsterdam: University of Amsterdam, 1982.
Lajnat al-Khidmat. *Tanmiyat al-Mar'a ka-Madkhal li-l-Tanmiya al-Shamila*. Silsilat Taqarir Majlis al-Shura. Cairo: Matbuʿat al-Shaʿb, 1984.
Lalevée, Thierry. "Egypt and the IMF: Is a Break Coming?" *Executive Intelligence Review* 12, no. 39 (October 4, 1985): 11.
Landes, Joan B. "The Public and the Private Sphere: A Feminist Reconsideration." In *Feminists Read Habermas: Gendering the Subject of Discourse*. New York: Routledge, 1995.
Lane, Edward William. *Arabic-English Lexicon*. Beirut: Librairie du Liban, 1968.
Lasch, Christopher. *Haven in a Heartless World: The Family Besieged*. New York: Norton, 1995.
League of Arab States, UNICEF, and Markaz al-Dawli li-l-Taʿlim al-Wazifi li-l-Kitab fi al-ʿAlam al-ʿArabi. *al-Mar'a al-ʿArabiyya wa-l-Tanmiya al-Qawmiyya: Halqa Dirasiyya*. Cairo: UNICEF, 1972.
LeVine, Mark. "The UN Arab Human Development Report: A Critique." *Middle East Research and Information Project* (July 26, 2002).
Lewis, Reina. "Marketing Muslim Lifestyle: A New Media Genre." *Journal of Middle East Women's Studies* 6, no. 3 (Fall 2010): 58–90.
Lia, Brynjar. *The Society of the Muslim Brothers in Egypt: The Rise of an Islamic Mass Movement 1928–1942*. Reading, UK: Ithaca Press, 2006.
Lorde, Audre. *Sister Outsider: Essays and Speeches*. New York: Ten Speed Press, 1984.
Losurdo, Domenico. *Liberalism: A Counter-History*. Translated by Gregory Elliott. London: Verso, 2014.
Lukács, Georg. *The Theory of the Novel: A Historico-Philosophical Essay on the Forms of Great Epic Literature*. Translated by Anna Bostock. Cambridge, MA: MIT Press, 1974.

Lutfi, ʿAli. *al-Tanmiya al-Iqtisadiyya: Dirasa Tahliliyya.* Cairo: Maktabat ʿAin Shams, 1982.
———. *al-Tatawwur al-Iqtisadi: Dirasa Tahliliyya li-Tarikh Urubba wa Misr al-Iqtisadi.* Cairo: Dar al-Qurʿan, 1976.
———. *La technique élevée à la suprême puissance: la planification de l'économie.* Geneva: Droz, 1964.
MacLeod, Arlene Elowe. *Accommodating Protest: Working Women, the New Veiling, and Change in Cairo.* New York: Columbia University Press, 1991.
Mahmood, Saba. *Politics of Piety: The Islamic Revival and the Feminist Subject.* Princeton, NJ: Princeton University Press, 2005.
———. "Preface to the 2012 Edition." In *Politics of Piety: The Islamic Revival and the Feminist Subject.* Princeton, NJ: Princeton University Press, 2012.
———. "Questioning Liberalism, Too: A Response to 'Islam and the Challenge of Democracy.' " *Boston Review* (May 2003).
———. "Secularism, Hermeneutics, Empire: The Politics of Islamic Reformation." *Public Culture* 18, no. 2 (2006): 323–47.
al-Majlis al-Aʿla li-l-Thaqafa. *Miʾat ʿAm ʿAla Tahrir al-Marʾa.* Cairo: al-Majlis al-Aʿla li-l-Thaqafa, 2001.
al-Majlis al-Qawmi li-l-Marʾa. *al-Marʾa wa-Suq al-ʿAmal: al-Qitaʿ al-Rasmi wa-Ghayr al-Rasmi.* Cairo: al-Majlis al-Qawmi li-l-Marʾa, 2001.
Malti-Douglas, Fedwa. "Faces of Sin: Corporeal Geographies in Contemporary Islamist Discourse." In *Religious Reflections on the Human Body,* edited by Jane Marie Law. Bloomington: Indiana University Press, 1995.
———. *Medicines of the Soul: Female Bodies and Sacred Geographies in a Transnational Islam.* Berkeley: University of California Press, 2001.
———. *Woman's Body, Woman's Word: Gender and Discourse in Arabo-Islamic Writing.* Princeton, NJ: Princeton University Press, 1991.
———. *A Woman and Her Sufis.* Washington, DC: Georgetown University Center for Contemporary Arab Studies, 1995.
Mantena, Karuna. *Alibis of Empire: Henry Maine and the Ends of Liberal Imperialism.* Princeton, NJ: Princeton University Press, 2010.
Maraghi, Abu al-Wafaʾ. *Mabadiʾ al-Islam fi Tanzim al-Usra.* Cairo: al-Majlis al-Aʿla li-l-Shuʾun al-Islamiyya, 1962.
Maraʿi, Samah Hasan. *Yaqazat al-ʿIffa: Rihlati min al-Sufur ila al-Hijab.* Beirut: Dar al-ʿUlum li-l-Tahqiq wa-l-Tibaʿa wa-l-Nashr wa-l-Tawziʿ, 2004.
Masʿud, Jibran. *al-Raʾid: Muʿjam Lughawi ʿAsri.* Beirut: Dar al-ʿIlm, 1965.
McLarney, Ellen. "The Islamic Public Sphere and the Discipline of Adab." *International Journal of Middle Eastern Studies* 42, no. 4 (Fall 2011).
———. "Private Is Political: Women and Family in Intellectual Islam." Special Issue on Arab Feminisms. *Feminist Theory* (2010): 129–48.
———. "The Socialist Romance of the Postcolonial Arabic Novel." *Research in African Literatures* 40, no. 3 (2009): 186–205.
———. "Women's Rights in the Egyptian Constitution: (Neo)Liberalism's Family Values," May 22, 2013. http://www.jadaliyya.com/pages/index/11852/womens-rights-in-the-egyptian-constitution_(neo)li.
McMorris, Christine McCarthy. "Grappling with Islam: Bush and the Burqa." *Religion in the News* 5, no. 1 (Spring 2002).

Meet Asmaa Mahfouz and the Vlog That Helped Spark the Revolution, 2011. http://www.youtube.com/watch?v = SgjIgMdsEuk&feature = youtube_gdata _player.

Mehta, Uday Singh. *Liberalism and Empire: A Study in Nineteenth-Century British Liberal Thought*. Chicago: University of Chicago Press, 1999.

Mendieta, Eduardo, and Jonathan VanAntwerpen, eds. *The Power of Religion in the Public Sphere*. New York: Columbia University Press, 2011.

Mies, Maria. *Patriarchy and Accumulation on a World Scale: Women in the International Division of Labour*. New York: Palgrave Macmillan, 1999.

Ministry of Information. *al-Marʾa al-Misriyya: Mishwar Tawil min al-Hijab ila ʿAsr al-ʿUbur*. Cairo: Public Information Council, 1976.

Mink, Gwendolyn. *Welfare's End*. Ithaca, NY: Cornell University Press, 2002.

Mir-Hosseini, Ziba. "Beyond 'Islam' vs 'Feminism.' " *IDS Bulletin* 42, no. 1 (2011): 67–77.

Misri, Sana. *Khalf al-Hijab: Mawqif al-Jamaʿat al-Islamiyya min Qadiyyat al-Marʾa*. al-Qasr al-ʿAyni, Cairo: Sinaʿ li-l-Nashr, 1989.

Mitchell, Timothy. "L'expérience de l'emprisonement dans le discours islamiste: une lecture d'Ayyam min Hayati de Zaynab al-Ghazzali." In *Intellectuels et militants de l'Islam contemporain*, edited by Gilles Kepel and Yann Richard. Paris: Éditions du Seuil, 1990.

———. *Rule of Experts: Egypt, Techno-Politics, Modernity*. Berkeley: University of California Press, 2002.

Mittermaier, Amira. "Dreams from Elsewhere: Muslim Subjectivities beyond the Trope of Self-Cultivation." *Journal of the Royal Anthropological Institute* 18, no. 2 (2012): 247–65.

Moghadam, Valentine M. "Islamic Feminism and Its Discontents." *Signs: Journal of Women in Culture and Society* 27, no. 4 (2002): 1135–71.

———. *Modernizing Women: Gender and Social Change in the Middle East*. Boulder, CO: Lynne Rienner, 2003.

———. *Women, Work, and Economic Reform in the Middle East and North Africa*. Boulder, CO: Lynne Rienner, 1998.

Mojab, Shahrzad. "Theorizing the Politics of 'Islamic Feminism.' " *Feminist Review* no. 69 (2001): 124–46.

Moll, Yasmin. "Islamic Televangelism: Religion, Media, and Visuality in Contemporary Egypt." *Arab Media and Society* no. 10 (2010): 1–27.

Momani, Bessma. *IMF-Egyptian Debt Negotiations*. Cairo Paper in Social Science. Cairo: American University in Cairo Press, 2005.

Moosa, Ebrahim. "The Ethical Soundscape: Cassette Sermons and Islamic Counterpublics. By Charles Hirschkind." *Journal of the American Academy of Religion* 80, no. 1 (2012): 252–54.

———. *Ghazali and the Poetics of Imagination*. Chapel Hill, NC: University of North Carolina Press, 2005.

Moyn, Samuel. *The Last Utopia: Human Rights in History*. Cambridge, MA: Belknap Press of Harvard University Press, 2012.

Muderrisoglu, Gaye, and Jonathan Hanson. "Authoritarian States and IMF Conditionality." Presented at the Midwest Political Science Association, Chicago, April 22, 2010.

Muhammad, Yahya. *al-Taswir al-Islami li-l-Mujtamaʿ: Dirasa Ijtimaʿiyya li-Kull min al-Tasawwur wa-l-Manhaj wa-l-Qawanin*. Beirut: Muʾassasat Ahl al-Bayt, 1980.

Muhriz, Jamal Muhammad. *al-Taswir al-Islami wa-Madarisuhu*. Cairo: al-Muʾassasa al-Misriyya al-ʿAmma, 1962.

Muqaddam, Muhammad ibn Ahmad ibn Ismaʿil. *Bal al-Niqab Wajib! Al-Radd al-ʿIlmi ʿala Kitab "Tadhkir al-Ashab bi-Tahrim al-Niqab."* Alexandria: Dar al-Manar al-Salafi, 1991.

———. *Dafʿ al-Saʾil ʿala Mashruʿiyyat al-Hijab al-Kamil*. Alexandria: Dar al-Khulafaʾ al-Rashidin, 2009.

———. *al-Hayaʾ: Khuluq al-Islam*. Cairo: Dar al-Haramayn li-l-Tibaʿa, 1993.

Mustafa, Iman Muhammad. *Imbaraturiyyat al-Nisaʾ al-ʿAmilat*. Madinat Nasr, Cairo: al-Zahraʾ li-l-Iʿlam al-ʿArabi, 1991.

———. "*Imbaraturiyyat al-Nisaʾ al-ʿAmilat*." *al-Ahram al-Iqtisadi* 1077 (September 4, 1989).

Mustafa, Kamal Judah Abu al-Maʿati. *Wazifat al-Marʾa fi Nazar al-Islam*. Cairo: Dar al-Huda li-l-Tibaʿa, 1980.

Nadir, Muthni Amin, and Muhammad ʿImara. *Harakat Tahrir al-Marʾa min al-Musawaa ila al-Jindar: Dirasa Islamiyya Naqdiyya*. Cairo: Dar al-Qalam, 2004.

Nadwat al-Marʾa wa-l-Tanmiya al-Qawmiyya: Cairo, 10–11 Nufimbir 1984. Cairo: UNESCO, al-Markaz al-Iqlimi al-ʿArabi li-l-Buhuth wa-l-Tawthiq fi al-ʿUlum al-Ijtimaʿiyya, 1984.

El-Naggar, Mona. "Family Life According to the Brotherhood." *New York Times*, September 4, 2012. http://www.nytimes.com/2012/09/05/world/middleeast/05iht-letter05.html.

Najmabadi, Afsaneh. "Crafting an Educated Housewife in Iran." In *Remaking Women: Feminism and Modernity in the Middle East*, edited by Lila Abu-Lughod. Princeton, NJ: Princeton University Press, 1998.

Nasif, ʿImad, and Amal Khudayr. *Fannanat Taʾibat: Iʿtirafat lam Tunshar*. Cairo: Dar al-Kutub wa-l-Wathaʾiq, 1991.

Nelson, Cynthia. *Doria Shafik, Egyptian Feminist: A Woman Apart*. Cairo: University of Cairo Press, 1996.

Nichols, Bill. "Film Theory and the Revolt against Master Narratives." In *Reinventing Film Studies*, edited by Christine Gledhill and Linda Williams, 34–52. Oxford: Oxford University Press, 2000.

Nicholson, Linda. *Gender and History*. New York: Columbia University Press, 1986.

Nieuwkerk, Karin van. *Performing Piety: Singers and Actors in Egypt's Islamic Revival*. Austin: University of Texas Press, 2013.

Nye, Joseph. *Soft Power: The Means to Success in World Politics*. New York: PublicAffairs, 2005.

Okin, Susan Moller. *Justice, Gender, and the Family*. New York: Basic Books, 1991.

Omran, Abdel R. *Family Planning in the Legacy of Islam*. London: Routledge, United Nations Population Fund, 1992.

"100 Most Powerful Arab Women 2011." *ArabianBusiness*. Accessed March 21, 2012. http://www.arabianbusiness.com/100-most-powerful-arab-women-2011-384182.html?view=profile&itemid=384141.

Pateman, Carole. "Feminist Critiques of the Public/Private Dichotomy." In *Public and Private in Social Life*, edited by S. I. Benn and G. F. Gaus. London: St. Martin's Press, 1983.

———. *The Sexual Contract*. Stanford, CA: Stanford University Press, 1988.

Pitts, Jennifer. *A Turn to Empire: The Rise of Imperial Liberalism in Britain and France*. Princeton, NJ: Princeton University Press, 2006.

al-Qaradawi, Yusuf. "Fatwa hawl Musharakat al-Nisaʾ fi al-ʿAmaliyyat al-Istishhadiyya." *Filastin al-Muslima*, March 2002.

al-Qaradawi, Yusuf, et al. *Tahrir al-Marʾa fi al-Islam: Muʾtamar 22–23 Fabrayir 2003*. al-Safat, Kuwait: Dar al-Qalam, al-Lajna al-Islamiyya al-ʿAlamiyya li-l-Marʾa wa-l-Tifl, 2004.

Qindil, Amani, and ʿUla Abu Zayd. *al-Marʾa al-Misriyya wa-l-ʿAmal al-ʿAmm: Ruʾya Mustaqbaliyya*. Cairo: Jamiʿat al-Qahira, Kulliyyat al-Iqtisad wa-l-ʿUlum al-Siyasiyya, Markaz al-Buhuth wa-l-Dirasat al-Siyasiyya, 1995.

Qutb, Muhammad. *Qadiyyat Tahrir al-Marʾa*. Nahw Fiqh Rashid. Fairfax, Va.: Maʿhad al-ʿUlum al-Islamiyya wa-l-ʿArabiyya fi Amrika, 1990.

Qutb, Sayyid. *al-ʿAdala al-Ijtimaʿiyya fi al-Islam*. Cairo: Maktabat Misr, 1949.

———. *al-ʿAdala al-Ijtimaʿiyya fi al-Islam*. Cairo: Dar al-Shuruq, 1975.

———. *In the Shade of the Qurʾan*. Trans. Adil Salahi and Ashur Shamis. Leicester: Islamic Foundation, 2001.

———. *Khasaʾis al-Tasawwur al-Islami wa-Muqawwimatuhu*. Cairo: ʿIsa al-Babi al-Halabi, 1962.

———. *al-Shatiʾ al-Majhul*. Cairo: 1932.

———. *Social Justice in Islam*. Oneonta, NY: Islamic Publications International, 2000.

———. *al-Taswir al-Fanni fi al-Qurʾan*. Cairo: Dar al-Maʿarif, 1945.

al-Quwwa al-Naʿima. Waqf Foundation, 2011. http://www.youtube.com/watch?v=UGcNTE1T1jo&feature=youtube_gdata_player.

"al-Quwwa al-Naʿima: Siyasat Sitt al-Hajja." *TheRamadanComedy*, August 2, 2011.

Rabiʿ, Muhammad Shihata. *Dawr al-Umm fi ʿAmaliyyat al-Tatbiʿ al-Ijtimaʿi*. Cairo: Jamiʿat al-Azhar, Kulliyyat al-Banat al-Islamiyya, Markaz Dirasat al-Marʾa wa-l-Tanmiya, 1977.

Radwan, Zaynab. *Bahth Zahirat al-Hijab bayn al-Jamiʿiyyat*. Cairo: al-Markaz al-Qawmi li-l-Buhuth al-Ijtimaʿiyya wa-l-Jinaʾiyya, 1982.

———. *Bahth Zahirat al-Hijab bayn al-Jamiʿiyyat: al-Buʿd al-Dini li-Zahirat al-Hijab bayn al-Mihniyyat*. Cairo: al-Markaz al-Qawmi li-l-Buhuth al-Ijtimaʿiyya wa-l-Jinaʾiyya, 1984.

Rahman, Fazlur, ed. *Avicenna's Psychology*. London: Oxford University Press, 1952.

Ramdun, ʿAbd al-Baqi. *Khatar al-Tabarruj wa-l-Ikhtilat*. Beirut: Muʾassasat al-Risala, 1974.

Raouf Ezzat, Heba. "al-Dawla al-Diniyya wa-l-Dawla al-Madaniyya." Presented at the Barnamaj al-Tathqif al-Siyasi, Bibliotheca Alexandrina, May 19, 2011.

———. "DrHRaouf's Channel—YouTube." Accessed March 21, 2012. http://www.youtube.com/user/DrHRaouf?ob=0&feature=results_main.

———. "Hawl al-Dawla wa-l-Mujtamaʿ wa-l-Umma." Center for Civilization Studies and Dialogue of Cultures, Faculty of Economics and Political Science, Cairo University, May 16, 2011.

———. *Hawl Mawaqif al-Quwa al-Siyasiyya, Khassatan al-Harakat al-Islamiyya wa-l-Harakat al-Diniyya, min Tamkin al-Nisaʾ fi al-Buldan al-ʿArabiyya*. Background Paper. Arab Human Development Report: Toward the Rise of Women in the Arab World, 2005.

———. "Hiwarat fi-l-Nahda: Nahw Idrak Jadid li-l-Marhala." Yaqazat al-Fikr and al-Markaz al-Thaqafi al-ʿArabi bi-Ittihad al-Atbaʾ al-ʿArab, July 20, 2012.

———. "Islam and Equality." In *Islam and Equality: Debating the Future of Women's and Minority Rights in the Middle East and North Africa*. New York: Lawyers Committee for Human Rights, 1998.

———. "Islamic Media in a Secular Environment." Presented at the Deutsche Welle Global Media Forum 2011: Human Rights in a Globalized World, Challenges for the Media, Bonn, Germany, June 20, 2011.

———. *al-Marʾa wa-l-ʿAmal al-Siyasi: Ruʾya Islamiyya*. Herndon, VA: Institute of Islamic Thought, 1995.

———. "al-Marʾa wa-Mustaqbal al-ʿAmal al-Siyasi." *al-Maktaba al-ʿAmma, al-Mahalla al-Kubra*, April 20, 2011.

———. "al-Nahda wa-Usturat al-Tahakkum al-Kamil." *al-Wasat*. April 21, 2009.

———. "Politics of Informality: On the Power of the Public Spheres of Egypt." Alwaleed Bin Talal Center for Muslim-Christian Understanding, Georgetown University, Washington, DC, February 15, 2012.

———. "al-Quwwa al-Naʿima." Al-Jazeera Center for Studies, October 13, 2011. http://studies.aljazeera.net/files/2011/08/20118872345213170.htm.

———. "Rethinking Secularism . . . Rethinking Feminism." *SuhaibWebb.com Your Virtual Mosque* (December 11, 2008). http://www.suhaibwebb.com/islam-studies/rethinking-secularism-%E2%80%A6-rethinking-feminism-by-dr-heba-raouf-ezzat/.

———. "Secularism, the State and the Social Bond: The Withering Away of the Family." In *Islam and Secularism in the Middle East*, edited by Azzam Tamimi and John L. Esposito. New York: New York University Press, 2000.

———. "al-Siyasi wa-l-Insani wa-l-Ghayr Rasmi." Presented at the Peaceful Revolution in Egypt: Lessons Learned, Center for Civilization Studies and Dialogue of Cultures, Faculty of Economics and Political Science, Cairo University, June 6, 2011.

———. "Tanazuʿ al-Afkar . . . al-Dawla al-Madaniyya (Contending Ideas . . . the Civil State)." Accessed April 5, 2012. http://www.heba-ezzat.com.

———. "Toward a Culture of Shura: Citizenship and Democracy Reform from a Muslim Woman's Perspective." *Arab Reform Initiative*. Critical Dialogue between Different Intellectual Movements: The Experience in the Arab World (July 2010). http://www.arab-reform.net/.

———. "al-Usra wa-l-Taghyir al-Siyasi: Ruʾya Islamiyya." *Islamiyyat al-Maʿrifa* 2 (2007). http://www.eiiit.org/resources/eiiit/eiiit/eiiit_article_read.asp?articleID=804.

Raouf Ezzat, Heba, and Ahmed Mohamed Abdallah. "Towards an Islamically Democratic Secularism." In *Faith and Secularism*, edited by Rosemary Bechler. London: British Council, 2004.

Raouf Ezzat, Heba, and Emran Qureshi. "Are Sharia Laws and Human Rights Compatible?" *Qantara.de*, October 4, 2004. http://en.qantara.de/Are-Sharia-Laws-and-Human-Rights-Compatible/7606c43/index.html.

Raouf Ezzat, Heba, and ʿUla Abu Zayd. *al-Muwatana al-Misriyya wa-Mustaqbal al-Dimuqratiyya: Ruʾa Jadida li-ʿAlam Mutaghayyir: Aʿmal al-Muʾtamar al-Sanawi al-Sabiʿ ʿAshar li-l-Buhuth al-Siyasiyya, 21–23 Disimbir 2003*. Giza: Jamiʿat al-Qahira, Kulliyyat al-Iqtisad wa-l-ʿUlum al-Siyasiyya, Markaz al-Buhuth wa-l-Dirasat al-Siyasiyya, 2005.

Rached, Tahani. *Four Women of Egypt*. Cairo: Elixir Productions, 2006.

Rida, Abeya to Shaykh Fathi Amin Uthman. "Sira Dhatiyya li-l-Sayyida Niʿmat Sidqi," n.d.

Rida, Rashid. *Nidaʾ li-l-Jins al-Latif*. Cairo: Matbaʿat al-Manar, 1932.

Ridha, Niʿmah Rasyid. *Tabarruj*. Jakarta: Pustaka Al-Kautsar, 1990.

"Risala ila ʿAyni: Adab al-Nazar." *El Eman*, n.d. http://www.al-eman.com.

"Risala ila ʿAyni: Adab al-Nazar." *Kalemat*, n.d. http://www.kalemat.org/sections.php?so = va&aid = 546.

"Risala ila ʿAyni: Adab al-Nazar." *Musslima*, n.d. http://musslima.net/forum/showthread.php?t = 4523.

"Risala ila ʿAyni: Adab al-Nazar," n.d. http://fr-fr.facebook.com/note.php?note_id = 149966085063928.

Roded, Ruth. "Bint al-Shatiʾ's 'Wives of the Prophet': Feminist or Feminine?" *British Journal of Middle Eastern Studies* 33, no. 1 (2006): 51–66.

Roschelle, Anne R. "Gender, Family Structure, and Social Structure: Racial Ethnic Families in the United States." In *Revisioning Gender*, edited by Myra Marx Ferree, Judith Lorber, and Beth B. Hess. Thousand Oaks, CA: Sage, 1999.

Rose, Nikolas S. *Powers of Freedom: Reframing Political Thought*. Cambridge: Cambridge University Press, 1999.

Rosen, Lawrence. *Bargaining for Reality: The Construction of Social Relations in a Muslim Community*. Chicago: University of Chicago Press, 1984.

Rugh, Andrea B. *Family in Contemporary Egypt*. Syracuse, NY: Syracuse University Press, 1984.

———. *Women in Development Projects in Egypt: Final Report*. Washington, DC: USAID, May 31, 1979.

El Saadawi, Nawal. *Imraʾa ʿind Nuqtat al-Sifr*. Beirut: Dar al-Adab, 1977.

———. *al-Wajh al-ʿAri li-l-Marʾa al-ʿArabiyya*. Beirut: al-Muʾassasa al-ʿArabiyya li-l-Dirasat wa-l-Nashr, 1977.

El Saadawi, Nawal, and Heba Raouf Ezzat. *al-Marʾa wa-l-Din wa-l-Akhlaq*. Damascus: Dar al-Fikr, 2000.

Sabʿ, Tawfiq Muhammad. *Nufus wa-Durus fi-Itar al-Taswir al-Qurʾani*. Cairo: Majmaʿ al-Buhuth al-Islamiyya, 1971.

Safran, Nadav. "The Abolition of the Shariʿa Courts in Egypt." *Muslim World* 48 (1958): 20–28.

Sahiron, Syamsuddin. "An Examination of Bint al-Shatiʾ's Method of Interpreting the Qurʾan." MA thesis, McGill University, 1998.

Sakr, Naomi. *Satellite Realms: Transnational Television, Globalization and the Middle East*. London: I. B. Tauris, 2002.

Salih, Sara. "On Judith Butler and Performativity." In *Sexualities and Communication in Everyday Life*, edited by Karen E. Lovaas and Mercilee M. Jenkins. Thousand Oaks, CA: Sage Publications, 2007.

Salime, Zakia. *Between Feminism and Islam: Human Rights and Sharia Law in Morocco*. Minneapolis: University of Minnesota Press, 2011.

al-Salmi, ibn ʿAbd al-ʿAziz ibn ʿUbayd. *al-Tabarruj wa-l-Ihtisab ʿalayhi*. Beirut: Maktabat al-Haramayn, 1987.

Salvatore, Armando, and Dale F. Eickelman. "Muslim Publics." In *Public Islam and the Common Good*. Leiden: Brill, 2004.

Salvatore, Armando, and Mark LeVine. "Reconstructing the Public Sphere in Muslim Majority Societies." In *Religion, Social Practice, and Contested Hegemonies: Reconstructing the Public Sphere in Muslim Majority Societies*. New York: Palgrave Macmillan, 2005.

———, eds. *Religion, Social Practice, and Contested Hegemonies: Reconstructing the Public Sphere in Muslim Majority Societies*. New York: Palgrave Macmillan, 2005.

Saqr, ʿAtiyya. *al-Hijab wa-ʿAmal al-Marʾa*. Cairo: Jumhuriyyat Misr al-ʿArabiyya, Wizarat al-Awqaf, al-Majlis al-Aʿla li-l-Shuʾun al-Islamiyya, 1983.

Scholte, Jan Aart. *Democratizing the Global Economy: The Role of Civil Society*. Translated by Ola Abou Zeid. Coventry: Centre for the Study of Globalisation and Regionalisation, University of Warwick, 2004.

Scott, Joan Wallach. *Only Paradoxes to Offer: French Feminists and the Rights of Man*. Cambridge, MA: Harvard University Press, 1997.

———. *Parite!: Sexual Equality and the Crisis of French Universalism*. Chicago: University of Chicago Press, 2005.

Segal, Jerome M. *The Employment Problem in Egypt: The Extent of Non-Productive Labor Force*. Washington, DC: Bureau for Program and Policy Coordination, United States Agency for International Development, September 1981.

Selim, Samah. "Politics of Piety: The Islamic Revival and the Feminist Subject." *Jadaliyya* (October 13, 2010). http://www.jadaliyya.com/pages/index/235/politics-of-piety_the-islamic-revival-and-the-femi.

Shaʿban, Rida Muhammad. *ʿAmr Khalid Shahid ʿala Hijab al-Fannanat wa-Iʿtizal al-Nujum*. Cairo: Dar Hiwar li-l-Nashr wa-l-Tawziʿ, 2007.

Shafiq, Durriya, and Ibrahim ʿAbduh. *Tatawwur al-Nahda al-Nisaʾiyya fi Misr min ʿAhd Muhammad ʿAli ila ʿAhd al-Faruq*. Cairo: Maktabat al-Adab, 1945.

El Shakry, Omnia. *The Great Social Laboratory: Subjects of Knowledge in Colonial and Postcolonial Egypt*. Stanford, CA: Stanford University Press, 2007.

———. "Schooled Mothers and Structured Play: Child Rearing in Turn-of-the-Century Egypt." In *Remaking Women: Feminism and Modernity in the Middle East*, edited by Lila Abu-Lughod. Princeton, NJ: Princeton University Press, 1998.

Shalabi, ʿAbd al-Wadud, and ʿAli Ahmad Khatib. *Fi Masʾalat al-Sufur wa-l-Hijab*. Cairo: Majallat al-Azhar, 1985.

Shalabi, Raʾuf. *Shaykh al-Islam ʿAbd al-Halim Mahmud: Siratuhu wa-Aʿmaluhu*. Kuwait: Dar al-Qalam, 1982.

Sharabasi, Ahmad. *al-Din wa-Tanzim al-Usra*. Cairo: Dar wa-Matabiʿ al-Shaʿb, 1965.

Sharaf, Hifni Muhammad. *al-Taswir al-Bayani: Min al-Balagha al-ʿArabiyya*. Cairo: Maktabat al-Shabab, 1969.

Sharma, Aradhana. *Logics of Empowerment: Development, Gender, and Governance in Neoliberal India*. Minneapolis: University of Minnesota Press, 2008.

Shepard, William E. *Sayyid Qutb and Islamic Activism: A Translation and Critical Analysis of* Social Justice in Islam. Leiden: E. J. Brill, 1996.
Sherif, Mohamed Ahmed. *Ghazali's Theory of Virtue*. New York: SUNY Press, 1975.
Sibaʿi, Muhammad Ahmad. *al-Marʾa bayn al-Tabarruj wa-l-Tahajjub*. Cairo: al-Azhar, Majmaʿ al-Buhuth al-Islamiyya, 1981.
Sidqi, Niʿmat. *Badiʿ Sunʿ Allah fi al-Barr wa-l-Bahr*. Cairo: Dar al-Iʿtisam, 1980.
———. *Bersolek (Tabarruj)*. Kuala Lumpur: Dewan Pustaka Fajar, 1988.
———. *al-Jihad fi Sabil Allah*. Cairo: Dar al-Iʿtisam, 1975.
———. *Min Tarbiyat al-Qurʾan*. Cairo: ʿAlam al-Kutub, 1970.
———. *Muʿjizat al-Qurʾan*. Cairo: ʿAlam al-Kutub, 1971.
———. *Niʿmat al-Qurʾan*. Cairo: Matbaʿat al-Sunna al-Muhammadiyya, 1968.
———. *Raʾaytu wa-Samiʿtu*. Cairo: ʿAlam al-Kutub, 1973.
———. *al-Shuʿa min al-Qurʾan*. Cairo: Dar al-Iʿtisam, 1975.
———. *al-Tabarruj*. Cairo: Matbaʿat al-ʿAsima, 1971.
Singerman, Diane. *Avenues of Participation: Family, Politics, and Networks in Urban Quarters of Cairo*. Princeton, NJ: Princeton University Press, 1996.
Siraj al-Din, Saʿd. *Awraq Shams al-Barudi*. Azbakiyya, Egypt: al-Rawda li-l-Nashr wa-l-Tawziʿ, 1993.
Slaughter, Anne-Marie. "Why Women Still Can't Have It All." *Atlantic*, August 2012.
Smith, Charles D. "The Crisis of Orientation: The Shift of Egyptian Intellectual to Islamic Subjects in the 1930s." *International Journal of Middle Eastern Studies* 4 (1973): 382–410.
———. " 'Cultural Construct' and Other Fantasies: Imagined Narratives in Imagined Communities." *International Journal of Middle Eastern Studies* 31 (1999): 95–102.
———. *Islam and the Search for Social Order in Modern Egypt: A Biography of Muhammad Husayn Haykal*. Albany: State University of New York Press, 1983.
Smith, Sidonie A., and Julia Watson. "Situating Subjectivity in Women's Autobiographical Practices." In *Women, Autobiography, Theory: A Reader*, edited by Sidonie A. Smith and Julia Watson. Madison: University of Wisconsin Press, 1998.
Solh, Camillia Fawzi. *al-Marʾa wa-l-Faqr fi Mintaqat ESCWA: Qadaya wa-Ihtimamat*. Studies of the Arab Woman in Development. New York: Economic and Social Commission for Western Asia, United Nations, 1995.
Stowasser, Barbara. "Gender Issues in Contemporary Qurʾan Interpretation." In *Islam, Gender, and Social Change*, edited by Yvonne Haddad and John Esposito. Oxford: Oxford University Press, 1998.
———. "Religious Ideology, Women, and the Family: The Islamic Paradigm." In *The Islamic Impulse*. Washington, DC: Georgetown University Press, 1987.
———. "Women and Citizenship in the Qurʾan." In *Women, the Family, and Divorce Laws in Islamic History*. Ed. Amira El Azhary Sonbol. Syracuse, NY: Syracuse University Press, 1996.
———. *Women in the Qurʾan, Traditions, and Interpretation*. New York: Oxford University Press, 1996.

Tartoussieh, Karim. "Pious Stardom: Cinema and the Islamic Revival in Egypt." *Arab Studies Journal* 15, no. 1 (April 1, 2007): 30–43.

Taylor, Charles. *Modern Social Imaginaries*. Durham, NC: Duke University Press, 2003.

Tinker, Irene, and Arvonne Fraser, eds. *Developing Power: How Women Transformed International Development*. New York: Feminist Press at CUNY, 2004.

Tucker, Judith E. "Decline of the Family Economy in Mid-Nineteenth Century Egypt." In *The Modern Middle East*, edited by Albert Hourani, Phillip Khoury, and Mary Wilson. Berkeley: University of California Press, 1993.

———. "Problems in the Historiography of Women in the Middle East: The Case of Nineteenth-Century Egypt." *International Journal of Middle East Studies* 15, no. 3 (1983): 321–36.

———. *Women in Nineteenth-Century Egypt*. Cambridge: Cambridge University Press, 2002.

Tuwayjiri, Hammud ibn ʿAbd Allah. *al-Sarim al-Mashhur ʿala Ahl al-Tabarruj wa-l-Sufur: Wa-fihi al-Radd ʿala Kitab al-Hijab li-l-Albani*. Aleppo: Maktabat al-Huda, 1974.

Tyan, E. "Bayʿa." *Encyclopaedia of Islam*, 2nd ed. Leiden: Brill Online, n.d.

ʿUkasha, Tharwat. *al-Taswir al-Islami, al-Dini wa-l-ʿArabi*. Cairo: Dar al-Maʿarif, 1977.

United Nations. *Ijtimaʿ Majmuʿat al-ʿAmal hawl Tatwir al-Muʾashshirat wa-Tahsin al-Ihsaʾat al-Khassa bi-Wadʿ al-Marʾa al-ʿArabiyya: 15–19 Uktubir 1989*. Cairo: Markaz al-Qawmi li-l-Buhuth al-Ijtimaʿiyya wa-l-Jinaʾiyya, 1990.

United Nations Development Programme, Regional Bureau for Arab States, and Arab Fund for Economic and Social Development. *The Arab Human Development Report 2005: Towards the Rise of Women in the Arab World*. New York: United Nations, 2005.

USAID/Cairo Development Information Center. *Women in Development: Special Bibliography*. USAID, May 1980.

Voll, John O. "Renewal and Reform in Islamic History: Tajdid and Islah." In *Voices of Resurgent Islam*, edited by John L. Esposito. Oxford: Oxford University Press, 1983.

Wadud, Amina. *Qurʾan and Woman: Rereading the Sacred Text from a Woman's Perspective*. New York: Oxford University Press, 1999.

Wafi, ʿAli ʿAbd al-Wahid. *Bayt al-Taʿa wa-Taʿaddud al-Zawjat wa-l-Talaq fi al-Islam*. Maʿ al-Islam. Cairo: Muʾassasat al-Matbuʿat al-Haditha, 1960.

———. *Contribution à une théorie sociologique de l'esclavage: étude des situations génératrices de l'esclavage*. Paris: A. Mechelinck, 1931.

———. *Huquq al-Insan fi al-Islam*. Cairo: Maktabat Nahdat Misr, 1957.

———. *al-Marʾa fi al-Islam*. Cairo: Maktabat Gharib, 1971.

———. *al-Musawaa fi al-Islam*. Iqraʾ. Cairo: Dar al-Maʿarif, 1962.

Wahyudi, Yudian. "Ali Shariati and Bint al-Shatiʾ on Free Will: A Comparison." *Journal of Islamic Studies* 9, no. 1 (1998): 35.

Wajdi, Muhammad Farid. *Al-Marʾa al-Muslima*. Cairo: Matbaʿat al-Taraqqi, 1901.

al-Wakil, ʿAbd al-Rahman ʿAbd al-Wahhab. "Introduction." In *Niʿmat al-Qurʾan*, by Niʿmat Sidqi. Cairo: Matbaʿat al-Sunna al-Muhammadiyya, 1968.

Warner, Michael. "'An Evangelical Public Sphere' (lecture)." Presented at the Critical Speaker Series, University of North Carolina, Chapel Hill, September 23, 2011.

———. *Publics and Counterpublics*. New York: Zone Books, 2002.

Weeks, Kathi. *The Problem with Work: Feminism, Marxism, Antiwork Politics, and Postwork Imaginaries*. Durham, NC: Duke University Press, 2011.

Weidemann, Jean C., and Zohra Merabet. *Egyptian Women and Microenterprise: The Invisible Entrepreneurs*. Development Alternatives, Inc. Growth and Equity through Microenterprise Investment. Washington, DC: USAID Office of Women in Development, March 1992.

Welchman, Lynn, ed. *Women's Rights and Islamic Family Law: Perspectives on Reform*. New York: Zed Books, 2004.

Werbner, Pnina. "Political Motherhood and the Feminisation of Citizenship." In *Women, Citizenship and Difference*, edited by Pnina Werbner and Nira Yuval Davis. London: Zed Books, 1999.

White House Working Group on the Family. *The Family: Preserving America's Future: A Report to the President*. Washington, DC: United States Department of Education, 1986.

Wickham, Carrie Rosefsky. *Mobilizing Islam: Religion, Activism, and Political Change in Egypt*. New York: Columbia University Press, 2002.

Youssef, Nadia. "The Interrelationship between the Division of Labour in the Household, Women's Roles, and Their Impact on Fertility." In *Women's Roles and Population Trends in the Third World*, edited by Richard Anker and Mayra Buvinic. London: Routledge, 1982.

———. *Women and Work in Developing Societies*. Population Monograph Series. Berkeley: Berkeley Institute of International Studies, University of California, 1974.

———. "Women Workers and Economic Development: A Comparative Study of Latin America and the Middle East." PhD dissertation, University of California, 1970.

Youssef, Nadia Haggag, and Carol B. Hetler. *Rural Households Headed by Women: A Priority Concern for Development*. World Employment Programme Research, Working Paper. Geneva: International Labour Office, 1984.

Zerilli, Linda. *Feminism and the Abyss of Freedom*. Chicago: University of Chicago Press, 2005.

Zizek, Slavoj. *Did Somebody Say Totalitarianism? Five Interventions in the (Mis)Use of a Notion*. New York: Verso, 2001.

Zuhur, Sherifa. *Revealing Reveiling: Islamist Gender Ideology in Contemporary Egypt*. Albany, NY: State University of New York Press, 1992.

Index

Princeton Studies in Muslim Politics

Diane Singerman, *Avenues of Participation: Family, Politics, and Networks in Urban Quarters of Cairo*
Tone Bringa, *Being Muslim the Bosnian Way: Identity and Community in a Central Bosnian Village*
Dale F. Eickelman and James Piscatori, *Muslim Politics*
Bruce B. Lawrence, *Shattering the Myth: Islam beyond Violence*
Ziba Mir-Hosseini, *Islam and Gender: The Religious Debate in Contemporary Iran*
Robert W. Hefner, *Civil Islam: Muslims and Democratization in Indonesia*
Muhammad Qasim Zaman, *The 'Ulama in Contemporary Islam: Custodians of Change*
Michael G. Peletz, *Islamic Modern: Religious Courts and Cultural Politics in Malaysia*
Oskar Verkaaik, *Migrants and Militants: Fun and Urban Violence in Pakistan*
Laetitia Bucaille, *Growing Up Palestinian: Israeli Occupation and the Intifada Generation*
Robert W. Hefner, ed., *Remaking Muslim Politics: Pluralism, Contestation, Democratization*
Lara Deeb, *An Enchanted Modern: Gender and Public Piety in Shi'i Lebanon*
Roxanne L. Euben, *Journeys to the Other Shore: Muslim and Western Travelers in Search of Knowledge*
Robert W. Hefner and Muhammad Qasim Zaman, eds., *Schooling Islam: The Culture and Politics of Modern Muslim Education*
Loren D. Lybarger, *Identity and Religion in Palestine: The Struggle between Islamism and Secularism in the Occupied Territories*
Augustus Norton, *Hezbollah: A Short History*
Bruce K. Rutherford, *Egypt after Mubarak: Liberalism, Islam, and Democracy in the Arab World*
Emile Nakhleh, *A Necessary Engagement: Reinventing America's Relations with the Muslim World*
Roxanne L. Euben and Muhammad Qasim Zaman, eds., *Princeton Readings in Islamist Thought: Texts and Contexts from al-Banna to Bin Laden*
Irfan Ahmad, *Islamism and Democracy in India: The Transformation of Jamaat-e-Islami*
Kristen Ghodsee, *Muslim Lives in Eastern Europe: Gender, Ethnicity, and the Transformation of Islam in Postsocialist Bulgaria*
John R. Bowen, *Can Islam Be French? Pluralism and Pragmatism in a Secularist State*
Thomas Barfield, *Afghanistan: A Cultural and Political History*
Sara Roy, *Hamas and Civil Society in Gaza: Engaging the Islamist Social Sector*

Michael Laffan, *The Makings of Indonesian Islam: Orientalism and the Narration of a Sufi Past*

Jonathan Laurence, *The Emancipation of Europe's Muslims: The State's Role in Minority Integration*

Jenny White, *Muslim Nationalism and the New Turks*

Lara Deeb and Mona Harb, *Leisurely Islam: Negotiating Geography and Morality in Shi'ite South Beirut*

Ësra Özyürek, *Being German, Becoming Muslim: Race, Religion, and Conversion in the New Europe*

Ellen Anne McLarney, *Soft Force: Women in Egypt's Islamic Awakening*

Avi Max Spiegel, *Young Islam: The New Politics of Religion in Morocco and the Arab World*

Nadav Samin, *Of Sand or Soil: Genealogy and Tribal Belonging in Saudi Arabia*